PRIMER ON
OCCUPATIONAL SAFETY AND
HEALTH

PRIMER ON OCCUPATIONAL SAFETY AND HEALTH

Fred Blosser

Program Advisor
Office of Research and Development
United States Environmental Protection Agency

formerly Staff Editor
Occupational Safety and Health Reporter

The Bureau of National Affairs, Inc., Washington, D.C.

Copyright © 1992
The Bureau of National Affairs, Inc.

Fourth Printing, October 1997

Library of Congress Cataloging-in-Publication Data

Blosser, Fred.
  Primer on occupational safety and health / by Fred Blosser.
  Includes index.
  ISBN 0-87179-741-0
  1. Industrial safety—Law and legislation—United States.
  2. Industrial hygiene—Law and legislation—United States.
  3. United States. Occupational Safety and Health Administration.
  4. United States. Occupational Safety and Health Review
Commission.
  I. Title.
KF3570.B54   1992
344.73'0465—dc20
[347.304465]   91-43769
                                                          CIP

Copyrights and Acknowledgments

Annals of the New York Academy of Sciences, Copyright © 1989
by the New York Academy of Sciences.

"What to Do When the OSHA Inspector Appears at Your Door:
A Guide from A to Z," prepared by Shaw, Pittman, Potts, &
Trowbridge, Washington, D.C., for The Workplace Health &
Safety Council, Washington, D.C.

Published by BNA Books
1250 23rd St., N.W., Washington, D.C. 20037-1165

Printed in the United States of America

PREFACE

Safety and health conditions in the workplace have been regulated to some extent in the United States for more than a century. But early regulation—mostly at the state level—was inconsistent and generally weak. It was only in 1970, with the passage of the Occupational Safety and Health Act (OSHA), that the federal government assumed the primary responsibility for setting and enforcing minimum standards to protect most private-sector workers from job-related injuries and illnesses.

To carry out those duties, the authors of the law created the Occupational Safety and Health Administration, a new agency within the U.S. Department of Labor. Now, as OSHA enters its third decade of activity, observers can point to achievements that are attributable, either directly or indirectly, to the agency and its parent statute. Among these are hundreds of standards covering an array of hazardous industrial processes, chemicals, and equipment; active research programs in government, university, and industry laboratories; and a heightened public awareness of the importance of safety on the job.

However, the OSH Act has not provided definitive answers to the problem of controlling workplace hazards. Workers continue to suffer injuries and illnesses, and the controversies that occasioned OSHA's birth still generate debate among business and union leaders, government officials, and scientists: How best can job-related hazards be corrected? How far should the government's police powers extend in this respect? How can problems arising from new technologies and changing work-force demographics be identified in advance and ultimately be avoided?

This book is intended to serve as an introduction to occupational safety and health regulation for readers who seek basic knowledge of this subject area. It provides an overview of current government programs, how these programs came to be, how they have changed over time, and how they may change in the future.

As the following chapters try to make clear, health and safety regulation is not a static discipline: as a science, it evolves with every advancement in industrial technology, and as an area of public policy, it changes with every new presidential administration and each shift in congressional priorities.

Although the Primer covers several federal programs, it focuses mainly on those programs administered under the OSH Act, in particular the enforcement activities of OSHA and the adjudicatory procedures of the Occupational Safety and Health Review Commission. This approach seemed to be the logical one to take with an introductory volume intended for a nonspecialized audience.

Cites in this book are to the Code of Federal Regulations (C.F.R.) for federal standards and regulations, the Federal Register (Fed. Reg.) for official publication of government notices, and the OSHA Field Operations Manual (F.O.M.) and compliance directives (C.P.L.) for OSHA administrative guidelines. I have cited to BNA's *Occupational Safety and Health Reporter* for source material that may not be readily available in public, college, or law libraries or from the government itself. Similarly, where applicable, references to court decisions include cites to BNA's *Occupational Safety and Health Cases*.

Please note that I wrote this book as an individual. No official support or endorsement by the EPA is intended or should be conferred.

—FRED BLOSSER

CONTENTS

1
OVERVIEW

Like wages, hours, collective bargaining, and job discrimination, occupational safety and health is an employment issue regulated by law. A variety of federal statutes require employers in nearly every type of workplace in the United States to protect their employees from job-related hazards that could cause injury, illness, or death.

The first occupational safety and health laws in this country were enacted at the state level in the late 1800s. Federal laws began appearing a few years later. But all of these laws protected only a relatively small number of workers, in the most heavily industrialized states and only in specialized occupations such as mining and railroading.

Comprehensive federal regulation came in 1970 with the passage of the Occupational Safety and Health Act. The OSH Act remains the most extensive piece of safety and health legislation in the United States, regulating conditions in six million private business establishments, including manufacturing, construction, service, and other industries. Other statutes—many of which predate the OSH Act—cover workers in mining, railroading, nuclear power, asbestos removal, and the maritime trades.

HEALTH AND SAFETY LAWS BEFORE 1970

The first occupational safety and health laws in the United States date back to the post–Civil War period, when the nation entered an era of significant industrial growth. Initially, these measures were enacted at the state level. In 1877, Massachusetts passed a factory inspection law that required employers to put barriers or guards around moving parts of heavy machinery. In 1869, Pennsylvania passed the country's first coal mine inspection act.

Federal regulation began in 1893 with the Safety Appliances Act, a measure regulating the safety of employees on interstate railroad systems. After the turn of the century, with the expansion of labor unions and the Progressive Era's trend toward social legislation, states such as New York and Wisconsin enacted comprehensive occupational safety and health laws. At the same time, safety and health research programs were created in the Departments of the Interior and Health, Education, and Welfare (now the Department of Health and Human Services), but these federal research programs did not set any regulatory requirements for employers.

President Franklin D. Roosevelt's New Deal programs of the 1930s gave proponents of occupational safety and health regulation an opportunity to advance safety and health standards as a condition for granting government contracts to private employers. The Walsh-Healey Act of 1936 stated that private companies working under federal contract could not require employees to work in conditions that were "unsanitary, or hazardous or dangerous to . . . heath and safety."

In the 1940s and 1950s, other laws were passed that required employers in certain industries to protect workers from hazards on the job. Beginning with the Coal Mine Inspection and Investigation Act of 1941, a series of laws were enacted that were intended to prevent explosions and other disasters in mines. The Atomic Energy Act of 1954 set standards for the then–new nuclear industry, including requirements for protecting employees at nuclear installations.

The 1950s also brought a push for general regulation of worker safety and health. Senator Hubert Humphrey (D-Minn.) introduced a bill in 1951, calling for uniform safety codes and enforcement. Responding to an industrial disaster in St Louis, Representative Lenore Sullivan (D-Mo.) introduced legislation in 1958 to set mandatory standards for the safe use of hazardous materials in industry. Neither bill passed, but the push for nationwide standards continued through the 1960s as concern over industrial accident rates persisted. Economic prosperity enabled labor unions to call for worker rights beyond wage-and-hour issues, and growing public support for environmental protection gave rise to a parallel concern about exposure to harmful chemicals and other contaminants on the job.

THE OCCUPATIONAL SAFETY AND HEALTH ACT OF 1970

President Lyndon B. Johnson's agenda of social programs in the 1960s—"The Great Society"—included a proposal for a federal occupational safety and health regulatory program. In 1968, the Johnson Administration called for legislation that would authorize the Department of Labor to set and enforce standards, and to impose penalties against employers that violated those rules.

Legislation to establish such a program was introduced in Congress, but failed to pass. However, the enactment of the Federal Coal Mine Health and Safety Act of 1969, spurred by a November 1968 West Virginia mine explosion that killed 78 miners, set the stage for serious congressional debate on legislation to establish a comprehensive regulatory program.

Like the earlier Johnson Administration proposal, a Senate bill (S. 2193) introduced in May 1969 by Democratic Senators Harrison Williams (N.J.), Edward Kennedy (Mass.), Walter Mondale (Minn.), and Ralph Yarborough (Texas) as "the Occupational Safety and Health Act of 1969" proposed that the Department of Labor (DOL) be authorized to set standards, inspect workplaces, propose citations and fines for violations, and adjudicate employer challenges to those sanctions. Republicans were concerned about the concentration of authority in DOL. Senator Jacob Javits (R-N.Y.) introduced a bill (S. 2788) to give DOL enforcement authority only, and to create an independent National Occupational Safety and Health Board to set standards and adjudicate challenges. Senator Peter Dominick (R-Colo.) introduced a bill (S. 4404) that would have assigned various responsibilities to three bodies: standards-setting to a National Occupational Safety and Health Board, enforcement to DOL, and adjudication to an Occupational Safety and Health Appeals Commission.

Eventually, the Senate passed an amended version of S. 2193 that—in a provision introduced by Javits—resolved the conflict over delegation of authority by calling for DOL to issue and enforce standards, and for an independent panel to adjudicate employer challenges. In the meantime, the House approved a measure (H.R. 19200), introduced by Representative William Steiger (R-Wis.), that gave standards-setting, enforcement, and adjudicatory authority to three different agencies.

Final compromise legislation—approved by the Senate on December 15, 1970, and by the House two days later—followed the approach of the Senate bill. It created a new agency in the Department of Labor, the Occupational Safety and Health Administration, to set and enforce standards, and a new independent panel, the Occupational Safety and Health Review Commission, to adjudicate challenges. On December 28, 1970, President Nixon signed the Occupational Safety and Health Act into law (Pub. L. No. 91-596).

The Act authorized OSHA to regulate private employers in the 50 states, the District of Columbia, the Virgin Islands, American Samoa, Puerto Rico, Guam, and the Trust Territories of the Pacific Islands. According to 1990 figures from the Department of Labor, 89 million workers are covered by the Act. The statute also authorized the government to conduct research on occupational hazards and ways to correct them, and to oversee and approve state regulatory programs.

Three agencies administer the major requirements of the OSH Act: the Occupational Safety and Health Administration (OSHA), the National Institute for Occupational Safety and Health (NIOSH), and the Occupational Safety and Health Review Commission (OSHRC).

Occupational Safety and Health Administration

An agency of the Department of Labor, OSHA carries out the regulatory functions of the Act. It:

- Sets the health and safety standards that employers must meet to be considered in compliance with the act;
- Enforces those standards by inspecting workplaces in private industry and citing conditions that fail to meet the requirements. OSHA generally proposes monetary fines for violations that it deems to be serious;
- Monitors the performance of state agencies that wish to set and enforce their own standards. Under the OSH Act, states may establish their own regulatory programs, but only if their standards are at least as effective as OSHA's, and if they gain federal approval through a specified process;
- Requires employers to maintain records that may be used to judge compliance and to measure the incidence of work-related injuries and illnesses;
- Inspects federal workplaces under certain circumstances (although the OSH Act does not permit the agency to levy penalties against federal employers as it is authorized to do against private-sector employers);
- Coordinates its regulatory activity with the activities of other federal agencies that regulate workplace safety and health in certain industries, by entering into agreements that delineate the responsibilities of the respective agencies, to avoid confusion and duplication of effort;
- Furthers health and safety training for employers and employees by conducting training at a facility in Des Plaines, Illinois, and by funding courses through grants to other organizations;
- Investigates complaints by employees who claim that they have suffered retaliation from their employers for reporting safety hazards or asking OSHA to inspect their workplace.

OSHA is administered by an Assistant Secretary of Labor for Occupational Safety and Health, who reports to the Secretary of Labor. Agency policies are formulated at headquarters in Washington, D.C., and inspections are carried out by a field staff in 85 area offices.

Although OSHA's duties are prescribed by the OSH Act, the statute also gives the agency flexibility in determining how it should carry out those duties, including which standards it should issue, and how those standards should be enforced. As a result, OSHA's policies and priorities have changed over time.

For example, the agency's initial standards generally addressed safety hazards, and set detailed requirements for protecting workers against those dangers—such as stating how close ladder rungs should be to each other, and how large the letters should be on the warning signs of welding gas cylinders. Beginning, however, in the mid-1970s, the agency began to devote more time and attention to developing standards to address toxic substances and other health hazards.

Similarly, after its first few years of existence, the agency began to abandon the practice of setting highly detailed rules called specification standards because they require employers to comply with specific requirements. Responding to criticism that these rules often result in OSHA spending too much time regulating conditions that pose no serious risk to workers, and that they bar employers from pursuing innovative safety measures, it instead began to issue performance standards that set general safety objectives and gave employers greater latitude in deciding how to meet those goals.

Enforcement policies have changed as well. Criticized in the 1970s by industry officials for using what they termed heavy-handed inspection practices, OSHA was redirected in the early 1980s during the Reagan Administration's first term. Pursuing its campaign pledge to reduce what it saw as overly burdensome government regulation, the administration decreased OSHA's inspection force, exempted some businesses from comprehensive inspections, and instituted new programs to encourage voluntary compliance by industry.

However, the late 1980s marked a return to more aggressive enforcement after the Bhopal, India, chemical disaster in December 1984 generated new concerns about the safety of U.S. chemical plants, the 1987 collapse of a building under construction in Connecticut raised questions about construction safety, and labor unions and local government authorities began to report that some unsafe workplaces had escaped inspection under the more lenient policies. The agency did away with its recent inspection exemptions and sought significantly higher fines for flagrant safety violations.

In the late 1980s OSHA began to address emerging workplace hazards such as repetitive-motion disorders, indoor air contamination, and infectious bloodborne diseases. Reflecting the growth of office work, health care, and other service industries in the United States since the 1970s, these concerns have demanded increasing attention from occupational safety and health professionals over the past decade.

National Institute for Occupational Safety and Health

NIOSH, an institute of the Centers for Disease Control in the U.S. Department of Health and Human Services, is the leading federal occupational safety and health research agency. The institute, based in Atlanta, Georgia, conducts laboratory research at two facilities, in Cincinnati, Ohio, and Morgantown, West Virginia; funds studies at universities across the United States; and conducts investigations called health hazard evaluations. For these evaluations, which are done at the invitation of an employer or employee, NIOSH researchers go to a business establishment, evaluate potential hazards there, and recommend ways to correct any dangers that may be found.

On the basis of its own studies and research by other scientists, NIOSH develops criteria documents, or formal recommendations for new or revised OSHA standards. The institute also prepares reports called current intelligence bulletins that alert employers and employees to specific hazards and describe ways to avoid or correct the problems.

Occupational Safety and Health Review Commission

OSHRC is an independent, adjudicatory agency, separate from OSHA, that hears challenges by employers to OSHA citations and proposed fines. The commission is composed of three members or commissioners, one of whom, as chairperson, also is responsible for overseeing the agency's administrative functions.

Challenges or contests to citations are first heard by the commission's administrative law judges (ALJs). A ruling by an administrative law judge either upholding, modifying, or vacating a citation may be reviewed by the three commissioners. Rulings by the commission may be appealed to a U.S. court of appeals.

Commissioners are appointed by the President, with the advice and consent of the Senate, each for a six-year term.

OTHER STATUTES

Workers in the mining, nuclear power, agricultural, asbestos abatement, hazardous waste, transportation, and maritime industries are covered, either completely or in part, by statutes other than the OSH Act. This is because section 4(b)(1) of the Act prohibits OSHA from exercising jurisdiction over "working conditions of employees with respect to which other Federal agencies . . . exercise statutory authority to prescribe or enforce standards or regulations affecting occupational safety or health."

Some of these other laws predate the OSH Act, while others are more recent. They include:

- *The Federal Mine Safety and Health Act*, which requires owners and operators of coal, metal, and non-metal mines to protect their employees from hazards involved in mining. This law, which was passed in 1977, but amended the earlier Federal Coal Mine Health and Safety Act of 1969, is administered by the Mine Safety and Health Administration (MSHA) in the Department of Labor (Pub. L. No. 95-164, 30 U.S.C. § 801 et seq.).
- *The Energy Reorganization Act of 1974* (Pub. L. No. 93-438, 42 U.S.C. § 2201 et seq.) and *The Department of Energy Organization Act of 1977* (Pub. L. No. 95-91, 40 U.S.C. § 486(c) and 42 U.S.C. § 2201 et seq.), which require the Nuclear Regulatory Commission (NRC) and the Department of Energy (DOE), respectively, to protect the health and safety of employees who work with radioactive materials.
- *The Asbestos Hazard Emergency Response Act*, which requires states to accredit private contractors engaged in

removing or otherwise treating asbestos in school buildings. As a requirement for certification, contractors must
train their employees in the safe handling of the cancer-
causing material (Pub. L. No. 99-519, 15 U.S.C. § 2641
et seq.).

- *The Federal Insecticide, Fungicide, and Rodenticide Act*, which
sets safety regulations for pesticide application to protect
agricultural workers from health hazards (Pub. L. No.
88-305, 7 U.S.C. § 136 et seq.).
- *The Superfund Amendments and Reauthorization Act*, which
authorizes OSHA and the Environmental Protection
Agency (EPA) to set standards to protect workers engaged in cleaning up hazardous waste or responding to
emergency situations involving chemical spills (Pub. L.
No. 99-499, *amending* 42 U.S.C. § 9601 et seq.).
- *The Federal Aviation Act*, which requires the Federal Aviation Administration (FAA) to regulate worker as well as
passenger safety in air travel (Pub. L. No. 85-726, 49
U.S.C. app. § 421 et seq.).
- *The Federal Railroad Safety Act*, which authorizes the Federal Railroad Administration (FRA) to regulate the safety
of railroad employees (Pub. L. No. 91-458, 45 U.S.C.
§ 421 et seq.).
- *The Motor Carrier Safety Act*, which requires employers to
comply with commercial motor vehicle safety regulations
issued by the Federal Highway Administration (FHwA)
(Pub. L. No. 98-554, U.S.C. app. § 2501 et seq.).
- *The Hazardous Materials Transportation Act*, which regu-
lates the interstate transportation of hazardous materials
(Pub. L. No. 93-633, 49 U.S.C. app. § 1801 et seq.).
- *The Natural Gas Pipeline Safety Act*, which regulates the
safety of natural gas pipeline facilities and transportation
(Pub. L. No. 90-481, 49 U.S.C. app. § 1671 et seq.).
- *Maritime safety statutes* that give the U.S. Coast Guard
authority over worker safety on tank and passenger ves-
sels (46 U.S.C. § 21 et seq.).
- *The Outer Continental Shelf Lands Act*, which gives the
Coast Guard and the Department of the Interior's Min-

erals Management Service the authority to regulate employee safety in drilling operations on the Outer Continental Shelf (43 U.S.C. § 1331 et seq.).

More detail on these non-OSHA programs appears in Chapter 9.

2

OSHA STANDARDS

OSHA standards are important because they form the cornerstone of the agency's enforcement program. They set the requirements that employers must meet in order to be in compliance with the OSH Act.

Unlike some other labor laws, such as the Fair Labor Standards Act, the OSH Act does not prescribe specific standards. In writing the statute, Congress reasoned that workplace hazards are so "complex and changing" that "they cannot be solved by a lengthy list of prohibitions spelled out in a statute" (*Congressional Record*, Oct. 8, 1970, p. S. 17470).

Rather, the Act directs OSHA to develop and issue standards through a public rule-making process. Employers must comply with those standards as they would with any statutory requirement.

OSHA has issued hundreds of standards covering a wide range of hazards, including toxic chemicals, hazardous equipment and processes, and unsafe workplace conditions. These standards require employers to use appropriate "practices, means, methods, operations, or processes" to protect employees from the risk of injury, illness, or death (29 U.S.C. § 652). For example:

- If an employee is working with a chemical that is toxic or cancer-causing at a given exposure level, the employer must keep worker exposure within safe limits.
- If the hazard involves a tool or machine that can crush, cut, burn, or otherwise injure the worker if not used

properly, the employer must ensure that the tool or machine meets recognized safety design criteria and is used in a safe manner.

- If the hazard involves an integral feature or condition of the workplace, the employer must correct the feature (for example, keeping floors dry to avoid slipping, or bracing the sides of trenches to keep them from collapsing).

PERFORMANCE AND SPECIFICATION STANDARDS

OSHA standards sometimes are categorized as to whether they are specification or performance rules. Specification standards set forth detailed means by which employers must protect workers. For example, OSHA's rules on walking-working surfaces (29 C.F.R. § 1910.21 et seq.) set specific dimensions for ladders and guardrails. Those items must meet the specified dimensions in order to comply with the standards. (See Appendix B for a copy of the walking-working surface rules as an example of specification standards.)

Most of the agency's earliest safety standards were specification rules. In some instances, employers have complained that such highly detailed requirements compel them to go to needless lengths to address insignificant safety problems.

In some instances, OSHA has agreed with this criticism. Since the late 1970s, the agency has revoked many of the provisions in its original specification standards after concluding that these requirements were not necessary to protect workers from serious injuries. The agency has made greater use of performance standards, which require employers to address given hazards but provide flexibility in meeting this goal.

One such rule is the OSHA hazard communication standard (29 C.F.R. § 1910.1200), which requires chemical manufacturers to prepare labels and material safety data sheets (MSDSs) for toxic and cancer-causing chemicals, and requires employers to use these and other means to warn workers about the hazardous properties of particular chemicals found on the job. The standard gives employers flexibility in designing hazard-notification programs, as long as certain types of information are provided. (The hazard communication standard is reprinted in Appendix C as an example of a performance standard.)

INDUSTRY CLASSIFICATIONS FOR STANDARDS

OSHA standards fall into four broad industry classifications. These distinctions are made because a standard intended for one type of industry may not be applicable to a different industry with its own unique working conditions and work practices.

General Industry Standards

General industry standards are the broadest category of OSHA regulations. These rules generally apply to all industries, but especially to manufacturing and service-industry workplaces. They include two subcategories of rules:

- Specific standards for certain industry segments: pulp, paper, and paperboard mills (29 C.F.R. § 1910.261); textile manufacturing (29 C.F.R. § 1910.262); bakery equipment (29 C.F.R. § 1910.263); laundry machines and operations (29 C.F.R. § 1910.264); sawmills (29 C.F.R. § 1910.265); pulpwood logging (29 C.F.R. § 266); telecommunications (29 C.F.R. § 1910.268); and grain-handling facilities (29 C.F.R. § 1910.272). These regulations are called vertical standards because they cover only certain industries, addressing unique conditions in those workplaces.
- Standards that cut across industry boundaries and apply to conditions in many different types of workplaces, including toxic chemicals (for example, exposure standards for formaldehyde at 29 C.F.R. § 1910.1048); hazardous materials (for example, regulations on compressed gases at 29 C.F.R. § 1910.101); personal protective equipment (29 C.F.R. § 1910.132–1910.140), machine guarding (29 C.F.R. § 1910.211–1910.222), and electrical systems (29 C.F.R. § 1910.301–1910.330). These are called horizontal standards because they apply to a broad range of industries.

If a particular type of hazard is addressed by both a vertical and a horizontal standard, the vertical standard will take precedence for the industry covered by that particular rule (29 C.F.R. § 1910.5(c)(1)). To the extent that an industry-specific standard fails to address a particular hazard, OSHA will apply the general industry rule pertaining to that hazard. For example, OSHA's standard for noise exposure (29 C.F.R. § 1910.95) regulates conditions in sawmills as well as textile plants (29 C.F.R. § 1910.5(c)(2)).

Construction Standards

The second broad classification of OSHA standards are construction standards that govern safety and health conditions at building sites. Included in this category are standards for ladders and scaffolding (29 C.F.R. § 1926.450–1926.452), asbestos (29 C.F.R. § 1926.58), excavations and trenches (29 C.F.R. § 1926.650–1926.653), explosives (29 C.F.R. § 1926.900–1926.914), and other conditions and equipment found in the building trades.

OSHA's earliest construction standards incorporated regulations issued by the Department of Labor under the Construction Safety Act of 1969. The predecessor regulations applied only to private employers performing construction work for the federal government under contract.

Maritime Standards

The third major category of standards comprises maritime standards that apply to workplaces involved in water-borne commerce conducted within the United States. These rules pertain to:

- Work at *shipyards*—namely, ship building, repairing, and breaking (the breaking down of a vessel's structure for the purpose of scrapping the vessel, including the removal of gear, equipment, or component parts) (29 C.F.R. § 1915.2(a)).
- Operations at *marine terminals*—wharves, bulkheads, piers, docks, or other berthing locations where cargo

is moved from vessel to shore or vice versa (29 C.F.R. § 1917.1(a)).

- *Longshoring* activities—loading or unloading from on board the vessel (29 C.F.R. § 1918.3(d)).
- *Gear certification*—affirming the safety of equipment used in loading or unloading ships. Under these rules, OSHA accredits persons who are responsible for determining if equipment is in working order (29 C.F.R. § 1919.3– 1919.9), and details the procedures that those persons are to follow in carrying out their duties (29 C.F.R. § 1919.13–1919.90).

Agriculture Standards

Safety and health rules for agricultural operations include standards for roll-over protective structures for tractors (29 C.F.R. § 1928.51–1928.53), field-sanitation rules for farm laborers (29 C.F.R. § 1928.110), and standards for guarding farm field equipment, farmstead equipment, and cotton gins (29 C.F.R. § 1928.57).

The construction, maritime, and agricultural standards also are considered to be vertical standards, and take precedence over general industry rules that cover similar hazards.

DEVELOPING OSHA STANDARDS

Section 6 of the OSH Act provides the framework under which OSHA develops its safety and health standards. The agency's very first rules, issued in 1971, were "start-up" standards promulgated from existing national consensus standards and established federal rules.

The standards adopted since then have been developed through a process in which OSHA determines that requirements are needed to protect workers from a safety or health hazard, the agency proposes a standard, public comment on the proposal is sought, and a final rule that takes the public input into account is issued.

OSHA's start-up standards generally addressed safety hazards. In the mid-1970s, as labor unions criticized the agency for failing to do enough to address hazards from toxic and cancer-causing substances, and information came to light on the harmful effects of chemicals such as vinyl chloride and 1,2-dibromo-3-chloropropane, the agency began to give more attention to health standards. More recently, labor unions and public interest groups have increasingly asked OSHA to regulate conditions unique to the growing white-collar industries, such as video display terminals and indoor air quality.

Section 6(a) Standards

In drafting the OSH Act, Congress decided that OSHA would need a quick way of setting an initial body of standards, so the agency could expeditiously enforce the new law. Section 6(a) of the act provided that mechanism.

The provision required OSHA "as soon as practicable" after April 28, 1971, the effective date of the act, but no later than April 28, 1973, to "promulgate as an occupational safety or health standard any national consensus standard, and any established Federal standard, unless [it] determines that the promulgation of such a standard would not result in improved safety or health for specifically designated employees" (29 U.S.C. § 655(a)).

"National consensus standards" are voluntary guidelines developed by non-governmental standards-setting organizations such as the American National Standards Institute Inc. and the National Fire Protection Association. These guidelines are adopted under procedures intended to ensure that diverse views have been considered and that interested and affected parties have reached substantial agreement on the standards. Therefore, Congress reasoned, OSHA should be able to incorporate such rules as mandatory start-up standards without first having to gather further public input through lengthy notice-and-comment rulemaking procedures (Senate Labor Committee Report on the Occupational Safety and Health Act, S. Rep. No. 1282, ¶ 32).

OSHA was also authorized to use voluntary "proprietary standards" developed by professional societies and associations as interim start-up standards. According to Congress, these standards, adopted by such organizations as the American Conference of Governmental Industrial Hygienists, "have gained wide acceptance by American Industry" (S. Rep. No. 1282, ¶ 34).

Similarly, Congress felt that industry "should be readily able to adapt itself to Federal standards since many voluntary industrial standards have been incorporated by reference into numerous Federal safety laws" ("Interim Standards," House Labor Committee Report on the Occupational Safety and Health Act, H.R. Rep. No. 1291).

OSHA issued its section 6(a) standards in May 1971, a month after the OSH Act went into effect. These rules addressed basic safety concerns such as walking-working surfaces, fire protection, personal protective equipment, and machine guarding, as well as health concerns of exposure to air contaminants. The safety standards incorporated various consensus standards originally developed by the American National Standards Institute (ANSI) and the National Fire Protection Association. The air contaminants standards—which set exposure limits for such substances as carbon monoxide, nitric acid, silica dust, and sulfur dioxide—were derived from ANSI standards and recommended exposure limits (called "threshold limit values") developed by the American Conference of Governmental Industrial Hygienists. Previously, these rules had served as mandatory standards for government contractors under the Walsh-Healey Act.

Through the 1970s, section 6(a) standards came in for criticism from employers and labor unions alike. Critics argued that many of the standards set unnecessarily detailed requirements that had little real value for protecting workers against serious hazards. In the case of the air contaminants standards, critics noted that many of the exposure limits adopted by OSHA had become outdated as new research showed the need to set more stringent limits. Employers complained that OSHA's detailed requirements discouraged industry from exploring and using other, possibly more effective, means for correcting hazards.

Consequently, beginning in the late 1970s, OSHA has been revising these standards. In 1978, the agency deleted some 600 standards that were found to be outdated, unrelated to worker safety, or otherwise of little value for protecting workers from serious job-related hazards. Similarly, in 1989, OSHA updated and tightened exposure standards for almost 400 air contaminants. The agency also has undertaken comprehensive revisions of some groups of standards, such as those pertaining to electrical hazards and fire protection.

Section 6(b) Standards

All of OSHA's permanent standards since 1971 have been issued under section 6(b) of the OSH Act. This section:

- Allows private individuals and organizations to petition OSHA to set standards (29 U.S.C. § 655(b)(1));
- Requires OSHA to give the public adequate opportunity to participate in the development of a new standard (29 U.S.C. § 655(b)(2)–(3)); and
- Requires OSHA, in respect to standards for toxic substances or harmful physical agents, to set rules that "most adequately [assure], to the extent feasible, on the basis of the best available evidence, that no employee will suffer material impairment of health or functional capacity" (29 U.S.C. § 655(b)(5)).

Initiating Standards

OSHA may begin development of a standard on its own volition, or it may do so in response to requests from outside organizations. As one former OSHA administrator has noted, news media coverage of significant outbreaks or occurrences of work-related injuries and illnesses has prompted OSHA to initiate rulemaking in several instances:

> Such crises often bring outrage from the citizens, and various organized groups can be an enormous stimulus for passage of a specific standard, notably with asbestos and DBCP [dibromochloropropane]. The fact that the media was heavily involved in reporting episodes involving DBCP and asbestos clearly served as pressure to regulate.

(Eula Bingham, *Workplace Regulation Gone Wrong*, in OCCUPATIONAL HEALTH IN THE 1990s, 64)

Some critics have charged that OSHA's standards-setting agenda is too often set on the basis of pressure from outside parties, and that the agency needs to set long-range regulatory goals itself.

Public Participation

Whatever the stimulus for a new standard, OSHA must involve outside parties once it begins rulemaking.

To solicit input, OSHA may convene a standards advisory committee to provide expert opinions on new standards for specific hazards.

An advisory committee may include a maximum number of 15 members. An equal number of members must represent employers and employees, respectively, and the committee must include at least one representative each from the Department of Health and Human Services and state government, respectively. Meetings must be open to the public, and an accurate record kept and made available (29 U.S.C. § 656(b)). An advisory committee must submit its recommendations within 90 days of its appointment or within a shorter or longer period set by the Secretary of Labor, but at any rate no longer than 270 days from its appointment (29 U.S.C. § 655(b)(1)).

A similar process—used by OSHA in two instances—is negotiated rulemaking, which differs in some technical ways from the advisory committee process but also involves the convening of a group of experts representing different interests. OSHA first used negotiated rulemaking in 1986 in an effort to develop a benzene standard that would be acceptable to both labor and industry. The effort was unsuccessful because the participants failed to agree on certain key provisions. In 1987, another effort was more successful in helping OSHA develop a standard for 4,4'-methylenedianiline (MDA).

Aside from standards advisory committees and negotiated rulemaking, OSHA is required by the OSH Act to involve the general public in standards-setting through notice-and-comment rulemaking. The agency must publish a proposed rule in the *Federal Register* and allow at least 30 days for public comment (29 C.F.R. § 655(b)(2)).

This procedure usually involves these actions:

- First, OSHA publishes in the *Federal Register* an advance notice of proposed rulemaking (ANPRM) or request for information. This announces that it is considering the development of a particular standard and asks for information or comment that would help determine, at an early stage, whether the rule is necessary or feasible, and if so, what requirements should be set.

- If OSHA decides to proceed with rulemaking on the basis of the response to the advance notice, agency staff members may write a draft proposed standard and circulate it informally to interested outside parties for comment.

- Next, with a notice of proposed rulemaking (NPRM), the agency formally publishes a proposed standard and again asks for public comment (29 U.S.C. § 655(b)(2)).

- If, during the comment period, an interested party requests a public hearing on the proposed standard, OSHA must grant the request and specify a time and place for the hearing (29 U.S.C. § 655(b)(3)).

Other Requirements

OSHA's standards-setting procedures also are guided by three requirements imposed generally on federal regulatory agencies:

- Under the National Environmental Policy Act, OSHA must prepare an environmental impact statement for each proposed standard and certify that the rule will not have a significant adverse impact on the general environment (42 U.S.C. § 4332; 29 C.F.R. § 1999.1–1999.8).

- Executive Order No. 12,291, issued February 19, 1981, as a "regulatory reform" effort by the Reagan Administration and continued under the Bush Administration, requires OSHA to prepare a "regulatory impact analysis" that describes the potential benefits of the proposed standard, its potential costs, alternative ways to control the hazard, and why the approach chosen by OSHA is preferable to the alternatives (46 Fed. Reg. 13,193 (1981)).

- The Paperwork Reduction Act requires OSHA to ensure that the proposed standard will not require employers to keep unnecessary records (44 U.S.C. § 3501 et seq.).

Developmental Process

OSHA standards are written by staff members in the agency's two directorates, or units, for safety and health standards development. Whether a given standard is intended to protect workers from a safety hazard (unsafe equipment, processes, or physical conditions in the workplace) or a health hazard (toxic, cancer-causing, or otherwise harmful chemicals and physical agents), determines the involvement of staff members from either the Directorate of Safety Standards Programs or the Directorate of Health Standards Programs.

Attorneys from the Department of Labor's Office of the Solicitor (the department's legal counsel) also are involved in the development of standards, beginning in early stages of the process. Where OSHA staff members provide technical expertise, the attorneys provide legal advice to ensure that the rule will not violate legal or procedural strictures.

Before publication, proposed and final standards must be approved by the Policy Review Board, a Department of Labor executive panel; the Secretary of Labor; and the White House Office of Management and Budget (OMB). Under Executive Order No. 12,291, OMB is authorized to assess the regulatory impact of each standard.

Final Standards

Final standards are published in the *Federal Register*, as required by section 6(b)(4) of the OSH Act (29 U.S.C. § 655(b)(4)). As required by the Administrative Procedure Act, every final OSHA rule is published with a preamble in which the agency discusses the provisions of the standard, reviews the public comments received on the proposed version, and explains why given requirements were chosen over alternative approaches that may have been recommended in the comments.

For major standards—those setting extensive requirements and resulting in significant costs for employers where equipment must be fitted with new controls, workplaces must be redesigned, and protective clothing and equipment must be provided to employees—it generally takes OSHA two years or longer to progress from an advance notice of proposed rulemaking to a final rule.

Typically, an OSHA standard will require employers to use engineering controls to correct or prevent hazards. This means that the employer must control the hazard at its source. If the hazard is a toxic chemical, for example, the employer must use ventilation, closed systems, or similar approaches to keep airborne concentrations at low levels or otherwise protect the employee from harmful direct contact.

If the hazard involves a safety risk (for example, exposure to moving parts of heavy machinery), the employer may be required to use barriers or "guards" to physically separate the work from the source of risk.

Generally, OSHA standards allow employers to use personal protective equipment (such as protective clothing, face shields, and respirators) only as a secondary or emergency measure. In line with traditional industrial hygiene policy, OSHA has concluded that engineering controls, as a rule, are more effective than personal protective equipment for safeguarding workers.

In issuing a new standard, OSHA may delay enforcement of the rule for a maximum of 90 days (29 U.S.C. § 655(b)(4)). This lead time is intended to ensure that employers and employees have an opportunity to become familiar with the standard. The agency also may phase in compliance over a longer period of time.

Under the OSH Act, the agency must set standards that "most adequately [ensure], to the extent feasible, on the basis of the best available evidence, that no employee will suffer material impairment of health or functional capacity even if such employee has regular exposure to the hazard dealt with by such standard" (29 U.S.C. § 655(b)(5)).

Emergency Temporary Standards

To meet an "obvious need for quick response to new safety and health findings" (House Education and Labor Committee Rep. No. 1291), the OSH Act gives OSHA the authority to set emergency temporary standards under certain circumstances. These rules may be put into effect immediately without going through normal section 6(b) notice-and-comment procedures. The Act authorizes emergency rulemaking if:

- Employees are at "grave danger" from exposure to toxic or physically harmful substances or agents, or from "new hazards," and
- An emergency standard is necessary to protect employees from that danger (29 U.S.C. § 655(c)(1)).

As soon as the emergency rule is published in the *Federal Register*, OSHA must begin proceedings to set a permanent standard under normal notice-and-comment procedures, using the emergency rule as a proposed permanent standard. A final permanent standard must be issued no later than six months after publication of the emergency rule (29 U.S.C. § 655(c)(3)).

Under the Act, an emergency standard may remain in effect until OSHA issues a permanent rule (29 U.S.C. § 655(c)(2)).

VARIANCES

Employers who find it difficult to comply with a new standard by the given effective date, or believe that other means exist for more effectively protecting workers than are provided for in a standard may seek exemptions or variances from those requirements if certain conditions are met.

Temporary Variance Order

If an employer believes it is unable to comply with a new standard by the given effective date, it may seek a temporary variance order from OSHA. Such an order would give the employer additional time to come into compliance (29 U.S.C. § 655(b)(6)(A)).

To qualify for such an order, the employer must show that it:

- Is unable to comply by the effective date because necessary personnel, materials, or equipment are not available, or because needed workplace construction or renovation cannot be completed by then;
- Is taking all available steps to protect employees from the hazard covered by the standard;
- Has an effective program for coming into compliance as quickly as it can; and
- Has informed employees about the request for a temporary variance.

OSHA also is authorized to grant a temporary variance if it determines, or the Department of Health and Human Services certifies, that such an order is necessary to permit the employer to participate in an experiment approved by the secretary of labor or the secretary of health and human services that is designed to demonstrate or validate "new and improved techniques to safeguard the health or safety of workers" (29 U.S.C. § 655(b)(6)(C)).

A temporary variance may remain in effect for as long as it takes to achieve compliance, or for one year, whichever is shorter. However, an order may be renewed twice, as long as the request for renewal is filed at least 90 days before the scheduled expiration date of the order (29 U.S.C. § 655(b)(6)(A)).

Permanent Variance

An employer may seek a permanent variance from a standard if it can show by "a preponderance of the evidence" that it uses other means to protect employees from the hazard covered by the standard and that those means are as effective as those required by the standard (29 U.S.C. § 655(d)).

The request for a permanent variance must:

- Describe the processes, conditions, operations, practices, means, or methods used or proposed to be used by the applicant (29 C.F.R. § 1905.11(b)(3));

- Show how these approaches would protect workers as effectively as the standard (29 C.F.R. § 1905.11(b)(4)); and
- Certify that the applicant has informed its employees of the request for variance (29 C.F.R. § 1905.11(b)(5)).

An employer seeking a variance also may request an interim order providing an exemption from the standard in question until the application for a variance is acted upon (29 C.F.R. § 1905.11(c)).

If OSHA finds that an application for a variance does not contain the information required for a determination, it may deny the application (29 C.F.R. § 1905.14(a)(1)); such a denial does not bar the employer from filing another application later (29 C.F.R. § 1905.14(a)(4)).

If the application is adequate, OSHA must publish a notice in the *Federal Register* that the application has been filed, describing the application and inviting comment from interested parties (29 C.F.R. § 1905.14(b)(1)–(2)).

Any employer, employee, or state agency having jurisdiction over the place of employment covered by the variance request may ask OSHA to hold a hearing on the application (29 C.F.R. § 1905.15(a)).

CHALLENGING STANDARDS

Persons or organizations "adversely affected" by an OSHA standard may challenge the rule in federal appeals court. Lawsuits must be filed within 60 days of the time the standard appeared in the *Federal Register*, and they must be filed in the federal judicial circuit in which the challenger "resides or has his principal place of business" (29 U.S.C. § 655(f)).

Typically, whenever an OSHA standard is challenged in court, petitions for review are filed by several parties, each of which cites its own reasons for seeking judicial review of the rule. Often, these petitions are filed in different judicial circuits, raising the question of which circuit should properly have venue.

Until 1988, venue was decided by determining which circuit had *first* been petitioned (28 U.S.C. § 2112). All challenges then would be consolidated in that circuit. However, this procedure for resolving questions of venue (which applied to other federal regulatory programs as well as OSHA's) created further problems. It usually resulted in a "race to the courthouse," in which each party would try to file first in the circuit believed to be most receptive to its challenge.

Congress took a critical look at the "race to the courthouse" process in 1987, and found that this system had significant drawbacks. Races to the courthouse "detract from the public's perception of the Federal courts as impartial, consistent arbiters of justice" (S. Rep. No. 263). In addition, the report noted, such races "produce no economic benefit . . . yet often cost private participants tens of thousands of dollars," and lead to "wasteful litigation to determine who 'won' the race."

The procedure for determining venue in multiple-appeal cases was revised in January 1988 by the "Act Affecting Selection of Court for Multiple Appeals" (Pub. L. No. 100-236). Now, when petitions are filed in more than one circuit, OSHA must notify a judicial panel on multidistrict litigation—a panel of seven circuit and district judges designated by the Chief Justice of the United States (28 U.S.C. § 1407(d)). By random selection, the panel will select one court of appeals from among those in which the petitions were filed (28 U.S.C. § 2112(a)(3)).

An OSHA standard can be challenged as soon as it is issued—that is, when it is officially filed in the Office of the Federal Register (29 C.F.R. § 1911.18). Under an unpublished opinion by the U.S. Court of Appeals for the First Circuit, this occurs when the date of receipt is stamped on the standard by the staff of the *Federal Register,* and the document is made available for public review (*American Textile Manufacturers Institute v. Bingham*). This may occur one or several days before the document is actually published in the *Federal Register.*

Whenever a standard is challenged, the reviewing court must find OSHA's reasons for setting the rule "conclusive" if those reasons are "supported by substantial evidence in the record [of rulemaking] considered as a whole" (29 U.S.C. § 655(f)).

A challenge to a standard may be carried beyond a court of appeals to the U.S. Supreme Court. Two landmark standards cases have been heard by the Supreme Court:

- *American Textile Manufacturers Institute v. Donovan,* in which the Supreme Court upheld OSHA's standard for exposure to cotton dust in textile mills after concluding that the rule was technologically and economically feasible.
- *Industrial Union Department v. American Petroleum Institute,* in which the high court vacated OSHA's benzene standard after concluding that the agency failed to show that the rule would protect workers from a "significant risk" of harm.

Staying a Standard

The filing of a challenge against a standard does not automatically stay or delay enforcement of the rule pending a decision on the suit, unless the court itself grants a stay (29 U.S.C. § 655(f)). In seeking a stay, the petitioner must show that:

- There is a substantial likelihood the petitioner will win the challenge on the merits of its argument;
- The petitioner will suffer "irreparable harm" if the stay is not granted;
- The issuance of a stay will not substantially harm any other parties in the case; and
- The issuance of a stay will not interfere with the "public interest" (*Taylor Diving and Salvage Co. v. Department of Labor*).

A stay, if granted, may remain in effect as long as the court deems necessary, but does not constitute a decision on the merits of the challenge (*American Iron and Steel Institute v. OSHA*).

ADMINISTRATIVE GUIDELINES

OSHA standards often are supplemented by administrative guidelines developed by agency staff at OSHA headquarters and issued to compliance officers and other field staff. These guidelines are used to clarify possible ambiguities in the wording of standards and to provide further guidance to field staff on enforcing the requirements.

These guidelines usually are issued first as program directives or instructions. Directives with long-term application may be incorporated later into OSHA's *Field Operations Manual*, which details the procedures that compliance officers should follow in conducting inspections.

For example, OSHA instruction STD 1-1.12 clarifies the standard on fixed ladders for walking-working surfaces, by providing further guidance on the use of fixed ladders as escape mechanisms for employees in emergencies. (The instruction is reprinted in Appendix D.)

All OSHA directives and instructions are reprinted in BNA's *Occupational Safety and Health Reporter* (O.S.H. Rep. Ref. File (BNA) No. 21, 8001–9966) as is the OSHA *Field Operations Manual* (O.S.H. Rep. Ref. File (BNA) No. 77, 1–3604).

GENERAL DUTY CLAUSE

OSHA standards are not all-inclusive. To address hazards not covered by a particular standard, OSHA may cite section 5(a)(1) of the OSH Act.

This provision is called the general duty clause because it imposes on employers the general obligation of furnishing workplaces that are "free from recognized hazards that are causing or are likely to cause death or serious physical harm" (29 U.S.C. § 654(a)(1)).

In its deliberations on the OSH Act in 1970, the Senate Labor Committee reasoned that "precise standards to cover every conceivable situation will not always exist. This legislation would be seriously deficient if any employee were killed or seriously injured on the job simply because there was no specific standard applicable to a recognized hazard" (S. Rep. No. 1282).

However, the committee added that the general duty clause was not meant to be "a general substitute" for standards, but simply would help protect employees working in "special circumstances for which no standard has yet been adopted."

Section 5(a)(1) cannot be cited when a particular standard applies to a given condition (*Brisk Waterproofing Co.*) and may be invoked only where:

- The employer failed to keep the workplace free from a hazard to which its employees were exposed;
- The hazard was recognized;
- The hazard caused or was likely to cause death or serious physical harm to workers; and
- A feasible or useful method for correcting the hazard existed (OSHA *Field Operations Manual*, ch. IV, (A)(2), O.S.H. Rep. Ref. File (BNA) No. 77, at 2502).

Each challenge to a section 5(a)(1) citation is litigated on the unique facts at that particular workplace.

3

OSHA RECORD KEEPING REQUIREMENTS

Section 8(c) of the OSH Act requires employers to maintain records deemed necessary or appropriate for enforcing the Act and for developing information regarding the causes and prevention of occupational accidents and illnesses (29 U.S.C. § 657(c)).

Generally speaking, two kinds of records are required by OSHA under regulations issued by the agency under the authority of section 8(c):

- Affidavits, certificates, medical forms, measurements, and other such documentation that help the agency gauge the employer's compliance with specific safety and health standards, and
- Logs and supporting documents showing the number, nature, and circumstances of injuries and illnesses that occur in the workplace.

The Senate and House labor committees, in approving their respective versions of the OSH legislation in 1970, underscored the importance of information collected in such records. In its report on the Senate bill, the Senate Labor and Public Welfare Committee stated:

Full and accurate information is a fundamental precondition for meaningful administration of an occupational safety and health program. At the present time, however, the Federal government and most of the states have inadequate information on the in-

31

cidence, nature, or causes of occupational injuries, illnesses, and deaths (S. Rep. No. 1282 (1970)).

Section 8(c) was meant to correct this deficiency of information by requiring employers to document, for example, the levels of toxic substances present in their workplaces, and the circumstances surrounding injuries to their workers, and to make these data available to OSHA and to their own employees.

Looking at such information from individual workplaces, OSHA can determine more readily whether the employer is providing safe and healthful working conditions. Moreover, when analyzed with similar data from other workplaces, the information gives researchers a valuable tool for monitoring injury and illness trends, evaluating the safety record of various industries, and determining whether particular safeguards are effective in protecting workers from dangerous machinery or toxic chemicals.

Providing data to employees themselves also is important, according to OSHA:

> . . . [G]iving employees and their designated representatives the right to see relevant exposure and medical information . . . will make it easier for employees to identify worksite hazards, particularly workplace exposures which impair their health or functional capacity. Increased awareness of workplace hazards will also make it more likely that prescribed work and personal hygiene practices will be followed (43 Fed. Reg. 31,371 (1978)).

RECORDS REQUIRED UNDER OSHA STANDARDS

Employers must maintain documents under various OSHA standards. Generally, this record keeping falls into several categories, including the types discussed in the following sections.

Equipment Certification

Regulations covering certain types of potentially hazardous equipment require employers to examine the machinery periodically and certify that it is in safe working condition. Equipment to which such requirements pertain include cranes

(29 C.F.R. § 1910.180(d)(6)), slings (29 C.F.R. § 1910.184(e)(3)), and power presses (29 C.F.R. § 1910.217(h)).

Exposure Records

OSHA standards covering hazardous workplace substances require that employers measure worker exposure to these substances to ensure that exposure does not exceed allowable limits. Measurements must be recorded.

Exposure records include:

- Results of personal, grab, area, wipe, or other types of sampling, and the related calculations used to interpret those samples;
- Biological monitoring results that interpret the effects of a toxic substance or harmful physical agent on the body;
- Material safety data sheets indicating that a given substance may pose a hazard to worker health (a material safety data sheet is a form that provides information about the physical properties, appearance, and effects of a chemical substance); and
- In the absence of any of these documents, a chemical inventory or other record that identifies any harmful substances used in the workplace, and when and where they were used.

Because cancer and other diseases may take several years to develop, the harmful effects of a given chemical or physical agent may not become apparent until decades after the victim was first exposed. In recognition of this latency period, OSHA requires employers generally to keep exposure records for at least 30 years, so that data will be available for research if—years after its first use—a chemical is suspected of causing harm to employees who worked with it (29 C.F.R. § 1910.20(d)(1)(ii)). There are some exceptions to this requirement:

- Background documents such as laboratory reports and worksheets need be kept for only one year, as long as sampling results associated with those documents, a description of the methodologies used for sampling and analysis, and a summary of other relevant information are kept for at least 30 years.

- Material safety data sheets for materials not currently in use need not be retained for any specified period, as long as the employer maintains for at least 30 years some record of the materials and when and where they were used.
- Biological monitoring results designated as exposure records under individual OSHA health standards must be maintained as required by the specific standard.

Medical Records

OSHA health standards also require that employers conduct periodic medical tests to monitor the health effects of potentially toxic or carcinogenic workplace substances, and document the results of these tests. These medical records include:

- Medical and employment questionnaires and histories, including job descriptions and occupational exposures related to those jobs;
- Results of medical examinations and laboratory tests;
- Medical opinions, diagnoses, progress notes, and recommendations;
- First-aid records;
- Descriptions of treatments and prescriptions; and
- Employee medical complaints.

Like exposure documents, medical records may have long-term value for researchers. Consequently, in most instances, they must be kept for at least as long as the employee works for the employer, plus an additional 30 years (29 C.F.R. § 1910.20(d)(1)(i)). However, there are three exceptions to that requirement:

- Health insurance claims maintained apart from the employer's medical surveillance program need not be retained for any specific period of time.
- First-aid records involving one-time treatment of minor injuries such as cuts, scratches, and burns need not be kept for any specific length of time, if the injury did not

involve medical treatment, loss of consciousness, restriction of work or motion, or transfer to another job; if the records were made on-site by persons who were not physicians; and if the records were kept separately from the employer's medical surveillance program.

• Medical records for persons employed for less than a year need not be kept by the employer beyond the period of employment, as long as copies were given to the worker at the termination of employment.

If the employer uses exposure or medical records to analyze potential workplace hazards, copies of those analyses must also be kept for at least 30 years (29 C.F.R. § 1910.20(d)(1)(iii)).

If a company goes out of business, its exposure and medical records must be transferred to the company that absorbs or buys it (29 C.F.R. § 1910.20(h)(1)). If there is no successor company, the employer must notify workers that they have a right of access to the records, at least three months before the employer ceases to do business (29 C.F.R. § 1910.20(h)(2)). In that instance, the employer also must transfer the records to NIOSH, if required to do so by a specific health standard (29 C.F.R. § 1910.20(h)(3)).

Miscellaneous Records

Some OSHA regulations require employers to keep other records to document that employers have taken specific steps to protect employees from certain hazards. For example:

• The standard for commercial diving operations requires employers to record dives, decompression analyses, and employee hospitalizations (29 C.F.R. § 1910.440).

• Under the fire protection standard, employers must certify that fire extinguishers have been tested at required intervals (29 C.F.R. § 1910.157(f)(16)).

• The standard for hazardous waste operations requires employers to develop written work plans that describe cleanup operations at specific hazardous waste sites, including precautions taken to protect workers from hazards (29 C.F.R. § 1910.120(b)(3)).

ACCESS TO EXPOSURE AND MEDICAL RECORDS

Employers are required to give OSHA access to records under section 8(c)(1) of the OSH Act. In 1980, OSHA issued regulations to give employees similar access to exposure and medical records. This step was needed, OSHA said, to give workers the ability to "play a meaningful role in their own health management" and to "become directly involved in the discovery and control of occupational health hazards." In issuing the regulations, OSHA said it had found that denial of employee access to records was "commonplace, if not the universal practice of industry."

Employee Access to Records

Although subject to some constraints, OSHA's regulations give an employee access to his or her own medical and exposure records. They also provide access for employee representatives. A representative can be "any individual or organization to whom an employee gives written authorization" for access to records. A recognized or certified collective bargaining agent must be regarded by the employer automatically as a representative of employees who belong to the union's bargaining unit, regardless of whether the union has the employee's written authorization (29 C.F.R. § 1910.20(c)(3)).

When an employee or employee representative seeks access to records, OSHA requires the employer to provide the documents in a reasonable time, place, and manner. If access cannot reasonably be provided within 15 working days of the request, the employer must explain the reasons for the delay and indicate the earliest date on which the records can be made available.

OSHA prohibits employers from demanding needless information from employees or employee representatives concerning the records that are being sought. The employer may demand only information that will be readily known to the person making the request, or necessary for locating the pertinent documents—for example, the dates and locations of relevant employment (29 C.F.R. § 1910.20(e)(1)(ii)).

The employer must provide copies of records at no charge, make copying facilities available at no cost, or loan records "for a reasonable time" to allow the employee or the representative to make a copy (29 C.F.R. § 1910.20(e)(1)(iii)). There are two exceptions to this rule:

- If the record is an original X-ray, the employer may require the employee or representative to examine it on-site, or may make arrangements for a temporary loan.
- If the record was provided to the same person before at no cost, the employer may charge "reasonable, non-discriminatory" fees for additional copies, covering such expenses as search time and photocopying costs. However, the employer cannot charge for new information that supplements the earlier data, and cannot charge for a first-time request by a recognized bargaining agent.

If records relevant to a particular employee's job-related exposures are not available, OSHA requires the employer to provide records of other employees who had similar job duties or were in similar working conditions (29 C.F.R. § 1910.20(e)(2)). This information must be provided to the extent needed to show what substances or physical agents the employee was exposed to, and to what extent he or she was exposed.

An employee may request exposure records that indicate the types and concentrations of toxic substances or harmful physical agents present in the work areas to which he or she is being newly assigned or transferred.

If a designated representative seeks access to an employee's medical records without the worker's written consent, the request must specify what records are being sought and what "occupational health need" provides the basis for the request. If the representative has the employee's written consent, the authorization must include the name and signature of the worker, a general description of the medical information sought, and a general description of the purpose for the request, among other information.

Because medical records may contain sensitive or highly technical information, OSHA permits physicians retained by employers to suggest—when asked to provide access to such documents—that the employee or representative:

- Consult with the physician to review or discuss the records;
- Accept a summary of "material facts and opinions" in place of the records themselves; or
- Accept release of the records only to a physician or other designated representative.

If a physician representing the employer believes that direct disclosure of information pertinent to a diagnosis of a terminal illness or a psychiatric condition would be detrimental to the employee's health, the employer may deny direct access to the worker. However, in those instances, the employer must also state that the information may be provided to a designated representative having the worker's written consent. The representative must be given access if he or she has this consent, even if the employer knows that the information subsequently will be passed along to the employee.

Physicians, nurses, or other health care personnel who maintain records may delete from requested records the name of any family member, friend, or fellow worker who has provided confidential information about the employee's health.

Any health or hazard analyses prepared by the employer using information from an employee's medical records must be provided to the employee or an authorized representative on request. However, the employer must first remove any information that would identify other employees. If that step is not feasible, the employer is not required to provide access to those portions of the analysis.

OSHA Access to Records

Except where the request would infringe on the employer's constitutional rights, an employer must assure that OSHA representatives have prompt access to employee exposure and medical records, and to employer analyses using those records. Because medical documents sometimes contain sensitive information, OSHA has established strict procedures governing its access to such records in order to protect employees' right of privacy.

Written Access Order

In seeking access, OSHA representatives generally must have either the employee's written consent or a written access order approved by the administrator of the agency on the recommendation of OSHA's medical records officer. The latter specialist is an OSHA official specifically experienced or trained in the evaluation, use, and privacy protection of such records.

The agency may seek disclosure of records without a written access order or the employee's consent only if an OSHA staff physician or a doctor under contract to the agency is consulting with the employer's physician on a health or safety issue. Then employee medical documents can be examined, and necessary personal notes can be made on the findings. However, no records may be taken off site without a written order or worker consent, and no notes concerning personally identifiable medical information may leave the OSHA physician's control without the permission of the agency's medical records officer.

Before approving an access order, the OSHA administrator and the medical records officer must determine that:

- The information is relevant to an investigation or study involving worker health and safety;
- Personally identifiable medical information (i.e., medical data accompanied by the employee's name, address, or other details through which the worker could be identified) to be examined and copied is limited to data needed to accomplish OSHA's purpose; and
- Personnel authorized to review or analyze the information are limited to those who have a bona fide need for access and appropriate professional qualifications (for example, a doctor, nurse, industrial hygienist, or toxicologist).

A written access order must state:

- The purpose for which the information is sought;
- A general description of the kind of data sought, and why OSHA needs to examine personally identifiable data;

- Whether medical information will be examined at the employer's workplace, and what type of data will be copied and taken elsewhere;
- The name, address, and phone number of the OSHA representative responsible for assuring that the information will be used in the manner described in the access order, and similar identification of anyone else who is expected to analyze the information;
- The name, address, and phone number of the OSHA medical records officer; and
- The length of time that OSHA expects to retain the information in a personally identifiable form.

Presenting the Order

Under agency procedures, the OSHA investigator must present at least two copies of the written access order to the employer, with a cover letter, before the employer is required to divulge any records. The cover letter must summarize the medical records access rules and advise the employer to direct any questions or objections about the order to the principal agency investigator or the medical records officer.

The investigator also must give a copy of the order and the cover letter to each collective bargaining agent representing the employees whose records are sought. This copy of the order, and at least one of the copies given to the employer, must omit information that would enable others to identify the specific employees. The employer's copy, from which the information is deleted, must be posted promptly in the place of business.

If the investigator decides, after consultation with the employer and the union, that it is appropriate to notify each employee affected by the access order, the employer must do so. The employer may notify individual workers by contacting them directly, or by placing a copy of the order in the employee's medical file.

Even if the employer raises an objection to the access order, OSHA has the authority to proceed with its investigation. The medical records officer must respond in writing to any written objections by the employer or union. If the medical records officer finds the objection valid, he or she may revoke the access order and direct the investigator to return the information to the original record holder, or destroy it if it is in the form of a copy.

OSHA's procedures call for the agency to take care in handling information that could be used to identify specific employees:

- Whenever such information is taken off the employer's premises, OSHA must code the data, using a code number for each employee. Only personnel with a need to know the information, as part of OSHA's investigation, may be given access to the identifiers that could be used to translate the code.
- Files containing the information must be separated from other OSHA files and secured in a locked cabinet or vault. The agency must keep a log of the utilization of the data, and any transfers of the information. Only OSHA personnel, contractors for the agency, or Labor Department attorneys with a "need to know" may be given access to it.
- When personally identifiable information and lists of codes are no longer needed, they must be returned to the original record holder or destroyed.

OSHA is not permitted to transfer personally identifiable information to another agency, unless the recipient is:

- A public health agency that needs the data for an important health purpose, will not use the information to make decisions that could be detrimental to the employees affected, and has procedures, comparable to OSHA's, for protecting the data;
- NIOSH; or
- The Department of Justice (DOJ), in situations in which DOJ needs the data for specific action under the OSH Act, such as prosecuting employers for criminal violations of the Act.

Trade Secrets

In giving the agency access to exposure or medical records, as in any situation in which an employer is required to divulge information to OSHA, there is a fear of disclosing trade secrets. To address this concern, the agency permits employers to withhold such information if:

- The employer can support the assertion that the data involve a trade secret;
- The employer releases all other information on the properties and effects of a toxic substance for which a trade secret is claimed; and
- The employer informs the party that requested the data— OSHA, an employee, or an employee representative— that the information is being withheld as a trade secret.

However, if deletion of trade secret information would impair OSHA's ability to evaluate employee exposure to a harmful substance or physical agent, the employer still must provide alternative data that would enable the agency to determine where and when an exposure occurred.

In some instances, OSHA still may require employers to provide the agency, employees, or employee representatives with access to information claimed as trade secrets. In an emergency—a situation in which a doctor or nurse would need to know the identity of a chemical in order to treat an employee immediately for an injury or illness caused by exposure to the substance—the employer must disclose the information to the doctor or nurse. As soon as circumstances permit, the doctor or nurse may be required by the employer to provide a written request stating why the information is needed, and a written confidentiality agreement indicating that the data will not be used except for that purpose.

If the information is needed to monitor worker exposure, assess the effects of a substance, or protect or treat employees—but immediate access is not crucial—the employer may be required to disclose the information after a statement of need and a confidentiality agreement are presented.

To help protect the employer's interests, the confidentiality agreement may authorize the employer to seek appropriate legal remedies if the agreement is violated, including stipulation of a reasonable preestimate of the damages the employer probably would suffer if the trade secret were disclosed improperly.

If the employer denies a request for disclosure of a chemical identity, it must do so within 30 days of the request. The denial must be in writing and must include evidence to support a trade secret claim.

An employee, employee representative, or health professional denied access may refer the action to OSHA for review. The employer may be subject to citation if the agency determines that:

- The information is not a true trade secret; or
- Even if it is a trade secret, (1) the requesting party has a legitimate need for the information, (2) the party has executed a written confidentiality agreement, and (3) the party has shown adequate means for complying with the agreement.

What if the employer can show that a confidentiality agreement would not provide sufficient protection for a trade secret? In this instance, OSHA may set additional conditions for the requesting party to ensure that the party's needs are met without causing undue harm to the employer.

INJURY AND ILLNESS RECORDS

Employers generally are required to keep records of work-related injuries, illnesses, and deaths of their employees. This information is deemed "necessary and appropriate" for developing data on the causes and preventions of such incidents, and for maintaining a nationwide program for collecting and analyzing job safety and health statistics (29 C.F.R. § 1904.1).

Only employers that have employed fewer than ten workers at any time during the preceding calendar year, and those in low-hazard industries such as retail trade, finance, insurance, real estate, and services, are exempted from these requirements. However, they still are required to report to OSHA any accident that results in a fatality or the hospitalization of five or more workers.

OSHA routinely inspects injury and illness logs when conducting inspections. For individual workplaces, these records help alert the agency to particular hazards at these sites. The data, when aggregated with similar information from other workplaces, also help the government determine which industries pose the greatest risk of injury or illness, and consequently help OSHA determine to which types of workplaces it should give priority attention in scheduling inspections.

Since 1986, OSHA has emphasized the importance of accurate injury and illness records by proposing large fines against companies that keep incomplete or inaccurate logs.

Reporting and Forms

Employers are required to record injuries and illnesses on the government's OSHA Form 200 (see Appendix E), or on an equivalent document that is as readable and comprehensive.

When a work-related injury or illness occurs, it must be entered on the form as early as practicable, but in no event any later than six days after the employer has learned of the incident.

If a worker dies in a job-related fatality, or five or more employees are hospitalized as a result of a workplace accident, the death or injuries must be reported within 48 hours, either orally or in writing, to the nearest OSHA area office.

Along with Form 200, which is called the log and summary of occupational injuries and illnesses, employers must keep a supplementary record for each incident. The supplementary record is intended to provide further information about the employer, the affected employee, the circumstances of the injury or illness, any medical treatment provided to the worker, and the name of the person completing the form.

Employers may use government document, OSHA Form 101 (see Appendix E), or equivalent documents such as workers' compensation and insurance reports for the supplementary record, as long as these forms provide the same information required by the 101 form.

Employers also are required to use Form 200 to compile an annual summary of injuries and illnesses, which must be posted in the workplace on February 1 of the year following the year covered by the summary and remain posted until March 1. (For example, the annual summary covering 1991 would need to be posted from February 1, 1992, to March 1, 1992.) The employer must mail copies to workers who do not report to a single establishment or who do not report to a fixed establishment on a regular basis.

Recordable Injuries and Illnesses

OSHA requires employers to keep injury and illness records for five years following the year to which they relate. Incidents must be recorded if they:

- Result in a fatality, regardless of the time between the injury and the resulting death, or the length of the illness;
- Cause the victim to lose any days of work;
- Result in transfer to another job or termination of employment, medical treatment other than first aid, loss of consciousness, or restriction of motion or work; or
- In the case of diagnosed occupational illnesses, are reported to the employer but are not classified as fatalities or lost work day incidents (29 C.F.R. § 1904.12(c)).

For further guidance, OSHA recommends that employers consult a booklet prepared by the U.S. Bureau of Labor Statistics (BLS), "Record Keeping Guidelines for Occupational Injuries and Illnesses" (U.S. Bureau of Lab. Stat. No. LAB-441, 1986).[1]

Enforcement

In the earliest years of the agency, injury and illness records became an integral part of OSHA's enforcement program when the government used industry-wide injury incidence rates calculated from injury-record data to identify particularly hazardous industries for priority inspection. In 1981, record-keeping assumed even greater importance for employers when OSHA began exempting some workplaces from comprehensive inspections if their records showed an injury rate lower than the national average.

---

[1]This booklet is available from OSHA, U.S. Department of Labor, Washington, D.C. 20212, or from OSHA area offices.

OSHA rescinded that policy in 1988 (see Chapter 4, OSHA Enforcement), but inspectors continue to examine injury and illness records as a part of each inspection. To emphasize the importance of accurate records, in 1986, OSHA began to assess large penalties for alleged instances of inaccurate or incomplete record keeping. Of the 25 largest penalties proposed by OSHA in 1986 and 1987, 17 involved alleged record keeping violations, including 2 proposed fines of more than $1 million each. Numerous other major record keeping penalties have been proposed since 1987.

Industry and organized labor both have criticized OSHA's record keeping system. Employers charge that in some instances, the agency requires them to record minor injuries that do not give a true indication of a company's overall safety experience, and that some of the requirements are ambiguous or confusing. Labor unions charge that employers fail to report most injuries and illnesses to OSHA.

Since 1987, OSHA and other agencies have taken steps to address both sets of concerns. The Bureau of Labor Statistics, after revising its record keeping guidelines in 1986, held meetings and seminars with employers around the United States to explain and clarify the guidelines. Another revision is expected to be undertaken in 1992 by OSHA, to which the Labor Department, in January 1991, transferred responsibility for providing record keeping guidance to employers.

Other agencies have begun to look at ways to collect additional workplace illness data to supplement OSHA's. For example, the National Center for Health Statistics has added questions relating to job-related illnesses to some of its national health surveys, and NIOSH has encouraged state health agencies to begin collecting occupational illness data.

Annual Survey

Industry-wide injury and illness statistics are calculated by the government through an annual survey conducted by BLS. The survey is based on a questionnaire, OSHA Form 200-S, that about 200,000 employers are asked to complete. Different employers are asked to participate each year, and are sent the questionnaire in February following the year covered by the survey. (A copy of the survey form appears in the O.S.H. Rep. Ref. File (BNA) No. 27, at 1261.)

Usually, information for the questionnaire can be copied directly from OSHA Form 200. Sometimes, BLS asks employers not normally required to keep injury and illness records (for example, small businesses and employers in low-hazard industries) to participate in the survey. If these employers are asked to participate, they are required to do so. However, BLS will notify these businesses of this duty a year beforehand, and will supply the necessary forms and instructions for completing the questionnaire.

4

OSHA ENFORCEMENT

The OSH Act gives OSHA the authority to go into workplaces, inspect worksite conditions, cite employers found to be in violation of agency standards, and levy monetary penalties for those infractions. Although OSHA's police powers have generated controversy since the agency's inception, Congress determined that citations were important for deterring reckless disregard for employee safety.

"American industry cannot be made safe and healthful solely by enacting a Federal law which emphasizes punishment," the House Education and Labor Committee said in approving the OSH Act in 1970. "Nevertheless, this measure recognizes that effective enforcement and sanctions are necessary for serious cases" (H.R. Rep. No. 1291 (1970)).

OSHA has never had enough inspectors to oversee every business establishment under its jurisdiction. Consequently, in conducting inspections, it gives first priority to accidents and employee safety complaints, and conducts programmed or scheduled inspections at selected work sites in those industries having the highest accident rates, such as construction and heavy manufacturing. Some workplaces in industries with lower than average injury rates have been exempted from OSHA inspections every year since 1976 through appropriations bills for the agency.

In states that have their own OSHA-approved safety and health enforcement programs, inspections are conducted by state personnel. More information on state programs appears in Chapter 6.

The OSH Act sets maximum penalty levels for safety and health violations, but OSHA has the authority to calculate specific penalty amounts within those limits. Employers have the right to challenge citations, proposed fines, and abatement periods before the Occupational Safety and Health Review Commission.

OSHA traditionally has been criticized by industry groups for being unreasonably strict in its enforcement program, and alternately, by labor unions for not being stringent enough. In the early 1980s in response to industry complaints, OSHA instituted a policy under which some workplaces were exempted from complete inspections. Compliance officers were instructed to examine employer injury records and then to terminate the inspection if the documents showed the establishment had a lower than average injury rate. However, in the late 1980s, that policy was abandoned and full inspections reinstituted for all workplaces after an employee died in a workplace that OSHA had not inspected thoroughly.

In recent years, OSHA has utilized new procedures to set higher penalties for particularly serious violations, and Congress, in 1990, increased significantly the maximum fine for all types of infractions.

GROUNDS FOR INSPECTIONS

Under section 8(a) of the OSH Act, OSHA inspectors may enter a workplace after presenting their credentials to the person in charge of the site. Inspectors may examine the equipment, materials, conditions, and structures at the site, and question management and workers to determine if the site is in compliance with pertinent safety and health standards (29 U.S.C. § 657(a)).

OSHA inspections fall into two categories: programmed and unprogrammed. Programmed inspections are scheduled in advance by the agency. Unprogrammed inspections are unplanned, resulting when OSHA learns that a workplace may be in violation of agency standards.

Unprogrammed Inspections

Unprogrammed inspections normally have priority over scheduled ones. They are conducted as a result of:

- Reports of an imminent danger threatening employees at a particular work site;
- Fatalities or catastrophes at a work site;
- Formal complaints made to OSHA by employees under section 8(f) of the OSH Act about dangerous conditions at a site, or referrals from other safety and health agencies; or
- Reports in the news media about an accident at a particular workplace (*FOM* II(E), O.S.H. Rep. Ref. File (BNA) No. 77, at 2202).

Programmed Inspections

In scheduling programmed inspections, OSHA attempts to concentrate on high-hazard workplaces, or work sites in industries that historically have conditions that pose an increased risk to workers' health or safety. For inspection purposes, the construction and maritime industries are considered by OSHA to be high-hazard industries, as is oil and gas extraction (*FOM* II(E)(2), O.S.H. Rep. Ref. File (BNA) No. 77, at 2204).

In terms of safety, a high-hazard industry is one whose injury rate is equal to or higher than the lowest average injury rate for industry as a whole, as determined by the Bureau of Labor Statistics. In terms of health hazards, a high-hazard industry is one with a history of OSHA citations for serious health violations.

OSHA inspections are scheduled in cycles. Simply put, OSHA compiles lists of business establishments and schedules them randomly for inspection, giving first priority to those in high-hazard industries. Two cycles of inspections are scheduled for each fiscal year. The agency conducted 44,000 inspections in fiscal 1991 (as a mid-year estimate), and plans to conduct 47,000 in fiscal 1992.

Occasionally, under special emphasis programs, the agency gives particular priority to workplaces in certain industries after deciding that those industries may pose higher than average risks to employees. Among the industries that have been singled out for increased attention are trench excavation in construction (1973), foundries (1975), chemical manufacturing (1985), petrochemical operations (1990), and meatpacking (1991). Special emphasis programs usually are triggered by catastrophes (the 1985 chemical industry inspections resulted from the 1984 toxic chemical leak in Bhopal, India) or reports about previously neglected hazards in particular industries (for example, the meatpacking inspection program resulted from union complaints that serious injuries were unreported in meatpacking plants).

INSPECTION EXEMPTIONS

Since 1976, Congress has provided special exemptions from programmed OSHA inspections to some industries that otherwise might be scheduled for inspection. These exemptions have been put into effect each year through provisions in annual legislation appropriating operating funds for OSHA.

The most recent OSHA appropriations measure, as of this writing, signed November 5, 1990, covers fiscal year 1991, (Pub. L. No. 101-517), and exempts:

- Work activities involving hunting, shooting, and fishing;
- Employers having ten or fewer employees, in industry categories having a lost-workday occupational injury rate lower than the most recently published national average rate; and
- Farming operations that do not maintain temporary labor camps and which employ ten or fewer employees (in essence, family farms).

These provisions are intended to apply to small businesses, which complained in the early 1970s that they were being subjected to an undue number of OSHA inspections. The provisions do not, however, completely exempt such businesses from OSHA visits; OSHA may still enter these workplaces to:

- Provide consultation or technical assistance;
- Conduct surveys such as the BLS annual survey of occupational injuries and illnesses;
- Respond to imminent dangers, health hazards, accidents resulting in at least one employee death or the hospitalization of at least five employees; and
- Investigate employee discrimination complaints.

Voluntary Compliance

OSHA also exempts some workplaces from scheduled inspections under its voluntary protection programs (VPP). These programs, instituted in 1982, encourage employers to develop their own comprehensive safety programs. Applicants must have lower than average accident rates, written safety programs, injury and exposure records available for OSHA scrutiny; must inform employees of the employer's participation in the VPP program and the employees' rights under the OSH Act; and must notify OSHA every year of their annual injury rates (50 Fed. Reg. 43,804 et seq. (1985)).

The VPP program frees OSHA's inspection resources for visits to establishments that are less likely to meet the requirements of the OSHA standards.

As with workplaces exempted from routine OSHA inspections under the yearly appropriations measures, work sites participating in VPP are still subject to inspection if OSHA receives employee complaints about safety conditions at the site, or if a fatality or catastrophe occurs at the site. A VPP agreement ends if the participating site is sold to another company, and an agreement may be terminated by OSHA if the participant fails to meet the requirements of the program.

CONDUCTING AN INSPECTION

Generally, OSHA does not notify an employer in advance that the employer's place of business has been scheduled for an inspection. In hearings on the then-proposed OSH Act, labor unions complained that employers were sometimes tipped off in advance of inspections, giving them time to cover up hazardous conditions. The OSH Act sets a maximum fine of

$1,000 and a maximum jail term of six months for any person who provides advance notice of an inspection without the agency's authorization (29 C.F.R. § 1903.6(c)).

Only in four instances may advance notice be given:

- To enable an employer to correct an imminent danger as quickly as possible;
- If an inspection can be conducted most effectively after normal business hours, or if special precautions by the inspector are necessary;
- To ensure the presence of employer or employee representatives or other necessary participants; or
- In other circumstances in which the OSHA area director determines that advance notice would enhance the effectiveness of the inspection (29 C.F.R. § 1903.6(a)).

In such instances, advance notice must be authorized by the area director, or—in cases of imminent danger—by a compliance officer if the area director is not immediately available. If advance notice is given, the employer must then inform an authorized employee representative.

Entry to the Workplace

Section 8(a) of the Act gives inspectors the right to enter a workplace "without delay" (29 U.S.C. § 657(a)(1)). However, critics in the early 1970s charged that this provision violated the right of businesses under the Fourth Amendment to protection from unreasonable searches and seizures. The provision was eventually challenged in court by an Idaho company, Barlow's Inc., whose owner refused to allow an inspector into the business establishment without a search warrant.

In this landmark 1978 ruling, the U.S. Supreme Court upheld the owner's action. The court ruled that an inspector generally must obtain a search warrant if refused the right to enter (*Marshall v. Barlow's Inc.*).

The court found that a warrant protects an employer's Fourth Amendment rights by curbing "the almost unbridled discretion" that "[t]he authority to make warrantless searches devolves . . . upon executive and administrative officers, particularly those in the field."

To obtain a warrant, OSHA must present a U.S. district judge or U.S. magistrate with evidence that the employer is violating a standard, or that the inspection is based on reasonable legislative or administrative standards. In the *Barlow's* ruling, for example, the Supreme Court suggested that a written, signed complaint by an employee, alleging unsafe conditions at a site, might satisfy this requirement for evidence.

The court further ruled, however, that OSHA does not need to obtain a warrant, even if the employer fails to consent to an inspection, if:

- An authorized third party consents (in a 1984 case, *Donovan v. Beiro*, a court upheld an inspection at a construction site, even though one contractor there had not consented, because the other contractors had consented);
- An emergency exists, and there is no time to obtain a warrant; or
- The conditions at the work site are observable to the public or are in "plain, obvious view" of OSHA inspectors while they are lawfully on the premises.

If an employer turns away an inspector and refuses to permit the execution of a warrant, OSHA will petition the U.S. district court in which the warrant was issued to hold the employer in civil contempt (*Rockford Drop Forge Co. v. Donovan*). OSHA may also seek to hold the employer in criminal contempt. The agency rarely pursues this course, although a court may convert a civil petition to a criminal proceeding (*In re Establishment Inspection of Consolidated Rail Corp.*).

Conducting the Inspection

When an inspector arrives at a work site to begin an inspection, he or she must first locate the owner, operator, or agent in charge of the site, and present his or her credentials. If the person in charge or another management official cannot be found, the OSHA *Field Operations Manual* directs the inspector to contact the employer by phone and request the presence of the owner or another management representative.

Additionally, the inspector tries to determine the identity of the employees' representative. This may be a union, an

INSPECTION CHECKLIST FOR EMPLOYERS

From the Workplace Health and Safety Council

CHECK LIST

Preparation before inspection

☐ Identify the employer representative who will work with and accompany the inspector.

☐ Identify the employee representative who will be notified of the inspection and accompany the inspector.

☐ Discuss with supervisors the need to continue enforcing all health and safety rules during an inspection.

☐ Know location of records required to be kept by OSHA.

☐ Identify sources and areas of confidential and proprietary information.

Start of inspection/opening conference

☐ Notify employee representative.

☐ Get inspector's name, agency, address, and telephone number.

☐ Establish whether the inspector has a warrant.

☐ Establish the purpose and scope of the inspection.

☐ Determine which documents the inspector wishes to review and under what regulatory authority.

☐ Ask what triggered the inspection.

☐ Identify sources of confidential and proprietary information for the inspector.

☐ Write opening conference information down.

Advise legal counsel of the inspection

INSPECTION CHECKLIST FOR EMPLOYERS (cont.)

During the inspection

☐ Accompany the inspector.

☐ Take notes on:
   ☐ What is seen
   ☐ Who is spoken to
   ☐ What is said
   ☐ Samples and pictures taken
   ☐ Documents reviewed

☐ When in doubt, ask the inspector to put questions in writing for review by counsel.

Post inspection/closing conference

☐ Provide additional relevant information that might have been overlooked.

☐ Don't make admissions or argue your case.

☐ Request receipt for any documents copied.

☐ Request copies of photographs or videotapes.

☐ Request copies of sample reports.

If there is a citation

☐ Promptly post the citation.

☐ Schedule the informal conference.

☐ If indicated, have notice of contest filed within 15 working days.

☐ Remedy the uncontested violations within the stated abatement period.

employee member of a joint labor-management committee who has been selected by the workers as their representative in OSHA related matters, or an employee who has been selected by the workers as their representative for this particular inspection.

OSHA regulations entitle an employee representative to accompany a compliance officer during an inspection (29 C.F.R. § 1903.8(a), pursuant to section 8(e) of the Act, 29 U.S.C. § 657(e)). The same rules authorize an employer representative to accompany the inspector as well.

The OSHA inspector holds an opening conference in which he or she informs the employer of the nature of the inspection, seeks to obtain the employer's consent to include a worker representative, and notifies the employer of its right to participate in the inspection.

The two primary components of an inspection are:

- A records check, in which the inspector examines the employer's injury, illness, medical, monitoring, and certification records to determine whether applicable standards have been met, and to assess the employer's injury and illness rates; and
- A walkaround, in which the inspector examines the actual working conditions at the site and evaluates the employer's safety training and enforcement, accident investigation, and related programs. When inspectors note possible violations of OSHA standards, they are instructed by the *Field Operations Manual* to document the details of the alleged violation on a worksheet.

From October 1981 through March 1988, an OSHA policy ended inspections at manufacturing sites after the records check, if the records showed the establishment had a lower-than-average injury rate. A similar approach had been proposed in a 1979 bill by Representative Richard Schweiker (R-Pa.), but drew union criticism and never received final congressional approval. OSHA's administrative policy also came under fire from labor unions and public interest organizations, which charged that some employers were keeping inaccurate and incomplete records in order to escape full inspections.

In 1986, in the wake of widespread public concern about the safety of chemical plants following the catastrophic 1984 chemical leak in Bhopal, India, OSHA modified its policy and directed inspectors to do a complete workplace assessment with every tenth general industry inspection, whatever the establishment's injury rate.

In March 1988, the agency completely abandoned the records-check-only policy. The agency's reason for doing so, officials said, involved reports that OSHA inspectors had failed to comprehensively inspect a suburban Chicago company where a worker subsequently died of cyanide poisoning. Critics charged that the agency would have found unsafe conditions at the plant, where cyanide was used, if inspectors had not ended the inspection after looking at records indicating a low injury rate.

Following the records check and the walkthrough inspection, the inspector holds a closing conference with the employer and employee representatives. The inspector:

- Describes the apparent violations found during the inspection, if any;
- Describes ways to abate the violations;
- Provides the employer representative with a publication, "Employer Rights and Responsibilities Following an OSHA Inspection," discusses the information in the booklet, and answers any questions the employer representative may have; and
- Notifies the employee representative of his or her rights in the event the employer challenges any citations that may result from the inspection: the right to be notified if a challenge, or notice of contest, is filed, and to seek "party status" as a participant in the adjudication of that challenge before the Occupational Safety and Health Review Commission. Employee representatives also are notified of their right to challenge the abatement date set by OSHA in a citation—the schedule by which a violation is to be corrected by the employer—and their right under section 11(c) of the Act to protection from retaliation by their employer for any OSHA-related activity.

After a citation is issued (either immediately after the inspection, or delivered later to the employer by mail), employer or employee representatives may request an additional informal conference to discuss any issues raised by the citation, such as the proposed penalty or an employer notice of contest to the citation. (For more information on citations, penalties, or the contest procedure, see the next section of this chapter.)

OSHA may also hold a follow-up inspection to determine if the employer has corrected the conditions noted in the citation. OSHA inspectors are prohibited from conducting new inspection activity in conjunction with the follow-up, unless he or she determines that significant changes have occurred in the workplace that warrant further examination. In such instances, the inspector must consult his or her supervisor before starting any new investigation.

Imminent Dangers

During an inspection, a compliance officer may find a condition that appears to pose an immediate or imminent danger of death or serious physical harm to employees. OSHA does not have the authority to immediately order workers to be removed from the location or to shut down the operation. Instead, it must file a petition for an injunction with the U.S. district court having jurisdiction over the region where the work site is located (29 U.S.C. § 662(a)).

When inspectors determine that conditions require such action, they must notify the employer and affected employees of the danger, and the inspector's recommendation that the court respond with an injunction (29 U.S.C. § 662(c)).

OSHA's authority to deal with imminent dangers was an issue of controversy in 1970 during deliberations on the OSH Act, and it continues to generate disagreement between labor and business interests. An early draft of the Act would have allowed an inspector to shut down an operation for 72 hours, after which the order could be challenged in court by the employer. However, opponents argued successfully that giving the agency this power without first involving the courts could deprive employers of their due process rights in a situation where an immediate danger might not, in fact, exist.

Labor advocates have sought new laws and programs that would give workers the right to walk off a job to avoid a perceived danger of death or serious injury. Workers currently have this right only under narrowly defined circumstances. Further discussion of this issue appears in Chapter 5.

Unlike OSHA, the Mine Safety and Health Administration does have the power to order employers under its jurisdiction—mine owners and operators—to withdraw employees from work areas where an imminent danger is found to exist (see Chapter 9).

Fatality Investigations

When investigating fatal accidents, OSHA has the additional duty of contacting the family of a worker who died from a work-related injury or illness. Under procedures adopted in April 1990, the agency contacts the next-of-kin at the outset of the investigation by letter, and offers to meet with the family personally to answer questions. The agency also provides the survivors with copies of citations issued as a result of the investigation (OSHA Instruction CPL 2.89, April 13, 1990, O.S.H. Rep. Ref. File (BNA) No. 21, at 9641).

OSHA adopted this policy after incurring criticism for failing, in many instances,to keep family members apprised of its investigations. Some critics contend that OSHA should go further and involve survivors in discussions with employers about monetary penalties for violations that result in worker deaths. OSHA has resisted that suggestion, saying it would be inappropriate to involve the families of workers in such negotiations, just as it is inappropriate to involve crime victims or their families in plea bargainings.

CITATIONS

OSHA citations describe the violations found during inspections (detailing both the circumstances of the infraction, and the particular standard alleged to have been violated) and set abatement dates, or deadlines for correcting the violations. The OSH Act requires that such deadlines be reasonable (29 U.S.C. § 658(a)). In setting these dates, the agency considers such factors as the seriousness of the alleged violation; the availability of needed equipment, materials, or personnel; the time needed for delivery, installation, modification, or construction of parts or equipment; and the training of personnel.

The OSH Act requires OSHA to issue citations with reasonable promptness and sets a six-month time limit for issuance from the occurrence of the violation. Several employers have challenged citations that were not issued until several weeks or even months after an inspection, contending that such delays prejudiced the employer's defense in challenging the citation. Rulings in these cases have held that the length of elapsed time, by itself, is not necessarily detrimental to the employer, but that a long delay may be prejudicial if, for example, it becomes difficult to locate witnesses when a delay occurs (*Havens Steel Co. v. OSHRC* and *Secretary of Labor v. E.C. Ernst Inc.*).

Employers must post copies of citations at or near the locations where the violations occurred, and must keep them posted for three working days or until the violations are corrected, whichever is longer (29 U.S.C. § 658(b), 29 C.F.R. § 1903.16(b)). Employers may be liable for civil penalties and may lose the right to pursue a challenge to a citation for violating these posting requirements (29 U.S.C. § 666(i)) (*Secretary of Labor v. C & H Erection Co.*).

Categories of Violations

OSHA categorizes violations according to the degree of risk they pose. The categories are:

- *De minimis*—conditions that violate a standard but have no direct or immediate relationship to safety or health. Such a violation may occur, for example, where an employer uses a ladder whose rungs are 13 inches apart, although a standard requires that they be no more than 12 inches apart. OSHA requires inspectors to document such violations, but not to include them on a citation.

- *Other-than-serious*—conditions that would probably not cause serious injury or death, but still would affect the safety or health of employees.
- *Serious*—conditions involving a substantial probability of death or serious physical harm.
- *Repeat*—conditions substantially similar to ones noted in earlier citations involving the same employer that have become final orders.
- *Willful*—violations involving an intentional and knowing disregard of the OSH Act, in which the employer knew that a hazard existed and that it violated a standard or other requirement of the OSH Act, but failed to make a reasonable effort to correct it.
- *Criminal/willful*—violations that were willful and resulted in the death of an employee (*FOM* IV(B), O.S.H. Rep. Ref. File (BNA) No. 77, 2508–13).

In writing a citation, OSHA may combine multiple instances in which a standard is alleged to have been violated. For example, if an inspection found unguarded, open-sided platforms at five places within the same site, the violations could be combined into one item on the citation, with each instance listed as a part of that item. The agency also may group different but related violations into one citation item; for example, failure to provide safety guards and work rests for an abrasive wheel could be grouped into one item. OSHA may decide to group violations in situations where the infractions are so closely related that they constitute a single dangerous condition, or where the hazards, though nonserious if considered individually, create a probable risk of death or serious injury in the aggregate.

PENALTIES

OSHA citations are a catalyst for employer action by the assessment of monetary penalties for infractions. The OSH Act set maximum penalty levels for different categories of violations, but, within these limits, left the assessment of proposed fines to OSHA.

Penalty amounts in individual cases are based on four factors for proposed penalties:

- The gravity of the alleged violation;
- The size of the business;
- The employer's good faith in having shown genuine and effective efforts to comply with the OSH Act before the inspection, and evidence of a desire to comply with the law during and after the inspection; and
- The employer's history of previous violations (*FOM* VI(A)(2)(a), O.S.H. Rep. Ref. File (BNA) No. 77, at 2701).

Originally the OSH Act allowed OSHA to propose civil penalties up to $1,000 for nonserious and serious violations, up to $10,000 for repeated or willful infractions, and up to $1,000 per day for failure to abate violations. The Act also provided for a maximum criminal penalty of $10,000, six months' imprisonment, or both, for first offenses, and up to $20,000 per year and one year's imprisonment for second convictions.

In the late 1980s, critics increasingly charged that these levels were inadequate as meaningful deterrents. Monetary fines for criminal violations were increased under the Comprehensive Crime Control Act of 1984 to $500,000 for companies and $250,000 for individual corporate executives convicted of criminal violations. However, critics said even these changes were insufficient because they did not expand prison sentences.

Congress acted in 1990 to address these concerns. Advocates of increased penalties utilized the Omnibus Budget Reconciliation Act of 1990 to raise OSHA fines sevenfold. Under this provision, effective March 1, 1991, and applicable to violations that occurred on or after November 5, 1990, the date the budget act was signed, the maximum penalty for willful and repeat violations is $70,000, and maximum penalties for serious, nonserious, failure-to-abate, and failure-to-post-citation violations are $7,000. The budget act also set a minimum penalty level of $5,000 for willful violations.

OSHA is continuing to adjust penalties in individual cases on the basis of the size of the business, the employer's good faith, and the company's history of compliance (OSHA Instruction CPL 2.45B, CH-2; 20 O.S.H. Rep. (BNA) 1313).

Shortly after the new penalty levels went into effect, the Department of Labor's Office of the Solicitor predicted the higher penalties could increase the number of companies contesting citations—up to 25 percent of cited companies from about 8 percent before the budget act took effect. However, former OSHA Administrator Gerard F. Scannell said he expected the penalty increases to be accepted if the agency was reasonable in assessing penalties.

Egregious-Case Policy

OSHA also has assessed heavier than normal penalties for particularly serious violations through an egregious-case policy. Under this procedure, applied to particularly egregious violations, OSHA assesses a separate penalty for each instance of a violation, instead of combining violations and proposing an aggregate fine. For example, in a citation alleging that employees were exposed to a toxic substance knowingly, a separate violation would be cited for each source of air contamination and for each employee exposed to the toxic substance. Normally failure to control emissions or high concentrations of a contaminant would count as one violation, regardless of the number of emission sources, or the number of workers exposed. If the violations were classified as willful, a $70,000 penalty might be proposed for each individual violation, instead of one aggregate fine of $70,000.

The egregious-case policy was first used by OSHA in 1986 to cite alleged record keeping violations by Union Carbide Corporation at two plants in West Virginia. The agency decided the hazard posed by possible chemical accidents (the plants had been inspected shortly after the catastrophic chemical leak in Bhopal, India) was so serious that large penalties were needed to convince employers to comply with OSHA rules. As of May 1, 1990, OSHA issued approximately 100 such penalties to some 90 employers, with some of the proposed fines greater than $1 million.

OSHA applies egregious-case penalties in cases in which:

- The employer knew of the violation when it occurred. This can be shown by previous citations, accident history, or the fact that OSHA had given special attention to the hazard in other workplaces through widely publicized enforcement programs;
- The employer intentionally had made no reasonable effort to correct the violation;
- The violation resulted in worker fatalities, a catastrophe, or a large number of illnesses and injuries;
- The employer has an extensive history of prior violations;
- The employer has intentionally disregarded its safety and health responsibilities;
- The employer's conduct as a whole shows clear bad faith in complying with OSHA requirements; or
- The employer has committed so many violations that the effectiveness of its safety and health program is undermined (OSHA Instruction CPL 2.80, Oct. 1, 1990, O.S.H. Rep. Ref. File (BNA) No. 21, 9649 et seq.).

CONTESTING A CITATION

After receiving a citation, an employer has 15 working days in which to challenge or contest it. The employer may contest the allegation of a violation, the abatement period, or both. Employee representatives may challenge the period of time set for abatement.

Filing a Notice of Contest

A notice of contest must be presented, in writing, to the OSHA area director from whose office the citation was issued. In turn, the area director transmits the notice to the Occupational Safety and Health Review Commission. The same procedure is followed by employee representatives who challenge an abatement period (29 C.F.R. § 1903.17).

When the commission receives a notice of contest, it informs the employer that the case has been filed, and that employees exposed to the alleged hazard must be told they have the right to participate in the Commission's proceedings. An employer is not required to abate an alleged hazard while the citation is being contested.

Within 30 days of the filing of the notice of contest with the commission, the Secretary of Labor files a written complaint detailing the alleged violations and stating that the abatement period and the amount of the proposed penalty are appropriate. A copy also must be sent to the employer, who has 30 days from service to file a written response.

The response must answer every allegation, specifically admitting or denying it. If the employer has no knowledge of the facts surrounding a specific allegation, the response must state this position, which will be regarded by OSHRC as a denial.

Each case involving a notice of contest is assigned to an OSHRC administrative law judge (ALJ), who designates a time and location for a hearing. The commission's rules of procedure state that the administrative law judge must notify the parties of the hearing date at least 30 days before that date. In practice, an administrative law judge usually sets a hearing date several months in the future.

Between the time an employer files an answer to OSHA's complaint, and the time a hearing is held, the parties may ask each other for additional information or documents under the process of discovery (29 C.F.R. § 2200.52(a)). Such documents—for example, notes taken by the OSHA compliance officer during the inspection, or company documents pertaining to the alleged hazard—may help one party find weak points in the other's case. The hearing judge or the commission may set limitations on such requests, however, to protect either OSHA or the employer from annoyance, embarassment, or undue expense, or to protect confidential information.

Hearings

Much like a proceeding in a court, a hearing on a notice of contest is presided over by the administrative law judge handling the case, and is transcribed. Exhibits are introduced, witnesses are called and questioned, and the parties involved have the right to cross-examine each other's witnesses.

After a hearing, the administrative law judge may give the parties an opportunity to file posthearing briefs by a certain date. Subsequently, the judge issues a decision that includes findings and conclusions on the material issues in the case, and an order affirming, modifying, or vacating each contested citation item and proposed penalty. Copies of the decision must be mailed to each party (29 C.F.R. § 2200.90).

Review by OSHRC

An ALJ's ruling can be and often is reviewed by a higher authority—the three-member Review Commission. This may occur in either of two ways:

- A commissioner on his or her own motion may issue a direction for review if the case raises novel questions of law or policy, or questions involving conflict with other ALJ decisions. This is rarely done.
- As is more likely to occur, a commissioner may issue a direction for review if one of the parties in the case believes itself adversely affected or aggrieved by the ALJ's ruling and seeks review. Such a request must be filed within 20 days after the decision has been transmitted to all the parties.

If an ALJ's decision is not called for review through either of these procedures, it becomes a final order of the commission (29 U.S.C. § 661(j)).

In reviewing a case, the commission ordinarily asks the parties to file briefs. It also may call for oral argument, either at the request of an involved party or on its own volition. Normally, on review, the commission will examine only the issues that were raised before the ALJ.

Until 1990 OSHRC's rules of procedure discouraged oral argument. However, on June 4, 1990, the commission issued new rules to remove those strictures:

> As the complexity of the cases coming before the Commission has increased . . . it has become apparent that the Commission's decision-making process would be substantially facilitated by having the parties participate in oral argument. The Commission

anticipates using oral argument to supplement the briefs by giving the parties an opportunity to answer questions on matters raised, but not fully explored, in their briefs (55 Fed. Reg. 22,780 (1990)).

The commission can render a decision in a case only if a quorum of its members—two out of the three commissioners—vote in agreement. If the commission splits equally on a vote (which may occur if the three members hand down three differing decisions, or only two members participate because a third commissioner's term has expired, or the third member has been disqualified from the case), the hearing judge's decision becomes, in effect, a final order of the commission. However, it is given less value as a precedent for future cases than an opinion rendered by the commission (*Secretary of Labor v. Life Science Products Co.*). Many ALJ orders became final commission orders in this manner in the late 1980s, when delays in filling vacant OSHRC seats left the commission without a quorum for more than two years.

Settlements

At any stage of the hearing process, OSHA may withdraw a citation, the employer may withdraw its notice of contest, or the two parties may enter into a settlement agreement to resolve the dispute. More than 90 percent of all cases disposed of by OSHRC administrative law judges are terminated prior to a hearing through such actions.

Under a settlement agreement, OSHA generally reduces its proposed penalties in return for a pledge by the employer to correct the cited condition. As a rule, the agreement also stipulates that the employer's action does not represent an acknowledgment that a violation occurred.

Representatives of employees affected by the agreement must be given a copy of the pact. However, regulations do not require nor do they prohibit employee involvement in the negotiations (29 C.F.R. § 2200.100).

Since the late 1980s, OSHA has made frequent use of corporate-wide settlement agreements to resolve employer challenges to citations charging egregious violations. In such instances, the company's pledge to correct conditions cited by

OSHA at one workplace extends to similar conditions at its other places of business as well.

According to OSHA, corporate-wide settlements are particularly useful for resolving challenges to citations alleging egregious violations of record keeping regulations: "Because record keeping regulations and guidelines are straightforward and relatively unambiguous, they can be implemented uniformly in a variety of workplaces, without regard to differences in product, establishment size, or technology" (OSHA Dir. CPL 2.90, June 3, 1991).

Corporate-wide settlements, according to OSHA administrative guidelines, must specify the specific steps the employer plans to take to abate the cited conditions, and the dates by which abatement will occur (OSHA Dir. CPL 2.90). OSHA contends that such agreements are useful because they help the agency avoid protracted litigation, and provide for company-wide correction of hazards without the necessity of additional OSHA inspections.

However, labor unions have criticized this approach because settlements usually are negotiated without input from affected employees. Unions also are critical of the fact that a corporate-wide settlement removes from OSHA's inspection schedule workplaces that may not have been inspected previously. Further, they charge, OSHA's monitoring of abatement relies too much on a review of progress reports from the employer, and provides too little direct monitoring by the agency itself.

An OSHA reform bill endorsed by the AFL-CIO and introduced August 1, 1991, by Senators Edward M. Kennedy (D-Mass.) and Howard Metzenbaum (D-Ohio) in the Senate (S. 1622) and Representatives William Ford (D-Mich.) and Joseph Gaydos (D-Pa.) in the House (H.R. 3160) would allow affected employees to seek OSHRC review of corporate-wide and other types of settlement agreements.

JUDICIAL REVIEW

An OSHRC ruling can be appealed to a federal court by any party adversely affected or aggrieved by the order. An employer in a case may file an appeal in any of three places:

- The U.S. court of appeals for the circuit in which the violation was alleged to have occurred;
- The circuit in which the employer has its principal offices; or
- The U.S. Court of Appeals for the District of Columbia Circuit.

The Secretary of Labor can file only in the circuit in which the violation was alleged to have occurred, or the circuit in which the employer has its principal office. So as not to require an employer to come to Washington, D.C., to defend a case, the OSH Act does not allow the Secretary to file in the D.C. Circuit in cases involving employers located outside that area.

Unions that have elected party status in a case are entitled to judicial review of an OSHRC ruling as well, the District of Columbia Circuit concluded in a 1982 ruling (*Oil, Chemical & Atomic Workers v. OSHRC*). A union's rights in this regard are "subject to two conditions, derived from the general statutory scheme and purpose of the Act," according to the ruling:

> First, the union must give the Secretary notice of its intention to appeal and must serve him with copies of all the pleadings. . . . Second, the case may become moot in those instances when the Secretary, participating in the appeal as an amicus curiae or as an intervenor, provides th[e] court with a clear and unconditional statement that he will not prosecute the claim regardless of the disposition of the appeal by th[e] court.

Appeals must be filed within 60 days of the issuance of the Review Commission's order (29 U.S.C. § 660(a)).

A party seeking judicial review of a citation must take its challenge through the Review Commission first. This procedure must be followed so as "to allow the administrative agency to perform functions within its special competence—to make a factual record, to apply its expertise and to correct its own errors so as to moot judicial controversies," the U.S. Court of Appeals for the Seventh Circuit ruled in 1979 (*Continental Can Co. U.S.A. v. Marshall*).

An employer or the Department of Labor may appeal a federal appellate court decision to the U.S. Supreme Court (29 U.S.C. § 660(a)). Such requests have been made of the Supreme Court numerous times since OSHA's inception, but only three enforcement cases have ever been heard by the high court:

- *Atlas Roofing Co. v. OSHRC*, dealing with the speed of the commission's hearing procedures (decided in 1977);
- *Cuyahoga Valley Railway v. United Transportation Union*, in which the Supreme Court held that the review commission has no authority to entertain a union's request to review a decision by DOL not to issue or withdraw a citation (decided in 1985); and
- *Secretary of Labor v. OSHRC*, in which the Supreme Court ruled, per curiam, that a court reviewing a challenge to an OSHA citation must defer to a reasonable interpretation of a standard by the Secretary of Labor where that interpretation differs from one by OSHRC (decided in 1991).

CRIMINAL PROSECUTION

One of the most controversial areas of OSHA regulation in recent years has been the question of criminal penalties for violations of safety and health standards. In the late 1980s, OSHA came under criticism by labor unions and some members of Congress for not being aggressive enough in pursuing criminal sanctions against employers in cases where workers were killed in work related incidents. An October 4, 1988, report by the House Government Operations Committee stated:

> OSHA's record with respect to seeking criminal penalties for workplace safety violations and fatalities is dismal. Since its creation by Congress in 1970, OSHA has referred only 42 cases to the Justice Department for possible criminal action. Only 14 of those cases were prosecuted, resulting in 10 convictions, but no jail sentences. No one has ever spent a day in jail for violating the OSH Act (H.R. Rep. No. 1051).

OSHA itself does not have the authority to bring criminal cases in U.S. courts. Instead, it must refer a case to the U.S. Justice Department for prosecution. Critics have charged that the Justice Department gives insufficient attention to criminal cases under the OSH Act, and that Justice and OSHA have not worked together efficiently enough in pursuing such cases. Some state prosecutors have shared these opinions, and since the mid–1980s have been increasingly active in bringing criminal charges under state laws. These activities in turn have raised the question of whether these state laws are preempted by the OSH Act (see Chapter 6 for further discussion of this issue).

OSHA and Justice Department officials have defended their record on criminal prosecutions, contending that the OSH Act's definition of a criminal violation—a willful infraction that results in the death of an employee—is so restrictive that it makes prosecution difficult. In some states, by way of contrast, criminal charges can be brought for negligent behavior by an employer that results in an employee death—an easier charge to prove, according to federal prosecutors.

Since the issuance of the House Government Operations Committee report, OSHA has increased the number of cases referred to the Justice Department for prosecution. In one of these cases, a company president pled guilty and was sentenced to six months in jail (*U.S. v. Elliott*). However, critics say that improvements in the OSH Act's criminal provisions still are needed.

Three bills to toughen these provisions were introduced in Congress in 1991: S. 445, by Senator Howard Metzenbaum (D-Ohio); H.R. 549, by Representative Charles Schumer (D-NY); and H.R. 4050, by Representative Tom Lantos (D-Calif.). Both House measures would extend criminal sanctions to willful violations that resulted in serious bodily injury to workers or recklessly endangered an employee's life. The Senate bill would extend sanctions to cover serious bodily injury, but not reckless endangerment. S. 445 and H.R. 4050 would increase the penalty for a willful violation that led to a worker death from 3 months to up to 10 years in prison. H.R. 549 would raise the penalty up to 20 years in prison. A hearing only on S. 445 had been held at the time of this writing.

5

ANTIDISCRIMINATION PROVISIONS

In crafting the Occupational Safety and Health Act, Congress considered the question of whether an employee should be allowed—without fear of losing his or her job or otherwise being punished—to refuse to undertake a task that would require exposure to a perceived risk of serious injury or death.

Congress ultimately decided not to incorporate such a provision. However, in section 11(c) of the Act, it did provide a clause that explicitly forbids employers from punishing or otherwise discriminating against workers for exercising their rights under the legislation, and gives workers a means of recourse for challenging such actions when they occur.

Section 11(c) allows workers to file a complaint with OSHA if they feel they have been discriminated against for undertaking safety-related actions, including, in certain situations, refusing to perform unsafe work. OSHA is required to investigate such complaints, and seek judicial review of cases that it feels are valid.

Similar protections for workers who are fired or disciplined for refusing to work under dangerous conditions are also provided by the National Labor Relations Act. OSHA and the National Labor Relations Board have worked out an agreement for handling such cases without overlap or duplication.

Labor unions, however, contend that workers still need proactive laws that will allow them to refuse hazardous work—so-called right-to-act legislation.

PROTECTED ACTIVITIES

Under section 11(c) and OSHA regulations (29 C.F.R. Pt. 1977) protected activities include situations in which an employee:

- Requests an OSHA inspection or otherwise files a complaint under or related to the OSH Act (*Donovan v. R.D. Andersen Construction Co.*, which held that complaining to the news media about a workplace hazard would be an activity related to the Act (10 O.S.H. Cas. (BNA) 2025));
- Complains about safety and health hazards to any other federal or state agency that has the authority to investigate such hazards;
- Complains to the employer about safety and health conditions (employees are covered even if their concerns prove to be unwarranted, as long as the complaint was made in good faith (*Marshall v. Klug & Smith Co.*));
- Contests an abatement date in an OSHA citation, initiates proceedings for issuing a new standard, asks OSHA to modify or revoke a variance granted to the employer, challenges a standard in court, or appeals an Occupational Safety and Health Review Commission ruling;
- Testifies or plans to testify in proceedings related to the OSH Act, including statements given in the course of an inspection, standards-setting proceedings, and adjudicative functions;
- Requests information from OSHA; or
- Refuses in good faith, having no reasonable alternative, to be exposed to a job-related condition that poses a threat of serious injury or death, if there is insufficient time to correct the hazard through normal regulatory channels (for example, by asking OSHA to investigate the problem), and the employee has tried unsuccessfully to convince the employer to correct the hazard.

The refusal-to-work provision was challenged twice in the 1970s. The first case, *Marshall v. Daniel Construction Co.*, resulted in a decision by the U.S. Court of Appeals for the Fifth Circuit that vacated the regulation as being beyond OSHA's statutory authority. Two years later, in 1979, the U.S. Court of Appeals for the Sixth Circuit disagreed and upheld the rule in *Marshall v. Whirlpool Corp.* The U.S. Supreme Court subsequently upheld the *Whirlpool* ruling.

Whirlpool Corporation, in challenging the Sixth Circuit's ruling, argued that the OSHA provision was inconsistent with the legislative history of the OSH Act, in that Congress had rejected proposals to allow employees to refuse to work for safety or health reasons. However, the Supreme Court found that Congress had rejected a strike-with-pay provision that would have required employers to pay workers who had walked off the job:

> When it rejected the "strike with pay" concept, therefore, Congress very clearly meant to reject a law unconstitutionally imposing upon employers an obligation to continue to pay employees their regular pay checks when they absented themselves from work for reasons of safety. But the regulation at issue here does not require employers to pay workers who refuse to perform their assigned tasks in the face of imminent danger. It simply provides that in such cases the employer may not "discriminate" against employees involved. An employer "discriminates" against an employee only when he treats that employee less favorably than he treats others similarly situated (*Whirlpool Corp. v. Marshall*).

Because section 11(c) broadly states that "no person shall discharge or otherwise discriminate against an employee" for engaging in protected activities, the antidiscrimination provisions do not pertain solely to retaliation by an employer. The agency also prohibits such action by:

- An employer discriminating against an employee of another company;
- An employer discriminating against a person who had applied for a job but who has not yet been hired;
- Other individuals; and
- Unions and employment agencies.

State, county, and municipal employees are not protected directly by section 11(c). Consequently, OSHA does not have authority to investigate complaints by such employees. However, states that maintain their own OSHA-approved safety and health regulatory programs (see Chapter 6) are required to have antidiscrimination provisions as effective as those under section 11(c), including protections for public employees. Complaints by public employees may be referred by OSHA to the appropriate state agency for investigation.

PROCEDURES FOR FILING A COMPLAINT

Ordinarily an employee must file a complaint within 30 days of the time the alleged discriminatory action occurred. This schedule allows OSHA to decline complaints that have become stale, and consequently difficult to investigate or substantiate.

However, this restriction may be relaxed if there are extenuating circumstances—for example, if the employer had misled the employee about the true grounds for the adverse action.

A complaint may be filed by the employee, or by a representative authorized to do so on the employee's behalf, such as a union official. It must be filed with the director of the OSHA area office responsible for enforcement activity in the geographical location where the action occurred. No particular form is required for the complaint. Complaints, in fact, may be made orally to the agency, but OSHA prefers written complaints to determine more easily when the complaint was filed, and thus ensure timely filings.

INVESTIGATING A COMPLAINT

Once the area office receives a complaint, it refers it to the regional office for investigation. Each regional office has a regional supervisory investigator (RSI) who oversees the program in that region and assigns each complaint to a staff investigator.

Initially a complaint will be screened by the RSI or the investigator to determine if, on its face, the case appears to be valid. OSHA is not required to investigate complaints if:

- In the absence of mitigating circumstances, the complaint was not filed within the 30-day allowable period;
- The employee is not covered by the OSH Act; or

• The complaint does not involve a protected activity.

If OSHA decides that it has reason to pursue the complaint, it will notify the employer and promptly begin an investigation. OSHA's *Field Operations Manual* calls for investigators to identify and contact witnesses. If the employer wishes to retain legal counsel, the *FOM* calls for the investigator to arrange for a return visit, to give the employer time to do so (*FOM* X(3)(1), O.S.H. Rep. Ref. File (BNA) No. 77, at 3103).

The OSH Act requires the agency to notify a complainant within 90 days of receiving the complaint as to whether it determined the employee's charge to be valid (29 U.S.C. § 660(c)). Section 11(c) disputes may be resolved in either of two ways:

• OSHA may negotiate a settlement that provides terms agreeable to both the complainant and the employer; or
• If a settlement cannot be reached, the regional solicitor of labor will file suit in federal district court against the employer.

As a rule, according to OSHA, settlements are easiest to reach in the earlier stages of the process, before the positions of the parties harden and the employer becomes liable for large amounts of back pay to the complainant (*FOM* X(7), O.S.H. Rep. Ref. File (BNA) No. 77, at 3105). If a case is taken to court and the court rules in favor of the complainant, the employer may be ordered to provide all appropriate relief, including reinstatement of the employee with back pay (29 U.S.C. § 660(c)(2)).

OSHA regulations allow employees to ask that a discrimination complaint, once filed, be withdrawn. However, because OSHA may find that good reason exists for pursuing an investigation (for example, there may be some question as to whether the employee was coerced into trying to withdraw the complaint), the agency is not required to end the case. But regulations require OSHA to give consideration to voluntary and uncoerced requests for withdrawal.

PROCEDURES OUTSIDE OSHA

According to OSHA statistics, the number of section 11(c) cases filed with the agency declined in the 1980s, but began to rise again slightly toward the end of the decade:

Fiscal Year	New Cases Filed
1980	4,029
1981	3,055
1982	2,405
1983	2,522
1984	2,981
1985	2,433
1986	2,612
1987	2,872
1988	3,324
1989	3,342

OSHA officials and labor union representatives theorize that the drop in new filings reflected a growing preference by workers and unions for pursuing other antidiscrimination processes outside the section 11(c) program. Relatively few cases are found by OSHA to have merit under section 11(c), either because the complainant failed to present enough prima facie evidence to support a discrimination charge, or because the case failed to fit the section 11(c) eligibility criteria, according to officials:

Fiscal Year	Merit Cases
1980	586
1981	386
1982	327
1983	370
1984	309
1985	283
1986	352
1987	325
1988	484
1989	559

Because section 11(c) cases are difficult to bring, workers have tended to turn instead to two other avenues of recourse: antidiscrimination provisions of the National Labor Relations Act (NLRA), and provisions under individual collective bargaining contracts.

NLRA Procedures

Section 7 of the NLRA gives employees the right "to engage in . . . concerted activities for the purpose of . . . mutual aid and protection." The U.S. Supreme Court has held that the rule gives employees the right to refuse work when faced with what they believe to be unsafe or unhealthy conditions, and that employers violate the provision by disciplining workers who engage in such activity (29 U.S.C. § 147). (See also *NLRB v. Washington Aluminum*.)

One issue that has generated litigation is whether the definition of concerted activities extends NLRA protection to workers who act alone. The definition in the statute is unclear. The issue came before the U.S. Supreme Court in *NLRB v. City Disposal Systems, Inc.*, in which a truck driver claimed that he was protected by NLRA when he refused to drive a vehicle that he believed to be unsafe because of defective brakes. The high court found nothing in the Act's legislative history that specifically expresses what Congress meant in enacting the provision. It ruled that the driver was engaged in concerted activity when he refused to operate the truck.

The National Labor Relations Board (NLRB)—which adjudicates labor disputes under the NLRA—has suggested various interpretations. In 1975, with a ruling in *Alleluia Cushion Co.*, the National Labor Relations Board adopted a broad interpretation, finding that a single worker engaged in safety-related activity was involved in concerted activity unless fellow employees disavowed the activity.

However, the Board put forth a new, more stringent interpretation in 1984, in *Meyers Industries Inc.* In that ruling the Board found that an action is concerted only if it is "engaged in, with, or on, the authority of other employees, and not solely by and on behalf of the employee himself."

The *Meyers* interpretation was eventually upheld on review in *Prill v. NLRB*. Quoting from *City Disposal*, the court said: "It is clear that 'Congress sought generally to equalize the bargaining power of the employee with that of his employer *by allowing employees to band together in confronting an employer* regarding the terms and conditions of their employment.' . . . By requiring that workers actually band together, the NLRB has adopted a reasonable—but by no means the only reasonable—interpretation of section 7."

Another part of NLRA, section 502, permits workers to stop work because of abnormally dangerous conditions at the work site, even if the employees are covered by a no-strike clause in their collective bargaining contract that otherwise would prohibit a work stoppage (29 U.S.C. § 143).

Employees may file complaints concurrently under the OSH Act and the NLRA. OSHA's authority to investigate a section 11(c) complaint is independent of the NLRB's jurisdiction (20 C.F.R. § 1977.18(a)(1)). However, under a 1975 memorandum of agreement between the two agencies, NLRB will defer or dismiss a charge if it has received a complaint involving the same situation addressed in a section 11(c) complaint. If no complaint has been filed with OSHA, the board will inform the complainant of the right to proceed under section 11(c). If the complaint falls within the Board's exclusive jurisdiction but involves possible retaliation for safety-related activity, the two agencies will consult.

OSHA, at its discretion, may postpone a determination on a section 11(c) complaint pending an NLRB proceeding, or may defer to the Board. Before the agency does so, it must be clear that:

- The Board's review deals adequately with all factual issues in the case;
- The Board's procedures are fair, regular, and free of procedural shortcomings; and
- The outcome of those proceedings are not contrary or detrimental to the purpose of the OSH Act.

Contract Provisions

According to union officials, contract provisions allowing workers to refuse to perform what they see as unsafe tasks grew stronger in the 1980s. Unions say that arbitration under such provisions is faster than the section 11(c) process, and does not put the burden solely on the employee to justify a work stoppage. Under contract provisions, an employee may refuse to perform work that presents risks beyond those normally inherent in the operation. Thus, for example, a worker would not be able to refuse to work on a properly erected scaffold, but could refuse to work on one that was insecurely or poorly erected. If any disciplinary action followed, the dispute would be arbitrated.

Right to Act

Protective contract provisions pertain to a relatively small number of employees. A 1989 Bureau of National Affairs (BNA) analysis of a cross-section of 400 contracts found that only 26 percent of the agreements place some restrictions on an employee's performance of alleged hazardous work (*Basic Patterns in Union Contracts*, 12th Ed.; The Bureau of National Affairs, Inc., 1989).

In the mid-1980s, labor advocates began to call for right-to-act laws to give all workers the authority to refuse to perform hazardous tasks without fear of employer retaliation. As of this writing, only one such measure has been enacted. This measure, "An Act Concerning An Employee's Right to Act" (Pub. L. No. 91-33), is a Connecticut statute that allows workers in that state to refuse to perform a task if (1) the worker reasonably believes that the task poses a risk of serious injury or illness, (2) the task involves a violation of a safety or health standard or a contract provision, and (3) the employer has failed to correct the hazardous condition. The measure was signed April 22, 1991, and went into effect October 1, 1991.

In the meantime, bills introduced in the House and the Senate on August 1, 1991, would add right-to-act provisions to the federal Occupational Safety and Health Act as part of a larger "OSHA reform" effort by congressional Democrats who want to see stronger federal safety and health requirements.

The bills—S. 1622, introduced by Senators Edward Kennedy (D-Mass.) and Howard Metzenbaum (D-Ohio), and H.R. 3160, introduced by Representatives William Ford (D-Mich.) and Joseph Gaydos (D-Pa.)—would add new paragraphs to the OSH Act to prohibit employers from discharging or otherwise discriminating against any worker who, after failing to obtain corrective action, "refused to perform duties that he reasonably believes would expose employees to a bona fide danger of injury or serious impairment of health" (21 O.S.H. Rep. (BNA) 314). Hearings on the bills began in late 1991 and, as of this writing, were scheduled to continue in early 1992.

Employer groups have expressed opposition to the right-to-act concept, claiming that it would be an unwarranted interference with traditional management prerogatives and that OSHA and NLRB procedures already offer adequate protection for workers.

SURFACE TRANSPORTATION ACT

In addition to the section 11(c) program, OSHA also administers a discrimination-complaint investigation program for employees in the trucking industry. OSHA was given this responsibility under section 405 of the Surface Transportation Act of 1982. Procedures are similar to those under section 11(c), except that OSHA has the authority to order an employer to reinstate a discharged worker, with back pay, if the case is found to have merit, instead of having to take the case to court.

Employees who may file complaints under this program include drivers (including independent contractors) of commercial motor vehicles in private industry, mechanics, freight handlers, and any other individual other than an employer who works for a commercial motor carrier.

OSHA prefers that complaints be filed with the director of the OSHA area office responsible for enforcement in the geographical locale where the employee works or resides. However, employees are not prohibited from filing with any other agency officer or employee.

Section 405 gives employees more time to file a complaint than section 11(c) does—within 180 days after the alleged violation occurred. However, as with the 30-day limit under the OSH Act provision, complaints may still be considered after 180 days if there are extenuating circumstances—for example, if the employer misled the worker about the grounds for the adverse action.

OSHA's regulations for administering the program call for the agency to investigate and to notify the employer. Within 20 days of receiving notification, the employer may give OSHA a written statement explaining or defending its position in the matter. The employer also may request a meeting with OSHA.

If, after the investigation, OSHA finds reasonable cause to believe that discriminatory action has occurred, it must give the employer an opportunity to respond, meet with the investigators, and present statements from rebuttal witnesses.

OSHA's rules call for the agency to issue written findings within 60 days of the filing of the complaint. If the agency determines that discrimination occurred, it will issue a preliminary order calling for the complainant to be restored to his or her position, with back pay and compensatory damages.

The employer or the employee may file an objection to the order with the chief administrative law judge of the Department of Labor within 30 days of receiving the order. The chief ALJ will refer the case to a hearing judge, who must convene a hearing within 30 days unless the judge can show cause for a delay or the parties agree to a delay.

Regulations call for the judge to complete the case and close the record no more than 30 days after the filing of the objection, and issue a decision within 30 days after that. The decision is forwarded to the Secretary of Labor, who must file a final order within 120 days.

The Secretary's order, in turn, may be appealed to the U.S. court of appeals for the federal circuit in which the violation allegedly occurred, or in which the person appealing the order resided at the time of the alleged violation.

As in the section 11(c) process, the parties in a section 405 case can settle the dispute at any time in the process. An employee can withdraw a complaint prior to the filing of objections or the filing of a preliminary order.

OSH statistics show that 462 section 405 complaints were filed with the agency in fiscal 1990, 402 cases were completed that year, and 93 were found to have merit.

6

STATE PROGRAMS UNDER OSHA

Although the OSH Act gives the federal government the preeminent role in regulating worker safety and health, it also provides a way for states—with OSHA's oversight and approval—to assume a significant measure of authority themselves.

The Act allows states to establish their own programs for issuing and enforcing standards, subject to OSHA certification (29 U.S.C. § 667(b)). Within certain restrictions, states also may assert jurisdiction over health and safety issues for which OSHA has no federal standard, subject to OSHA approval (29 U.S.C. § 667(a)).

A significant number of states have launched OSHA-approved programs. Although organized labor has been critical of some state programs, contending that their enforcement efforts are weak, state officials contend that their OSHA-approved programs often are more effective than the federal program.

If a state chooses not to develop its own standards-setting and enforcement program, OSHA retains federal jurisdiction there. In the past decade, some states have come into conflict with the federal agency by issuing right-to-know regulations covering chemical hazards, or by attempting to prosecute health and safety violations under state criminal laws, without having developed OSHA-approved programs. Such conflicts have centered on the question of whether a state can take an action that OSHA claims is preempted by federal law.

STATE PLANS

States may seek authority to conduct their own occupational safety and health programs by submitting a state plan to OSHA. A state plan is a detailed description of how the state proposes to develop and enforce its own standards, how it will fund the program, and how it will provide adequate staffing.

In the state plan, the state must:

- Designate an agency or agencies to administer the proposed program;
- Provide for the development of standards that will be at least as effective as OSHA's, but at the same time, when applied to products that are distributed or used in interstate commerce, will not unduly disrupt business;
- Provide for a right of entry by state inspectors into workplaces;
- Assure OSHA that it will have adequate funding and qualified personnel for carrying out the program;
- Agree to develop an effective and comprehensive safety and health program for state and local employees (who otherwise are not covered by OSHA);
- Require employers to provide reports (such as injury and illness records) to the U.S. Department of Labor just as they would if the federal government were exerting its jurisdiction in the state.

Steps Toward Approval

To seek OSHA approval for a plan, the state must submit a copy of the plan to the regional administrator in the OSHA office covering the geographical area in which the state is located. The plan must include supporting documents and copies of the standards that will be enforced by the state.

If the regional administrator finds any defect in the plan, he or she must offer to help the state correct the shortcoming. Then the plan is submitted to OSHA's Office of State Programs.

If the agency finds no reason to reject the plan, it will publish a notice in the *Federal Register*:

- Announcing receipt of the plan and describing its contents and the subjects or issues involved;
- Informing interested parties that the plan is available for inspecting and copying at OSHA headquarters, the OSHA regional office, and the office of the state agency that will administer the program;
- Giving parties an opportunity to comment on the plan;
- Announcing a hearing on the plan if the OSHA administrator believes that such a step is necessary; and
- Giving parties an opportunity to request a hearing if one has not already been scheduled.

If the agency receives any adverse comments on the plan, it must give the state an opportunity to modify or clarify its proposal before beginning any proceedings to reject the plan (29 C.F.R. § 1902.12).

Developmental Period

OSHA may grant initial approval to a plan even if, at the time the plan was submitted, the state had not accomplished all the steps promised. OSHA's approval is conditioned on the state's promise to have all elements of its program in place within three years.

Each time a state completes one of these steps, it must give OSHA a state plan supplement that describes the step taken, and must provide the agency with relevant documentation. OSHA notes its approval of each step by publishing a notice in the *Federal Register*. During the developmental period, the state begins to exercise enforcement authority concurrently with OSHA, and begins to receive federal matching grants to help fund the program.

State Certification

Once a state plan completes all its developmental steps, OSHA publishes in the *Federal Register* a state plan certification, which:

- Lists all the developmental steps;
- Notes any changes in the state plan that have been approved by OSHA; and
- Describes the scope of the plan.

To date, 24 state programs have been certified: Alaska, Arizona, California, Connecticut, Hawaii, Indiana, Iowa, Kentucky, Maryland, Michigan, Minnesota, Nevada, New Mexico, North Carolina, Oregon, Puerto Rico, South Carolina, Tennessee, Utah, Vermont, the Virgin Islands, Virginia, Washington, and Wyoming. (Puerto Rico and the Virgin Islands fall within the OSH Act's definition of "states," as do the District of Columbia, American Samoa, Guam, and the Trust Territory of the Pacific Islands.)

Connecticut's state plan covers only public employees, as does a New York state plan that has been approved but not certified. OSHA retains the authority in those two states for regulating private-sector workplaces.

Section 18(e) Approval

The state's next step is to obtain final approval of its plan under section 18(e) of the Act. Before granting final approval, OSHA must determine that the state program is as effective as its own. The agency considers whether:

- The state has enough trained or competent personnel to carry out its responsibilities;
- The state has adhered to the procedures adopted under its plan;
- The state has adopted all federal standards, or standards as effective as OSHA's, in a timely way;
- The state's interpretation of the federal standards is consistent with OSHA's;
- The state has taken action to correct any deficiencies found in its program;
- In granting any permanent variances from its standards, the state has ensured that the employer is providing conditions as safe as those required under the standard;

- In granting a temporary variance, the state has ensured that the employer will come into compliance with the standard as soon as possible;
- The state allocates sufficient resources for inspecting industries or health hazards that have been targeted for special enforcement attention, while giving adequate time to other inspections as well;
- The state has appropriately exercised its right of entry into a workplace whenever that right was challenged;
- State inspectors conduct inspections in a competent way;
- The state issues citations, fines, and notices for failure to abate violations in a timely way;
- The state's proposed penalties are at least as effective as OSHA's;
- The state ensures that employers correct cited hazards;
- Whenever appropriate, the state has sought administrative or judicial review of any adjudicative decisions unfavorable to the state program; and
- Trends in state injury and illness rates compare favorably with those in states where OSHA retains enforcement authority.

Once OSHA grants final approval, the state assumes responsibility for setting and enforcing standards, except to the extent that OSHA needs to conduct inspections to monitor the program's performance. OSHA also may complete any enforcement activities that began before the time approval was granted.

To date, 14 states have received final approval: Alaska, Arizona, Hawaii, Indiana, Iowa, Kentucky, Maryland, Minnesota, South Carolina, Tennessee, Utah, the Virgin Islands, Virginia, and Wyoming.

Benchmarks

One issue in the approval process that has generated particular controversy over the past two decades has been the OSH Act's criterion that a state provide an adequate number of staff personnel to carry out its program.

In construing the requirements of the Act, OSHA determined that states needed enough personnel to ensure that their programs would be at least as effective as OSHA's would be in the absence of a state program.

However, the AFL-CIO, in a lawsuit filed in federal court, challenged OSHA's interpretation. The labor federation argued that, because federal OSHA had only limited resources to carry out its own program, its interpretation meant that states would have to provide fewer staff personnel than would optimally be required for an effective program.

The U.S. Court of Appeals for the District of Columbia Circuit, in *AFL-CIO v. Marshall*, agreed with the AFL-CIO's argument. It found that OSHA had a duty to set staffing criteria that would ensure a fully effective enforcement effort by the states. The court ordered OSHA to calculate new personnel levels, or benchmarks, for the state programs in accordance with its finding.

Responding to that order in April 1980, OSHA announced new calculations that substantially increased target levels for state staffing over previous figures, for most states. State agencies criticized OSHA's calculations, arguing that they were adopted without proper notice-and-comment procedures and that they set unrealistic levels.

In consultation with the states, OSHA subsequently revised its calculations again to allow states to set their benchmarks for fully effective staffing based on a mutually agreed upon formula.

Withdrawal Procedures

States may withdraw from OSHA plan agreements. Conversely, OSHA may withdraw its approval of a state plan. To date, eight states have withdrawn from agreements: Colorado, Connecticut, Illinois, Montana, New Jersey, North Dakota, New York, and New Jersey. Connecticut and New York (which withdrew their plans in regard to private-sector regulation, but still maintain plans covering public employees) took action even after their plans had received final OSHA approval. All eight withdrawals occurred in the 1970s and generally resulted from the states' unwillingness or inability to fund their programs.

OSHA has never withdrawn approval of a state plan, but the OSH Act sets procedures that it must follow if it decides to do so. To withdraw approval, OSHA must first give the state an opportunity to show why the action is not warranted. Then it must publish a notice of proposed withdrawal in the *Federal Register*. An administrative law judge will be appointed by the Labor Department to preside over the proceedings. The ALJ has the authority to gather information and evidence, and—unless the state and OSHA resolve the dispute—to hold a hearing at which the parties have the right to present testimony, rebut each other's position, and conduct cross-examination.

After a transcript of the hearing has been filed with the judge, along with any other findings that the state and OSHA may be permitted to submit, the judge will reach a decision. If any party disputes the ruling, the case will be reviewed by the Secretary of Labor, who will issue a final ruling.

OSHA may withdraw its approval of a plan even after it has granted final section 18(e) approval. Factors that would trigger such a decision could include:

- Failure by the state over a period of time to enforce standards effectively;
- Actions by the state that limit the effectiveness of the program by limiting the rights of employees;
- Failure to maintain the state program in accordance with changes in the federal program; and
- Failure to ensure an adequate number of personnel or enough funding for the program.

If the secretary's decision calls for a withdrawal of approval, the state may appeal the ruling to the U.S. court of appeals for the circuit in which the state is located. The appeal court's decision in turn may be appealed to the U.S. Supreme Court.

Monitoring

Even after OSHA grants final approval to a state program, it retains the authority to monitor the effectiveness of the plan. To conduct monitoring, OSHA may:

- Gather quarterly and annual reports from the state regarding activity under the program;
- Visit the state program agency;
- Evaluate the performance of state inspectors on the job; and
- Investigate complaints about state program administration.

Complaints about State Program Administration

Any person who perceives shortcomings in a state's administration of its OSHA-approved plan may file a Complaint about State Program Administration (CASPA). A complaint may be made orally, or filed in writing with the assistant regional administrator for the OSHA region in which the state is located.

OSHA regulations call for CASPAs to describe the grounds for the complaint and to specify the aspects of the state program alleged to be inadequate.

In determining whether the complaint warrants investigation, the assistant regional director will consider such factors as:

- The extent to which the alleged problem affects a substantial number of people;
- The number of other complaints received on the same or similar issues, and whether the complaints related to conditions at a particular workplace;
- Whether the complainant has exhausted all channels for requesting a state investigation and correction of the problem; and
- The extent to which the subject matter of the complaint affects the carrying out of federal safety and health policy.

To investigate a CASPA, OSHA may obtain supporting evidence by making spot checks of workplaces, reviewing relevant state files, and discussing the investigation with employers, employees, state officials, and members of the public.

If OSHA determines that no reasonable grounds exist for an investigation, it must notify the complainant of that decision. At the request of the complainant, the agency may hold an informal conference and, after considering all oral and written comments, decide whether to affirm, modify, or reverse its determination.

Grants to States

To give states an incentive to participate in the state plan process, OSHA awards grants to help fund their programs. OSHA calculates the amount of a grant on the basis of the cost necessary to cover the direct expenses of the program, along with indirect expenses as determined by OSHA.

From 1971 to 1973, OSHA was authorized to award grants to provide seed money to states interested in developing plans. Those grants could cover as much as 90 percent of the cost of developing a program. The Act currently authorizes OSHA to fund 50 percent of the cost of administering and enforcing a state program.

The cost of running a safety and health program, OSHA grants notwithstanding, has made state plan agreements vulnerable to state budget cutters. California's program was eliminated in July 1987 in a budgetary move, then restored in November 1988 when organized labor successfully marshalled public support for a ballot initiative that called for reinstatement of the program. Michigan's governor proposed in January 1991 to eliminate that state's program, but the Michigan Labor Department arranged alternative funding for fiscal 1991 until a decision can be made on whether to continue the program.

State officials say that OSHA needs to increase its share of funding to better support state programs. Although OSHA has raised its funding by an additional $2 million to $2.5 million per year in recent years, a larger increase of $10 million is needed, according to these officials.

STATE STANDARDS

To gain OSHA approval, state standards must be at least as effective as the federal agency's program. When OSHA adopts a new standard, states with approved programs must issue a corresponding rule. By and large, state standards are identical to OSHA's. However, in a 1990 report, the Occupational Safety and Health State Plan Association (OSHSPA), an organization of state plan administrators, cited instances in which some states have standards that exceed OSHA's:

- Oregon and Washington have had comprehensive safety standards for logging since the early 1970s. OSHA only regulates pulpwood logging at present, although it recently proposed a more comprehensive rule.
- Maryland has had safety standards for work in confined spaces since 1976. OSHA did not propose a confined spaces standard until 1989.
- Michigan's standards on logging, fire fighting, and automotive safety operations are more stringent than OSHA's.

The OSH Act sets one restriction on state standards: if a rule affects a product used in interstate commerce, it must be justified by compelling local conditions and may not unduly burden interstate commerce. In one instance, industry groups used this provision for urging that OSHA reject a 1981 California rule for the fumigant ethylene dibromide (EDB) that was considerably more stringent than the corresponding OSHA standard. Business groups argued that California's action would disrupt interstate commerce involving EDB-treated produce. OSHA, which seeks public comment on all state rules that differ from federal standards, eventually approved the stricter state standard, finding that it was justified by local conditions and that industry critics failed to prove their assertions.

STATE ENFORCEMENT

Labor union officials have charged that some state programs do not provide adequate enforcement. However, state-plan administrators contend that their enforcement record surpasses federal OSHA's. In fiscal 1989 state-plan agencies conducted 113,582 inspections, compared with 54,557 by OSHA in the same period, and cited employers for 386,723 alleged violations, compared with 184,620 cited by OSHA.

State-plan programs will be required to set higher minimum fines for safety and health violations, to reflect higher fines that OSHA has been directed by Congress to levy (see Chapter 4). State officials say this requirement may provide an incentive for more states to enter into plan agreements with OSHA, if legislatures see higher penalties as a way of raising new revenues for their state governments.

FEDERAL PREEMPTION

Section 18(b) of the OSH Act reads:

Any State which, at any time, desires to assume responsibility for development and enforcement therein of occupational safety and health standards relating to any occupational safety or health issue with respect to which a Federal Standard has been promulgated under section 6 shall submit a State plan for the development of such standards and their enforcement (29 U.S.C. § 667(b)).

Some observers have read this section as giving a state the authority to set and enforce safety and health standards only if it has entered into a state-plan agreement with OSHA. In the 1980s two controversies raised the question of whether a state is always preempted from regulating a workplace hazard if it has not entered into a plan agreement. One controversy involved the promulgation of state right-to-know regulations, and the other pertained to state prosecutions of health and safety violations under state criminal statutes.

Right-to-Know

In 1983, as OSHA issued a hazard communication standard that required employers to notify workers of the identities and hazards of chemicals used on the job, several states similarly were developing right-to-know regulations pertaining to industrial chemicals. Many of these rules went beyond OSHA's by requiring disclosure of chemical information to workers in non-manufacturing industries (such as construction sites and offices) and to residents in communities near chemical plants, but they often overlapped the OSHA rule as well.

Industry groups filed suit against these state rules, contending that the existence of the OSHA standard pre-empted the states' authority to develop their own regulations.

This argument was upheld by the U.S. Court of Appeals for the Third Circuit in *United Steelworkers of America v. Auchter* (12 O.S.H. Cas. 1337) on May 24, 1985, in regard to workplaces *explicitly* covered by the OSHA rule. The court found that the federal regulation "preempts state hazard disclosure laws with respect to disclosure to employees in the manufacturing sector."

Two other rulings held that states may issue right-to-know provisions that are *outside* the scope of the OSHA standard, however. In *New Jersey Chamber of Commerce v. Hughey* (13 O.S.H. Cas. 1593), the U.S. District Court for New Jersey upheld portions of the New Jersey Workers and Community Right-to-Know Law that required the labeling of substances that present environmental hazards, and the universal labeling of all chemical containers in a workplace, regardless of whether all the containers held hazardous substances.

The court, in findings upheld by the U.S. Court of Appeals for the Third Circuit in February 1983 (13 O.S.H. Cas. 2040) rejected industry complaints that two labeling systems would confuse workers:

> The OSHA label can be distinguished from other labels by proper formatting and positioning, and since it is in the manufacturer's interests to alert his workers to potential hazards, there is no reason to believe [that] proper and effective formatting and positioning will not be the rule. Further, OSHA mandated training is designed to complement proper formatting and positioning.

The U.S. Supreme Court, on July 3, 1989, declined to review the case, allowing the decision favoring state authority to stand (19 O.S.H. Rep. 176).

Similarly, the Third Circuit in *Manufacturers Association of Tri-County v. Knepper*, on Sept. 12, 1986, upheld provisions in the Pennsylvania Right-to-Know Act requiring employers to complete hazardous substance surveys in their workplaces and post results of those surveys. In addition, chemical manufacturers are required to provide material-safety data sheets to public safety officials and include information such as chemical abstract service numbers. The court found that these provisions either pertained to disclosures outside the workplace, or set requirements that—even though affecting chemicals used on the job—would not be confusing to workers.

Criminal Prosecution

In the mid-1980s, state and local prosecutors in California, Illinois, Michigan, New York, Texas, and Wisconsin, began to press charges against employers under state criminal laws in cases involving death or the possibility of serious injury to workers from hazards on the job. Employers challenged the actions, contending that the criminal penalties provision of the OSH Act (29 U.S.C. § 666(e)) preempt a state from exercising prosecutorial authority over work-related hazards.

A series of court rulings reached differing conclusions over the question. In *Colorado v. Kelran Construction Co.*, *Sabine Consolidated Inc. v. Texas*, and *Michigan v. Hegedus*, courts in Colorado, Texas, and Michigan found that state prosecutions were preempted by the federal law.

However, rulings in *Illinois v. Chicago Magnet Wire Inc.*, *Wisconsin ex rel Cornellier v. Black*, and *Pymm v. State of New York* found that the OSH Act does not preclude state prosecutions.

Two of these rulings—*Chicago Magnet Wire* and *Pymm*—have been appealed to the U.S. Supreme Court. In each instance, the Supreme Court declined to review the lower court rulings that upheld state prosecution authority.

Proponents of state prosecution contend that district attorneys and prosecuting attorneys have shown more interest in applying criminal statutes to workplace safety violations than the federal government has. They also note that state prosecutions generally are easier to bring than criminal action under the OSH Act. Where criminal penalties under the OSH Act are limited to willful violations that result in the death of an employee, some state laws impose less stringent criteria that allow prosecution for negligent action that results in a safety violation.

On May 1, 1990, in testimony before the Senate Labor and Human Resources Subcommittee on Labor, former OSHA Administrator Gerard F. Scannell said there may be instances in which states may exercise prosecutorial authority without being challenged by OSHA:

> We agree that states should not be pre-empted for enforcing criminal laws of general applicability, such as those dealing with murder, manslaughter, or assault. However, to the extent that

states enact criminal laws which are purely regulatory in nature—that is, laws which make it a crime for employers to violate particular health or safety standards or to kill or injure an employee by committing such a violation—such laws should be preempted unless they are part of an OSHA-approved state plan. We believe that authorizing prosecution by the states, in appropriate cases, would serve as a complement to the predominantly civil federal enforcement scheme, providing that such prosecutions do not interfere with ongoing civil cases.

CONSULTATION PROGRAMS

Outside of enforcement, the OSH Act also provides for state and federal cooperation by allowing OSHA to use state personnel to provide free assistance to employers in identifying and correcting potential hazards (29 U.S.C. § 656(c), 670(c)). State personnel may provide such assistance through consultation programs conducted at an employer's work site, or by telephone or correspondence, or at the offices of the state agency in charge of the consultation program.

Consultation programs are kept separate from federal and state enforcement activity. Consultative visits can be made only at the request of an employer, and information from consultative activities cannot be provided to OSHA or state enforcement staffs, unless:

- The employer fails to correct a condition that the consultant identifies as an imminent danger to employees, or
- The employer wishes to use the results of the consultation to support a request for exemption from OSHA inspections for one year following the end of the consultative assistance.

Consultative programs are funded under cooperative agreements between OSHA and the states involved, with OSHA covering 90 percent of the cost of the state program.

7

FEDERAL AGENCY SAFETY AND HEALTH

The OSH Act requires heads of federal agencies to establish and maintain comprehensive, effective safety and health programs consistent with the requirements set for private industry employers by OSHA (29 U.S.C. § 668(a)). Specifically, the Act requires agency heads to:

- Acquire, maintain, and require the use of safety equipment, personal protective equipment, and other devices reasonably necessary to protect their employees from on-the-job hazards;
- Keep adequate records of all work-related injuries and illnesses;
- Consult with the Secretary of Labor on the proper form and content of those records; and
- Submit an annual report to the Secretary of Labor on the agency's program and on occupational injuries and illnesses among agency employees.

Through the 1970s, OSHA was criticized by federal employee unions for failing to set detailed requirements to carry out the mandate of the Act. In 1980, President Jimmy Carter issued Executive Order No. 12,196, which set several specific requirements for agency heads, including periodic inspection of agency workplaces. The executive order was followed by a set of OSHA standards in October 1980.

OSHA has the authority to inspect federal workplaces under certain circumstances, but not to levy penalties against federal agencies for safety or health hazards. Although federal officials make an effort to keep their workplaces safe, labor critics charge that agency heads do not give safety a high priority, and therefore, OSHA should be given the power to impose fines as an incentive for compliance.

PROGRAM ADMINISTRATION

The head of each federal agency (including the U.S. Postal Service) must designate a health and safety official who will administer the safety and health program for that agency. The designated official must hold the position of assistant secretary or its equivalent (29 C.F.R. § 1960.6(a)), and must be assured by the agency of sufficient financial and other resources to effectively administer the program (29 C.F.R. § 1960.7(a)).

Safety and Health Committees

Agencies may, but are not required to, establish safety and health committees to monitor and assist their programs. Such committees are viewed by OSHA as vehicles to help agencies maintain an open channel of communication between employees and management on safety and health matters. This allows employees to use their knowledge of workplace operations to improve working conditions (29 C.F.R. § 1960.36(a)).

If an agency decides to utilize such committees, it must establish them at both the national level and—if the agency has field offices—at other appropriate levels consistent with the size, mission, organization, and collective bargaining structure of the agency (29 C.F.R. § 1960.37(a)).

Committees must have equal numbers of member representing employees and management (29 C.F.R. § 1960.37(b)). If employees in the agency are represented by a union, the employee members must be appointed by the union (29 C.F.R. § 1960.37(b)(2)(i)). If the employees are not represented by a union, employee members must be determined through agency procedures that will provide for effective representation of all employees (29 C.F.R. § 1960.37(b)(2)(ii)). If some employees are covered by a collective bargaining contract, but others are not, committee members must be representative of both groups (29 C.F.R. § 1960.37(b)(2)(iii)).

Duties of a committee include:

- Monitoring and assisting agency safety and health initiatives;
- At the local level, participating in inspections of the particular workplace where the committee exists; and
- Reporting deficiencies in the agency's safety and health program to the Secretary of Labor (29 C.F.R. § 1960.40–41).

STANDARDS

Agencies must comply with OSHA standards or with alternative standards set through a prescribed procedure. After first notifying the Secretary of Labor, an agency may set more stringent exposure levels for hazardous substances and physical agents than OSHA does, or may require more frequent monitoring of employees than OSHA (29 C.F.R. § 1960.16).

Alternative and Supplementary Standards

Federal agency standards are generally similar to OSHA's. However, agencies are permitted to set alternative standards to OSHA's, or rules that supplement OSHA's. To obtain approval from the Secretary of Labor for setting alternative regulations, an agency must:

- Explain why it cannot comply with the comparable OSHA rule, or why it wishes to adopt a different standard;
- Describe the alternative standard;
- Explain how the alternative would be as protective as, or more protective than, OSHA's;
- Describe interim measures the agency would take to protect employees until the Secretary could decide whether to grant the request; and

- Provide a written summary of comments on the alternative from interested employees, employee representatives, and safety and health committees.

To adopt supplementary standards covering hazards not addressed by OSHA rules, the agency must send the final draft of the proposed supplementary regulation to the Secretary of Labor, along with any comments from employees, employee representatives, and safety and health committees. If the Secretary finds the rule inconsistent with any OSHA regulation or government policy, the Secretary has 15 working days to notify the agency of the finding. The agency must be given an opportunity to modify the standard. It also may request technical assistance from the Secretary to help develop a standard (29 C.F.R. § 1960.18(a)–(b)).

INSPECTIONS

A Presidential Executive Order requires agency heads to allow inspections of agency workplaces to be conducted by personnel with equipment and competence to recognize hazards (Exec. Order No. 12,196, § 1–201(g)). These persons must be safety or occupational health specialists, or other persons with sufficient training or experience to recognize hazards and suggest general abatement procedures (29 C.F.R. § 1960.28(a)).

All agency workplaces, including office work sites, must be inspected at least annually. More frequent inspections must be conducted in workplaces where an increased risk of accident, injury, or illness exists (29 C.F.R. § 1960.25(c)).

Inspections must be conducted in a way similar to OSHA inspections in private industry workplaces. The inspector has the authority to confer with employer and employee representatives, to conduct exposure monitoring, and to inform management of conditions that pose a hazard to workers (29 C.F.R. § 1960.26(b)(1)–(4)).

If an inspection finds a hazard that could reasonably be expected to cause death or serious physical harm immediately, the inspector must inform the affected employees and the official in charge of the workplace. That official must begin immediate abatement of the hazard and withdraw employees who are not necessary for corrective action (29 C.F.R. § 1960.26(b)(5)).

After concluding an inspection, the inspector must confer with the official in charge of the workplace and with an appropriate employee representative, and advise them of any hazards found (29 C.F.R. § 1960.26(b)(6)).

Notice of Unsafe Conditions

Agencies must establish procedures for the issuance of Notices of Unsafe or Unhealthful Working Conditions describing any hazards found by the inspector. Such notices must be based on written reports by inspectors (29 C.F.R. § 1960.26(c)(1)).

Notices must be issued within 15 days after completion of inspections for safety violations and within 30 days for health violations. If there are compelling reasons for a delay, those reasons must be explained to the person in charge of the inspected workplace, the employee representative who participated in the closing conference, and the safety and health committee, if any exists. Notices must:

- Be in writing and describe with particularity the nature and degree of seriousness of the hazard, including a reference to relevant standards or other requirements;
- Fix a reasonable time for abating the hazard; and
- Be sent to the official in charge of the inspected workplace, the employee representative who participated in the closing conference, and the safety and health committee if one exists (29 C.F.R. § 1960.26(c)(2)).

The official in charge of the workplace must post the notice immediately at or near the location where the hazard was found, or, if that requirement is not practicable, in a prominent place where it will readily be observed by affected employees. The notice must be posted for three working days or until the violation is corrected, whichever is later, and a copy must be kept on file for five years after abatement of the violation (29 C.F.R. § 1960.26(c)(3)–(4)).

OSHA Inspections

If an agency does not have a safety and health committee, OSHA may, and sometimes does, conduct an inspection. OSHA also may conduct inspections:

- In response to a request from at least 50 percent of the membership of a safety and health committee;
- In response to an employee's report of an imminent danger; and
- As an integral part of an evaluation of the agency's safety and health program.

Accident Investigations

OSHA requires that federal agencies investigate any accidents that result in a fatality or the hospitalization of five or more employees. Agencies are encouraged, but not required, to investigate less serious accidents, including those that involve only property damage.

When looking into an accident, agency investigators must prepare a report that includes documentation on the accident, information from interviews with employees and witnesses, measurements, and other pertinent data. Copies of the report must be given to the official in charge of the workplace, the safety and health committee, the employee representative, if any, and (on request) the Secretary of Labor.

Accidents resulting in the death of one or more employees or the hospitalization of five or more employees must be reported to OSHA within 48 hours after the accident occurs (29 C.F.R. § 1960.70(a)). Agencies also must report within 48 hours any occupational illness that results in the death of an employee (29 C.F.R. § 1960.70(a)).

EMPLOYEE REPORTS OF HAZARDS

Federal employees are authorized to report perceived hazards to agency safety and health officials and request an inspection of the workplace (29 C.F.R. § 1960.28(c)).

Agency inspections must be conducted within 24 hours in response to complaints involving imminent dangers, within three working days for potentially serious hazards, and within 20 working days for other-than-serious hazards (29 C.F.R. § 1960.28(d)(3)).

Protection from Discrimination

Agencies are required to establish procedures to protect employees' rights to engage in safety and health activities, and to protect employees from reprisals or discrimination for such activities. This includes the right of an employee to refuse to perform an assigned task when the employee has a reasonable belief that the activity involves an imminent risk of death or serious injury, and the employee has insufficient opportunity to seek redress through normal channels (29 C.F.R. § 1960.46(a)).

8

NIOSH RESEARCH

Seeing the need for more federal research on occupational safety and health, Congress included in the OSH Act a provision that created a new agency specifically responsible for research: the National Institute for Occupational Safety and Health.

Section 22 of the Act (29 C.F.R. § 671) authorizes NIOSH to:

- Develop recommendations for OSHA standards;
- Develop information on safe levels of exposure to toxic materials and harmful physical agents and substances;
- Conduct research on new safety and health problems;
- Conduct on-site investigations to determine the toxicity of materials used in workplaces; and
- Fund research by other agencies or private organizations through grants, contracts, and other arrangements.

The Federal Mine Safety and Health Amendments Act of 1977 delegated additional authority to NIOSH for coal mine health research. The mine health and safety law authorized NIOSH to:

- Develop recommendations for mine health standards for the Mine Safety and Health Administration;
- Administer a medical surveillance program for miners, including chest X-rays to detect pneumoconiosis (black lung disease) in coal miners;
- Conduct on-site investigations in mines similar to those authorized for general industry under the OSH Act; and

- Test and certify personal protective equipment and hazard-measurement instruments.

NIOSH, a unit of the Department of Health and Human Services (HHS), evolved from an earlier agency in the department, the Bureau of Occupational Health and Safety. The role of the institute under the Act was intended to "elevate the status of occupational safety and health research to place it on an equal footing with the research conducted by the HEW [the Department of Health, Education, and Welfare, as HHS was known in 1970] into other matters of vital social concern, particularly in the health area" (S. Rep. No. 91-1282).

ORGANIZATION

Originally located within the Health Services and Mental Health Administration, NIOSH was transferred, in 1973, to the Centers for Disease Control (CDC), the federal government's lead agency for control and eradication of infectious and communicable diseases. Critics have charged that the placement of NIOSH in the CDC (itself a component of the Public Health Service) does not give the institute needed prestige and autonomy for carrying out its duties. However, departmental officials have contended that NIOSH's activities complement those of other CDC units that address infectious, communicable, and environmental diseases.

Since 1981, NIOSH headquarters have been located at CDC headquarters in Atlanta, Georgia. The institute's actual research is conducted by seven divisions, some of which are located in Cincinnati, Ohio, and others in Morgantown, West Virginia. The divisions consist of Biomedical and Behavioral Science; Physical Sciences and Engineering; Respiratory Diseases Studies; Safety Research; Standards Development and Technology Transfer; Surveillance, Hazard Evaluations, and Field Studies; and Training and Manpower Development.

In large measure, the efforts of these divisions are focused on 10 problems that NIOSH has ranked as the leading types of work-related injuries and illnesses:

- Occupational lung disease;
- Musculoskeletal injuries;

- Occupational cancers;
- Occupational cardiovascular disease;
- Severe job-related traumatic injuries;
- Reproductive disorders;
- Neurotoxic disorders;
- Noise-induced hearing loss;
- Dermatological conditions; and
- Psychological disorders.

Division of Biomedical and Behavioral Science

This division conducts research on toxicology, stress, ergonomics, and the effects of physical agents, including studies on:

- Developing and evaluating methods for assessing adverse effects of job-related exposure to reproductive and neurotoxic hazards;
- The mental and emotional effects of new technology in the workplace;
- Reducing musculoskeletal strains from poor tool and work station design, or job tasks requiring repetitive, forceful movements; and
- The adequacy of current practices for protecting workers' hearing from loud noise on the job.

Division of Physical Sciences and Engineering

This division conducts research to develop procedures and equipment for measuring and controlling occupational health hazards, including:

- Developing methods for analyzing toxic substances through state-of-the-art instrumentation;
- Assisting small companies and other employers to improve design and operations of their businesses; and
- Evaluating the competency of analytical laboratories, and helping labs improve their performance.

Division of Respiratory Diseases Studies

This unit designs, conducts, and interprets studies on job-related respiratory diseases, such as black lung and silicosis. It also plans, coordinates, and performs other tasks related to medical examinations required under the Federal Mine Safety and Health Amendments Act, and certifies the medical facilities and doctors who participate in the program.

Division of Safety Research

This division is NIOSH's lead unit for safety research. Its duties include:

- Maintaining data bases for monitoring work-related injuries, which can be used to identify particular safety problems and set research priorities;
- Conducting general injury surveillance, and working with states to improve their own surveillance programs;
- Providing technical assistance on safety issues; and
- Evaluating and certifying respirators and instruments used for measuring dust in coal mines.

Division of Standards Development and Technology Transfer

This unit is the focal point for development and review of NIOSH scientific policy. Among other activities, the division:

- Maintains information on the numbers of workers potentially exposed to specific types of hazardous materials, the toxicity of these materials, and the status of research studies on them;
- Prepares criteria documents, or detailed reports on particular hazards that include information on exposure limits, protective equipment, and other worker-protection issues, which may be used as a basis for new OSHA standards;
- Develops other types of documents, including current intelligence bulletins, which disseminate new information on workplace hazards, and alerts, which are intended to help safety engineers, industrial hygienists,

or other safety and health professionals take direct action to reduce or eliminate a particular kind of workplace hazard;

- Maintains and annually revises the NIOSH "Registry of Toxic Effects of Chemical Substances," a toxic substances list that NIOSH is required to keep under section 20(a)(6) of the OSH Act; and
- Maintains a clearinghouse for NIOSH technical information.

Division of Surveillance, Hazard Evaluations, and Field Studies

This division conducts on-site investigations of health problems at workplaces called health hazard evaluations (HHEs), at the request of employers or employees. (Further discussion of HHEs appears later in this chapter.)

The division also conducts industry-wide occupational health studies to help make recommendations about safe levels of exposure to potentially hazardous substances in particular industries. Additionally, it provides technical assistance and consultation to other agencies, organizations, employers, and workers.

Division of Training and Manpower Development

This unit administers a number of training programs, carrying out requirements in section 21 of the OSH Act for such services in order to provide an adequate supply of occupational safety and health specialists, and information on the proper use of health and safety equipment.

The division's efforts include short-term training programs, such as seminars and specialized workshops, as well as long-term administration of training grants. NIOSH grants support academic programs, called Educational Resource Centers (ERCs), at 14 universities across the United States.

NIOSH ENTRY INTO WORKPLACES

Court cases have arisen regarding NIOSH's authority to enter a workplace to conduct an investigation. These cases have upheld NIOSH warrants to enter the workplace, and have found that the institute has the right to enter a workplace under authority of an administrative search warrant based on probable cause for believing that a problem exists at the workplace.

Because NIOSH does not have the authority to issue citations and penalties, it does not have to show evidence of a safety or health violation at the workplace, as does OSHA in obtaining a warrant under the *Barlow's* decision (see Chapter 4). The courts have held that, like OSHA, NIOSH, under the *Barlow's* standard, must show that its investigations are based on "reasonable legislative or administrative standards" (*In re Establishment Inspection of Keokuk Steel; In re Inland Steel Co.; In re Pfister & Vogel Tanning Co.*). But the courts have held that the necessary legislative standards are found in the OSH Act, which authorizes the institute to make on-site health hazard evaluations (29 U.S.C. § 669(a)(6)), and that the necessary administrative standards are found in the NIOSH regulations that implement the OSH Act provision (42 C.F.R. pts. 85 and 85a).

In the *Keokuk Steel* decision, a federal court ruled that for a request for an HHE to be valid, the request must be made by a single employee, if there are three or fewer employees in the particular workplace; by an employee who has been authorized by others to ask for an HHE; or by an authorized representative of the employee's local or parent international union.

For an investigation conducted by NIOSH as part of a planned research program, the court held in *Pfister & Vogel Tanning* that a NIOSH request for a warrant will be valid if the site was chosen as part of "a general administrative plan for the enforcement of the [OSH] Act derived from neutral sources." In issuing a warrant, the court said, the magistrate must determine that a reasonable legislative or administrative inspection program exists, and that the inspection fits within that program.

Legal questions also have arisen as to whether an employer may refuse to give NIOSH access to employee records on the grounds that such access would violate an employee's right of privacy. In the first ruling on this question, *E.I. du*

Pont de Nemours v. Finklea, a court found that disclosure would not violate employee's privacy because NIOSH assured the court that the information would be treated as confidential.

In *United States v. Westinghouse Electric Corp.,* the U.S. Court of Appeals for the Third Circuit went a step further and ordered NIOSH to notify the affected employees that it intended to review company medical records, and that employees would have the opportunity to object to the disclosure of sensitive medical information. If employees did not reply to the notice, their consent for release would be implied, and the company would have to release the records.

REGULATORY PROGRAMS BEYOND OSHA

Working conditions in some industries are regulated, either in part or completely, by statutes other than the Occupational Safety and Health Act. These industries include mining, nuclear materials, agriculture, asbestos removal, transportation, hazardous waste cleanup and emergency response, and offshore oil drilling.

In most instances (as in the mining, transportation, and nuclear industries), these laws predate the OSH Act. In other cases (as in asbestos removal and hazardous waste cleanup), the statutes were issued after the enactment of the OSH Act, and were intended to address problems that aroused public concern during the 1970s and 1980s.

In some of these industries, some activities are regulated by OSHA and other activities are regulated by other agencies. This division of authority occurs for a variety of reasons:

- If a hazard affects both the safety of the general public and the safety of workers, OSHA shares enforcement authority but is limited to conditions affecting employees (such as worker safety during hazardous waste cleanup activities);
- OSHA assumes responsibility for worker safety if another agency has not set standards to regulate a specific hazard (as it has done under the Outer Continental Shelf

Lands Act in regard to certain hazards at offshore drilling sites); and

- Some safety conditions in specialized industries are more typical of those normally regulated by OSHA than by another agency (for example, safety conditions in nuclear plants that are not related to the handling of radioactive substances, such as toxic, nonradioactive chemicals).

Under the OSH Act, OSHA is prohibited from exercising statutory authority over operations that another federal agency chooses to regulate (29 U.S.C. § 653(b)(1)). In some instances, where the division of authority between OSHA and another agency has been unclear, OSHA has entered into agreements or memoranda of understanding to clarify the lines of jurisdiction.

FEDERAL MINE SAFETY AND HEALTH ACT

Conditions in the mining industry are regulated by the Federal Mine Safety and Health Act of 1977 (P.L. No. 95-164). This law, whose enactment was prompted by a series of mine disasters in the 1970s, amended the Federal Coal Mine Health and Safety Act of 1969 and repealed the Metal and Nonmetallic Mine Act of 1966, bringing under one system of regulation many types of mines that previously had been covered by a variety of earlier laws.

Under the earlier statutes, regulations were set by the Mining Enforcement and Safety Administration (MESA), an agency of the U.S. Department of the Interior. Critics charged that Interior, which was the parent department of the Bureau of Mines, an agency concerned with mining productivity, was not the proper location for a mine safety agency.

Consequently, the 1977 law transferred mine safety responsibility to the Department of Labor, created a new Mine Safety and Health Administration (MSHA) in that department to set and enforce standards, and established an independent Federal Mine Safety and Health Review Commission to hear challenges to MSHA citations.

MSHA has jurisdiction not only over work activities in mines, but also over work activities on the roads leading to and from mines; on the roads belonging to the mine property; the lands, structures, equipment, and property used in connection with mines, including milling operations; and the work of preparing coal or other mined minerals, including custom coal preparation facilities (30 U.S.C. § 802(h)(1)).

Standards

The mine act's provisions on standards-setting are similar to those set by the OSH Act for OSHA. MSHA must publish a proposed standard in the *Federal Register* for comment (30 U.S.C. § 811(a)(2)), and give interested parties the opportunity to request a hearing (30 U.S.C. § 811(a)(3)).

MSHA may issue emergency temporary standards where it determines that miners are "exposed to grave danger from exposure to substances or agents determined to be toxic or physically harmful, or to other hazards," and that emergency action is needed to protect the miners. However, the agency must begin permanent rulemaking to address the hazard as soon as it publishes the emergency rule, and must issue a permanent standard no more than nine months later (30 U.S.C. § 811(b)).

MSHA may modify the application of a permanent standard when petitioned to do so by a mine operator or a representative of the miners employed at the mine, if it finds that an alternative, equally effective means of protecting the miners exists. Before granting such an exception, the agency must give public notice of the petition, provide an opportunity for a public hearing, and otherwise gather information on the request, in a process similar to that used by OSHA for variances from OSHA standards (see Chapter 4). MSHA's findings must be made public, and made available to representatives of affected miners at the mine (30 U.S.C. § 811(c)).

Any party that may be adversely affected by a standard may challenge the validity of the regulation in the U.S. Court of Appeals for the District of Columbia Circuit or in the district in which the person resides or has his or her principal place of business. Unless otherwise ordered by the court, the filing of a petition may not delay the effective date of the rule (30 U.S.C. § 811(d)).

Enforcement

The Mine Safety Act requires MSHA to inspect every underground mine at least four times a year, and every surface mine at least two times a year. In 1985, an investigation by the government's General Accounting Office found that the agency had conducted only about 64 percent of the required inspections during fiscal 1984, and a similar proportion in fiscal 1983.

According to the agency, improvements were made in the inspection program, and in 1991 the agency was making about 98 percent of the required inspections. (The 2 percent shortfall was due to the fact that some mines either opened or closed during the year, making it difficult for the agency to schedule them for inspections.) The agency expected to conduct about 74,000 inspections during fiscal 1991.

A miner or the miners' representative may request an immediate inspection by MSHA if reasonable grounds exist for believing that a health or safety violation or an imminent danger exists at a mine. The request must be made in writing and signed. A copy must be presented to the operator or the operator's agent no later than the time of the inspection; if the complainant alleges that an imminent danger exists, the operator or the agent must be notified "forthwith." The names of the complainant or other individual miners must be deleted from any copy or notification provided to the operator (30 U.S.C. § 813(g)).

Whenever MSHA finds that dangerous levels of explosive gases exist at a mine, or that a serious explosion resulting from the ignition of such gases has occurred at the mine in the past five years, or that some other especially hazardous condition exists, it must conduct at least one spot inspection at irregular intervals every 5, 10, or 15 working days, depending on the amount of gas found. The inspections will continue until the MSHA district manager in charge is satisfied that the hazard has been corrected or that the concentration of gas has subsided to a safe level (30 U.S.C. § 813(i)).

In the event of an accident at a mine, the operator must notify MSHA and take steps to prevent the destruction of any evidence that would assist in determining the cause or causes of the accident. If appropriate, MSHA may direct rescue and recovery operations (30 U.S.C. § 813(j)).

Citations and Orders

If, after an inspection, MSHA determines that a safety or health violation exists, it must issue a citation describing the alleged violation and setting a reasonable time for abatement (30 U.S.C. § 814(a)).

If, after a follow-up inspection, the agency finds that a cited hazard has not been completely abated and additional time for correction should not be granted, it may order the operator or the agent to immediately withdraw employees from the affected area until the agency determines that the violation has been abated (30 U.S.C. § 814(b)).

Withdrawal orders also may be issued where:

- MSHA, in the course of an inspection, finds more than one violation that poses a significant hazard, which has resulted from an unwarrantable failure of the operator to comply with safety and health regulations;
- MSHA, on reinspecting a mine within 90 days of the issuance of a citation, finds a violation of another standard that is significant and has resulted from an unwarrantable failure to comply; or
- MSHA finds a condition that poses an imminent danger of death or serious physical harm (30 U.S.C. § 814(d)(1), 817(a)).

Miners idled by a withdrawal order must be given full compensation for the time they are idled (30 U.S.C. § 821).

Penalties

The mine act allows MSHA to propose a penalty of up to $10,000 for a violation. Each occurrence of the violation may be regarded as a separate offense (30 U.S.C. § 820(a)).

Where an operator fails to correct a cited violation within the time alloted for abatement, MSHA may issue a penalty of up to $1,000 a day for each day the violation continues to be unabated (30 U.S.C. § 820(b)).

In 1982, MSHA revised its penalty structure to include a $20 single penalty for nonsignificant violations that were abated in a timely way (47 Fed. Reg. 22,286 (1982)). The United Mine Workers of America and the Coal Employment Project challenged the $20 penalty policy in 1988, and in 1989 the U.S. Court of Appeals for the District of Columbia Circuit ordered the agency to amend the policy. The court found that MSHA failed to take an operator's safety history into consideration in calculating $20 penalties, and failed to include $20 violations in considering a mine operator's safety history when levying regular penalties.

Therefore, in December 1989, MSHA issued an interim final rule in which it said it would begin to consider past penalties for nonsignificant violations in computing subsequent fines for operators. It also proposed, in December 1990, to increase penalty assessments for mines with a history of excessive safety violations.

The December 1990 proposal was issued a month after Congress, in the Omnibus Budget Reconciliation Act of 1990, increased maximum MSHA fines from $10,000 to $50,000 for a violation, and increased the maximum fine for failure to correct a violation from $1,000 a day to $5,000 per day (the same measure similarly increased OSHA penalties—see Chapter 4). The proposal asked for public comment on the proposed increases in penalty assessments (55 Fed. Reg. 53,482, (1990)).

The Mine Safety Act also allows MSHA to propose criminal penalties for knowing violations of standards or refusals to comply with orders issued by the agency. MSHA can propose a fine of up to $25,000, imprisonment for up to a year, or both, for a first offense. If a repeated infraction is alleged, MSHA can propose a fine of up to $50,000, imprisonment of up to five years, or both (30 U.S.C. § 820(d)).

According to MSHA statistics, as of July 1991, 46 successful criminal cases have been brought under the Mine Safety Act against coal mine operators, and three against metal/nonmetal mine operators.

Contesting Citations

Mine operators are given until 30 days after the issuance of a citation to notify MSHA if they wish to contest it (30 U.S.C. § 815(a)).

Challenges to MSHA citations are heard by the five-member Federal Mine Safety and Health Review Commission (FMSHRC) (30 U.S.C. § 816(d)). These procedures are similar to those followed by the Occupational Safety and Health Review Commission in hearing contests to OSHA citations.

Initially, a contest is heard by an administrative law judge, who will hold a hearing and then issue a written decision (30 U.S.C. § 823(d)(1); 29 C.F.R. § 2700.65). The judge's decision will become a final order of the commission, unless the commission orders a review. The commission may order a decision reviewed if:

- Any person or party adversely affected by the judge's decision petitions for a review of the decision within 30 days of its issuance; or
- The commission, at its own discretion, orders review on the grounds that the ruling was contrary to law or FMSHRC policy, or raised a novel question of policy (30 U.S.C. § 823(d)(2)(A)–(B)).

The commission, a five-member, independent panel appointed by the President with the consent of the Senate, may gather evidence and hold hearings in a manner similar to that followed by OSHRC in proceedings under the OSH Act (30 U.S.C. § 823(e)).

If the commission declines review of an ALJ decision, or if it reviews the decision and issues a ruling, any person or party aggrieved by the decision may seek review in a U.S. court of appeals in the region where the violation was alleged to have occurred, or in the U.S. Court of Appeals for the District of Columbia Circuit (30 U.S.C. § 816(a)(1)).

MSHA/OSHA Interagency Agreement

An interagency agreement signed between OSHA and MSHA on March 29, 1979, clarifies the jurisdictional authorities of the two agencies.

As a general principle, the agreement specifies that MSHA will exercise its authority on mine sites and in milling operations. However, where the provisions of the mine act do not cover or otherwise do not apply to job-related hazards at these sites (for example, hazards to employees in hospitals on mine sites), or where MSHA has statutory jurisdiction but no MSHA standards exist that are applicable to particular working conditions, the OSH Act will apply.

Further, OSHA may exercise its authority over an employer who has control over working conditions at a mining or milling site, if that employer is neither a mine operator nor an independent contractor subject to the mine act, if application of the OSH Act to this type of employer would provide a more effective remedy than citing a mine operator or independent contractor that does not have direct control over those conditions (48 Fed. Reg. 7521 (1979), O.S.H. Rep. Ref. File (BNA) No. 21, at 7071).

FIFRA

Under the authority of provisions in the Federal Insecticide, Fungicide, and Rodenticide Act (FIFRA) (7 U.S.C. § 136w), the Environmental Protection Agency (EPA) enforces standards to protect the health of workers engaged in hand labor operations in fields treated with pesticides.

The agency prohibits agricultural employers from applying pesticides in a way that will expose unprotected workers—either directly or through drifting of vapors—to pesticides. The area being treated must be vacated by unprotected workers (40 C.F.R. § 170.3(a)).

The standards also prohibit employers from allowing workers not wearing protective clothing to reenter a treated field until after the pesticides have dried or settled. The standards set specific reentry limits of one day for certain pesticides and two days for others (40 C.F.R. § 170.3(b)).

Employers also are required to give appropriate and timely warning to workers who are expected to be working in a field that has been treated or is about to be treated. The warning may be given either orally or through signs posted at usual points of entrance to the field, or on bulletin boards at areas where workers usually assemble for instructions. If the employer has reason to believe that a worker is unable to read, the warning must be given orally to that worker, and, if appropriate, in a language other than English. Workers should be informed of areas or fields that they must not enter without protective clothing, the period for which the area or field should be vacated, and actions to take in case of accidental exposure (40 C.F.R. § 170.5).

SARA

Under the Superfund Amendments and Reauthorization Act of 1986 (SARA), OSHA and EPA are required to protect employees engaged in hazardous waste and emergency response operations. Specific duties include:

- Response operations under the Comprehensive Environmental Response, Compensation, and Liability Act (CERCLA), including initial investigation at CERCLA-regulated waste sites before the actual presence or absence of hazardous substances has been ascertained;
- Hazardous waste clean-up operations under the Resource Conservation and Recovery Act (RCRA);
- Operations involving hazardous waste storage, disposal, and treatment regulated under RCRA, except for operations that generate only small quantities of hazardous waste and employers having less than 90 days' accumulation of hazardous wastes;
- Hazardous waste operation sites that have been designed for clean-up by state or local authorities; and
- Emergency response operations for releases or substantial threats of release of hazardous substances, and post-

emergency response operations for such releases (29 C.F.R. § 1910.120(a)(1)).

To enforce SARA, OSHA issued standards requiring employers to develop site-specific plans for worker protection at hazardous waste sites and in emergency response operations, and to provide training, medical surveillance, protective equipment, and engineering controls for hazards. SARA also requires OSHA to set maximum exposure limits for workers engaged in hazardous waste and emergency response operations, and to set requirements for the handling, transportation, labeling, and disposal of hazardous wastes (Pub. L. No. 99-499, § 126).

EPA incorporated OSHA's standards (29 C.F.R. § 1910.120), by reference, to protect employees who do not fall within OSHA's jurisdiction—state and local government employees involved in hazardous waste and emergency response operations in states that do not have approved state plans (40 C.F.R. § 311).

AHERA

The Asbestos Hazard Emergency Response Act of 1986 (AHERA), which requires school systems to inspect school buildings for asbestos hazards and to abate those hazards through removal, replacement, encapsulation, or other appropriate actions, addresses potential hazards to public and worker health resulting from such activities. The act requires contractors who perform such activities to be accredited through state governments (Pub. L. No. 99-519, § 206(a)).

The law required EPA to develop model accreditation programs for the states. Contractors are required, under those accreditation plans, to pass an examination addressing such elements of asbestos safety as:

- Recognition of asbestos-containing materials and knowledge of asbestos health hazards;
- Assessing the risk of asbestos exposure through a knowledge of the friability of asbestos-containing materials, the age of those materials, and the relative advantages and disadvantages of dry and wet processes for removing asbestos, among other subjects;

- Knowledge of respirators and appropriate work practices and hazard-control measures; and
- Knowledge of ways to correctly prepare an area for response action, and of proper asbestos disposal (Pub. L. No. 99-519, § 206(b)(1)(B)).

NUCLEAR SAFETY

The Atomic Energy Act of 1954 originally conferred on the Atomic Energy Commission (AEC) the authority to regulate all aspects of safety in the then–new nuclear industry, including worker safety at nuclear facilities. In an overhaul of federal energy policy in 1974, the Energy Reorganization Act abolished the AEC and transferred worker safety functions to the Nuclear Regulatory Commission (NRC) and the Energy Research and Development Administration (ERDA). ERDA functions were then transferred to the newly created Department of Energy under the Department of Energy Organization Act of 1977.

Nuclear Regulatory Commission

NRC is responsible for licensing and regulating nuclear facilities (mainly nuclear power plants) and nuclear materials used in hospital equipment, gauges, and other commercial applications. Under the Atomic Energy Act, as amended, the NRC can set standards it "may deem necessary or desirable to promote the common defense and security or to protect health or to minimize danger to life or property" (42 U.S.C. § 2201(b)).

The commission requires operators of nuclear facilities to inform employees, working in areas where nuclear materials are used, about the storage, transfer, and use of such materials in the particular area where the employee works, the health hazards associated with exposure to radioactive materials, and the purposes and functions of protective devices (10 C.F.R. § 19.12).

NRC also sets and enforces exposure limits for radioactive materials used in licensed facilities and applications (10 C.F.R. § 20.101 et seq.) and requires operators of nuclear facilities to:

- Conduct surveys to determine potential hazards from radioactive materials and other radiation sources (10 C.F.R. § 20.201);
- Monitor workers' exposures to radiation (10 C.F.R. § 20.202); and
- Use signs, labels, and signals to identify radioactive materials and areas in which they are used (10 C.F.R. § 20.203).

According to NRC statistics, the commission regulates 111 commercial nuclear power plants and has issued about 8,200 licenses for the use of radioactive materials. Some 29 states, under agreements with the commission, have issued an additional 15,000 licenses for applications within their jurisdictions.

Some labor unions and citizens' groups have charged that NRC enforcement at licensed facilities is not stringent enough, and that its exposure standards are too lax. On May 21, 1991, NRC issued more stringent standards, reflecting "developments and scientific knowledge underlying radiation protection that have occurred since Part 20 was issued more than 30 years ago. These developments not only include updated scientific information on radionuclide uptake and metabolism, but also reflect changes in the basic philosophy of radiation protection" (56 Fed. Reg. 23,360 (1991), O.S.H. Rep. Ref. File (BNA) No. 21, 7211–14).

OSHA/NRC Memorandum of Understanding

Because workers in nuclear facilities may encounter work-related hazards that do not involve nuclear materials, NRC and OSHA have defined their respective areas of jurisdiction over safety and health in those plants.

In an October 21, 1988, memorandum of understanding, the agencies agreed that NRC's jurisdiction extends to:

- Radiation hazards from radioactive materials;
- Chemical risks from those materials; and
- Plant conditions that affect the safety of radioactive materials and thus present an increased risk of exposure to radiation—for example, conditions that may lead to fires

or explosions that in turn may release radioactive materials or damage reactors.

OSHA's authority extends to hazards unrelated to the safety of radioactive materials, such as exposure to toxic, nonradioactive substances.

Also under OSHA's jurisdiction are employee exposures to radiation sources not regulated by NRC, including X-ray equipment and naturally occurring radioactive materials such as radium (O.S.H. Rep. Ref. File (BNA) No. 21, at 7211).

Department of Energy

The Energy Department regulates worker safety at 23 sites involved in nuclear weapons production. These sites—called GOCO (government-owned, contractor-operated) facilities—are owned by DOE but operated by private companies under contract to the government. These sites employ 18,748 DOE employees and 140,693 contract workers, according to DOE figures.

As owner of these plants, DOE has responsibility for all health and safety concerns there. The department's safety regulations are disseminated to facility operators in the form of DOE orders.

As with NRC, critics have charged that DOE health and safety programs are not stringent enough, and have urged that the department's authority be transferred to OSHA. The government's own Defense Nuclear Facilities Safety Board, an independent agency created in 1988 to review DOE safety performance, issued recommendations in 1991 for strengthening DOE safety management.

Responding to the board on May 17, 1991, DOE said that it was:

- Centralizing the responsibility for safety policy coordination and development in the office of the Assistant Secretary for Nuclear Energy;
- Issuing updated safety orders without delay;
- Preparing an order to require line management at nuclear facilities to document and ensure the use of na-

tional and international consensus standards in the design, construction, and operation of facilities; and
- Drafting a rule to explain the process under which safety violations at DOE facilities may result in civil penalties for contractors.

DOE also noted that it had revised its radiation standards in 1988 to reflect recent scientific thinking. The DOE exposure standards are identical to those that NRC adopted on May 21, 1991, for facilities under its jurisdiction (56 Fed. Reg. 22,860 (1991)).

FEDERAL AVIATION ACT

Under the Federal Aviation Act of 1958, the Federal Aviation Administration (FAA) is authorized to "promote safety of flight of civil aircraft in air commerce" by issuing standards and regulations covering such subjects as aircraft design, construction, and performance; aircraft inspection and servicing; and hours of service for air carrier employees (49 U.S.C. § 1421(a)).

Pursuant to this provision, FAA enforces standards regarding aircraft airworthiness (14 C.F.R. § 121.211–291), instrument and equipment performance (14 C.F.R. § 121.301–360), aircraft maintenance (14 C.F.R. § 121.361–380a), crew member qualifications (14 C.F.R. § 121.431–457), flight time limitations (14 C.F.R. § 121.500–525), flight operations (14 C.F.R. § 121.531–590), and records and reports, including aircraft alteration and repair documents, and mechanical reliability reports (14 C.F.R. § 121.681–715).

OSHRC has issued rulings in two notable cases regarding OSHA's and FAA's respective lines of authority in regulating conditions that affect the safety of employees in air commerce.

In *Secretary of Labor v. Allegheny Airlines*, the commission examined a dispute in which Allegheny Airlines, Inc., contested a citation which alleged that the company's practice of locking exit doors in a flight departure lounge at an airport violated OSHA fire safety regulations. Allegheny contended that the OSHA rules were preempted by FAA security regulations ordering that such areas be properly controlled against unauthorized entrance.

OSHRC upheld the citation, finding that the FAA rules were directed toward a different hazard than that addressed by the OSHA standards (9 O.S.H. Cas. (BNA) 1623).

In *Northwest Airlines,* Northwest contested a citation involving an alleged safety hazard to ground aircraft maintenance personnel. The airline argued that the aircraft operations and maintenance manuals that it is required to keep under FAA regulations (14 C.F.R. § 121.131–144) constitute an exercise of FAA jurisdiction over the safety of ground maintenance personnel, preempting OSHA authority.

OSHRC found that the manuals met the requirements for preemption of OSHA under the OSH Act because FAA has the authority to penalize airlines for failing to comply with these manuals (which are generally based on information provided by aircraft manufacturers), just as OSHA may cite an employer for failing to comply with safety specifications developed by the manufacturers of equipment used in the employer's place of business (8 O.S.H. Cas. (BNA) 1982).

RAILWAY SAFETY STATUTES

Rail carriers are required to protect employees and the general public from safety and health hazards, under three statutes:

- The Federal Railroad Safety Act of 1970 authorizes the federal government to take actions to promote safety in "all areas of railroad operations" (45 U.S.C. § 421) and authorizes the Federal Railroad Administration to develop "appropriate rules, regulations, orders, and standards for all areas of railroad safety" (45 U.S.C. § 431);
- The Federal Safety Appliance Act requires rail carriers engaged in interstate commerce to equip their cars with safety devices and appliances, and to maintain these appliances in adequate condition (45 U.S.C. § 1–7); and
- The Boiler Inspection Act provides safety requirements to be followed in operating a locomotive (45 U.S.C. § 14).

Under the Federal Railroad Safety Act, the Federal Railroad Administration (FRA) enforces standards covering noise hazards (49 C.F.R. § 210), track safety (49 C.F.R. § 213), freight car safety (49 C.F.R. § 215), railroad operations (49 C.F.R. § 217), radio standards and procedures (49 C.F.R. § 220), rear-end marking devices for trains (49 C.F.R. § 221), car window safety glazing (49 C.F.R. § 223), accident investigations (49 C.F.R. § 224), locomotive safety (49 C.F.R. § 229), safety appliances (49 C.F.R. § 231), power brakes and drawbars (49 C.F.R. § 232), and installation, inspection, maintenance, and repair of signal and train control systems, devices, and appliances (49 C.F.R. § 236).

OSHRC and some federal courts have held, however, that OSHA may cite hazards in railroad maintenance shops because FRA has not issued standards specifically covering conditions in those workplaces (*Southern Pacific Transportation Co. v. Usery and OSAHRC; Southern Railway Co. v. OSAHRC and Brennan; Baltimore & Ohio Railroad Co. v. OSAHRC*).

MOTOR CARRIER SAFETY ACT

Under the Motor Carrier Safety Act, employers are required to comply with commercial motor vehicle safety standards issued by the Department of Transportation's Federal Highway Administration (FHwA). In addition to protecting public safety, one of the purposes of the act is to "minimize dangers to the health of operators of commercial motor vehicles and other employees whose employment directly affects motor carrier safety" (49 U.S.C. app. § 2501).

In addition to vehicle operators, the law also pertains to the safety of independent contractors operating commercial motor vehicles, mechanics, freight handlers, and other employees in the motor carrier trade (49 U.S.C. app. § 2503).

Among the standards issued by FHwA under the statute are rules pertaining to parts and accessories needed for safe operation of commercial vehicles (49 C.F.R. § 393.1–209), hours of service for drivers (49 C.F.R. § 395.1–15), inspection, maintenance, and repair of vehicles (49 C.F.R. § 396.1–23), and safety requirements for steps, handholds, and decks on commercial vehicles (49 C.F.R. § 399.201–211).

HAZARDOUS MATERIALS TRANSPORTATION ACT

The Department of Transportation's Research and Special Programs Administration has the authority under the Hazardous Materials Transportation Act to regulate the transportation of materials "in a quantity and form which may pose an unreasonable risk to health and safety or property when transported in commerce" (49 U.S.C. §§ 1801, 1802(1)).

Among the regulations issued under this authority are standards for shipments and packaging (49 U.S.C. § 173.1–1201), and loading, handling, and other requirements for transportation of hazardous materials by rail (49 C.F.R. § 174.1–840), aircraft (49 C.F.R § 175.1–705), vessel (49 C.F.R. § 176.1–906), and public highway (49 C.F.R. § 177.800–861).

NATURAL GAS PIPELINE SAFETY ACT

Under another statute, the Natural Gas Pipeline Safety Act, the Research and Special Programs Administration (RSPA) also regulates the safety of gas pipeline facilities and gas transportation. The statute ordered the Department of Transportation (DOT) to adopt minimum safety standards (49 U.S.C. § 1672) and requires companies engaged in the transportation of gas or the ownership of pipeline facilities to comply with those regulations (49 U.S.C. § 1677).

Among RSPA's standards are regulations pertaining to pipe design (49 C.F.R. § 195.100–132), construction (49 C.F.R. § 195.200–266), hydrostatic testing (49 C.F.R. § 195.300–310), facility design (49 C.F.R. § 193.2101–2233), facility construction (49 C.F.R. § 193.2301–2329), facility equipment (49 C.F.R § 193.2401–2445), and facility operations (49 C.F.R. § 193.2501–2521).

Although RSPA's standards preempt OSHA rules in regard to pipeline operations, contractors engaged in repairing pipelines are covered by OSHA (*Secretary of Labor v. Texas Trans-*

mission Corp.; Northern Border Pipeline Co. v. Jackson County; Columbia Gas v. Marshall).

VESSEL INSPECTION

Under U.S. maritime law, the U.S. Coast Guard has authority over safety on tank and passenger vessels (14 U.S.C. § 1 et seq.). Among Coast Guard standards pertaining to the safety of maritime employees are those regulating lifesaving equipment on tank vessels (46 C.F.R. § 33), fire-fighting equipment on tank vessels (46 C.F.R. § 34), lifesaving equipment on passenger vessels (46 C.F.R. § 75), fire protection equipment on passenger vessels (46 C.F.R. § 76), and special construction arrangements and other provisions for carrying anhydrous ammonia, combustible liquids, and other dangerous cargoes in bulk (46 C.F.R § 98).

In a March 17, 1983, memorandum of understanding, OSHA and the Coast Guard stated that OSHA retains its authority under the OSH Act to respond to complaints by seamen aboard Coast Guard-inspected vessels regarding alleged discrimination for safety-related activity. OSHA also has the authority to order vessel owners to post notices informing employees of their right to complain about working conditions to the Coast Guard, OSHA, or to the employer, and to be free from retaliatory discrimination (48 Fed. Reg. 11,550 (1983), O.S.H. Rep. Ref. File (BNA) No. 21, at 7161).

OUTER CONTINENTAL SHELF LANDS ACT

The Outer Continental Shelf Lands Act gives the Coast Guard and the Department of the Interior's Minerals Management Services (MMS) the authority to set and enforce standards to regulate hazardous working conditions on the outer continental shelf (43 U.S.C. § 1347, 1348).

MMS' standards pertain to safety in drilling operations by offshore rigs (30 C.F.R. § 250.50–67), well completion (30 C.F.R. § 250.70–87), and well workover (30 C.F.R. § 250.90–98); production safety systems (30 C.F.R. § 250.120–127); platforms and structures, including inspection and maintenance (30 C.F.R. § 250.130–144); and employee training (30 C.F.R. § 250.210–212).

The Coast Guard's regulations pertain to mobile offshore units—vessels engaged in drilling operations, rather than stationary rigs. They include rules for inspection and certification of vessels, including testing of fire-fighting equipment and lifeboats (46 C.F.R. § 107.01–413), design and equipment, including location of fire-fighting equipment and lifeboats (46 C.F.R. § 108.101–719), and operations, including practice drills and stowage of safety equipment (46 C.F.R. § 109.101–585).

Under memoranda of understanding signed December 19, 1979, and January 20, 1982, OSHA and the Coast Guard agreed that OSHA would enforce standards covering working conditions for which the Coast Guard has no specific standards of its own. The Coast Guard agreed to notify OSHA whenever a Coast Guard inspection found apparent violations of OSHA rules, and to cooperate with any subsequent enforcement activity that OSHA might undertake (45 Fed. Reg. 9142 (1980), O.S.H. Rep. Ref. File (BNA) No. 21, at 7101).

Appendix A

OCCUPATIONAL SAFETY AND HEALTH ACT OF 1970

OCCUPATIONAL SAFETY AND HEALTH ACT OF 1970

(Enacted by Public Law 91–596, 84 Stat. 1590, December 29, 1970; 29 USC 651 et. seq.; amended by P.L. 93–237, January 2, 1974; P.L. 95–251, March 27, 1978; P.L. 96–88, October 17, 1979; P.L. 97–375, December 21, 1982; P.L. 98–620, November 8, 1984; P.L. 101–508, November 5, 1990)

AN ACT to assure safe and healthful working conditions for working men and women; by authorizing enforcement of the standards developed under the Act; by assisting and encouraging the States in their efforts to assure safe and healthful working conditions; by providing for research, information, education, and training in the field of occupational safety and health; and for other purposes.

Be it enacted by the Senate and House of Representatives of the United States of America in Congress assembled, That this Act may be cited as the "Occupational Safety and Health Act of 1970."

CONGRESSIONAL FINDINGS AND PURPOSE

Sec. (2) The Congress finds that personal injuries and illnesses arising out of work situations impose a substantial burden upon, and are a hindrance to, interstate commerce in terms of lost production, wage loss, medical expenses, and disability compensation payments.

(b) The Congress declares it to be its purpose and policy, through the exercise of its powers to regulate commerce among the several States and with for-eign nations and to provide for the general welfare, to assure so far as possible every working man and woman in the Nation safe and healthful working conditions and to preserve our human resources—

(1) by encouraging employers and employees in their effort to reduce the number of occupational safety and health hazards at their places of employment, and to stimulate employers and employees to institute new and to perfect existing programs for providing safe and healthful working conditions;

(2) by providing that employers and employees have separate but dependent responsibilities and rights with respect to achieving safe and healthful working conditions;

(3) by authorizing the Secretary of Labor to set mandatory occupational safety and health standards applicable to businesses affecting interstate commerce, and by creating an Occupational Safety and Health Review Commission for carrying out adjudicatory functions under the Act;

(4) by building upon advances already made through employer and employee initiative for providing safe and healthful working conditions;

138

Published by THE BUREAU OF NATIONAL AFFAIRS, INC., Washington, D.C. 20037

(5) by providing for research in the field of occupational safety and health, including the psychological factors involved, and by developing innovative methods, techniques, and approaches for dealing with occupational safety and health problems;

(6) by exploring ways to discover latent diseases, establishing causal connections between diseases and work in environmental conditions, and conducting other research relating to health problems, in recognition of the fact that occupational health standards present problems often different from those involved in occupational safety;

(7) by providing medical criteria which will assure insofar as practicable that no employee will suffer diminished health, functional capacity, or life expectancy as a result of his work experience;

(8) by providing for training programs to increase the number and competence of personnel engaged in the field of occupational safety and health;

(9) by providing for the development and promulgation of occupational safety and health standards;

(10) by providing an effective enforcement program which shall include a prohibition against giving advance notice of any inspection and sanctions for any individual violating this prohibition;

(11) by encouraging the States to assume the fullest responsibility for the administration and enforcement of their occupational safety and health laws by providing grants to the States to assist in identifying their needs and responsibilities in the area of occupational safety and health, to develop plans in accordance with the provisions of this Act, to improve the administration and enforcement of State occupational safety and health laws, and to conduct experimental and demonstration projects in connection therewith;

(12) by providing for appropriate reporting procedures with respect to occupational safety and health which pro-

cedures will help achieve the objectives of this Act and accurately describe the nature of the occupational safety and health problem;

(13) by encouraging joint labor-management efforts to reduce injuries and disease arising out of employment.

DEFINITIONS

Sec. 3. For the purposes of this Act—

(1) The term "Secretary" mean the Secretary of Labor.

(2) The term "Commission" means the Occupational Safety and Health Review Commission established under this Act.

(3) The term "commerce" means trade, traffic, commerce, transportation, or communication among the several States, or between a State and any place outside thereof, or within the District of Columbia, or a possession of the United States (other than the Trust Territory of the Pacific Islands), or between points in the same State but through a point outside thereof.

(4) The term "person" means one or more individuals, partnerships, associations, corporations, business trusts, legal representatives, or any organized group of persons.

(5) The term "employer" means a person engaged in a business affecting commerce who has employees, but does not include the United States or any State or political subdivision of a State.

(6) The term "employee" means an employee of an employer who is employed in a business of his employer which affects commerce.

(7) The term "State" includes a State of the United States, the District of Columbia, Puerto Rico, the Virgin Islands, American Samoa, Guam, and the Trust Territory of the Pacific Islands.

(8) The term "occupational safety and health standard" means a standard which requires conditions, or the adoption or use of one or more practices, means, methods, operations, or process-

139

es, reasonably necessary or appropriate to provide safe or healthful employment and places of employment.

(9) The term "national consensus standard" means any occupational safety and health standard or modification thereof which (1), has been adopted and promulgated by a nationally recognized standards-producing organization under procedures whereby it can be determined by the Secretary that persons interested and affected by the scope or provisions of the standard have reached substantial agreement on its adoption, (2) was formulated in a manner which afforded an opportunity for diverse views to be considered and (3) has been designated as such a standard by the Secretary, after consultation with other appropriate Federal agencies.

(10) The term "established Federal standard" means any operative occupational safety and health standard established by any agency of the United States and presently in effect, or contained in any Act of Congress in force on the date of enactment of this Act.

(11) The term "Committee" means the National Advisory Committee on Occupational Safety and Health established under this Act.

(12) The term "Director" means the Director of the National Institute for Occupational Safety and Health.

(13) The term "Institute" means the National Institute for Occupational Safety and Health established under this Act.

(14) The term "Workmen's Compensation Commission" means the National Commission on State Workmen's Compensation Laws established under this Act.

APPLICABILITY OF THIS ACT

Sec. 4. (a) This Act shall apply with respect to employment performed in a workplace in a State, the District of Columbia, the Commonwealth of Puerto Rico, the Virgin Islands, Ameri-

can Samoa, Guam, the Trust Territory of the Pacific Islands, Wake Island, Outer Continental Shelf lands defined in the Outer Continental Shelf Lands Act, Johnston Island, and the Canal Zone. The Secretary of the Interior shall, by regulation, provide for judicial enforcement of this Act by the courts established for areas in which there are no United States district courts having jurisdiction.

(b)(1) Nothing in this Act shall apply to working conditions of employees with respect to which other Federal agencies, and State agencies acting under section 274 of the Atomic Energy Act of 1954, as amended (42 U.S.C. 2021), exercise statutory authority to prescribe or enforce standards or regulations affecting occupational safety or health.

(2) The safety and health standards promulgated under the Act of June 30, 1936, commonly known as the Walsh-Healey Act (41 U.S.C. 35 et seq.), the Service Contract Act of 1965 (41 U.S.C. 351 et seq.), Public Law 91–54, Act of August 9, 1969 (40 U.S.C. 333), Public Law 85–742, Act of August 23, 1958 (33 U.S.C. 941), and the National Foundation on Arts and Humanities Act (20 U.S.C. 951 et seq.) are superseded on the effective date of corresponding standards, promulgated under this Act, which are determined by the Secretary to be more effective. Standards issued under the laws listed in this paragraph and in effect on or after the effective date of this Act shall be deemed to be occupational safety and health standards issued under this Act, as well as under such other Acts.

(3) The Secretary shall, within three years after the effective date of this Act, report to the Congress his recommendations for legislation to avoid unnecessary duplication and to achieve coordination between this Act and other Federal laws.

(4) Nothing in this Act shall be construed to supersede or in any manner affect any workmen's compensation

law or to enlarge or diminish or affect in any other manner the common law or statutory rights, duties, or liabilities of employers and employers under any law with respect to injuries, diseases, or death of employees arising out of, or in the course of, employment.

DUTIES

Sec. 5. (a) Each Employer—

(1) shall furnish to each of his employees employment and a place of employment which are free from recognized hazards that are causing or are likely to cause death or serious physical harm to his employees;

(2) shall comply with occupational safety and health standards promulgated under this Act.

(b) Each employee shall comply with occupational safety and health standards and all rules, regulations, and orders issued pursuant to this Act which are applicable to his own actions and conduct.

OCCUPATIONAL SAFETY AND HEALTH STANDARDS

Sec. 6. (a) Without regard to chapter 5 of title 5, United States Code, or to the other subsections of this section, the Secretary shall, as soon as practicable during the period beginning with the effective date of this Act and ending two years after such date, by rule promulgate as an occupational safety or health standard federal any national consensus standard, and any established Federal standard, unless he determines that the promulgation of such a standard would not result in improved safety or health for specifically designated employees. In the event of conflict among any such standards, the Secretary shall promulgate the standard which assures the greatest protection of the safety or health of the affected employees.

(b) The Secretary may by rule promulgate, modify, or revoke any occupational safety or health standard in the following manner:

(1)Whenever the Secretary, upon the basis of information submitted to him in writing by an interested person, a representative of any organization of employers or employees, a nationally recognized standards-producing organization, the Secretary of Health and Human services, the National Institute for Occupational Safety and Health, or a State or political subdivision, or on the basis of information developed by the Secretary or otherwise available to him, determines that a rule should be promulgated in order to serve the objectives of this Act, the Secretary may request the recommendations of an advisory committee appointed under section 7 of this Act. The Secretary shall provide such an advisory committee with any proposals of his own or of the Secretary of Health, and Human Services together with all pertinent factual information developed by the Secretary or the Secretary of Health and Human Services, or otherwise available, including the results of research, demonstrations, and experiments. An advisory committee shall submit to the Secretary its recommendations regarding the rule to be promulgated within ninety days from the date of its appointment or within such longer or shorter period as may be prescribed by the Secretary, but in no event for a period which is longer than two hundred and seventy days.
[Sec. 6(b)(1) amended by P.L. 96–88, October 17, 1979]

(2) The Secretary shall publish a proposed rule promulgating, modifying, or revoking an occupational safety or health standard in the Federal Register and shall afford interested persons a period of thirty days after publication to submit written data or comments. Where an advisory committee is appointed and the Secretary determines that a rule should be issued, he shall publish the proposed rule within sixty days after the submission of the advisory committee's recommendations or the expiration of the period prescribed by the Secretary for such submission.

(3) On or before the last day of the period provided for the submission of written data or comments under paragraph (2), any interested person may file with the Secretary written objections to the proposed rule, stating the grounds therefore and requesting a public hearing on such objections. Within thirty days after the last day for filing such objections, the Secretary shall publish in the Federal Register a notice specifying the occupational safety or health standard to which objections have been filed and a hearing requested, and specifying a time and place for such hearing.

(4) Within sixty days after the expiration of the period provided for the submission of written data or comments under paragraph (2), or within sixty days after the completion of any hearing held under paragraph (3), the Secretary shall issue a rule promulgating, modifying, or revoking an occupational safety or health standard or make a determination that a rule should not be issued. Such a rule may contain a provision delaying its effective date for such period (not in excess of ninety days) as the Secretary determines may be necessary to insure that affected employers and employees will be informed of the existence of the standard and of its terms and that employers affected are given an opportunity to familiarize themselves and their employees with the existence of the requirements of the standard.

(5) The Secretary, in promulgating standards dealing with toxic materials or harmful physical agents under this subsection, shall set the standard which most adequately assures, to the extent feasible, on the basis of the best available evidence, that no employee will suffer material impairment of health or functional capacity even if such employee has regular exposure to the hazard dealt with by such standard for the period of his working life. Development of standards under this subsection shall be based upon research, demonstra-

tions, experiments, and such other information as may be appropriate. In addition to the attainment of the highest degree of health and safety protection for the employee, other considerations shall be the latest available scientific data in the field, the feasibility of the standards, and experience gained under this and other health and safety laws. Whenever practicable, the standard promulgated shall be expressed in terms of objective criteria and of the performance desired.

(6)(A) Any employer may apply to the Secretary for a temporary order granting a variance from a standard or any provision thereof promulgated under this section. Such temporary order shall be granted only if the employer files an application which meets the requirements of clause (B) and establishes that (i) he is unable to comply with a standard by its effective date because of unavailability of professional or technical personnel or of materials and equipment needed to come into compliance with the standard or because necessary construction or alteration of facilities cannot be completed by the effective date, (ii) he is taking all available steps to safeguard his employees against the hazards covered by the standard, and (iii) he has an effective program for coming into compliance with the standard as quickly as practicable. Any temporary order issued under this paragraph shall prescribe the practices, means, methods, operations, and processes which the employer must adopt and use while the order is in effect and state in detail his program for coming into compliance with the standard. Such a temporary order may be granted only after notice to employees and an opportunity for a hearing: *Provided,* That the Secretary may issue one interim order to be effective until a decision is made on the basis of the hearing. No temporary order may be in effect for longer than the period needed by the employer to achieve compliance with the standard or one year, whichever is shorter, except that such an order may be renewed not more than twice (I) so long as the requirements of this paragraph are met and (II) if an application for renewal is filed at least 90 days prior to the expiration date of the order. No interim renewal of an order may remain in effect for longer than 180 days.

(B) An application for a temporary order under this paragraph (6) shall contain:

(i) a specification of the standard or portion thereof from which the employer seeks a variance,

(ii) a representation by the employer, supported by representations from qualified persons having firsthand knowledge of the facts represented, that he is unable to comply with the standard or portion thereof and a detailed statement of the reasons thereof,

(iii) a statement of the steps he has taken and will take (with specific dates) to protect employees against the hazard covered by the standard,

(iv) a statement of when he expects to be able to comply with the standards and what steps he has taken what steps he will take (with dates specified) to come into compliance with the standard, and

(v) a certification that he has informed his employees of the application by giving a copy thereof to their authorized representative, posting a statement giving a summary of the application and specifying where a copy may be examined at the place or places where notices to employees are normally posted and by other appropriate means.

A description of how employees have been informed shall be contained in the certification. The information to employees shall also inform them of their right to petition the Secretary for a hearing.

(C) The Secretary is authorized to grant a variance from any standard or portion thereof whenever he determines, or the Secretary of Health and Human Services certifies, that such variance is necessary to permit an employer to participate in an experiment approved by him or the Secretary of Health and Human Services designed to demonstrate or validate new and improved techniques to safeguard the health or safety of workers.

[Sec. 6(b)(6)(c) amended by P.L. 96–88, October 17, 1979]

(7) Any standard promulgated under this subsection shall prescribe the use of labels or other appropriate forms of warning as are necessary to insure that employees are apprised of all hazards to which they are exposed, relevant symptoms and appropriate emergency treatment, and proper conditions and precautions of safe use or exposure. Where appropriate, such standard shall also prescribe suitable protective equipment and control or technological procedures to be used in connection with such hazards and shall provide for monitoring or measuring employee exposure at such locations and intervals, and in such manner as may be necessary for the protection of employees. In addition, where appropriate, any such standard shall prescribe the type and frequency of medical examinations or other tests which shall be made available, by the employer or at his cost, to employees exposed to such hazards in order to most effectively determine whether the health of such employees is adversely affected by such exposure. In the event such medical examinations are in the nature of research, as determined by the Secretary of Health and Human Services, such examinations may be furnished at the expense of the Secretary of Health and Human Services. The results of such examinations or tests shall be furnished only to the Secretary or the Secretary of Health and Human Services, and, at the request of the employee, to his physician. The Secretary, in consultation with the Secretary of Health and Human Services may by rule promulgated pursuant to section 553 of title 5, United States Code, make appropriate modifications in the foregoing require-

ments relating to the use of labels or other forms of warning, monitoring or measuring, and medical examinations, as may be warranted by experience, information, or medical or technological developments acquired subsequent to the promulgation of the relevant standards.

[Sec. 6(b)(7) amended by P.L. 96–88, October 17, 1979]

(8) Whenever a rule promulgated by the Secretary differs substantially from an existing national consensus standard, the Secretary shall, at the same time, publish in the Federal Register a statement of the reasons why the rule as adopted will better effectuate the purposes of this Act than the national consensus standard.

(c)(1) The Secretary shall provide, without regard to the requirements of chapter 5 title 5, United States Code, for an emergency temporary standard to take immediate effect upon publication in the Federal Register if he determines (A) that employees are exposed to grave danger from exposure to substances or agents determined to be toxic or physically harmful or from new hazards,and (B) that such emergency standard is necessary to protect employees from such danger.

(2) Such standard shall be effective until superseded by a standard promulgated in accordance with the procedures prescribed in paragraph (3) of this subsection.

(3) Upon publication of such standard in the Federal Register the Secretary shall commence a proceeding in accordance with section 6(b) of this Act, and the standard as published shall also serve as a proposed rule for the proceeding. The Secretary shall promulgate a standard under this paragraph no later than six months after publication of the emergency standard as provided in paragraph (2) of this subsection.

(d) Any affected employer may apply to the Secretary for a rule or order for a variance from a standard promul-

gated under this section. Affected employees shall be given notice of each such application and an opportunity to participate in a hearing. The Secretary shall issue such rule or order if he determines on the record, after opportunity for an inspection where appropriate and a hearing, that the proponent of the variance has demonstrated by a preponderance of the evidence that the conditions, practices, means, methods, operations,or processes used or proposed to be used by an employer will provide employment and places of employment to his employees which are as safe and healthful as those which would prevail if he complied with the standard. The rule or order so issued shall prescribe the conditions the employer must maintain, and the practices, means, methods, operations, and processes which he must adopt and utilize to the extent they differ from the standard in question. Such a rule or order may be modified or revoked upon application by an employer, employees, or by the Secretary on his own motion, in the manner prescribed for its issuance under this subsection at any time after six months from its issuance.

(e) Whenever the Secretary promulgates any standard, makes any rule, order, or decision, grants any exemption or extension of time, or compromises, mitigates, or settles any penalty assessed under this Act, he shall include a statement of the reasons for such action, which shall be published in the Federal Register.

(f) Any person who may be adversely affected by a standard issued under this section may at any time prior to the sixtieth day after such standard is promulgated file a petition challenging the validity of such standard with the United States court of appeals for the circuit wherein such person resides or has his principal place of business, for a judicial review of such standard. A copy of the petition shall be forthwith transmitted by the clerk of the court to the Secretary. The filing of such peti-

tion shall not, unless otherwise ordered by the court, operate as a stay of the standard. The determinations of the Secretary shall be conclusive if supported by substantial evidence in the record considered as a whole.
[Sec. 6(g) amended by P.L. 96–88, October 17, 1979]

(g) In determining the priority for establishing standards under this section, the Secretary shall give due regard to the urgency of the need for mandatory safety and health standards for particular industries, trades, crafts, occupations, businesses, workplaces or work environments. The Secretary shall also give due regard to the recommendations of the Secretary of Health and Human Services regarding the need for mandatory standards in determining the priority for establishing such standards.

ADVISORY COMMITTEES; ADMINISTRATION

Sec. 7 (a) (1) There is hereby established a National Advisory Committee on Occupational Safety and Health consisting of twelve members appointed by the Secretary, four of whom are to be designated by the Secretary of Health and Human Services, without regard to the provisions of title 5, United States Code, governing appointments in the competitive service, and composed of representatives of management, labor, occupational safety and occupational health professions, and of the public. The Secretary shall designate one of the public members as Chairman. The members shall be selected upon the basis of their experience and competence in the field of occupational safety and health.

(2) The Committee shall advise consult with and make recommendations to the secretary and the secretary of Health and Human Services on matters relating to the administration of the Act. The Committee shall hold no fewer than two meetings during each calendar year. All meetings of the Committee shall be open to the public

and a transcript shall be kept and made available for public inspection.
[Sec. 7(a)(1) and (2) amended by P.L. 96–88, October 17, 1979]

(3) The members of the Committee shall be compensated in accordance with the provisions of section 3109 of title 5, United States Code.

(4) The Secretary shall furnish to the Committee an executive secretary and such secretarial, clerical, and other services as are deemed necessary to the conduct of its business.

(b) An advisory committee may be appointed by the Secretary to assist him in his standard-setting functions under section 6 of this Act. Each such committee shall consist of not more than fifteen members and shall include as a member one or more designees of the Secretary of Health and Human Services, and shall include among its members an equal number of persons qualified by experience and affiliation to present the viewpoint of the employers involved, and of persons similarly qualified to present the viewpoint of the workers involved, as well as one or more representatives of health and safety agencies of the States. An advisory committee may also include such other persons as the Secretary may appoint who are qualified by knowledge and experience to make a useful contribution to the work of such committee, including one or more representatives of professional organizations of technicians or professionals specializing in occupational safety or health, and one or more representatives of nationally recognized standards-producing organizations, but the number of persons so appointed to any such advisory committee shall not exceed the number appointed to such committee as representatives of Federal and State agencies. Persons appointed to advisory committees from private life shall be compensated in the same manner as consultants or experts under section 3109 of title 5, United States Code. The Secretary shall pay to any State which is the employer of a member of such a committee who is a representative of the health or safety agency of that State, reimbursement sufficient to cover the actual cost to the State resulting from such representative's membership on such committee. Any meeting of such committee shall be open to the public and an accurate record shall be kept and made available to the public. No member of such committee (other than representation of employer and employees) shall have an economic interest in any proposed rule.

[Sec. 7(b) amended by P.L. 96–88, October 17, 1979]

(c) In carrying out his responsibilities under this Act, the Secretary is authorized to—

(1) use, with the consent of any Federal agency, the services, facilities, and personnel of such of such agency, with or without reimbursement, and with the consent of any State or political subdivision thereof, accept and use the services, facilities, and personnel of any agency of such State or subdivision with reimbursement; and

(2) employ experts and consultants or organizations thereof as authorized by section 3109 of title 5, United States Code, except that contracts for such employment may be renewed annually; compensate individuals so employed at rates not in excess of the rate specified at the time of service for grade GS–18 under section 5332 of title 5, United States Code, including traveltime, and allow them while away from their homes or regular places of business travel expenses (including per diem in lieu of subsistence) as authorized by section 5703 of title 5, United States Code, for persons in the Government service employed intermittently, while so employed.

INSPECTIONS, INVESTIGATIONS, AND RECORDKEEPING

Sec. 8.(a) In order to carry out the purposes of this Act., the Secretary, upon presenting appropriate credentials to the owner, operator, or agency in charge, is authorized—

(1) to enter without delay and at reasonable times any factory, plant, establishment, construction site, or other area, workplace or environment where work is performed by an employee of an employer; and

(2) to inspect and investigate during regular working hours and at other reasonable times, and within reasonable limits and in a reasonable manner, any such place of employment and all pertinent conditions, structures, machines, apparatus, devices, equipment, and materials therein, and to question privately any such employer, owner, operator, agent or employee.

(b) In making his inspections and investigations under this Act the Secretary may require the attendance and testimony of witnesses and the production of evidence under oath. Witnesses shall be paid the same fees and mileage that are paid witnesses in the courts of the United States. In case of a contumacy, failure, or refusal of any person to obey such an order, any district court of the United States or the United States courts of any territory or possession, within the jurisdiction of which such person is found, or resides or transacts business upon the application by the Secretary, shall have jurisdiction to issue to such person an order requiring such person to appear to produce evidence if, as, and when so ordered, and to give testimony relating to the matter under investigation or in question, and any failure to obey such order of the court may be punished by said court as a contempt thereof.

(c)(1) Each employer shall make, keep and preserve, and make available to the Secretary or the Secretary of Health and Human Services, such records regarding his activities relating to this Act as the Secretary, in cooperation with the Secretary of Health and Human Services, may prescribe by regulation as necessary or appropriate for the enforcement of this Act or for de-

veloping information regarding the causes and prevention of occupational accidents and illnesses. In order to carry out the provisions of this paragraph such regulations may include provisions requiring employers to conduct periodic inspections. The Secretary shall also issue regulations requiring that employers, through posting of notices or other appropriate means, keep their employees informed of their protections and obligations under this Act, including the provisions of applicable standards.
[Sec. 8(c)(1) amended by P.L. 96–88, October 17, 1979]

(2) The Secretary, in cooperation with the Secretary of Health and Human Services shall prescribe regulations requiring employers to maintain accurate records of, and to make periodic reports on, work-related deaths, injuries and illness other than minor injuries requiring only first aid treatment and which do not involve medical treatment, loss of consciousness, restriction of work or motion, or transfer to another job.

(3) The Secretary, in cooperation with the Secretary of Health and Human Services, shall issue regulations requiring employers to maintain accurate records of employee exposures to potentially toxic materials or harmful physical agents which are required to be monitored or measured under section 6. Such regulations shall provide employees or their representatives with an opportunity to observe such monitoring or measuring, and to have access to the records thereof. Such regulations shall also make appropriate provision for each employee or former employee to have access to such records as will indicate his own exposure to toxic materials or harmful physical agents. Each employer shall promptly notify any employee who has been or is being exposed to toxic materials or harmful physical agents in concentrations or at levels which exceed those prescribed by an applicable occupational safety and health standard promulgated under

section 6, and shall inform any employee who is being thus exposed of the corrective action being taken.

(d) Any information obtained by the Secretary, the Secretary of Health and Human Services, or a State agency under this Act shall be obtained with a minimum burden upon employers, especially those operating small businesses. Unnecessary duplication of efforts in obtaining information shall be reduced to the maximum extent feasible. [Sec. 7(d) amended by P.L. 96–88, October 17, 1979]

(e) Subject to regulations issued by the Secretary, a representative of the employer and a representative authorized by his employees shall be given an opportunity to accompany the Secretary or his authorized representative during the physical inspection of any workplace under subsection (a) for the purpose of aiding such inspection. Where there is no authorized employee representative, the Secretary or his authorized representative shall consult with a reasonable number of employees concerning matters of health and safety in the workplace.

(f)(1) Any employees or representative of employees who believe that a violation of a safety or health standard exists that threatens physical harm, or that an imminent danger exists, may request an inspection by giving notice to the Secretary or his authorized representative of such violation or danger. Any such notice shall be reduced to writing, shall set forth with reasonable particularity the grounds for the notice, and shall be signed by the employees or representative of employees, and a copy shall be provided the employer or his agent no later than at the time of inspection, except that, upon the request of the person giving such notice, his name and the names of individual employees referred to therein shall not appear in such copy or on any record published, released, or made available pursuant to subsection (g) of this section. If upon receipt of such notification the Secretary determines there are reasonable grounds to believe that such violation or danger exists, he shall make a special inspection in accordance with the provisions of this section as soon as practicable, to determine if such violation or danger exists. If the Secretary determines there are no reasonable grounds to believe that a violation or danger exists he shall notify the employees or representative of the employees in writing of such determination.

(2) Prior to or during any inspection of a workplace, any employees or representative of employees employed in such workplace may notify the Secretary or any representative of the Secretary responsible for conducting the inspection, in writing,of any violation of this Act which they have reason to believe exists in such workplace. The Secretary shall, by regulation, establish procedures for informal review of any refusal by a representative of the Secretary to issue a citation with respect to any such alleged violation and shall furnish the employees or representative of employees requesting such review a written statement of the reasons for the Secretary's final disposition of the case.

(g)(1) The Secretary and Secretary of Health and Human Services are authorized to compile, analyze, and publish, either in summary or detailed form, all reports or information obtained under this section. [Sec. 7(g)(1) amended by P.L. 96–88, October 17, 1979]

(2) The Secretary and the Secretary of Health and Human Services shall each prescribe such rules and regulations as he may deem necessary to carry out their responsibilities under this Act, including rules and regulations dealing with the inspection of an employer's establishment.

CITATIONS

Sec. 9. (a) If, upon inspection or investigation, the Secretary or his authorized representative believes that an employer has violated a requirement of section 5 of this Act, of any standard, rule or order promulgated pursuant to section 6 of this Act, or of any regulations prescribed pursuant to this Act, he shall with reasonable promptness issue a citation to the employer. Each citation shall be in writing and shall describe with particularly the nature of the violation, including a reference to the provision of the Act, standard, rule, regulation, or order alleged to have been violated. In addition, the citation shall fix a reasonable time for the abatement of the violation. The Secretary may prescribe procedures for the issuance of a notice in lieu of a citation with respect to de minimis violations which have no direct or immediate relationship to safety or health.

(b) Each citation issued under this section, or a copy or copies thereof, shall be prominently posted, as prescribed in regulations issued by the Secretary, at or near each place a violation referred to in the citation occurred.

(c) No citation may be issued under this section after the expiration of six months following the occurrence of any violation.

PROCEDURE FOR ENFORCEMENT

Sec. 10. (a) If, after an inspection or investigation, the Secretary issues a citation under Section 9(a), he shall, within a reasonable time after the termination of such inspection or investigation, notify the employer by certified mail of the penalty, if any, proposed to be assessed under section 17 and that the employer has fifteen working days within which to notify the Secretary that he wishes to contest the citation or proposed assessment of penalty. If, within fifteen working days from the receipt of the notice issued by the Secretary the employer fails to notify the Secretary that he intends to contest the citation or proposed assessment of penalty, and no notice is filed by any employee or representative of employees under subsection (c) within such time, the citation and the assessment, as proposed, shall be deemed a final order of the Commission and not subject to review by any court or agency.

(b) If the Secretary has reason to believe that an employer has failed to correct a violation for which a citation has been issued within the period permitted for its correction (which period shall not begin to run until the entry of a final order by the Commission in the case of any review proceedings under this section initiated by the employer in good faith and not solely for delay or avoidance of penalties), the Secretary shall notify the employer by certified mail of such failure and of the penalty proposed to be assessed under section 17 by reason of such failure, and that the employer has fifteen working days within which to notify the Secretary that he wishes to contest the Secretary's notification or the proposed assessment of penalty. If, within fifteen working days from the receipt of notification issued by the Secretary, the employer fails to notify the Secretary that he intends to contest the notification and assessment, as proposed, shall be deemed a final order of the Commission and not subject to review by any court or agency.

(c) If an employer notifies the Secretary that he intends to contest a citation issued under section 9 (a) or notification issued under subsection (a) or (b) of this section, or if, within fifteen working days of the issuance of a citation under section 9 (a), any employee or representative of employees files a notice with the Secretary alleging that the period of time fixed in the citation for the abatement of the violation is unreasonable, the Secretary shall immediately advise the Commission of such notification, and the Commission shall afford an opportunity for a hearing (in accordance with section 554 of title 5, United States Code, but without regard to subsection (a)(3) of such section). The Commission shall thereafter issue an order, based on findings of fact, affirming, modifying, or vacating the Secretary's citation or proposed penalty, or directing other appropriate relief, and such order shall become final thirty days after its issuance. Upon a showing by an employer of a good faith effort to comply with the abatement requirements of a citation, and that abatement has not been completed because of factors beyond his reasonable control, the Secretary, after an opportunity for a hearing as provided in this subsection, shall issue an order affirming or modifying the abatement requirements in such citation. The rules of procedure prescribed by the Commission shall provide affected employees or representatives of affected employees an opportunity to participate as parties to hearings under this subsection.

JUDICIAL REVIEW

Sec. 11. (a) Any person adversely affected or aggrieved by an order of the Commission issued under subsection (c) of section 10 may obtain a review of such order in any United States court of appeals for the circuit in which the violation is alleged to have occurred or where the employer has its principal office, or in the Court of Appeals for the District of Columbia Circuit, by filing in such court within sixty days following the issuance of such order a written petition praying that the order be modified or set aside. A copy of such petition shall be forthwith transmitted by the clerk of the court to the Commission and to the other parties, and thereupon the Commission shall file in the court the record in the proceeding as provided in section 2112 of title 28, United States Code. Upon such filing, the court shall have jurisdiction of the proceeding and of the question determined therein, and shall have power to grant such temporary relief or restraining order as it deems just and proper, and to make and enter upon the pleadings, testimony, and proceedings set forth in such record a decree affirming, modifying, or setting aside in whole or

in part, the order of the Commission and enforcing the same to the extent that such order is affirmed or modified. The commencement of proceedings under this subsection shall not, unless ordered by the court, operate as a stay of the order of the Commission. No objection that has not been urged before the Commission shall be considered by the court, unless the failure or neglect to urge such objection shall be excused because of extraordinary circumstances. The findings of the Commission with respect to questions of fact, if supported by substantial evidence on the record considered as a whole, shall be conclusive. If any party shall apply to the court for leave to adduce additional evidence and shall show to the satisfaction of the court that such additional evidence is material and that there were reasonable grounds for the failure to adduce such evidence in the hearing before the Commission, the court may order such additional evidence to be taken before the Commission and to be made a part of the record. The Commission may modify its findings as to the facts, or make new findings, by reason of additional evidence so taken and filed, and it shall file such modified or new findings, which findings with respect to questions of fact, if supported by substantial evidence on the record considered as a whole, shall be conclusive, and its recommendations, if any, for the modification or setting aside of its original order. Upon the filing of the record with it, the jurisdiction of the court shall be exclusive and its judgment and decree shall be final, except that the same shall be subject to review by the Supreme Court of the United States, as provided in section 1254 of title 28, United States Code.
[Sec. 11(a) amended by Public Law 98–620, November 8, 1984]

(b) The Secretary may also obtain review or enforcement of any final order of the Commission by filing a petition for such relief in the United States court of appeals for the circuit in which the alleged violation occurred or in which the employer has its principal office, and the provisions of subsection (a) shall govern such proceedings to the extent applicable. If no petition for review, as provided in subsection (a), is filed within sixty days after service of the Commission's order, the Commission's findings of fact and order shall be conclusive in connection with any petition for enforcement which is filed by the Secretary after the expiration of such sixty-day period. In any such case, as well as in the case of a noncontested citation or notification by the Secretary which has become a final order of the Commission under subsection (a) or (b) of section 10, the clerk of the court, unless otherwise ordered by the court, shall forthwith enter a decree enforcing the order and shall transmit a copy of such decree to the Secretary and the employer named in the petition. In any contempt proceeding brought to enforce a decree of a court of appeals entered pursuant to this subsection or subsection (a), the court of appeals may assess the penalties provided in section 17, in addition to invoking any other available remedies.

(c)(1) No person shall discharge or in any manner discriminate against any employee because such employee has filed any complaint or instituted or caused to be instituted any proceeding under or related to this Act or has testified or is about to testify in any such proceeding or because of the exercise by such employee on behalf of himself or others of any right afforded by this Act.

(2) Any employee who believes that he has been discharged or otherwise discriminated against by any person in violation of this subsection may, within thirty days after such violation occurs, file a complaint with the Secretary alleging such discrimination. Upon receipt of such complaint, the Secretary shall cause such investigation to be made as he deems appropriate. If upon

such investigation, the Secretary determines that the provisions of this subsection have been violated, he shall bring an action in any appropriate United States district court against such person. In any such action the United States district courts shall have jurisdiction, for cause shown to restrain violations of paragraph (1) of this subsection and order all appropriate relief including rehiring or reinstatement of the employee to his former position with back pay.

(3) Within 90 days of the receipt of a complaint filed under this subsection the Secretary shall notify the complainant of his determination under paragraph 2 of this subsection.

THE OCCUPATIONAL SAFETY AND HEALTH REVIEW COMMISSION

Sec. 12. (a) The Occupational Safety and Health Review Commission is hereby established. The Commission shall be composed of three members who shall be appointed by the President, by and with the advice and consent of the Senate, from among persons who by reason of training, education, or experience are qualified to carry out the functions of the Commission under this Act. The President shall designate one of the members of the Commission to serve as Chairman.

(b) The terms of members of the Commission shall be six years except that (1) the members of the Commission first taking office shall serve, as designated by the President at the time of appointment, one for a term of two years, one for a term of four years, and one for a term for six years, and (2) a vacancy caused by the death, resignation, or removal of a member prior to the expiration of the term for which he was appointed shall be filled only for the remainder of such unexpired term. A member of the Commission may be removed by the President for inefficiency, neglect of duty, or malfeasance in office.

(c) (1) Section 5314 of title 5, United States Code, is amended by adding at the end thereof the following new paragraph:

"(57) Chairman, Occupational Safety and Health Review Commission."

(2) Section 5315 of title 5, United States Code, is amended by adding at the end thereof the following new paragraph:

"(94) Members, Occupational Safety and Health Review Commission."

(d) The principal office of the Commission shall be in the District of Columbia. Whenever the Commission deems that the convenience of the public or of the parties may be promoted, or delay or expense may be minimized, it may hold hearings or conduct other proceedings at any other place.

(e) The Chairman shall be responsible on behalf of the Commission for the administrative operations of the Commission and shall appoint such administrative law judges and other employees as he deems necessary to assist in the performance of the Commission's functions and to fix their compensation in accordance with the provisions of chapter 51 and subchapter III of chapter 53 of title 5, United States Code, relating to classification and General Schedule pay rates: *Provided,* That assignment, removal and compensation of administrative law judges shall be in accordance with sections 3105, 3344, 5362, and 7521 of title 5, United State Code. [Sec. 12(e) amended by P.L. 95–251, March 27, 1978]

(f) For the purpose of carrying out its functions under this Act, two members of the Commission shall constitute a quorum and official action can be taken only on the affirmative vote of at least two members.

(g) Every official act of the Commission shall be entered of record, and its hearing and records shall be open to the public. The Commission is authorized to make such rules as are necessary for the orderly transaction of its proceedings. Unless the Commission has adopted a different rule, its proceedings shall be in accordance with the Federal Rules of Civil Procedure.

(h) The Commission may order testimony to be taken by deposition in any proceedings pending before it at any state of such proceeding. Any person may be compelled to appear and depose, and to produce books, papers, or documents, in the same manner as witnesses may be compelled to appear and testify and produce like documentary evidence before the Commission. Witnesses whose depositions are taken under this subsection, and the person taking such depositions, shall be entitled to the same fees as are paid for like services in the courts of the United States.

(i) For the purpose of any proceedings before the Commission, the provisions of section 11 of the National Labor Relations Act (29 U.S.C. 161) are hereby made applicable to the jurisdiction and powers of the Commission.

(j) An administrative law judge appointed by the Commission shall hear, and make a determination upon, any proceeding instituted before the Commission and any motion in connection therewith, assigned to such administrative law judge by the Chairman of the Commission, and shall make a report of any such determination which constitutes his final disposition of the proceedings. The report of the administrative law judge shall become the final order of the Commission within thirty days after such report by the administrative law judge, unless within such period any Commission member has directed that such report shall be reviewed by the Commission.
[Sec. 12(j) amended by P.L. 95–251, March 27, 1978]

(k) Except as otherwise provided in this Act, the administrative law judges shall be subject to the laws governing employees in the classified civil service, except that appointments shall be made without regard to section 5108 of title 5, United States Code. Each administrative law judge shall receive compensation at a rate not less than

that prescribed for GS-16 under section 5332 of title 5, United States Code.
[Sec. 12(k) amended by P.L. 95–251, March 27, 1978]

PROCEDURES TO COUNTERACT IMMINENT DANGERS

Sec. 13. (a) The United States district courts shall have jurisdiction, upon petition of the Secretary, to restrain any conditions or practices in any place of employment which are such that a danger exists which could reasonably be expected to cause death or serious physical harm immediately or before the imminence of such danger can be eliminated through the enforcement procedures otherwise provided by this Act. Any order issued under this section may require such steps to be taken as may be necessary to avoid, correct, or remove such imminent danger and prohibit the employment or presence of any individual in locations or under conditions where such imminent danger exists, except individuals whose presence is necessary to avoid, correct, or remove such imminent danger or to maintain the capacity of a continuous process operation to resume normal operations without a complete cessation of operations, or where a cessation of operations is necessary, to permit such to be accomplished in a safe and orderly manner.

(b) Upon the filing of any such petition the district court shall have jurisdiction to grant such injunctive relief or temporary restraining order pending the outcome of an enforcement proceeding pursuant to this Act. The proceeding shall be as provided by Rule 65 of the Federal Rules, Civil Procedure, except that no temporary restraining order issued without notice shall be effective for a period longer than five days.

(c) Whenever and as soon as an inspector concludes that conditions or practices described in subsection (a) exist in any place of employment, he shall inform the affected employees and employers of the danger and that he is recommending to the Secretary that relief be sought.

(d) If the Secretary arbitrarily or capriciously fails to seek relief under this section, any employee who may be injured by reason of such failure, or the representative of such employees, might bring an action against the Secretary in the United States district court for the district in which the imminent danger is alleged to exist or the employer has its principal office, or for the District of Columbia, for a writ of mandamus to compel the Secretary to seek such an order and for such further relief as may be appropriate.

REPRESENTATION IN CIVIL LITIGATION

Sec. 14. Except as provided in section 518(a) of title 28, United States Code, relating to litigation before the Supreme Court, the Solicitor of Labor may appear for and represent the Secretary in any civil litigation brought under this Act but all such litigation shall be subject to the direction and control of the Attorney General.

CONFIDENTIALITY OF TRADE SECRETS

Sec. 15. All information reported to or otherwise obtained by the Secretary or his representative in connection with any inspection or proceeding under this Act which contains or which might reveal a trade secret referred to in section 1905 of title 18 of the United States Code shall be considered confidential for the purpose of that section, except that such information may be disclosed to other officers or employees concerned with carrying out this Act or when relevant in any proceeding under this Act. In any such proceeding the Secretary, the Commission, or the court shall issue such orders as may be appropriate to protect the confidentiality of trade secrets.

VARIATIONS, TOLERANCES, AND EXEMPTIONS

Sec. 16. The Secretary, on the record, after notice and opportunity for a hearing may provide such reasonable limitations and may make such rules and regulations allowing reasonable variations, tolerances, and exemptions to and from any or all provisions of this Act as he may find necessary and proper to avoid serious impairment of the national defense. Such action shall not be in effect for more than six months without notification to affected employees and an opportunity being afforded for a hearing.

PENALTIES

Sec. 17. (a) Any employer who willfully or repeatedly violates the requirements of section 5 of this Act, any standard, rule, or order promulgated pursuant to section 6 of this Act, or regulations prescribed pursuant to this Act, may be assessed a civil penalty of not more than $70,000 for each violation but not less than $5,000 for each willful violation.
[Sec. 17(a)—(d) amended by PL 101-508]

(b) Any employer who has received a citation for a serious violation of the requirements of section 5 of this Act, of any standard, rule, or order promulgated pursuant to section 6 of this Act, or of any regulations prescribed pursuant to this Act, shall be assessed a civil penalty of up to $7,000 for each such violation.

(c) Any employer who has received a citation for a violation of the requirements of section 5 of this Act, of any standard, rule, or order promulgated pursuant to section 6 of this Act, or of regulations prescribed pursuant to this Act, and such violation if specifically determined not to be of a serious nature, may be assessed a civil penalty of up to $7,000 for each such violation.

(d) Any employer who fails to correct a violation for which a citation has been issued under section 9(a) within the period permitted for its correction (which period shall not begin to run until the date of the final order of the Commission in the case of any review proceeding under section 10 initiated by the employer in good faith and not solely for delay or avoidance of penalties), may be assessed a civil penalty of not more than $7,000 for each day during which such failure or violation continues.

(e) Any employer who willfully violates any standard, rule, or order promulgated pursuant to section 6 of this Act, or of any regulations prescribed pursuant to this Act, and that violation caused death to any employee, shall, upon conviction, be punished by a fine of not more than $10,000 or by imprisonment for not more than six months, or by both; except that if the conviction is for a violation committed after a first conviction of such person, punishment shall be by a fine of not more than $20,000 or by imprisonment for not more than one year, or by both.

(f) Any person who gives advance notice of any inspection to be conducted under this Act, without authority from the Secretary or his designees, shall, upon conviction, be punished by a fine of not more than $1,000 or by imprisonment for not more than six months, or by both.

(g) Whoever knowingly makes any false statement, representation, or certification in any application, record, report, plan, or other document filed or required to be maintained pursuant to this Act shall, upon conviction, be punished by a fine of not more than $10,000, or by imprisonment for not more than six months, or by both.

(h)(1) Section 1114 of title 18, United States Code, is hereby amended by striking out "designated by the Secretary of Health, Education, and Welfare to conduct investigations, or inspections under the Federal Food, Drug, and Cosmetic Act" and inserting in lieu thereof "or of the Department of Labor assigned to perform investigative, in-

spection, or law enforcement functions."

(2) Notwithstanding the provisions of sections 1111 and 1114 of title 18, United States Code, whoever, in violation of the provisions of section 1114 of such title, kills a person while engaged in or on account of the performance of investigative, inspection, or law enforcement functions added to such section 1114 by paragraph (1) of this subsection, and who would otherwise be subject to the penalty provisions of such section 1111, shall be punished by imprisonment for any term of years or for life.

(i) Any employer who violates any of the posting requirements, as prescribed under the provisions of this Act, shall be assessed a civil penalty of up to $7,000 for each violation.
[Sec. 17(i) amended by PL 101-508]

(j) The Commission shall have authority to assess all civil penalties provided in this section, giving due consideration to the appropriateness of the penalty with respect to the size of the business of the employer being charged, the gravity of the violation, the good faith of the employer, and the history of previous violations.

(k) For purposes of this section, a serious violation shall be deemed to exist in a place of employment if there is a substantial probability that death or serious physical harm could result from a condition which exists, or from one or more practices, means, methods, operations, or processes which have been adopted or are in use, in such place of employment unless the employer did not, and could not with the exercise of reasonable diligence, know of the presence of the violation.

(l) Civil penalties owed under this Act shall be paid to the Secretary for deposit into the Treasury of the United States and shall accrue to the United States and may be recovered in a civil action in the name of the United States brought in the United States district court for the district where the violation is alleged to have occurred or where the employer has its principal office.

STATE JURISDICTION AND STATE PLANS

Sec. 18.(a) Nothing in this Act shall prevent any State agency or court from asserting jurisdiction under State law over any occupational safety or health issue with respect to which no standard is in effect under section 6.

(b) Any State which, at any time, desires to assume responsibility for development and enforcement therein of occupational safety and health standards relating to any occupational safety or health issue with respect to which a Federal standard has been promulgated under section 6 shall submit a State plan for the development of such standards and their enforcement.

(c) The Secretary shall approve the plan submitted by a State under subsection (b), or any modification thereof, if such plan in his judgment —

(1) designates a State agency or agencies as the agency or agencies responsible for administering the plan throughout the State.

(2) provides for the development and enforcement of safety and health standards relating to one or more safety or health issues, which standards (and the enforcement of which standards) are or will be at least as effective in providing safe and healthful employment and places of employment as the standards promulgated under section 6 which relate to the same issues, and which standards, when applicable to products which are distributed or used in interstate commerce, are required by compelling local conditions and do not unduly burden interstate commerce,

(3) provides for a right of entry and inspection of all work-places subject to the Act which is at least as effective as that provided in section 8, and includes a prohibition on advance notice of inspections,

(4) contains satisfactory assurances that such agency or agencies have or will have the legal authority and qualified personnel necessary for the enforcement of such standards,

(5) gives satisfactory assurances that such State will devote adequate funds to the administration and enforcement of such standards.

(6) contains satisfactory assurances that such State will, to the extent permitted by its law, establish and maintain an effective and comprehensive occupational safety and health program applicable to all employees of public agencies of the State and its political subdivisions, which program is as effective as the standards contained in an approved plan,

(7) requires employers in the State to make reports to the Secretary in the same manner and to the same extent as if the plan were not in effect, and

(8) provides that the State agency will make such reports to the Secretary in such form and containing such information, as the Secretary shall from time to time require.

(d) If the Secretary rejects a plan submitted under subsection (b), he shall afford the State submitting the plan due notice and opportunity for a hearing before so doing.

(e) After the Secretary approves a State plan submitted under subsection (b), he may, but shall not be required to, exercise his authority under section 8, 9, 13, and 17 with respect to comparable standards promulgated under section 6, for the period specified in the next sentence. The Secretary may exercise the authority referred to above until he determines, on the basis of actual operations under the State plan, that the criteria set forth in subsection (c) are being applied, but he shall not make such determination for at least three years after the plan's approval under subsection (c). Upon making the determination referred to in the preceding sentence, the provisions of sections 5(a)(2), 8 (except for the purpose of carrying out subsection (f) of this section), 9, 10, 13, and 17, and standards promulgated under section 6 of this Act, shall not apply with respect to any occupational safety or health issues covered under the plan, but the Secretary may retain jurisdiction under the above provisions in any proceedings commenced under section 9 or 10 before the date of determination.

(f) The Secretary shall, on the basis of reports submitted by the State agency and his own inspections make a continuing evaluation of the manner in which each State having a plan approved under this section is carrying out such plan. Whenever the Secretary finds, after affording due notice and opportunity for a hearing, that in the administration of the State plan there is a failure to comply substantially with any provision of the State plan (or any assurance contained therein), he shall notify the State agency of his withdrawal of approval of such plan and upon receipt of such notice such plan shall cease to be in effect, but the State may retain jurisdiction in any case commenced before the withdrawal of the plan in order to enforce standards under the plan whenever the issues involved do not relate to the reasons for the withdrawal of the plan.

(g) The State may obtain a review of a decision of the Secretary withdrawing approval of or rejecting its plan by the United States court of appeals for the circuit in which the State is located by filing in such court within thirty days following receipt of notice of such decision a petition to modify or set aside in whole or in part the action of the Secretary. A copy of such petition shall forthwith be served upon the Secretary, and thereupon the Secretary shall certify and file in the court the record upon which the decision complained of was issued as provided in section 2112 of title 28, United States Code. Unless the court finds that the Secretary's decision in rejecting a proposed State plan or withdrawing his approval of such a plan is not supported by substantial evidence the court shall affirm the Secretary's decision. The judgment of the court shall be subject to review by the Supreme Court of the United States upon certiorari or certification as provided in section 1254 of title 28, United States Code.

(h) The Secretary may enter into an agreement with a State under which the State will be permitted to continue to enforce one or more occupational health and safety standards in effect in such State until final action is taken by the Secretary with respect to a plan submitted by a State under subsection (b) of this section, or two years from the date of enactment of this Act, whichever is earlier.

FEDERAL AGENCY SAFETY PROGRAMS AND RESPONSIBILITIES

Sec. 19.(a) It shall be the responsibility of the head of each Federal agency to establish and maintain an effective and comprehensive occupational safety and health program which is consistent with the standards promulgated under section 6. The head of each agency shall (after consultation with representatives of the employees thereof)—

(1) provide safe and healthful places and conditions of employment, consistent with the standards set under section 6;

(2) acquire, maintain, and require the use of safety equipment, personal protective equipment, and devices reasonably necessary to protect employees;

(3) keep adequate records of all occupational accidents and illnesses for proper evaluation and necessary corrective action;

(4) consult with the Secretary with regard to the adequacy as to form and content of records kept pursuant to subsection (a)(3) of this section; and

(5) make an annual report to the Secretary with respect to occupational accidents and injuries and the agency's

program under this section. Such report shall include any report submitted under section 7902(e)(2) of title 5, United States Code.

(b) The Secretary shall report to the President a summary or digest of reports submitted to him under subsection (a)(5) of this section, together with his evaluations of and recommendations derived from such reports. [Sec. 19(b) amended by P.L. 97–375, December 21, 1982]

(c) Section 7902(c)(1) of title 5, United States Code, is amended by inserting after "agencies" the following: "and of labor organizations representing employees."

(d) The Secretary shall have access to records and reports kept and filed by Federal agencies pursuant to subsections (a)(3) and (5) of this section unless those records and reports are specifically required by Executive order to be kept secret in the interest of the national defense or foreign policy, in which case the Secretary shall have access to such information as will not jeopardize national defense or foreign policy.

RESEARCH AND RELATED ACTIVITIES

Sec. 20.(a)(1) The Secretary of Health and Human Services after consultation with the Secretary and with other appropriate Federal departments or agencies, shall conduct (directly or by grants or contracts) research, experiments, and demonstrations relating to occupational safety and health, including studies of psychological factors involved, and relating to innovative methods, techniques, and approaches for dealing with occupational safety and health problems.

(2) The Secretary of Health and Human Services shall from time to time consult with the Secretary in order to develop specific plans for such research, demonstrations, and experiments as are necessary to produce criteria, including criteria identifying toxic substances, enabling the Secre-

tary to meet his responsibility for the formulation of safety and health standards under this Act; and the Secretary of Health and Human Services, on the basis of such research, demonstrations, and experiments and any other information available to him, shall develop and publish at least annually such criteria as will effectuate the purposes of this Act.

(3) The Secretary of Health and Human Services, on the basis of such research, demonstrations, and experiments, and any other information available to him, shall develop criteria dealing with toxic materials and harmful physical agents and substances which will describe exposure levels that are safe for various periods of employment, including but not limited to the exposure levels at which no employee will suffer impaired health or functional capacities or diminished life expectancy as a result of his work experience.

(4) The Secretary of Health and Human Services shall also conduct special research, experiments, and demonstrations relating to occupational safety and health as are necessary to explore new problems, including those created by new technology in occupational safety and health, which may require ameliorative action beyond that which is otherwise provided for in the operating provisions of this Act. The Secretary of Health and Human Services shall also conduct research into the motivational and behavioral factors relating to the field of occupational safety and health.

(5) The Secretary of Health and Human Services, in order to comply with his responsibilities under paragraph (2), and in order to develop needed information regarding potentially toxic substances or harmful physical agents, may prescribe regulations requiring employers to measure, record, and make reports on the exposure of employees to substances or physical agents which the Secretary of Health and Human Services reasonably be-

lieves may endanger the health or safety of employees. The Secretary of Health and Human Services also is authorized to establish such programs of medical examinations and tests as may be necessary for determining the incidence of occupational illnesses and the susceptibility of employees to such illnesses. Nothing in this or any other provision of this Act shall be deemed to authorize or require medical examination, immunization, or treatment for those who object thereto on religious grounds, except where such is necessary for the protection of the health or safety of others. Upon the request of any employer who is required to measure and record exposure of employees to substances or physical agents as provided under this subsection, the Secretary of Health and Human Services shall furnish full financial or other assistance to such employer for the purpose of defraying any additional expense incurred by him in carrying out the measuring and recording as provided in this subsection.

(6) The Secretary of Health and Human Services shall publish within six months of enactment of this Act and thereafter as needed but at least annually a list of all known toxic substances by generic family or other useful grouping, and the concentrations at which such toxicity is known to occur. He shall determine following a written request by any employer or authorized representative of employees, specifying with reasonable particularity the grounds on which the request is made, whether any substance normally found in the place of employment has potentially toxic effects in such concentrations as used or found; and shall submit such determination both to employers and affected employees as soon as possible. If the Secretary of Health and Human Services determines that any substance is potentially toxic at the concentrations in which it is used or

found in a place of employment, and such substance is not covered by an occupational safety or health standard promulgated under section 6, the Secretary of Health and Human Services shall immediately submit such determination to the Secretary, together with all pertinent criteria.

(7) Within two years of enactment of this Act, and annually thereafter the Secretary of Health and Human Services shall conduct and publish industrywide studies of the effect of chronic or low-level exposure to industrial materials, processes, and stresses on the potential for illness, disease, or loss of functional capacity in aging adults.

(b) The Secretary of Health and Human Services is authorized to make inspections and question employers and employees as provided in section 8 of this Act in order to carry out his functions and responsibilities under this section.

(c) The Secretary is authorized to enter into contracts, agreements, or other arrangements with appropriate public agencies or private organizations for the purpose of conducting studies relating to his responsibilities under this Act. In carrying out his responsibilities under this subsection, the Secretary shall cooperate with the Secretary of Health and Human Services in order to avoid any duplication of efforts under this section.

(d) Information obtained by the Secretary and the Secretary of Health and Human Services under this section shall be disseminated by the Secretary to employers and employees and organizations thereof.

(e) The functions of the Secretary of Health and Human Services under this Act shall, to the extent feasible, be delegated to the Director of the National Institute for Occupational Safety and Health established by section 22 of this Act.

[Sec. 20 amended by P.L. 96–88, October 17, 1979]

TRAINING AND EMPLOYEE EDUCATION

Sec. 21.(a) The Secretary of Health and Human Services after consultation with the Secretary and with other appropriate Federal departments and agencies, shall conduct, directly or by grants or contracts (1) education programs to provide an adequate supply of qualified personnel to carry out the purposes of this Act, and (2) informational programs on the importance of and proper use of adequate safety and health equipment.
[Sec. 21(a) amended by P.L. 96–88, October 17, 1979]

(b) The Secretary is also authorized to conduct, directly or by grants or contracts, short-term training of personnel engaged in work related to his responsibilities under this Act.

(c) The Secretary, in consultation with the Secretary of Health and Human Services, shall (1) provide for the establishment and supervision of programs for the education and training of employers and employees in the recognition, avoidance, and prevention of unsafe or unhealthful working conditions in employments covered by this Act, and (2) consult with and advise employers and employees, and organizations representing employers and employees as to effective means of preventing occupational injuries and illnesses.
[Sec. 21(c) amended by P.L. 96–88, October 17, 1979]

NATIONAL INSTITUTE FOR OCCUPATIONAL SAFETY AND HEALTH

Sec. 22. (a) It is the purpose of this section to establish a National Institute for Occupational Safety and Health in the Department of Health and Human Services in order to carry out the policy set forth in section 2 of this Act and to perform the functions of the Secretary of Health and Human Services under sections 20 and 21 of this Act.

(b) There is hereby established in the Department of Health and Human Services a National Institute for Occupational Safety and Health. The Institute shall be headed by a Director who shall be appointed by the Secretary of Health and Human Services, and who shall serve for a term of six years unless previously removed by the Secretary of Health and Human Services.
[Sec. 22(a) and (b) amended by P.L. 96–88, October 17, 1979]

(c) The Institute is authorized to—

(1) develop and establish recommended occupational safety and health standards; and

(2) perform all functions of the Secretary of Health and Human Services under sections 20 and 21 of this Act.
[Sec. 22(c)(2) amended by P.L. 96–88, October 17, 1979]

(d) Upon his own initiative, or upon the request of the Secretary or the Secretary of Health and Human Services, the Director is authorized (1) to conduct such research and experimental programs as he determines are necessary for the development of criteria for new and improved occupational safety and health standards, and (2) after consideration of the results of such research and experimental programs make recommendations concerning new or improved occupational safety and health standards. Any occupational safety and health standard recommended pursuant to this section shall immediately be forwarded pursuant to this section shall immediately be forwarded to the Secretary of Labor, and to the Secretary of Health and Human Services.
[Sec. 22(d) amended by P.L. 96–88, October 17, 1979]

(e) In addition to any authority vested in the Institute by other provisions of this section, the Director, in carrying out the functions of the Institute, is authorized to—

(1) prescribe such regulations as he deems necessary governing the manner in which its functions shall be carried out;

(2) receive money and other property donated, bequeathed, or devised, without condition or restriction other than that it be used for the purposes of the Institute and to use, sell, or otherwise dispose of such property for the purpose of carrying out its functions;

(3) receive (and use, sell, or otherwise dispose of, in accordance with paragraph (2)), money and other property donated, bequeathed, or devised to the Institute with a condition or restriction, including a condition that the Institute use other funds of the Institute for the purposes of the gift;

(4) in accordance with the civil service laws, appoint and fix the compensation of such personnel as may be necessary to carry out the provisions of this section;

(5) obtain the services of experts and consultants in accordance with the provisions of section 3109 of title 5, United States Code;

(6) accept and utilize the services of voluntary and noncompensated personnel and reimburse them for travel expenses, including per diem, as authorized by section 5703 of title 5, United States Code;

(7) enter into contracts, grants or other arrangements, or modifications thereof to carry out the provisions of this section, and such contracts or modifications thereof may be entered into without performance or other bonds, and without regard to section 3709 of the Revised Statutes, as amended (41 U.S.C. 5), or any other provision of law relating to competitive bidding;

(8) make advance, progress, and other payments which the Director deems necessary under this title without regard to the provisions of section 3648 of the Revised Statutes, as amended (31 U.S.C. 529); and

(9) make other necessary expenditures.

(f) The Director shall submit to the Secretary of Health and Human Services, to the President, and to the Congress an annual report of the operations of the Institute under this Act, which shall include a detailed statement of all private and public funds received and expended by it, and such recommendations as he deems appropriate.
[Sec 22(f) amended by P.L. 96–88, October 17, 1979]

GRANTS TO THE STATES

Sec. 23.(a) The Secretary is authorized, during the fiscal year ending June 30, 1971, and the two succeeding fiscal years, to make grants to the States which have designated a State agency under section 18 to assist them—

(1) in identifying their needs and responsibilities in the area of occupational safety and health,

(2) in developing State plans under section 118, or

(3) in developing plans for—

(A) establishing systems for the collection of information concerning the nature and frequency of occupational injuries and diseases;

(B) increasing the expertise and enforcement capabilities of their personnel engaged in occupational safety and health programs; or

(C) otherwise improving the administration and enforcement of State occupational safety and health laws, including standards thereunder, consistent with the objectives of this Act.

(b) The Secretary is authorized, during the fiscal year ending June 30, 1971, and the two succeeding fiscal years, to make grants to the States for experimental and demonstration projects consistent with the objectives set forth in subsection (a) of this section.

(c) The Governor of the State shall designate the appropriate State agency for receipt of any grant made by the Secretary under this section.

(d) Any State agency designated by the Governor of the State desiring a grant under this section shall submit an application therefor to the Secretary.

(e) The Secretary shall review the application, and shall, after consultation with the Secretary of Health and Human Services, approve or reject such application.
[Sec. 23(e) amended by P.L. 96–88. October 17, 1979]

(f) the Federal share for each State grant under subsection (a) or (b) of this section may not exceed 90 per centum of the total cost of the application. In the event the Federal share for all States under either such subsection is not the same, the differences among the States shall be established on the basis of objective criteria.

(g) The Secretary is authorized to make grants to the States to assist them in administering and enforcing programs for occupational safety and health contained in State plans approved by the Secretary pursuant to section 18 of this Act. The Federal share for each State grant under this subsection may not exceed 50 per centum of the total cost to the State of such a program. The last sentence of subsection (f) shall be applicable in determining the Federal share under this subsection.

(h) Prior to June 30, 1973, the Secretary shall, after consultation with the Secretary of Health and Human Services, transmit a report to the President and to the Congress, describing the experience under the grant programs authorized by this section and making any recommendations he may deem appropriate.

STATISTICS

Sec. 24. (a) In order to further the purposes of this Act, the Secretary, in consultation with the Secretary of Health and Human Services, shall develop and maintain an effective program of collection, compilation, and analysis of occupational safety and health statistics. Such program may cover all employments whether or not subject to any other provisions of this Act but shall not cover employments excluded by section 4 of the Act. The Secretary shall compile accurate statistics on work injuries and illnesses which shall include all disabling, serious, or significant injuries and illnesses, whether or not involving loss of time from work, other than minor injuries requiring only first aid treatment and which do not involve medical treatment, loss of consciousness, restriction of work or motion, or transfer to another job.
[Sec. 24(a) amended by P.L. 96–88, October 17, 1979]

(b) To carry out his duties under subsection (a) of this section, the Secretary may —

(1) promote, encourage, or directly engage in programs of studies, information and communication concerning occupational safety and health statistics:

(2) make grants to States or political subdivisions thereof in order to assist them in developing and administering programs dealing with occupational safety and health statistics; and

(3) arrange, through grants or contracts, for the conduct of such research and investigations as give promise of furthering the objectives of this section.

(c) The Federal share for each grant under subsection (b) of this section may be up to 50 per centum of the State's total cost.

(d) The Secretary may, with the consent of any State or political subdivision thereof, accept and use the services, facilities, and employees of the agencies of such State or political subdivision, with or without reimbursement, in order to assist him in carrying out his functions under this section.

(e) On the basis of the records made and kept pursuant to section 8(c) of this Act, employers shall file such reports with the Secretary as he shall prescribe by regulation, as necessary to carry out his functions under this Act.

(f) Agreements between the Department of Labor and States pertaining to the collection of occupational safety and health statistics already in effect on the effective date of this Act shall remain in effect until superseded by grants or contracts made under this Act.

AUDITS

Sec. 25. (a) Each recipient of a grant under this Act shall keep such records as the Secretary or the Secretary of Health and Human Services shall prescribe, including records which fully disclose the amount and disposition by such recipient of the proceeds of such grant, the total cost of the project or undertaking in connection with which such grant is made or used, and the amount of that portion of the cost of the project or undertaking supplied by other sources, and such other records as will facilitate an effective audit.

(b) The Secretary or the Secretary of Health and Human Services, and the Comptroller General of the United States, or any of their duly authorized representatives, shall have access for the purpose of audit and examination to any books, documents, papers, and records of the recipients of any grant under this Act that are pertinent to any such grant.

[Sec. 25 amended by P.L. 96–88, October 17, 1979]

ANNUAL REPORT

Sec. 26. Within one hundred and twenty days following the convening of each regular session of Congress, the Secretary and the Secretary of Health and Human Services shall each prepare and submit to the President for transmittal to the Congress a report upon the subject matter of this Act, the progress toward achievement of the purpose of this Act, the needs and requirements in the field of occupational safety and health, and any other relevant information. Such reports shall include information regarding occupational safety and health standards, and criteria for such standards, developed during the preceding year; evaluation of standards and criteria previously developed under this Act, defining areas

of emphasis for new criteria and standards; an evaluation of the degree of observance of applicable occupational safety and health standards, and a summary of inspection and enforcement activity undertaken; analysis and evaluation of research activities for which results have been obtained under governmental and nongovernmental sponsorship; an analysis of major occupational diseases; evaluation of available control and measurement technology for hazards for which standards or criteria have been developed during the preceding year; description of cooperative efforts undertaken between Government agencies and other interested parties in the implementation of this Act during the preceding year; a progress report on the development of an adequate supply of trained manpower in the field of occupational safety and health, including estimates of occupational safety and health, including estimates of future needs and the efforts being made by Government and others to meet those needs; listing of all toxic substances in industrial usage for which labeling requirements, criteria, or standards have not yet been established; and such recommendations for additional legislation as are deemed necessary to protect the safety and health of the worker and improve the administration of this Act.

[Sec. 26 amended by P.L. 96–88, October 17, 1979]

[Sec. 28–31—Omitted]

NATIONAL COMMISSION ON STATE WORKMEN'S COMPENSATION LAWS

Sec. 27. (a)(1) The Congress hereby finds and declares that—

(A) the vast majority of American workers, and their families, are dependent on workmen's compensation for their basic economic security in the event such workers suffer disabling injury or death in the course of their employment; and that the full protection of American workers from job-related injury or death requires an adequate, prompt, and equitable system of workmen's compensation as well as an effective program of occupational health and safety regulation; and

(B) in recent years serious questions have been raised concerning the fairness and adequacy of present workmen's compensation laws in the light of the growth of the economy, the changing nature of the labor force, increases in medical knowledge, changes in the hazards associated with various types of employment, new technology creating new risks to health and safety, and increases in the general level of wages and the cost of living.

(2) The purpose of this section is to authorize an effective study and objective evaluation of State workmen's compensation laws in order to determine if such laws provide an adequate, prompt, and equitable system of compensation for injury or death arising out of or in the course of employment.

(b) There is hereby established a National Commission on State Workmen's Compensation Laws.

(c)(1) The Workmen's Compensation Commission shall be composed of fifteen members to be appointed by the President from among members of State workmen's compensation boards, representatives of insurance carriers, business, labor, members of the medical profession having experience in industrial medicine or in workmen's compensation cases, educators having special expertise in the field of workmen's compensation, and representatives of the general public. The Secretary, the Secretary of Commerce, and the Secretary of Health and Human Services shall be ex officio members of the Workmen's Compensation Commission:

(2) Any vacancy in the Workmen's Compensation Commission shall not affect its powers.

(3) The President shall designate one of the members to serve as Chairman and one to serve as Vice Chairman of the Workmen's Compensation Commission.

(4) Eight members of the Workmen's Compensation Commission shall constitute a quorum.

(d)(1) The Workmen's Compensation Commission shall undertake a comprehensive study and evaluation of State workmen's compensation laws in order to determine if such laws provide an adequate, prompt, and equitable system of compensation. Such study and evaluation shall include, without being limited to, the following subjects: (A) the amount and duration of permanent and temporary disability benefits and the criteria for determining the maximum limitations thereon, (B) the amount and duration of medical benefits and provisions insuring adequate medical care and free choice of physician. (C) the extent of coverage of workers, including exemptions based on numbers or type of employment, (D) standards for determining which injuries or diseases should be deemed compensable, (E) rehabilitation, (F) coverage under second or subsequent injury funds, (G) time limits on filing claims, (H) waiting periods, (I) compulsory or elective coverage, (J) administration, (K) legal expenses, (L) the feasibility and desirability of a uniform system of reporting information concerning job-related injuries and diseases and the operation of workmen's compensation laws, (M) the resolution of conflict of laws, extraterritoriality and similar problems arising from claims with multistate aspects, (N) the extent to which private insurance carriers are excluded from supplying workmen's compensation coverage and the desirability of such exclusionary practices, to the extent they are found to exist, (O) the relationship between workmen's compensation on the one hand, and old-age, disability, and survivors insurance and other types of insurance, public or private, on the other hand, (P) methods of implementing the recommendations of the Commission.

(2) The Workmen's Compensation Commission shall transmit to the President and to the Congress not later than July 31, 1972, a final report containing a detailed statement of the findings and conclusions of the Commission, together with such recommendations as it deems advisable.

(e)(1) The Workmen's Compensation Commission or, on the authorization of the Workmen's Compensation Commission, any subcommittee or members thereof, may, for the purpose of carrying out the provisions of this title, hold such hearings, take such testimony, and sit and act at such times and places as the Workmen's Compensation Commission deems advisable. Any member authorized by the Workmen's Compensation Commission may administer oaths or affirmations to witness appearing before the Workmen's Compensation Commission or any subcommittee or members thereof.

(2) Each department, agency, and instrumentality of the executive branch of the Government, including independent agencies, is authorized and directed to furnish to the Workmen's Compensation Commission, upon request made by the Chairman or Vice Chairman, such information as the Workmen's Compensation Commission deems necessary to carry out its functions under this section.

(f) Subject to such rules and regulations as may be adopted by the Workmen's Compensation Commission, the Chairman shall have the power to—

(1) appoint and fix the compensation of an executive director, and such additional staff personnel as he deems necessary, without regard to the provisions of title 5, United States Code, governing appointments in the competitive service, and without regard to the provisions of chapter 51 and subchapter III of chapter 53 of such title relating to classification and General Schedule pay rates, but at rates not in excess of the maximum rate for GS-18 of the General Schedule under section 5332 of such title, and

(2) procure temporary and intermittent services to the same as is authorized by section 3109 of title 5, United States Code.

(g) The Workmen's Compensation Commission is authorized to enter into contracts with Federal or State agencies, private firms, institutions, and individuals for the conduct of research or surveys, the preparation of reports, and other activities necessary to the discharge of its duties.

(h) Members of the Workmen's Compensation Commission shall receive compensation for each day they are engaged in the performance of their duties as members of the Workmen's Compensation Commission at the daily rate prescribed for GS-18 under section 5332 of title 5, United State Code, and shall be entitled to reimbursement for travel subsistence, and other necessary expenses incurred by them in the performance of their duties as members of the Workmen's Commission.

(i) There are hereby authorized to be appropriated such sums as may be necessary to carry out the provisions of this section.

(j) On the ninetieth day after the date of submission of its final report to the President, the Workmen's Compensation Commission shall cease to exist.

SEPARABILITY

Sec. 32. If any provision of this Act, or the application of such provision to any person or circumstance, shall be held invalid, the remainder of this Act, or the application of such provision to persons or circumstances other than those as to which it is held invalid, shall not be affected thereby.

APPROPRIATIONS

Sec. 33. There are authorized to be appropriated to carry out this Act for each fiscal year such sums as the Congress shall deem necessary.

EFFECTIVE DATE

Sec. 34. This Act shall take effect one hundred and twenty days after the date of its enactment.

Appendix B

WALKING-WORKING SURFACES STANDARD (SPECIFICATION STANDARD)

OSHA SPECIFICATION STANDARD (EXAMPLE)

Editor's Note: This OSHA standard, which sets requirements for walking and working surfaces such as stairs, ladders, and scaffolds, is an example of a *specification standard* that sets highly detailed requirements with which employers must comply. This standard, for example, sets requirements for distances between rungs on ladders used in the workplace, and dimensions for scaffold components.

OCCUPATIONAL SAFETY AND HEALTH STANDARDS
SUBPART D — WALKING-WORKING SURFACES

(29 CFR 1910 — Subpart D; 36 FR 10466, May 29, 1971; Amended as shown in Code of Federal Regulations, Revised as of July 1, 1989; Amended by 55 FR 32014, August 6, 1990; Corrected by 55 FR 46053, November 1, 1990)

Subpart D—Walking-Working Surfaces

Authority: Secs. 4, 6, 8, Occupational Safety and Health Act of 1970 (29 U.S.C. 653, 655, 657); Secretary of Labor's Order No. 12-71 (36 FR 8754), 8-76 (41 FR 25059), 9-83 (48 FR 35736), or 1-90 (55 FR 9033), as applicable.

Sections 1910.23, 1910.24, 1910.25, 1910.26, and 1910.28 also issued under 29 CFR part 1911.

[Authority citation added by 51 FR 24525, July 7, 1986; revised by 53 FR 12121, April 12, 1988; republished by 55 FR 32014; August 6, 1990; Corrected by 55 FR 46053, November 1, 1990]

§1910.21 Definitions.

(a) As used in §1910.23, unless the context requires otherwise, floor and wall opening, railing and toe board terms shall have the meanings ascribed in this paragraph.

(1) *Floor hole.* An opening measuring less than 12 inches but more than 1 inch in its least dimension, in any floor, platform, pavement, or yard, through which materials but not persons may fall; such as a belt hole, pipe opening, or slot opening.

(2) *Floor opening.* An opening measuring 12 inches or more in its least dimension, in any floor, platform, pavement, or yard, through which persons may fall; such as a hatchway, stair or ladder opening, pit, or large manhole. Floor openings occupied by elevators, dumb waiters, conveyors, machinery, or containers are excluded from this subpart.

(3) *Handrail.* A single bar or pipe supported on brackets from a wall or partition, as on a stairway or ramp, to furnish persons with a handhold in case of tripping.

(4) *Platform.* A working space for persons, elevated above the surrounding floor or ground; such as a balcony or platform for the operation of machinery and equipment.

(5) *Runway.* A passageway for persons, elevated above the surrounding floor or ground level, such as a footwalk along shafting or a walkway between buildings.

(6) *Standard railing.* A vertical barrier erected along exposed edges of a floor opening, wall opening, ramp, platform, or runway to prevent falls of persons.

168

(7) *Standard strength and construction.* Any construction of railings, covers, or other guards that meets the requirements of §1910.23.

(8) *Stair railing.* A vertical barrier erected along exposed sides of a stairway to prevent falls of persons.

(9) *Toeboard.* A vertical barrier at floor level erected along exposed edges of a floor opening, wall opening, platform, runway, or ramp to prevent falls of materials.

(10) *Wall hole.* An opening less than 30 inches but more than 1 inch high, of unrestricted width, in any wall or partition; such as a ventilation hole or drainage scupper.

(11) *Wall opening.* An opening at least 30 inches high and 18 inches wide, in any wall or partition, through which persons may fall; such as a yardarm doorway or chute opening.

(b) As used in §1910.24, unless the context requires otherwise, fixed industrial stair terms shall have the meaning ascribed in this paragraph.

(1) *Handrail.* A single bar or pipe supported on brackets from a wall or partition to provide a continuous handhold for persons using a stair.

(2) *Nose, nosing.* That portion of a tread projecting beyond the face of the riser immediately below.

(3) *Open riser.* The air space between the treads of stairways without upright members (risers).

(4) *Platform.* An extended step or landing breaking a continuous run of stairs.

(5) *Railing.* A vertical barrier erected along exposed sides of stairways and platforms to prevent falls of persons. The top member of railing usually serves as a handrail.

(6) *Rise.* The vertical distance from the top of a tread to the top of the next higher tread.

(7) *Riser.* The upright member of a step situated at the back of a lower tread and near the leading edge of the next higher tread.

(8) *Stairs, stairway.* A series of steps leading from one level or floor to another, or leading to platforms, pits, boiler rooms, crossovers, or around machinery tanks, and other equipment that are used more or less continuously or routinely by employees, or only occasionally by specific individuals. A series of steps and landings having three or more risers constitutes stairs or stairway.

(9) *Tread.* The horizontal member of a step.

(10) *Tread run.* The horizontal distance from the leading edge of a tread to the leading edge of an adjacent tread.

(11) *Tread width.* The horizontal distance from the front to back of tread including nosing when used.

(c) As used in §1910.25, unless the context requires otherwise, portable wood ladders terms shall have the meanings ascribed in this paragraph.

(1) *Ladders.* A ladder is an appliance usually consisting of two side rails joined at regular intervals by crosspieces called steps, rungs, or cleats, on which a person may step in ascending or descending.

(2) *Stepladder.* A stepladder is a self-supporting portable ladder, nonadjustable in length, having flat steps and a hinged back. Its size is designated by the overall length of the ladder measured along the front edge of the side rails.

(3) *Single ladder.* A single ladder is a non-self-supporting portable ladder, nonadjustable in length, consisting of but one section. Its size is designated by the overall length of the side rail.

(4) *Extension ladder.* An extension ladder is a non-self-supporting portable ladder adjustable in length. It consists of two or more sections traveling in guides or brackets so arranged as to permit length adjustment. Its size is designated by the sum of the lengths of the sections measured along the side rails.

169

(5) *Sectional ladder.* A sectional ladder is a non-self-supporting portable ladder, nonadjustable in length, consisting of two or more sections of ladder so constructed that the sections may be combined to function as a single ladder. Its size is designated by the overall length of the assembled sections.

(6) *Trestle ladder.* A trestle ladder is a self-supporting portable ladder, nonadjustable in length, consisting of two sections hinged at the top to form equal angles with the base. The size is designated by the length of the side rails measured along the front edge.

(7) *Extension trestle ladder.* An extension trestle ladder is a self-supporting portable ladder, adjustable in length, consisting of a trestle ladder base and a vertically adjustable single ladder, with suitable means for locking the ladders together. The size is designated by the length of the trestle ladder base.

(8) *Special-purpose ladder.* A special-purpose ladder is a portable ladder which represents either a modification or a combination of design or construction features in one of the general-purpose types of ladders previously defined in order to adapt the ladder to special or specific uses.

(9) *Trolley ladder.* A trolley ladder is a semifixed ladder, nonadjustable in length, supported by attachments to an overhead track, the plane of the ladder being at right angles to the plane of motion.

(10) *Side-rolling ladder.* A side-rolling ladder is a semifixed ladder, nonadjustable in length, supported by attachments to a guide rail, which is generally fastened to shelving, the plane of the ladder being also its plane of motion.

(11) *Wood characteristics.* Wood characteristics are distinguishing features which by their extent and number determine the quality of a piece of wood.

(12) *Wood irregularities.* Wood irregularities are natural characteristics in or on wood that may lower its durability, strength, or utility.

(13) *Cross grain.* Cross grain (slope of grain) is a deviation of the fiber direction from a line parallel to the sides of the piece.

(14) *Knot.* A knot is a branch or limb, imbedded in the tree and cut through in the process of lumber manufacture, classied according to size, quality, and occurrence. The size of the knot is determined as the average diameter on the surface of the piece.

(15) *Pitch and bark pockets.* A pitch pocket is an opening extending parallel to the annual growth rings containing, or that has contained, pitch, either solid or liquid. A bark pocket is an opening between annual growth rings that contains bark.

(16) *Shake.* A shake is a separation along the grain, most of which occurs between the rings of annual growth.

(17) *Check.* A check is a lengthwise separation of the wood, most of which occurs across the rings of annual growth.

(18) *Wane.* Wane is bark, or the lack of wood from any cause, on the corner of a piece.

(19) *Decay.* Decay is disintegration of wood substance due to action of wood-destroying fungi. It is also known as dote and rot.

(20) *Compression failure.* A compression failure is a deformation (buckling) of the fibers due to excessive compression along the grain.

(21) *Compression wood.* Compression wood is an aberrant (abnormal) and highly variable type of wood structure occurring in softwood species. The wood commonly has density somewhat higher than does normal wood, but somewhat lower stiffness and tensile strength for its weight in addition to high longitudinal shrinkage.

(22) *Low density.* Low-density wood is that which is exceptionally light in weight and usually deficient in strength properties for the species.

(d) As used in §1910.26, unless the context requires otherwise, portable metal ladder terms shall have the meanings ascribed in this paragraph.

(1) *Ladder.* A ladder is an appliance usually consisting of two side rails joined at regular intervals by cross-pieces called steps, rungs, or cleats, on which a person may step in ascending or descending.

(2) *Step ladder.* A step ladder is a self-supporting portable ladder, nonadjustable in length, having flat steps and a hinged back. Its size is designated by the overall length of the ladder measured along the front edge of the side rails.

(3) *Single ladder.* A single ladder is a non-self-supporting portable ladder, nonadjustable in length, consisting of but one section. Its size is designated by the overall length of the side rail.

(4) *Extension ladder.* An extension ladder is a non-self-supporting portable ladder adjustable in length. It consists of two or more sections traveling in guides or brackets so arranged as to permit length adjustment. Its size is designated by the sum of the lengths of the sections measured along the side rails.

(5) *Platform ladder.* A self-supporting ladder of fixed size with a platform provided at the working level. The size is determined by the distance along the front rail from the platform to the base of the ladder.

(6) *Sectional Ladder.* A sectional ladder is a non-self-supporting portable ladder, non-adjustable in length, consisting of two or more sections so constructed that the sections may be combined to function as a single ladder. Its size is designated by the overall length of the assembled sections.

(7) *Trestle ladder.* A trestle ladder is a self-supporting portable ladder, nonadjustable in length, consisting of two sections, hinged at the top to form equal angles with the base. The size is designated by the length of the side rails measured along the front edge.

(8) *Extension trestle ladder.* An extension trestle ladder is a self-supporting portable ladder, adjustable in length, consisting of a trestle ladder base and a vertically adjustable single ladder, with suitable means for locking the ladders together. The size is designated by the length of the trestle ladder base.

(9) *Special-purpose ladder.* A special-purpose ladder is a portable ladder which represents either a modification or a combination of design or construction features in one of the general-purpose types of ladders previously defined, in order to adapt the ladder to special or specific uses.

(e) As used in §1910.27, unless the context requires otherwise, fixed ladder terms shall have the meanings ascribed in this paragraph.

(1) *Ladder.* A ladder is an appliance usually consisting of two side rails joined at regular intervals by cross-pieces called steps, rungs, or cleats, on which a person may step in ascending or descending.

(2) *Fixed ladder.* A fixed ladder is a ladder permanently attached to a structure, building, or equipment.

(3) *Individual-rung ladder.* An individual-rung ladder is a fixed ladder each rung of which is individually attached to a structure, building, or equipment.

(4) *Rail ladder.* A rail ladder is a fixed ladder consisting of side rails joined at regular intervals by rungs or cleats and fastened in full length or in sections to a building, structure, or equipment.

(5) *Railings.* A railing is any one or a combination of those railings constructed in accordance with §1910.23. A standard railing is a vertical barrier erected along exposed edges of floor openings, wall openings, ramps, platforms, and runways to prevent falls of persons.

(6) *Pitch.* Pitch is the included angle between the horizontal and the ladder, measured on the opposite side of the ladder from the climbing side.

(7) *Fastenings.* A fastening is a device to attach a ladder to a structure, building, or equipment.

(8) *Rungs.* Rungs are ladder crosspieces of circular or oval cross-section on which a person may step in ascending or descending.

(9) *Cleats.* Cleats are ladder crosspieces of rectangular cross-section placed on edge on which a person may step in ascending or descending.

(10) *Steps.* Steps are the flat crosspieces of a ladder on which a person may step in ascending or descending.

(11) *Cage.* A cage is a guard that may be referred to as a cage or basket guard which is an enclosure that is fastened to the side rails of the fixed ladder or to the structure to encircle the climbing space of the ladder for the safety of the person who must climb the ladder.

(12) *Well.* A well is a permanent complete enclosure around a fixed ladder, which is attached to the walls of the well. Proper clearances for a well will give the person who must climb the ladder the same protection as a cage.

(13) *Ladder safety device.* A ladder safety device is any device, other than a cage or well, designed to eliminate or reduce the possibility of accidental falls and which may incorporate such features as life belts, friction brakes, and sliding attachments.

(14) *Grab bars.* Grab bars are individual handholds placed adjacent to or as an extension above ladders for the purpose of providing access beyond the limits of the ladder.

(15) *Through ladder.* A through ladder is one from which a man getting off at the top must step through the ladder in order to reach the landing.

(16) *Side-step ladder.* A side-step ladder is one from which a man getting off at the top must step sideways from the ladder in order to reach the landing.

(f) As used in § 1910.28, unless the context requires otherwise, scaffolding terms shall have the meaning ascribed in this paragraph.

(1) *Bearer.* A horizontal member of a scaffold upon which the platform rests and which may be supported by ledgers.

(2) *Boatswain's chair.* A seat supported by slings attached to a suspended rope, designed to accommodate one workman in a sitting position.

(3) *Brace.* A tie that holds one scaffold member in a fixed position with respect to another member.

(4) *Bricklayers' square scaffold.* A scaffold composed of framed wood squares which support a platform limited to light and medium duty.

(5) *Carpenters' bracket scaffold.* A scaffold consisting of wood or metal brackets supporting a platform.

(6) *Coupler.* A device for locking together the component parts of a tubular metal scaffold. The material used for the couplers shall be of a structural type, such as a drop-forged steel, malleable iron, or structural grade aluminum. The use of gray cast iron is prohibited.

(7) *Crawling board or chicken ladder.* A plank with cleats spaced and secured at equal intervals, for use by a worker on roofs, not designed to carry any material.

(8) *Double pole or independent pole scaffold.* A scaffold supported from the base by a double row of uprights, independent of support from the walls and constructed of uprights, ledgers, horizontal platform bearers, and diagonal bracing.

(9) *Float or ship scaffold.* A scaffold hung from overhead supports by means of ropes and consisting of a substantial platform having diagonal bracing underneath, resting upon and securely fastened to two parallel plank bearers at right angles to the span.

(10) *Guardrail.* A rail secured to uprights and erected along the exposed sides and ends of platforms.

(11) *Heavy duty scaffold.* A scaffold designed and constructed to carry a working load not to exceed 75 pounds per square foot.

(12) *Horse scaffold.* A scaffold for light or medium duty, composed of horses supporting a work platform.

(13) *Interior hung scaffold.* A scaffold suspended from the ceiling or roof structure.

(14) *Ladder jack scaffold.* A light duty scaffold supported by brackets attached to ladders.

(15) *Ledger (stringer).* A horizontal scaffold member which extends from post to post and which supports the putlogs or bearer forming a tie between the posts.

(16) *Light duty scaffold.* A scaffold designed and constructed to carry a working load not to exceed 25 pounds per square foot.

(17) *Manually propelled mobile scaffold.* A portable rolling scaffold supported by casters.

(18) *Masons' adjustable multiple-point suspension scaffold.* A scaffold having a continuous platform supported by bearers suspended by wire rope from overhead supports, so arranged and operated as to permit the raising or lowering of the platform to desired working positions.

(19) *Maximum intended load.* The total of all loads including the working load, the weight of the scaffold, and such other loads as may be reasonably anticipated.

(20) *Medium duty scaffold.* A scaffold designed and constructed to carry a working load not to exceed 50 pounds per square foot.

(21) *Mid-rail.* A rail approximately midway between the guardrail and platform, used when required, and secured to the uprights erected along the exposed sides and ends of platforms.

(22) *Needle beam scaffold.* A light duty scaffold consisting of needle beams supporting a platform.

(23) *Outrigger scaffold.* A scaffold supported by outriggers or thrustouts projecting beyond the wall or face of the building or structure, the inboard ends of which are secured inside of such a building or structure.

(24) *Putlog.* A scaffold member upon which the platform rests.

(25) *Roofing bracket.* A bracket used in sloped roof construction, having provisions for fastening to the roof or supported by ropes fastened over the ridge and secured to some suitable object.

(26) *Runner.* The lengthwise horizontal bracing or bearing members or both.

(27) *Scaffold.* Any temporary elevated platform and its supporting structure used for supporting workmen or materials or both.

(28) *Single-point adjustable suspension scaffold.* A manually or power-operated unit designed for light duty use, supported by a single wire rope from an overhead support so arranged and operated as to permit the raising or lowering of the platform to desired working positions.

(29) *Single pole scaffold.* Platforms resting on putlogs or crossbeams, the outside ends of which are supported on ledgers secured to a single row of posts or uprights and the inner ends of which are supported on or in a wall.

(30) *Stone setters' adjustable multiple-point suspension scaffold.* A swinging-type scaffold having a platform supported by hangers suspended at four points so as to permit the raising or lowering of the platform to the desired working position by the use of hoisting machines.

(31) *Toeboard.* A barrier secured along the sides and ends of a platform, to guard against the falling of material. [Section 10.21(f)(3) amended at 39 FR 19468. June 3, 1974]

(32) *Tube and coupler scaffold.* An assembly consisting of tubing which serves as posts, bearers, braces, ties, and runners, a base supporting the posts, and special couplers which serve

to connect the uprights and to join the various members.

(33) *Tubular welded frame scaffold.* A sectional, panel, or frame metal scaffold substantially built up of prefabricated welded sections which consist of posts and horizontal bearer with intermediate members. Panels or frames shall be braced with diagonal or cross braces.

(34) *Two-point suspension-scaffold (swinging scaffold).* A scaffold, the platform of which is supported by hangers (stirrups) at two points, suspended from overhead supports so as to permit the raising or lowering of the platform to the desired working position by tackle or hoisting machines.

(35) *Window jack scaffold.* A scaffold, the platform of which is supported by a bracket or jack which projects through a window opening.

(36) *Working load.* Load imposed by men, materials, and equipment.

(g) As used in §1910.29, unless the context requires otherwise, manually propelled mobile ladder stand and scaffold (tower) terms shall have the meaning ascribed in this paragraph.

(1) *Bearer.* A horizontal member of a scaffold upon which the platform rests and which may be supported by ledgers.

(2) *Brace.* A tie that holds one scaffold member in a fixed position with respect to another member.

(3) *Climbing ladder.* A separate ladder with equally spaced rungs usually attached to the scaffold structure for climbing and descending.

(4) *Coupler.* A device for locking together the components of a tubular metal scaffold which shall be designed and used to safely support the maximum intended loads.

(5) *Design working load.* The maximum intended load, being the total of all loads including the weight of the men, materials, equipment, and platform.

(6) *Equivalent.* Alternative design or features, which will provide an equal degree or factor of safety.

(7) *Guardrail.* A barrier secured to uprights and erected along the exposed sides and ends of platforms to prevent falls of persons.

(8) *Handrail.* A rail connected to a ladder stand running parallel to the slope and/or top step.

(9) *Ladder stand.* A mobile fixed size self-supporting ladder consisting of a wide flat tread ladder in the form of stairs. The assembly may include handrails.

(10) *Ledger (stringer).* A horizontal scaffold member which extends from post to post and which supports the bearer forming a tie between the posts.

(11) *Mobile scaffold (tower).* A light, medium, or heavy duty scaffold mounted on casters or wheels.

(12) *Mobile.* "Manually propelled."

(13) *Mobile work platform.* Generally a fixed work level one frame high on casters or wheels, with bracing diagonally from platform to vertical frame.

(14) *Runner.* The lengthwise horizontal bracing and/or bearing members.

(15) *Scaffold.* Any temporary elevated platform and its necessary vertical, diagonal, and horizontal members used for supporting workmen and materials. (Also known as a scaffold tower.)

(16) *Toeboard.* A barrier at platform level erected along the exposed sides and ends of a scaffold platform to prevent falls of materials.
[Section 1910.21(g)(16) amended at 39 FR 19468, June 3, 1974]

(17) *Tube and coupler scaffold.* An assembly consisting of tubing which serves as posts, bearers, braces, ties, and runners, a base supporting the posts, and uprights, and serves to join the various members, usually used in fixed locations.

(18) *Tubular welded frame scaffold.* A sectional, panel, or frame metal scaffold substantially built up of prefabricated welded sections, which consist of

posts and bearers with intermediate connecting members and braced with diagonal or cross braces.

(19) *Tubular welded sectional folding scaffold.* A sectional, folding metal scaffold either of ladder frame or inside stairway design, substantially built of prefabricated welded sections, which consist of end frames, platform frame, inside inclined stairway frame and braces, or hinged connected diagonal and horizontal braces, capable of being folded into a flat package when the scaffold is not in use.

(20) *Work level.* The elevated platform, used for supporting workmen and their materials, comprising the necessary vertical, horizontal and diagonal braces, guardrails, and ladder for access to the work platform.

§1910.22 General requirements.

This section applies to all permanent places of employment, except where domestic, mining, or agricultural work only is performed. Measures for the control of toxic materials are considered to be outside the scope of this section.

(a) *Housekeeping.* (1) All places of employment, passageways, storerooms, and service rooms shall be kept clean and orderly and in a sanitary condition.

(2) The floor of every workroom shall be maintained in a clean and, so far as possible, a dry condition. Where wet processes are used, drainage shall be maintained, and false floors, platforms, mats, or other dry standing places should be provided where practicable.

(3) To facilitate cleaning, every floor, working place, and passageway shall be kept free from protruding nails, splinters, holes, or loose boards.

(b) *Aisles and passageways.* (1) Where mechanical handling equipment is used, sufficient safe clearances shall be allowed for aisles, at loading docks, through doorways and wherever turns or passage must be made. Aisles and passageways shall be kept clear and in good repairs, with no obstruction across or in aisles that could create a hazard.

(2) Permanent aisles and passageways shall be appropriately marked.

(c) *Covers and guardrails.* Covers and/or guardrails shall be provided to protect personnel from the hazards of open pits, tanks, vats, ditches, etc.

(d) *Floor loading protection.* (1) In every building or other structure, or part thereof, used for mercantile, business, industrial, or storage purposes, the loads approved by the building official shall be marked on plates of approved design which shall be supplied and securely affixed by the owner of the building, or his duly authorized agent, in a conspicuous place in each space to which they relate. Such plates shall not be removed or defaced but, if lost, removed, or defaced, shall be replaced by the owner or his agent.

(2) It shall be unlawful to place, or cause, or permit to be placed, on any floor or roof of a building or other structure a load greater than that for which such floor or roof is approved by the building official.

§1910.23 Guarding floor and wall openings and holes.

(a) *Protection for floor openings.* (1) Every stairway floor opening shall be guarded by a standard railing constructed in accordance with paragraph (e) of this section. The railing shall be provided on all exposed sides (except at entrance to stairway). For infrequently used stairways where traffic across the opening prevents the use of fixed standard railing (as when located in aisle spaces, etc.), the guard shall consist of a hinged floor opening cover of standard strength and construction and removable standard railings on all exposed sides (except at entrance to stairway).

(2) Every ladderway floor opening or platform shall be guarded by a standard railing with standard toeboard on all exposed sides (except at entrance to opening), with the passage through the railing either provided with a swinging

gate or so offset that a person cannot walk directly into the opening.

(3) Every hatchway and chute floor opening shall be guarded by one of the following:

(i) Hinged floor opening cover of standard strength and construction equipped with standard railings or permanently attached thereto so as to leave only one exposed side. When the opening is not in use, the cover shall be closed or the exposed side shall be guarded at both top and intermediate positions by removable standard railings.

(ii) A removable railing with toeboard on not more than two sides of the opening and fixed standard railings with toeboards on all other exposed sides. The removable railings shall be kept in place when the opening is not in use.

[Sec. 1910.23(a)(3)(ii) amended FR 5321, February 10, 1984]

Where operating conditions necessitate the feeding of material into any hatchway or chute opening, protection shall be provided to prevent a person from falling through the opening.

(4) Every skylight floor opening and hole shall be guarded by a standard skylight screen or a fixed standard railing on all exposed sides.

(5) Every pit and trapdoor floor opening, infrequently used, shall be guarded by a floor opening cover of standard strength and construction. While the cover is not in place, the pit or trap opening shall be constantly attended by someone or shall be protected on all exposed sides by removable standard railings.

[Sec. 1910.23(a)(5) amended by 49 FR 5321, February 10, 1984]

(6) Every manhole floor opening shall be guarded by a standard manhole cover which need not be hinged in place. While the cover is not in place, the manhole opening shall be constantly attended by someone or shall be protected by removable standard railings.

(7) Every temporary floor opening shall have standard railings, or shall be constantly attended by someone.

(8) Every floor hole into which persons can accidentally walk shall be guarded by either:

(i) A standard railing with standard toeboard on all exposed sides, or

(ii) A floor hole cover of standard strength and construction. While the cover is not in place, the floor hole shall be constantly attended by someone or shall be protected by a removable standard railing.

[Sec. 1910.23(a)(8)(ii) amended by 49 FR 5321, February 10, 1984]

(9) Every floor hole into which persons cannot accidentally walk (on account of fixed machinery, equipment, or walls) shall be protected by a cover that leaves no openings more than 1 inch wide. The cover shall be securely held in place to prevent tools or materials from falling through.

(10) Where doors or gates open directly on a stairway, a platform shall be provided, and the swing of the door shall not reduce the effective width to less than 20 inches.

(b) *Protection for wall openings and holes.* (1) Every wall opening from which there is a drop of more than 4 feet shall be guarded by one of the following:

(i) Rail, roller, picket fence, half door, or equivalent barrier. Where there is exposure below to falling materials, a removable toe board or the equivalent shall also be provided. When the opening is not in use for handling materials, the guard shall be kept in position regardless of a door on the opening. In addition, a grab handle shall be provided on each side of the opening with its center approximately 4 feet above level and of standard strength and mounting.

[Sec. 1910.23(b)(1)(i) amended by 49 FR 5321, February 10. 1984]

(ii) Extension platform onto which materials can be hoisted for handling, and which shall have side rails or equivalent guards of standard specifications.

(2) Every chute wall opening from which there is a drop of more than 4 feet shall be guarded by one or more of the barriers specified in paragraph (b)(1) of this section, or as required by the conditions.

(3) Every window wall opening at a stairway landing, floor, platform, or balcony, from which there is a drop of more than 4 feet, and where the bottom of the opening is less than 3 feet above the platform or landing, shall be guarded by standard slats, standard grill work (as specified in paragraph (e)(11) of this section), or standard railing. Where the window opening is below the landing, or platform, a standard toe board shall be provided.

(4) Every temporary wall opening shall have adequate guards but these need not be of standard construction.

(5) Where there is a hazard of materials falling through a wall hole, and the lower edge of the near side of the hole is less than 4 inches above the floor, and the far side of the hole more than 5 feet above the next lower level, the hole shall be protected by a standard toeboard, or an enclosing screen either of solid construction, or as specified in paragraph (e) (11) of this section.

(c) *Protection of open-sided floors, platforms, and runways.* (1) Every opensided floor or platform 4 feet or more above adjacent floor or ground level shall be guarded by a standard railing (or the equivalent as specified in paragraph (e)(3) of this section) on all open sides, except where there is entrance to a ramp, stairway, or fixed ladder. The railing shall be provided with a toeboard wherever, beneath the open sides.

(i) Persons can pass,

(ii) There is moving machinery, or

(iii) There is equipment with which falling materials could create a hazard.

(2) Every runway shall be guarded by a standard railing (or the equivalent as specified in paragraph (e)(3) of this section) on all open sides 4 feet or more above floor or ground level. Wherever tools, machine parts, or materials are likely to be used on the runway, a toeboard shall also be provided on each exposed side. Runways used exclusively for special purposes (such as oiling, shafting, or filling tank cars) may have the railing on one side omitted where operating conditions necessitate such omission, providing the falling hazard is minimized by using a runway of not less than 18 inches wide. Where persons entering upon runways become thereby exposed to machinery, electrical equipment, or other danger not a falling hazard, additional guarding than is here specified may be essential for protection.

(3) Regardless of height, open-sided floors, walkways, platforms, or runways above or adjacent to dangerous equipment, pickling or galvanizing tanks, degreasing units, and similar hazards shall be guarded with a standard railing and toe board.

(d) *Stairway railings and guards.* (1) Every flight of stairs having four or more risers shall be equipped with standard stair railings or standard handrails as specified in paragraphs (d)(1)(i) through (v) of this section, the width of the stair to be measured clear of all obstructions except handrails:

(i) On stairways less than 44 inches wide having both sides enclosed, at least one handrail, preferably on the right side descending.

(ii) On stairways less than 44 inches wide having one side open, at least one stair railing on open side.

(iii) On stairways less than 44 inches wide having both sides open, one stair railing on each side.

(iv) On stairways more than 44 inches wide but less than 88 inches wide, one handrail on each enclosed side and one stair railing on each open side.

(v) On stairways 88 or more inches wide, one handrail on each enclosed side, one stair railing on each open side, and one intermediate stair railing located approximately midway of the width.

(2) Winding stairs shall be equipped with a handrail offset to prevent walking on all portions of the treads having width less than 6 inches.

(e) *Railing, toe boards, and cover specifications.* (1) A standard railing shall consist of top rail, intermediate rail, and posts, and shall have a vertical height of 42 inches nominal from upper surface of top rail to floor, platform, runway, or ramp level. The top rail shall be smooth-surfaced throughout the length of the railing. The intermediate rail shall be approximately halfway between the top rail and the floor, platform, runway, or ramp. The ends of the rails shall not overhang the terminal posts except where such overhang does not constitute a projection hazard.

(2) A stair railing shall be of construction similar to a standard railing but the vertical height shall not be more than 34 inches nor less than 30 inches from upper surface of top rail to surface of tread in line with face of riser at forward edge of tread.

(3) [Revoked]

(i) For wood railings, the posts shall be of at least 2-inch by 4-inch stock spaced not to exceed 6 feet; the top and intermediate rails shall be of at least 2-inch by 4-inch stock. If top rail is made of two right-angle pieces of 1-inch by 4-inch stock, posts may be spaced on 8-foot centers, with 2-inch by 4-inch intermediate rail.

(ii) For pipe railings, post and top and intermediate railings shall be at least 1 1/2 inches nominal diameter with posts spaced not more than 8 feet on centers.

(iii) For structural steel railings, posts and top and intermediate rails shall be of 2-inch by 2-inch by 3/8-inch angles or other metal shapes of equivalent bending strength with posts spaced not more than 8 feet on centers.

(iv) The anchoring of posts and framing of members for railings of all types shall be of such construction that the completed structure shall be capable of withstanding a load of at least 200 pounds applied in any direction at any point on the top rail.

(v) Other types, sizes, and arrangements of railing construction are acceptable provided they meet the following conditions:

(a) A smooth-surfaced top rail at a height above floor, platform, runway, or ramp level of 42 inches nominal;

(b) A strength to withstand at least the minimum requirement of 200 pounds top rail pressure;

(c) Protection between top rail and floor, platform, runway, ramp, or stair treads, equivalent at least to that afforded by a standard intermediate rail;

(d) [Revoked]

(4) A standard toeboard shall be 4 inches nominal in vertical height from its top edge to the level of the floor, platform, runway, or ramp. It shall be securely fastened in place and with not more than 1/4-inch clearance above floor level. It may be made of any substantial material either solid or with openings not over 1 inch in greatest dimension. Where material is piled to such height that a standard toeboard does not provide protection, paneling from floor to intermediate rail, or to top rail shall be provided.

(5) (i) A handrail shall consist of a lengthwise member mounted directly on a wall or partition by means of brackets attached to the lower side of the handrail so as to offer no obstruction to a smooth surface along the top and both sides of the handrail. The handrail shall be of rounded or other section that will furnish an adequate

handhold for anyone grasping it to avoid falling. The ends of the handrail should be turned in to the supporting wall or otherwise arranged so as not to constitute a projection hazard.

(ii) The height of handrails shall be not more than 34 inches nor less than 30 inches from upper surface of handrail to surface of tread in line with face of riser or to surface of ramp.

(ii) The size of handrails shall be: When of hardwood, at least 2 inches in diameter; when of metal pipe, at least 1 ½ inches in diameter. The length of brackets shall be such as will give a clearance between handrail and wall or any projection thereon of at least 3 inches. The spacing of brackets shall not exceed 8 feet.

(iv) The mounting of handrails shall be such that the completed structure is capable of withstanding a load of at least 200 pounds applied in any direction at any point on the rail.

(6) All handrails and railings shall be provided with a clearance of not less than 3 inches between the handrail or railing and any other object.

(7) Floor opening covers may be of any material that meets the following strength requirements:

(i) Trench or conduit covers and their supports, when located in plant roadways, shall be designed to carry a truck rear-axle load of at least 20,000 pounds.

(ii) Manhole covers and their supports, when located in plant roadways, shall comply with local standard highway requirements if any; otherwise, they shall be designed to carry a truck rear-axle load of at least 20,000 pounds.

(iii) The construction of floor opening covers may be of any material that meets the strength requirements. Covers projecting not more than 1 inch above the floor level may be used providing all edges are chamfered to an angle with the horizontal of not over 30 degrees. All hinges, handles, bolts, or other parts shall set flush with the floor or cover surface.

(8) Skylight screens shall be of such construction and mounting that they are capable of withstanding a load of at least 200 pounds applied perpendicularly at any one area on the screen. They shall also be of such construction and mounting that under ordinary loads or impacts, they will not deflect downward sufficiently to break the glass below them. The construction shall be of grillwork with openings not more than 4 inches long or of slatwork with openings not more than 2 inches wide with length unrestricted.

(9) Wall opening barriers (rails, rollers, picket fences, and half doors) shall be of such construction and mounting that, when in place at the opening, the barrier is capable of withstanding a load of at least 200 pounds applied in any direction (except upward) at any point on the top rail or corresponding member.

(10) Wall opening grab handles shall be not less than 12 inches in length and shall be so mounted as to give 3 inches clearance from the side framing of the wall opening. The size, material, and anchoring of the grab handle shall be such that the completed structure is capable of withstanding a load of at least 200 pounds applied in any direction at any point of the handle.

(11) Wall opening screens shall be of such construction and mounting that they are capable of withstanding a load of at least 200 pounds applied horizontally at any point on the near side of the screen. They may be of solid construction, of grillwork with openings not more than 8 inches long, or of slatwork with openings not more than 4 inches wide with length unrestricted. [Sections 1910.23(e)(3) and (e)(3(v)(*d*) revoked at 43 FR 49726, October 24, 1978, effective November 24, 1978]

§1910.24 Fixed industrial stairs.

(a) *Application of requirements.* This section contains specifications for the safe design and construction of fixed general industrial stairs. This classification includes interior and exterior stairs around machinery, tanks, and other equipment, and stairs leading to or from floors, platforms, or pits. This section does not apply to stairs used for fire exit purposes, to construction operations to private residences, or to articulated stairs, such as may be installed on floating roof tanks or on dock facilities, the angle of which changes with the rise and fall of the base support.

(b) *Where fixed stairs are required.* Fixed stairs shall be provided for access from one structure level to another where operations necessitate regular travel between levels, and for access to operating platforms at any equipment which requires attention routinely during operations. Fixed stairs shall also be provided where access to elevations is daily or at each shift for such purposes as gauging, inspection, regular maintenance, etc., where such work may expose employees to acids, caustics, gases, or other harmful substances, or for which purposes the carrying of tools or equipment by hand is normally required. (It is not the intent of this section to preclude the use of fixed ladders for access to elevated tanks, towers, and similar structures, overhead traveling cranes, etc., where the use of fixed ladders is common practice.) Spiral stairways shall not be permitted except for special limited usage and secondary access situations where it is not practical to provide a conventional stairway. Winding stairways may be installed on tanks and similar round structures where the diameter of the structure is not less than five (5) feet.

(c) *Stair strength.* Fixed stairways shall be designed and constructed to carry a load of five times the normal live load anticipated but never of less strength than to carry safely a moving concentrated load of 1,000 pounds.

(d) *Stair width.* Fixed stairways, shall have a minimum width of 22 inches.

(e) *Angle of stairway rise.* Fixed stairs shall be installed at angles to the horizontal of between 30 ° and 50 °. Any uniform combination of rise/tread dimensions may be used that will result in a stairway at an angle to the horizontal within the permissible range. Table D —1 gives rise/tread dimensions which will produce a stairway within the permissible range, stating the angle to the horizontal produced by each combination. However, the rise/tread combinations are not limited to those given in Table D—1.

(f) *Stair treads.* All treads shall be reasonably slip-resistant and the nosings shall be of nonslip finish. Welded bar grating treads without nosing are acceptable providing the leading edge can be readily identified by personnel descending the stairway and provided the tread is serrated or is of definite nonslip design. Rise height and tread width shall be uniform throughout any flight of stairs including any foundation

TABLE D—1

Angle to horizontal	Rise (in inches)	Tread run (in inches)
30°35′	$6^1/2$	11
32°08′	$6^3/4$	$10^1/4$
33°41′	7	$10^1/2$
35°16′	$7^1/4$	$10^1/4$
36°52′	$7^1/2$	10
38°29′	$7^3/4$	$9^3/4$
40°08′	8	$9^1/2$
41°44′	$8^1/4$	$9^1/4$
43°22′	$8^1/2$	9
45°00′	$8^3/4$	$9^3/4$
46°38′	9	$8^1/2$
48°16′	$9^1/4$	$8^1/4$
49°54′	$9^1/2$	8

structure used as one or more treads of the stairs.

[Sec. 1910.24(f) amended by 49 FR 5321, February 10, 1984]

(g) *Stairway platforms.* Stairway platforms shall be no less than the width of a stairway and a minimum of

30 inches in length measured in the direction of travel.

[Sec. 1910.24(g) heading amended by 49 FR 5321, February 10, 1984]

(h) *Railings and handrails.* Standard railings shall be provided on the open sides of all exposed stairways and stair platforms. Handrails shall be provided on at least one side of closed stairways, preferably on the right side descending. Stair railings and handrails shall be installed in accordance with the provisions of §1910.23.

(i) *Vertical clearance.* Vertical clearance above any stair tread to an overhead obstruction shall be at least 7 feet measured from the leading edge of the tread.

(j) [Removed]

[Sec. 1910.24(j) deleted by 49 FR 5321, February 10, 1984]

(k) *General.* [Revoked]

[Section 1910.24(k) revoked at 43 FR 49726, October 24, 1978, effective November 24, 1978]

§1910.25 Portable wood ladders.

(a) *Application of requirements.* This section is intended to prescribe rules and establish minimum requirements for the construction, care, and use of the common types of portable wood ladders, in order to insure safety under normal conditions of usage. Other types of special ladders, fruitpicker's ladders, combination step and extension ladders, stockroom step ladders, aisle-way step ladders, shelf ladders, and library ladders are not specifically covered by this section.

(b) *Materials—(1) Requirements applicable to all wood parts.* (i) All wood parts shall be free from sharp edges and splinters; sound and free by accepted visual inspection from shake, wane, compression failures, decay, or other irregularities. Low-density wood shall not be used.

(c) Construction requirements.

(1) [Reserved]

(2) *Portable stepladders.* Stepladders longer than 20 feet shall not be supplied. Stepladders as hereinafter specified shall be of three types:

Type I —Industrial stepladder, 3 to 20 feet for heavy duty, such as utilities, contractors, and industrial use.

Type II —Commercial stepladder, 3 to 12 feet for medium duty, such as painters, offices, and light industrial use.

Type III —Household stepladder, 3 to 6 feet for light duty, such as light household use.

(i) *General requirements.*(a) [Revoked]

(b) A uniform step spacing shall be employed which shall be not more than 12 inches. Steps shall be parallel and level when the ladder is in position for use.

(c) The minimum width between side rails at the top, inside to inside, shall be not less than 11 1/2 inches. From top to bottom, the side rails shall spread at least 1 inch for each foot of length of stepladder.

(d) [Revoked]

(e) [Revoked]

(f) A metal spreader or locking device of sufficient size and strength to securely hold the front and back sections in open positions shall be a component of each stepladder. The spreader shall have all sharp points covered or removed to protect the user. For Type III ladder, the peil shelf and spreader may be combined in one unit (the so-called shelf-lock ladder).

(g) [Revoked]
(h) [Revoked]
(i) [Revoked]
(ii) *Type I industrial stepladder.*(a)
(1) [Revoked]
(2) [Revoked]
(b) [Revoked]
(c) [Revoked]
(1) [Revoked]
(2) [Revoked]
Tables D-2 and D-3 [Revoked]
(d) [Revoked]
(iii) *Type II commercial stepladder.*
(a) (1) [Revoked]
(2) [Revoked]
(b) [Revoked]
(c) [Revoked]
(1) (i) [Revoked]
(ii) [Revoked]
(2) [Revoked]
(3) [Revoked]
(iv) *Type III household stepladder.*
(a) [Revoked]
(b) [Revoked]
(c) [Revoked]
(1) [Revoked]
(2) [Revoked]
(3) *Portable rung ladders.*
(i) [Revoked]
(b) [Revoked]
(c) [Revoked]
(d) [Revoked]
(e) [Revoked]
(f) [Revoked]
(g) [Revoked]
(h) [Revoked]
(i) [Revoked]
(j) [Revoked]
(ii) *Single ladder.* (a) Single ladders longer than 30 feet shall not be supplied.
(b) [Revoked]
(c) [Revoked]
(d) [Revoked]
(iii) *Two-section ladder.* (a) Two-section extension ladders longer than 60 feet shall not be supplied. All ladders of this type shall consist of two sections, one to fit within the side rails of the other, and arranged in such a

manner that the upper section can be raised and lowered.
(b) [Revoked]
(c) [Revoked]
(d) [Revoked]
(e) [Revoked]
(f) [Revoked]
(g) (1) [Revoked]
(2) [Revoked]
(iv) *Sectional Ladder.* (a) Assembled combinations of sectional ladders longer than lengths specified in this subdivision shall not be used.
(b) [Revoked]
(c) [Revoked]
(1) [Revoked]
Table D-4 [Revoked]
(2) [Revoked]
(3) [Revoked]
(4) [Revoked]
(v) *Trestle and extension trestle ladder.* (a) Trestle ladders, or extension sections or base sections of extension trestle ladders longer than 20 feet shall not be supplied.
(b) [Revoked]
(c) [Revoked]
(d) [Revoked]
(e) [Revoked]
(f) [Revoked]
(g) [Revoked](4) *Special-purpose ladders.*
(i) [Revoked]
(a) [Revoked]
(b) [Revoked]
(c) [Revoked]
(d) [Revoked]
(e) [Revoked]
(f) [Revoked]
(ii) *Painter's stepladder.* (a) Painter's stepladders longer than 12 feet shall not be supplied.
(b) [Revoked]
(1) [Revoked]
(2) [Revoked]
(iii) *Mason's ladder.* A mason's ladder is a special type of single ladder intended for use in heavy construction work.

(a) Mason's ladders longer than 40 feet shall not be supplied.

(b) [Revoked]

(c) [Revoked]

(d) [Revoked](5) *Trolley and side-rolling ladders—(i) Length.* Trolley ladders and side-rolling ladders longer than 20 feet should not be supplied.

(ii) *Dimensions.* [Revoked]

(iii) *Width.* [Revoked]

(iv) *Step attachment.* [Revoked]

(v) *Locking device.* [Revoked]

(vi) *Tracks.*(a) [Revoked]

(b) [Revoked]

(c) [Revoked]

(d) [Revoked]

(vii) *Wheel carriages.*(a) [Revoked]

(b) [Revoked]

(c) [Revoked]

(d) [Revoked]

(e) [Revoked]

(f) [Revoked]

(d) *Care and use of ladders—(1) Care.* To insure safety and serviceability the following precautions on the care of ladders shall be observed:

(i) Ladders shall be maintained in good condition at all times, the joint between the steps and side rails shall be tight, all hardware and fittings securely attached, and the movable parts shall operate freely without binding or undue play.

(ii) Metal bearings of locks, wheels, pulleys, etc., shall be frequently lubricated.

(iii) Frayed or badly worn rope shall be replaced.

(iv) Safety feet and other auxiliary equipment shall be kept in good condition to insure proper performance.

(v) [Revoked]—(ix) [Reserved]

(x) Ladders shall be inspected frequently and those which have developed defects shall be withdrawn from service for repair or destruction and tagged or marked as "Dangerous, Do Not Use."

(xi) Rungs should be kept free of grease and oil.

(2) *Use.* The following safety precautions shall be observed in connection with the use of ladders:

(i) Portable rung and cleat ladders shall, where possible, be used at such a pitch that the horizontal distance from the top support to the foot of the ladder is one-quarter of the working length of the ladder (the length along the ladder between the foot and the top support). The ladder shall be so placed as to prevent slipping, or it shall be lashed, or held in position. Ladders shall not be used in a horizontal position as platforms, runways, or scaffolds;

(ii) Ladders for which dimensions are specified should not be used by more than one man at a time nor with ladder jacks and scaffold planks where use by more than one man is anticipated. In such cases, specially designed ladders with larger dimensions of the parts should be procured;

(iii) Portable ladders shall be so placed that the side rails have a secure footing. The top rest for portable rung and cleat ladders shall be reasonably rigid and shall have ample strength to support the applied load;

(iv) Ladders shall not be placed in front of doors opening toward the ladder unless the door is blocked upon, locked, or guarded.

(v) Ladders shall not be placed on boxes, barrels, or other unstable bases to obtain additional height;

(vi) [Removed]

[Sec. 1910.25(d)(2)(vi) deleted by 49 FR 5321, February 10, 1984]

(vii) [Removed]

[Sec.1910.25(d)(2)(vii) deleted by 49 FR 5321, February 10, 1984]

(viii) Ladders with broken or missing steps, rungs, or cleats, broken side rails, or other faulty equipment shall not be used; improvised repairs shall not be made.

(ix) Short ladders shall not be spliced together to provide long sections;

(x) Ladders made by fastening cleats across a single rail shall not be used;

(xi) Ladders shall not be used as guys, braces, or skids, or for other than their intended purposes;

(xii) Tops of the ordinary types of stepladders shall not be used as steps;

(xiii) On two-section extension ladders the minimum overlap for the two sections in use shall be as follows:

Size of ladder (feet):	Overlap (feet)
Up to and including 36	3
Over 36 up to and including 48	4
Over 48 up to and including 60	5

(xiv) Portable rung ladders with reinforced rails (see paragraphs (c) (3) (ii) (c) and (iii) (d) this section) shall be used only with the metal reinforcement on the under side. [Sec. 1910.25(d)(2)(xiv) amended by 49 FR 5321, February 10, 1984]

(xv) No ladder should be used to gain access to a roof unless the top of the ladder shall extend at least 3 feet above the point of support, at eave, gutter, or roof line;

(xvi) [Revoked] [Sec. 1910.25(d)(2)(xvi) deleted by 49 FR 5321, February 10, 1984]

(xvii) Middle and top sections of sectional or window cleaner's ladders should not be used for bottom section unless the user equips them with safety shoes.

(xviii) [Removed] [Sec. 1910.25(d)(2)(xviii) deleted by 49 FR 5321, February 10, 1984]

(xix) The user should equip all portable rung ladders with nonslip bases when there is a hazard of slipping. Nonslip bases are not intended as a substitute for care in safely placing, lashing, or holding a ladder that is being used upon oily, metal, concrete, or slippery surfaces.

(xx) The bracing on the back legs of step ladders is designed solely for increasing stability and not for climbing.

(xxi) [Revoked]

§1910.26 Portable metal ladders.

(a) *Requirements*—(1) *General.* Specific design and construction requirements are not part of this section because of the wide variety of metals and design possibilities. However, the design shall be such as to produce a ladder without structural defects or accident hazards such as sharp edges, burrs, etc. The metal selected shall be of sufficient strength to meet the test requirements, and shall be protected against corrosion unless inherently corrosion resistant.

(i) (ii) [Reserved]

(iii) The spacing of rungs or steps shall be on 12-inch centers.

(iv) [Reserved]

(v) Rungs and steps shall be corrugated, knurled, dimpled, coated with skid-resistant material, or otherwise treated to minimize the possibility of slipping.

(vi) [Reserved]

(2) *General specifications—straight and extension ladders*(i) The minimum width between side rails of a straight ladder or any section of an extension ladder shall be 12 inches.

(ii) The length of single ladders or individual sections of ladders shall not exceed 30 feet. Two-section ladders shall not exceed 48 feet in length and over two-section ladders shall not exceed 60 feet in length.

(iii) Based on the nominal length of the ladder, each section of a multisection ladder shall overlap the adjacent section by at least the number of feet stated in the following:

Nominal length of ladder (feet):	Overlap (feet)
Up to and including 36	*3*
Over 36, up to and including 48	*4*
Over 48, up to 60	*5*

(iv) Extension ladders shall be equipped with positive stops which will insure the overlap specified in the table above.

(3) *General specifications — step ladders.*

(i) (ii)[Reserved]

(iii) The length of a stepladder is measured by the length of the front rail. To be classified as a standard length ladder, the measured length shall be within plus or minus one-half inch of the specified length. Stepladders shall not exceed 20 feet in length.

(iv) -(vi) [Reserved]

(vii) The bottoms of the four rails are to be supplied with insulating non-slip material for the safety of the user.

(viii) A metal spreader or locking device of sufficient size and strength to securely hold the front and back sections in the open position shall be a component of each stepladder. The spreader shall have all sharp points or edges covered or removed to protect the user.

(4) *General specifications—trestles and extension trestle ladders.* (i) Trestle ladders or extension sections or base sections of extension trestle ladders shall be not more than 20 feet in length.

(ii) -(v) [Revoked]

(5) *General specifications—platform ladders.* (i) The length of a platform ladder shall not exceed 20 feet. The length of a platform ladder shall be measured along the front rail from the floor to the platform.

(b) [Reserved]

(c) *Care and maintenance of ladders* — (1) *General.* To get maximum service-ability, safety, and to eliminate unnecessary damage of equipment, good safe practices in the use and care of ladder equipment must be employed by the users.

The following rules and regulations are essential to the life of the equipment and the safety of the user.

(2) *Care of ladders.*

(i) -(iii) [Reserved]

(iv) Ladders must be maintained in good usable condition at all times.

[Sec. 1910.26(c)(2)(iv) amended by 49 FR 5321, February 10, 1984]

(v) [Removed]

[Sec. 1910.26(c)(2)(v) deleted by 49 FR 5321, February 10, 1984]

(vi) If a ladder is involved in any of the following, immediate inspection is necessary:

[Sec. 1910.26(c)(2)(vi) amended by 49 FR 5321, February 10, 1984]

(a) If ladders tip over, inspect ladder for side rails dents or bends, or excessively dented rungs; check all rung-to-side-rail connections; check hardware connections; check rivets for shear.

(b) [Removed]

(c) [Removed]

[Sec. 1910.26(c)(2)(vi)(b) and (c) removed by 49 FR 5321, February 10, 1984]

(d) If ladders are exposed to oil and grease, equipment should be cleaned of oil, grease, or slippery materials. This can easily be done with a solvent or steam cleaning.

(vii) Ladders having defects are to be marked and taken out of service until repaired by either maintenance department or the manufacturer.

(3) *Use of ladders.* (i) A simple rule for setting up a ladder at the proper angle is to place the base a distance from the vertical wall equal to one-fourth the working length of the ladder.

[Sec. 1910.26(c)(3)(i) amended by 49 FR 5321, February 10, 1984]

(ii) Portable ladders are designed as a one-man working ladder based on a 200-pound load.

(iii) The ladder base section must be placed with a secure footing.

[Sec. 1910.26(c)(3)(iii) amended by 49 FR 5321, February 10, 1984]

(iv) The top of the ladder must be placed with the two rails supported, unless equipped with a single supported, unless equipped with a single support attachment.

[Sec. 1910.26(c)(3)(iv) amended by 49 FR 5321, February 10, 1984]

(v) When ascending or descending, the climber must face the ladder.

(vi) Ladders must not be tied or fastened together to provide longer sections. They must be equipped with the hardware fittings necessary if the manufacturer endorses extended uses.

(vii) Ladders should not be used as a brace, skid, guy or gin pole, gangway, or for other uses than that for which they were intended, unless specifically recommended for use by the manufacturer.

(viii) See §1910.333(c) for work practices to be used when work is performed on or near electric circuits.
[Sec. 1910.26 (c)(3)(viii) revised by 55 FR 32014, August 6, 1990]

§ 1910.27 Fixed ladders.

(a) *Design requirements*—(1) *Design considerations.* All ladders, appurtenances, and fastenings shall be designed to meet the following load requirements:

(i) The minimum design live load shall be a single concentrated load of 200 pounds.

(ii) The number and position of additional concentrated live-load units of 200 pounds each as determined from anticipated usage of the ladder shall be considered in the design.

(iii) The live loads imposed by persons occupying the ladder shall be considered to be concentrated at such points as will cause the maximum stress in the structural member being considered.

(iv) The weight of the ladder and attached appurtenances together with the live load shall be considered in the design of rails and fastenings.

(2) *Design stresses.* Design stresses for wood components of ladders shall not exceed those specified in §1910.25. All wood parts of fixed ladders shall meet the requirements of §1910.25(b).

For fixed ladders consisting of wood side rails and wood rungs or cleats,

used at a pitch in the range 75 degrees to 90 degrees, and intended for use by no more than one person per section, single ladders as described in §1910.25(c)(3)(ii) are acceptable.

(b) *Specific features*—(1) *Rungs and cleats.* (i) All rungs shall have a minimum diameter of three-fourths inch for metal ladders, except as covered in paragraph (b)(7)(i) of this section and a minimum diameter of 1-1/8 inches for wood ladders.

(ii) The distance between rungs, cleats, and steps shall not exceed 12 inches and shall be uniform throughout the length of the ladder.

(iii) The minimum clear length of rungs or cleats shall be 16 inches.

(iv) Rungs, cleats, and steps shall be free of splinters, sharp edges, burrs, or projections which may be a hazard.

(v) The rungs of an individual-rung ladder shall be so designed that the foot cannot slide off the end. A suggested design is shown in figure D-1.

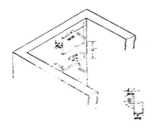

FIGURE D-1.—Suggested design for rungs on individual-rung ladders.

(2) *Side rails.* Side rails which might be used as a climbing aid shall be of such cross sections as to afford adequate gripping surface without sharp edges, splinters, or burrs.

(3) *Fastenings.* Fastenings shall be an integral part of fixed ladder design.

(4) *Splices.* All splices made by whatever means shall meet design requirements as noted in paragraph (a) of this section. All splices and connections shall have smooth transition with original members and with no sharp or extensive projections.

(5) *Electrolytic action.* Adequate means shall be employed to protect dissimilar metals from electrolytic action when such metals are joined.

(6) *Welding.* All welding shall be in accordance with the "Code for Welding in Building Construction" (AWSD1.0–1966).

(7) *Protection from deterioration.* (i) Metal ladders and appurtenances shall be painted or otherwise treated to resist corrosion and rusting when location demands. Ladders formed by individual metal rungs imbedded in concrete, which serve as access to pits and to other areas under floors, are frequently located in an atmosphere that causes corrosion and rusting. To increase rung life in such atmosphere individual metal rungs shall have a minimum diameter of 1 inch or shall be painted or otherwise treated to resist corrosion and rusting.

(ii) Wood ladders, when used under conditions where decay may occur, shall be treated with a nonirritating preservative, and the details shall be such as to prevent or minimize the accumulation of water on wood parts.

(iii) When different types of materials are used in the construction of a ladder, the materials used shall be so treated as to have no deleterious effect one upon the other.

(c) *Clearance*—(1) *Climbing side.* On fixed ladders, the perpendicular distance from the centerline of the rungs to the nearest permanent object on the climbing side of the ladder shall be 36 inches for a pitch of 76 degrees, and 30 inches for a pitch of 90 degrees (fig. D-2 of this section), with minimum clear-

ances for intermediate pitches varying between these two limits in proportion to the slope, except as provided in subparagraphs (3) and (5) of this paragraph.

(2) *Ladders without cages or wells.* A clear width of at least 15 inches shall be provided each way from the centerline of the ladder in the climbing space, except when cages or wells are necessary.

(3) *Ladders with cages or baskets.* Ladders equipped with cage or basket are excepted from the provisions of subparagraphs (1) and (2) of this paragraph, but shall conform to the provisions of paragraph (d)(1)(v) of this section. Fixed ladders in smooth-walled wells are excepted from the provisions of subparagraph (1) of this paragraph, but shall conform to the provisions of paragraph (d)(1)(vi) of this section.

(4) *Clearance in back of ladder.* The distance from the centerline of rungs,

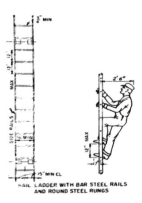

FIXED LADDER WITH BAR STEEL RAILS AND ROUND STEEL RUNGS

Fig. D-2
Minimum Ladder Clearances

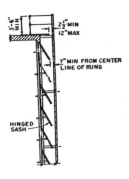

cleats, or steps to the nearest permanent object in back of the ladder shall be not less than 7 inches, except that when unavoidable obstructions are encountered, minimum clearances as shown in figure D-3 shall be provided.

(5) *Clearance in back of grab bar.* The distance from the centerline of the grab bar to the nearest permanent ob-

Fig. D-4
Ladder Far from Wall

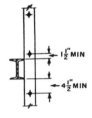

Fig. D-3
Clearance for Unavoidable Obstruction at Rear of Fixed Ladder.

(7) *Hatch cover.* Counterweighted hatch covers shall open a minimum of 60 degrees from the horizontal. The distance from the centerline of rungs or cleats to the edge of the hatch opening on the climbing side shall be not less than 24 inches for offset well or 30 inches for straight wells. There shall be no protruding potential hazards within 24 inches of the centerline of rungs or cleats; any such hazards within 30 inches of the centerline of the rungs or cleats shall be fitted with deflector plates placed at an angle of 60 degrees from the horizontal as indicated in figure D-5.

ject in back of the grab bars shall be not less than 4 inches. Grab bars shall not protrude on the climbing side beyond the rungs of the ladder which they serve.

(6) *Step-across distance.* The step-across distance from the nearest edge of ladder to the nearest edge of equipment or structure shall be not more than 12 inches, or less than 2 1/2 inches (fig. D-4).

Deflector Plates for Head Hazards
Fig. D-5

The relationship of a fixed ladder to an acceptable counterweighted hatch cover is illustrated in figure D-6.

(d) *Special requirements—(1) Cages or wells.* (i) Cages or wells (except on chimney ladders) shall be built, as shown on the applicable drawings, covered in detail in figures D-7, D-8, and D-9, or of equivalent construction.

(ii) Cages or wells (except as provided in subparagraph (5) of this paragraph) conforming to the dimensions shown in figures D-7, D-8, and D-9 shall be provided on ladders of more than 20 feet to a maximum unbroken length of 30 feet.

(iii) Cages shall extend a minimum of 42 inches above the top of landing, unless other acceptable protection is provided.

(iv) Cages shall extend down the ladder to a point not less than 7 feet nor more than 8 feet above the base of the ladder, with bottom flared not less than 4 inches, or portion of cage opposite ladder shall be carried to the base.

(v) Cages shall not extend less than 27 nor more than 28 inches from the centerline of the rungs of the ladder. Cage shall not be less than 27 inches in width. The inside shall be clear of projections. Vertical bars shall be located at a maximum spacing of 40 degrees around the circumference of the cage; this will give a maximum spacing of approximately 9½ inches, center to center.

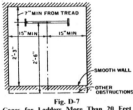

Fig. D-7
Cages for Ladders More Than 20 Feet High

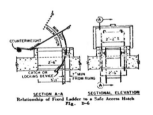

SECTION A-A   SECTIONAL ELEVATION
Relationship of Fixed Ladder to a Safe Access Hatch
Fig. D-6

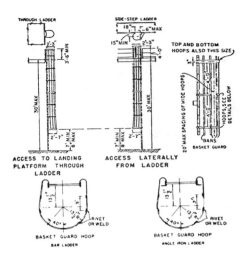

Clearance Diagram for Fixed Ladder in Well Figure D-8

[Sec. 1910.27 Figure D-8]

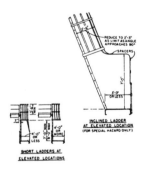

FIGURE D-9.—Cages—Special applications.

(vi) Ladder wells shall have a clear width of at least 15 inches measured each way from the centerline of the ladder. Smooth-walled wells shall be a minimum of 27 inches from the centerline of rungs to the well wall on the climbing side of the ladder. Where other obstructions on the climbing side of the ladder exist, there shall be a minimum of 30 inches from the centerline of the rungs.

(2) *Landing platforms.* When ladders are used to ascend to heights exceeding 20 feet (except on chimneys), landing platforms shall be provided for each 30 feet of height or fraction thereof, except that, where no cage, well, or ladder safety device is provided, land-

ing platforms shall be provided for each 20 feet of height or fraction thereof. Each ladder section shall be offset from adjacent sections. Where installation conditions (even for a short, unbroken length) require that adjacent sections be offset, landing platforms shall be provided at each offset.

(i) Where a man has to step a distance greater than 12 inches from the centerline of the rung of a ladder to the nearest edge of structure or equipment, a landing platform shall be provided. The minimum step-across distance shall be 2½ inches.

(ii) All landing platforms shall be equipped with standard railings and toeboards, so arranged as to give safe access to the ladder. Platforms shall be not less than 24 inches in width and 30 inches in length.

(iii) One rung of any section of ladder shall be located at the level of the landing laterally served by the ladder. Where access to the landing is through the ladder, the same rung spacing as used on the ladder shall be used from the landing platform to the first rung below the landing.

(3) *Ladder extensions.* The side rails of through or side-step ladder extensions shall extend 3 ½ feet above parapets and landings. For through ladder extensions, the rungs shall be omitted from the extension and shall have not less than 18 nor more than 24 inches clearance between rails. For side-step or offset fixed ladder sections, at landings, the side rails and rungs shall be carried to the next regular rung beyond or above the 3½ feet minimum (fig. D-10).

(4) *Grab bars.* Grab bars shall be spaced by a continuation of the rung spacing when they are located in the horizontal position. Vertical grab bars shall have the same spacing as the ladder side rails. Grab-bar diameters shall be the equivalent of the round-rung diameters.

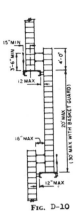

Fig. D-10

FIG. D-10 Offset Fixed Ladder Sections

(5) *Ladder safety devices.* Ladder safety devices may be used on tower, water tank, and chimney ladders over 20 feet in unbroken length in lieu of cage protection. No landing platform is required in these cases. All ladder safety devices such as those that incorporate lifebelts, friction brakes, and sliding attachments shall meet the design requirements of the ladders which they serve.

(e) *Pitch*—(1) *Preferred pitch.* The preferred pitch of fixed ladders shall be considered to come in the range of 75 degrees and 90 degrees with the horizontal (fig. D-11).

(2) *Substandard pitch.* Fixed ladders shall be considered as substandard if they are installed within the substandard pitch range of 60 and 75 degrees with the horizontal. Substandard fixed ladders are permitted only where it is

found necessary to meet conditions of installation. This substandard pitch range shall be considered as a critical range to be avoided, if possible.

(3) *Scope of coverage in this section.* This section covers only fixed ladders within the pitch range of 60 degrees and 90 degrees with the horizontal.

(4) *Pitch greater than 90 degrees.* Ladders having a pitch in excess of 90

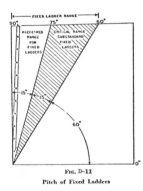

Fig. D-11

Pitch of Fixed Ladders

FIG. D-11 Pitch of Fixed Ladders

degrees with the horizontal are prohibited.

(f) *Maintenance.* All ladders shall be maintained in a safe condition. All ladders shall be inspected regularly, with the intervals between inspections being determined by use and exposure.

§1919.28 Safety requirements for scaffolding.

(a) *General requirements for all scaffolding (1) Scaffolds shall be furnished and erected in accordance with this standard for persons engaged in work that cannot be done safely from the ground or from solid construction, except that ladders used for such work shall conform to §1910.25 and §1910.26.*

(2) The footing or anchorage for scaffolds shall be sound, rigid, and capable of carrying the maximum intended load without settling or displacement. Unstable objects such as barrels, boxes, loose brick, or concrete blocks shall not be used to support scaffolds or planks.

(3) [Removed]
[Sec. 1910.28(a)(3) deleted by 49 FR 5321, February 10, 1984]

(4) Scaffolds and their components shall be capable of supporting without failure at least four times the maximum intended load.

(5) Scaffolds and other devices mentioned or described in this section shall be maintained in safe condition. Scaffolds shall not be altered or moved horizontally while they are in use or occupied.

(6) Any scaffold damaged or weakened from any cause shall be immediately repaired and shall not be used until repairs have been completed.

(7) Scaffolds shall not be loaded in excess of the working load for which they are intended.

(8) All load-carrying timber members of scaffold framing shall be a minimum of 1,500 f. (Stress Grade) construction grade lumber. All dimensions are nominal sizes as provided in the American Lumber Standards, except that where rough sizes are noted, only rough or undressed lumber of the size specified will satisfy minimum requirements. (NOTE: Where nominal sizes of lumber are used in place of rough sizes, the nominal size lumber shall be such as to provide equivalent strength to that specified in tables D-7 through D-12 and D-16.)

(9) All planking shall be Scaffold Grade as recognized by grading rules for the species of wood used. The maximum permissible spans for 2- × 9-inch

or wider planks are shown in the following table:

	Material				
	Full thickness undressed lumber			Nominal thickness lumber	
Working load (p.s.f.)	25	50	75	25	50
Permissible span (ft.)	10	8	6	8	6

The maximum permissible span for 1 $^1/_4$ × 9-inch or wider plank of full thickness is 4 feet with medium loading of 50 p.s.f.

(10) Nails or bolts used in the construction of scaffolds shall be of adequate size and in sufficient numbers at each connection to develop the designed strength of the scaffold. Nails shall not be subjected to a straight pull and shall be driven full length.

(11) All planking or platforms shall be overlapped (minimum 12 inches) or secured from movement.

(12) An access ladder or equivalent safe access shall be provided.

(13) Scaffold planks shall extend over their end supports not less than 6 inches nor more than 18 inches.

(14) The poles, legs, or uprights of scaffolds shall be plumb, and securely and rigidly braced to prevent swaying and displacement.

(15) Materials being hoisted onto a scaffold shall have a tag line.

(16) Overhead protection shall be provided for men on a scaffold exposed to overhead hazards.

(17) Scaffolds shall be provided with a screen between the toeboard and the guardrail, extending along the entire opening, consisting of No. 18 gauge U.S. Standard Wire one-half-inch mesh or the equivalent, where persons are required to work or pass under the scaffolds.

(18) Employees shall not work on scaffolds during storms or high winds.

(19) Employees shall not work on scaffolds which are covered with ice or snow, unless all ice or snow is removed and planking sanded to prevent slipping.

(20) Tools, materials, and debris shall not be allowed to accumulate in quantities to cause a hazard.

(21) Only treated or protected fiber rope shall be used for or near any work involving the use of corrosive substances or chemicals.

(22) Wire or fiber rope used for scaffold suspension shall be capable of supporting at least six times the intended load.

(23) When acid solutions are used for cleaning buildings over 50 feet in height, wire rope supported scaffolds shall be used.

(24) The use of shore scaffolds or lean-to scaffolds is prohibited.

(25) Lumber sizes, when used in this section, refer to nominal sizes except where otherwise stated.

(26) Scaffolds shall be secured to permanent structures, through use of anchor bolts, reveal bolts, or other equivalent means. Window cleaners' anchor bolts shall not be used.

(27) Special precautions shall be taken to protect scaffold members, including any wire or fiber ropes, when using a heat-producing process.

(b) *General requirements for wood pole scaffolds.* (1) Scaffold poles shall bear on a foundation of sufficient size and strength to spread the load from the poles over a sufficient area to prevent settlement. All poles shall be set plumb.

(2) Where wood poles are spliced, the ends shall be squared, and the upper section shall rest squarely on the lower section. Wood splice plates shall be provided on at least two adjacent sides and shall not be less than 4 feet 0 inches in length, overlapping the abutted ends equally, and have the same width and not less than the cross-sectional area of the pole. Splice plates of

other materials of equivalent strength may be used.

(3) Independent pole scaffolds shall be set as near to the wall of the building as practicable.

(4) All pole scaffolds shall be securely guyed or tied to the building or structure. Where the height or length exceeds 25 feet, the scaffold shall be secured at intervals not greater than 25 feet vertically and horizontally.

(5) Putlogs or bearers shall be set with their greater dimensions vertical, long enough to project over the ledgers of the inner and outer rows of poles at least 3 inches for proper support.

(6) Every wooden putlog on single pole scaffolds shall be reinforced with a $^3/_{16}$ ×2-inch steel strip or equivalent secured to its lower edge throughout its entire length.

(7) Ledgers shall be long enough to extend over two pole spaces. Ledgers shall not be spliced between the poles. Ledgers shall be reinforced by bearing blocks securely nailed to the side of the pole to form a support for the ledger.

(8) Diagonal bracing shall be provided to prevent the poles from moving in a direction parallel with the wall of the building, or from buckling.

(9) Cross bracing shall be provided between the inner and outer sets of poles in independent pole scaffolds. The free ends of pole scaffolds shall be cross braced.

(10) Full diagonal face bracing shall be erected across the entire face of pole scaffolds in both directions. The braces shall be spliced at the poles.

(11) Platform planks shall be laid with their edges close together so the platform will be tight with no spaces through which tools or fragments of material can fall.

(12) Where planking is lapped, each plank shall lap its end supports at least 12 inches. Where the ends of planks abut each other to form a flush floor, the butt joints shall be at the centerline

of a pole. The abutted ends shall rest on separate bearers. Intermediate beams shall be provided where necessary to prevent dislodgment of planks due to deflection, and the ends shall be nailed or cleated to prevent their dislodgment.

[Section 1910.28(b)(12) amended at 39 FR 19468, June 3, 1974]

(13) When a scaffold turns a corner, the platform planks shall be laid to prevent tipping. The planks that meet the corner putlog at an angle shall be laid first, extending over the diagonally placed putlog far enough to have a good safe bearing, but not far enough to involve any danger from tipping. The planking running in the opposite direction at right angles shall be laid so as to extend over and rest on the first layer of planking.

(14) When moving platforms to the next level, the old platform shall be left undisturbed until the new putlogs or bearers have been set in place, ready to receive the platform planks.

(15) Guardrails not less than 2 × 4 inches or the equivalent and not less than 36 inches or more than 42 inches high, with a mid-rail, when required, of 1 × 4-inch lumber or equivalent, and toeboards, shall be installed at all open sides on all scaffolds more than 10 feet above the ground or floor. Toeboards shall be a minimum of 4 inches in height. Wire mesh shall be installed in accordance with paragraph (a)(17) of this section.

(16) All wood pole scaffolds 60 feet or less in height shall be constructed and erected in accordance with tables D–7 through D –12 of this section. If they are over 60 feet in height they shall be designed by a registered professional engineer and constructed and erected in accordance with such design. A copy of the typical drawings and specifications shall be made available to the employer and for inspection purposes.

TABLE D–7 —MINIMUM NOMINAL SIZE AND MAXIMUM SPACING OF MEMBERS OF SINGLE POLE SCAFFOLDS LIGHT DUTY

	MAXIMUM HEIGHT OF SCAFFOLD	
	20 FEET	60 FEET
UNIFORMLY DISTRIBUTED LOAD	NOT TO EXCEED 25 POUNDS PER SQUARE FOOT.	
POLES OR UPRIGHTS	2 BY 4 IN	4 BY 4 IN.
POLE SPACING (LONGITUDINAL)	6 FT. 0 IN	10 FT. 0 IN.
MAXIMUM WIDTH OF SCAFFOLD	5 FT. 0 IN	5 FT. 0 IN.
BEARERS OR PUTLOGS TO 3 FT. 0 IN. WIDTH	2 BY 4 IN	2 BY 4 IN.
BEARERS OR PUTLOGS TO 5 FT. 0 IN. WIDTH	2 BY 6 IN. OR 3 BY 4 IN	2 BY 6 IN. OR 3 BY 4 IN.
LEDGERS	1 BY 4 IN	$1^1/4$ BY 9 IN.
PLANKING	$1^1/4$ BY 9 IN. (ROUGH)	2 BY 9 IN.
VERTICAL SPACING OF HORIZONTAL MEMBERS	7 FT. 0 IN	7 FT. 0 IN.
BRACING, HORIZONTAL AND DIAGONAL	1 BY 4 IN	1 BY 4 IN.
TIE-INS	1 BY 4 IN	1 BY 4 IN.
TOEBOARDS	4 IN. HIGH (MINIMUM)	1 IN. HIGH (MINIMUM).
GUARDRAIL	2 BY 4 IN	2 BY 4 IN.
ALL MEMBERS EXCEPT PLANKING ARE USED ON EDGE.		

(17) Wood-pole scaffolds shall not be erected beyond the reach of effective firefighting apparatus.

TABLE D–8 —MINIMUM NOMINAL SIZE AND MAXIMUM SPACING OF MEMBERS OF SINGLE POLE SCAFFOLDS MEDIUM DUTY

UNIFORMLY DISTRIBUTED...........	NOT TO EXCEED 50 POUNDS PER SQUARE FOOT.
MAXIMUM HEIGHT OF SCAFFOLD	60 FT.
POLES OR UPRIGHTS...........	4 BY 4 IN.
POLE SPACING (LONGITUDINAL)...................	8 FT. 0 IN.
MAXIMUM WIDTH OF SCAFFOLD.....	5 FT. 0 IN.
BEARERS OR PUTLOGS	2 BY 9 IN. OR 3 BY 4 IN.
SPACING OF BEARERS OR PUTLOGS	8 FT. 0 IN.
LEDGERS	2 BY 9 IN.
VERTICAL SPACING OF HORIZONTAL MEMBERS	9 FT. 0 IN.
BRACING, HORIZONTAL.............	1 BY 6 IN. OR $1^1/4$ BY 4 IN.
BRACING, DIAGONAL....................	1 BY 4 IN.
TIE-INS	1 BY 4 IN.
PLANKING	2 BY 9 IN.
TOEBOARDS...........	4 IN. HIGH (MINIMUM).
GUARDRAIL...........	2 BY 4 IN.

All members except planking are used on edge.

TABLE D–9 —MINIMUM NOMINAL SIZE AND MAXIMUM SPACING OF MEMBERS OF SINGLE POLE SCAFFOLDS

HEAVY DUTY

Uniformity distributed load.	Not to exceed 75 pounds per square foot.
Maximum height of scaffold..........	60 ft.
Poles or uprights...	4 by 4 in.
Pole spacing (longitudinal)...........	6 ft. 0 in.
Maximum width of scaffold..........	5 ft. 0 in.
Bearers or putlogs	2 by 9 in. or 3 by 5 in. (rough).
Spacing of bearers of putlogs.	6 ft. 0 in.
Ledgers	2 by 9 in.
Vertical spacing of horizontal members.....................	6 ft. 6 in.
Bracing, horizontal and diagonal.	2 by 4 in.
Tie-ins	1 by 4 in.
Planking................	2 by 9 in.
Toeboards..............	4 in. high (minimum).
Guardrail	2 by 4 in.

All members except planking are used on edge.

TABLE D–10 —MINIMUM NOMINAL SIZE AND MAXIMUM SPACING OF MEMBERS OF INDEPENDENT POLE SCAFFOLDS LIGHT DUTY

	Maximum height of scaffold	
	20 feet	60 feet
Uniformly distributed load	Not to exceed 25 pounds per square foot.	
Poles or uprights.................................	2 by 4 in.	4 by 4 in.
Pole spacing (longitudinal)................	6 ft. 0 in...............	10 ft. 0 in.
Pole spacing (transverse)....................	6 ft. 0 in...............	10 ft. 0. in.
Ledgers	1¼ by 4 in.	1¼ by 9 in.
Bearers to 3 ft. 0 in. span..................	2 by 4 in..............	2 by 4 in.
Bearers to 10 ft. 0. in. span...............	2 by 6 in. or 3 by 4 in	2 by 9 (rough) or 3 by 8 in.
Planking..	1¼ by 9 in	2 by 9 in.
Vertical spacing of horizontal members..	7 ft. 0 in...............	7 ft. 0 in.
Bracing, horizontal and diagonal	1 by 4 in..............	1 by 4 in.
Tie-ins	1 by 4 in..............	1 by 4 in.
Toeboards..	4 in. high	4 in. high (minimum).
Guardrail	2 by 4 in..............	2 by 4 in.

All members except planking are used on edge.

TABLE D–11 —MINIMUM NOMINAL
SIZE AND MAXIMUM SPACING OF
MEMBERS OF INDEPENDENT POLE
SCAFFOLDS
MEDIUM DUTY

Uniformly distrib-	Not to exceed 50 pounds per square foot.
uted load.	
Maximum height of scaffold.	60 ft.
Poles or uprights...	4 by 4 in.
Pole spacing (lon- gitudinal)..........	8 ft. 0 in.
Pole spacing (transverse).......	8 ft. 0 in.
Ledgers	2 by 9 in.
Vertical spacing of horizontal members.....................	6 ft. 0 in.
Spacing of bearers	8 ft. 0 in.
Bearers..................	2 by 9 in. (rough) or 2 by 10 in.
Bracing, horizon- tal	1 by 6 in. or 1 ¼ by 4 in.
Bracing, diagonal	1 by 4 in.
Tie-ins	1 by 4 in.
Planking................	2 by 9 in.
Toeboards..............	4 in. high (minimum).
Guardrail	2 by 4 in.

All members except planking are used on edge.

TABLE D–12 —MINIMUM NOMINAL
SIZE AND MAXIMUM SPACING OF
MEMBERS OF INDEPENDENT POLE
SCAFFOLDS
HEAVY DUTY

Uniformly distrib-	Not to exceed 75 pounds per square foot.
uted load.	
Maximum height of scaffold..........	60 ft.
Poles or uprights...	4 by 4 in.
Pole spacing (lon- gitundinal).........	6 ft. 0 in.
Pole spacing (transverse).......	8 ft. 0 in.
Ledgers	2 by 9 in.
Vertical spacing of horizontal members.....................	4 ft. 6 in.

TABLE D–12 —MINIMUM NOMINAL
SIZE AND MAXIMUM SPACING OF
MEMBERS OF INDEPENDENT POLE
SCAFFOLDS
HEAVY DUTY

Uniformly distrib-	Not to exceed 75 pounds per square foot.
uted load.	
Bearers..................	2 by 9 in. (rough).
Bracing, horizon- tal and diagonal.	2 by 4 in.
Tie-ins	1 by 4 in.
Planking................	2 by 9 in.
Toeboards..............	4 in. high (minimum).
Guardrail	2 by 4 in.

All members except planking are used on edge.

TABLE D–13—TUBE AND COUPLER
SCAFFOLDS LIGHT DUTY

Uniformly distrib- uted load	Not to exceed 25 p.s.f.
Post spacing (lon- gitudinal)..........	10 ft. 0 in.
Post spacing (transverse).......	6 ft. 0 in.

Working levels	Additional planked levels	Maximum height
1	8	125 ft.
2	4	125 ft.
3	0	91 ft. 0 in.

TABLE D–14—TUBE AND COUPLER
SCAFFOLDS MEDIUM DUTY

Uniformly distrib- uted load	Not to exceed 50 p.s.f.
Post spacing (lon- gitudinal)...........	8 ft. 0 in.
Post spacing (transverse).......	6 ft. 0 in.

Working levels	Additional planked levels	Maximum height
1	6	125 ft.
2	0	78 ft. 0 in.

TABLE D-15—TUBE AND COUPLER
SCAFFOLDS HEAVY DUTY

Uniformly distributed load	Not to exceed 75 p.s.f.
Post spacing (longitudinal)...........	6 ft. 6 in.
Post spacing (transverse)	6 ft. 0 in.

Working levels	Additional planked levels	Maximum height
1	6	125 ft.

(c) *Tube and coupler scaffolds.* (1) A light-duty tube and coupler scaffold shall have all posts, bearers, runners, and bracing of nominal 2-inch O.D. steel tubing. The posts shall be spaced no more than 6 feet apart by 10 feet along the length of the scaffold. Other structural metals when used must be designed to carry an equivalent load.

(2) A medium-duty tube and coupler scaffold shall have all posts, runners, and bracing of nominal 2-inch O.D. steel tubing. Posts spaced not more than 6 feet apart by 8 feet along the length of the scaffold shall have bearers of nominal 2 1/2-inch O.D. steel tubing. Posts spaced not more than 5 feet apart by 8 feet along the length of the scaffold shall have bearers of nominal 2-inch O.D. steel tubing. Other structural metals when used must be designed to carry an equivalent load.

(3) A heavy-duty tube and coupler scaffold shall have all posts, runners, and bracing of nominal 2-inch O.D. steel tubing, with the posts spaced not more than 6 feet apart by 6 feet 6 inches along the length of the scaffold. Other structural metals when used must be designed to carry an equivalent load.

(4) Tube and coupler scaffolds shall be limited in heights and working levels to those permitted in tables D-13, 14, and 15, of this section. Drawings and specifications of all tube and coupler scaffolds above the limitations in tables D-13, 14, and 15 of this section shall be designed by a registered professional engineer and copies made available to the employer and for inspection purposes.

(5) All tube and coupler scaffolds shall be constructed and erected to support four times the maximum intended loads as set forth in table D-13, 14, and 15 of this section, or as set forth in the specifications by a registered professional engineer, copies which shall be made available to the employer and for inspection purposes.

(6) All tube and coupler scaffolds shall be erected by competent and experienced personnel.

(7) Posts shall be accurately spaced, erected on suitable bases, and maintained plumb.

(8) Runners shall be erected along the length of the scaffold located on both the inside and the outside posts at even height. Runners shall be interlocked to form continuous lengths and coupled to each post. The bottom runners shall be located as close to the base as possible. Runners shall be placed not more than 6 feet 6 inches on centers.

(9) Bearers shall be installed transversely between posts and shall be securely coupled to the posts bearing on the runner coupler. When coupled directly to the runners, the coupler must be kept as close to the posts as possible.

(10) Bearers shall be at least 4 inches but not more than 12 inches longer than the post spacing or runner spacing. Bearers may be cantilevered for use as brackets to carry not more than two planks.

(11) Cross bracing shall be installed across the width of the scaffold at least every third set of posts horizontally and every fourth runner vertically. Such bracing shall extend diagonally from the inner and outer runners upward to the next outer and inner runners.

(12) Longitudinal diagonal bracing shall be installed at approximately a 45-degree angle from near the base of the first outer post upward to the ex-

treme top of the scaffold. Where the longitudinal length of the scaffold permits, such bracing shall be duplicated beginning at every fifth post. In a similar manner, longitudinal diagonal bracing shall also be installed from the last post extending back and upward toward the first post. Where conditions preclude the attachment of this bracing to the posts, it may be attached to the runners.

(13) The entire scaffold shall be tied to and securely braced against the building at intervals not to exceed 30 feet horizontally and 26 feet vertically.

(14) Guardrails not less than 2 ×4 inches or the equivalent and not less than 36 inches or more than 42 inches high, with a mid-rail, when required, of 1 ×4-inch lumber or equivalent, and toeboards, shall be installed at all open sides on all scaffolds more than 10 feet above the ground or floor. Toeboards shall be a minimum of 4 inches in height. Wire mesh shall be installed in accordance with paragraph (a)(17) of this section.

(d) *Tubular welded frame scaffolds.* (1) Metal tubular frame scaffolds, including accessories such as braces, brackets, trusses, screw legs, ladders, etc., shall be designed and proved to safely support four times the maximum intended load.

(2) Spacing of panels or frames shall be consistent with the loads imposed.

(3) Scaffolds shall be properly braced by cross bracing or diagonal braces, or both, for securing vertical members together laterally, and the cross braces shall be of such length as will automatically square and align vertical members so that the erected scaffold is always plumb, square, and rigid. All brace connections shall be made secure.

(4) Scaffold legs shall be set on adjustable bases or plain bases placed on mud sills or other foundations adequate to support the maximum intended load.

(5) The frames shall be placed one on top of the other with coupling or stacking pins to provide proper vertical alinement of the legs.

(6) Where uplift may occur, panels shall be locked together vertically by pins or other equivalent suitable means

(7) Guardrails not less than 2 ×4 inches or the equivalent and not less than 36 inches or more than 42 inches high, with a mid-rail, when required, of 1-×4-inch lumber or equivalent, and toeboards, shall be installed at all open sides on all scaffolds more than 10 feet above the ground or floor. Toeboards shall be a minimum of 4 inches in height. Wire mesh shall be installed in accordance with paragraph (a)(17) of this section.

(8) All tubular metal scaffolds shall be constructed and erected to support four times the maximum intended loads.

(9) To prevent movement, the scaffold shall be secured to the building or structure at intervals not to exceed 30 feet horizontally and 26 feet vertically.

(10) Maximum permissible spans of planking shall be in conformity with paragraph (a)(9) of this section.

(11) Drawings and specifications for all frame scaffolds over 125 feet in height above the base plates shall be designed by a registered professional engineer and copies made available to the employer and for inspection purposes.

(12) All tubular welded frame scaffolds shall be erected by competent and experienced personnel.

(13) Frames and accessories for scaffolds shall be maintained in good repair and every defect, unsafe condition, or noncompliance with this section shall be immediately corrected before further use of the scaffold. Any broken, bent, excessively rusted, altered, or otherwise structurally damaged frames or accessories shall not be used.

(14) Periodic inspections shall be made of all welded frames and accessories and any maintenance, including painting, or minor corrections autho-

rized by the manufacturer, shall be made before further use.

(e) *Outrigger scaffolds.* (1) Outrigger beams shall extend not more than 6 feet beyond the face of the building. The inboard end of outrigger beams, measured from the fulcrum point to the extreme point of support, shall be not less than one and one-half times the outboard end in length. The beams shall rest on edge, the sides shall be plumb, and the edges shall be horizontal. The fulcrum point of the beam shall rest on a secure bearing at least 6 inches in each horizontal dimension. The beam shall be secured in place against movement and shall be securely braced at the fulcrum point against tipping.

(2) The inboard ends of outrigger beams shall be securely supported either by means of struts bearing against sills in contact with the overhead beams or ceiling, or by means of tension members secured to the floor joists underfoot, or by both if necessary. The inboard ends of outrigger beams shall be secured against tipping and the entire supporting structure shall be securely braced in both directions to prevent any horizontal movement.

(3) Unless outrigger scaffolds are designed by a licensed professional engineer, they shall be constructed and erected in accordance with table D-16. Outrigger scaffolds designed by a registered professional engineer shall be constructed and erected in accordance with such design. A copy of the detailed drawings and specifications showing the sizes and spacing of members shall be kept on the job.

(4) Planking shall be laid tight and shall extend to within 3 inches of the building wall. Planking shall be nailed or bolted to outriggers.

(5) Where there is danger of material falling from the scaffold, a wire mesh or other enclosure shall be provided between the guardrail and the toeboard.

(6) Where additional working levels are required to be supported by the outrigger method, the plans and specifications of the outrigger and scaffolding structure shall be designed by a registered professional engineer.

TABLE D-16 —MINIMUM NOMINAL SIZE AND MAXIMUM SPACING OF MEMBERS OF OUTRIGGER SCAFFOLDS.

	Light duty	Medium duty
Maximum scaffold load.........	25 p.s.f	50 p.s.f.
Outrigger size..........	2×10 in	3×10 in.
Maximum outrigger spacing.	10 ft 0 in....	6 ft 0 in.
Planking.....	2×9 in	2×9 in.
Guardrail ...	2×4 in	2×4 in.
Guardrail uprights	2×4 in	2×4 in.
Toeboards...	4 in. (minimum)..........	4 in. (minimum).

(f) *Masons' adjustable multiple-point suspension scaffolds.* (1) The scaffold shall be capable of sustaining a working load of 50 pounds per square foot and shall not be loaded in excess of that figure.

(2) The scaffold shall be provided with hoisting machines that meet the requirements of a nationally recognized testing laboratory. Refer to §1910.7 for definition of nationally recognized testing laboratory. [1910.28 (f)(2) revised by 53 FR 12121, April 12, 1988]

(3) The platform shall be supported by wire ropes in conformity with paragraph (a)(22) of this section, suspended from overhead outrigger beams.

(4) The scaffold outrigger beams shall consist of structural metal securely fastened or anchored to the frame or floor system of the building or structure.

(5) Each outrigger beam shall be equivalent in strength to at least a standard 7-inch, 15.3-pound steel I-beam, be at least 15 feet long, and shall not project more than 6 feet 6 inches beyond the bearing point.

(6) Where the overhang exceeds 6 feet 6 inches, outrigger beams shall be composed of stronger beams or multiple beams and be installed in accordance with approved designs and instructions.

(7) If channel iron outrigger beams are used in place of I-beams, they shall be securely fastened together with the flanges turned out.

(8) All outrigger beams shall be set and maintained with their webs into vertical position.

(9) A stop bolt shall be placed at each end of every outrigger beam.

(10) The outrigger beams shall rest on suitable wood-bearing blocks.

(11) All parts of the scaffold such as bolts, nuts, fittings, clamps, wire rope, and outrigger beams and their fastenings, shall be maintained in sound and good working condition and shall be inspected before each installation and periodically thereafter.

(12) The free end of the suspension wire ropes shall be equipped with proper size thimbles and be secured by splicing or other equivalent means. The running ends shall be securely attached to the hoisting drum and at least four turns of rope shall at all times remain on the drum.

(13) Where a single outrigger beam is used, the steel shackles or clevises with which the wire ropes are attached to the outrigger beams shall be placed directly over the hoisting drums.

(14) The scaffold platform shall be equivalent in strength to at least 2-inch planking. (For maximum planking spans see paragraph (a)(9) of this section.)

(15) Guardrails not less than 2 ×4 inches or the equivalent and not less than 36 inches or more than 42 inches high, with a mid-rail, when required, of 1 ×4-inch lumber or equivalent, and toeboards, shall be installed at all open sides on all scaffolds more than 10 feet above the ground or floor. Toeboards shall be a minimum of 4 inches in height. Wire mesh shall be installed in accordance with paragraph (a)(17) of this section.

(16) Overhead protection shall be provided on the scaffold, not more than 9 feet above the platform, consisting of 2-inch planking or material of equivalent strength laid tight, when men are at work on the scaffold and an overhead hazard exists.

(17) Each scaffold shall be installed or relocated in accordance with designs and instructions, of a registered professional engineer, and supervised by a competent, designated person.

(g) *Two-point suspension scaffolds (swinging scaffolds).* (1) Two-point suspension scaffold platforms shall be not less than 20 inches nor more than 36 inches wide overall. The platform shall be securely fastened to the hangers by U-bolts or by other equivalent means.

(2) The hangers of two-point suspension scaffolds shall be made of wrought iron, mild steel, or other equivalent material having a cross-sectional area capable of sustaining four times the maximum intended load, and shall be designed with a support for guardrail, intermediate rail, and toeboard.

(3) When hoisting machines are used on two-point suspension scaffolds, such machines shall be of a design tested and approved by a nationally recognized testing laboratory. Refer to §1910.7 for definition of nationally recognized testing laboratory.
[1910.28(g)(3) revised by 53 FR 12121, April 12, 1988]

(4) The roof irons or hooks shall be of wrought iron, mild steel, or other equivalent material of proper size and design, securely installed and anchored. Tie-backs of three-fourth inch manila rope or the equivalent shall serve as a secondary means of anchorage, installed at right angles to the face of the building whenever possible and

secured to a structurally sound portion of the building.

(5) Guardrails not less than 2 ×4 inches or the equivalent and not less than 36 inches or more than 42 inches high, with a mid-rail, when required, of 1-×4-inch lumber or equivalent, and toeboards, shall be installed at all open sides on all scaffolds more than 10 feet above the ground or floor. Toeboards shall be a minimum of 4 inches in height. Wire mesh shall be installed in accordance with paragraph (a)(17) of this section.

(6) Two-point suspension scaffolds shall be suspended by wire or fiber ropes. Wire and fiber ropes shall conform to paragraph (a)(22) of this section.

(7) The blocks for fiber ropes shall be of standard 6-inch size, consisting of at least one double and one single block. The sheaves of all blocks shall fit the size of rope used.

(8) All wire ropes, fiber ropes, slings, hangers, platforms, and other supporting parts shall be inspected before every installation. Periodic inspections shall be made while the scaffold is in use.

(9) On suspension scaffolds designed for a working load of 500 pounds no more than two men shall be permitted to work at one time. On suspension scaffolds with a working load of 750 pounds, no more than three men shall be permitted to work at one time. Each workman shall be protected by a safety lifebelt attached to a lifeline. The lifeline shall be securely attached to substantial members of the structure (not scaffold), or to securely rigged lines, which will safely suspend the workman in case of a fall.

(10) Where acid solutions are used, fiber ropes are not permitted unless acid-proof.

(11) Two-point suspension scaffolds shall be securely lashed to the building or structure to prevent them from swaying. Window cleaners' anchors shall not be used for this purpose.

(12) The platform of every two-point suspension scaffold shall be one of the following types:

(i) The side stringer of ladder-type platforms shall be clear straight-grained spruce or materials of equivalent strength and durability. The rungs shall be of straight-grained oak, ash, or hickory, at least 1 1/8 inch in diameter, with seven-eighth inch tenons mortised into the side stringers at least seven-eighth inch. The stringers shall be tied together with the tie rods not less than one-quarter inch in diameter, passing through the stringers and riveted up tight against washers on both ends. The flooring strips shall be spaced not more than five-eighth inch apart except at the side rails where the space may be 1 inch. Ladder-type platforms shall be constructed in accordance with table D-17.

(ii) Plank-type platforms shall be composed of not less than nominal 2-×8-inch unspliced planks, properly cleated together on the underside starting 6 inches from each end; intervals in between shall not exceed 4 feet. The plank-type platform shall not extend beyond the hangers more than 18 inches. A bar or other effective means shall be securely fastened to the platform at each end, to prevent its slipping off the hanger. The span between hangers for plank-type platforms shall not exceed 10 feet.

(iii) Beam platforms shall have side stringers of lumber not less than 2 ×6 inches set on edge. The span between hangers shall not exceed 12 feet when beam platforms are used. The flooring shall be supported on 2- and 6-inch crossbeams, laid flat and set into the upper edge of the stringers with a snug fit, at intervals of not more than 4 feet, securely nailed in place. The flooring shall be of 1-×6-inch material properly nailed. Floorboards shall not be spaced more than one-half inch apart.

TABLE D-17—SCHEDULE FOR LADDER-TYPE PLATFORMS

	Length of platform (feet)				
	12	14 & 16	18 & 20	22 & 24	28 & 30
Side stringers, minimum cross section (finished sizes):					
At ends (in.)	$1^3/_4 \times 2^3/_4$	$1^3/_4 \times 2^3/_4$	$1^3/_4 \times 3$	$1^3/_4 \times 3$	$1^3/_4 \times 3^1/_2$
At middle (in)	$1^3/_4 \times 3^3/_4$	$1^3/_4 \times 3^2/_4$	$1^3/_4 \times 4$	$1^3/_4 \times 4^3/_4$	$1^3/_4 \times 5$
Reinforcing strip (minimum)..........	A $^1/_8 \times ^7/_8$-in. steel reinforcing strip or its equivalent shall be attached to the side or underside full length.				
Rungs..............	Rungs shall be $1^1/_8$-in. minimum, diameter with at least $^7/_8$-in. diameter tenons, and the maximum spacing shall be 12 in. center to center.				
Tie rods:					
Number (minimum)	3	4	4	5	6
Diameter (minimum)	$^1/_4$in.	$^1/_4$in.	$^1/_4$in.	$^1/_4$in.	$^1/_4$in.
Flooring, minimum finished size (in.)	$^1/_2 \times 2^3/_4$	$^1/_2 \times 2^3/_4$	$^1/_2 \times 2^3/_4$	$^1/_2 \times 2^3/_4$	$^1/_2 \times 2\ ^3/_4$

(h) *Stone setters' adjustable multiple-point suspension scaffolds*(1) The scaffold shall be capable of sustaining a working load of 25 pounds per square foot and shall not be overloaded. Scaffolds shall not be used for storage of stone or other heavy materials.

(2) The hoisting machine and its supports shall be of a type tested and listed by a nationally recognized testing laboratory. Refer to §1910.399(a)(77) for definition of listed, and §1910.7 for nationally recognized testing laboratory.
[1910.28(h)(2) revised by 53 FR 12121, April 12, 1988]

(3) The platform shall be securely fastened to the hangers by U-bolts or other equivalent means.

(4) The scaffold unit shall be suspended from metal outriggers, iron brackets, wire rope slings, or iron hooks which will safely support the maximum intended load.

(5) Outriggers when used shall be set with their webs in a vertical position, securely anchored to the building or structure and provided with stop bolts at each end.

(6) The scaffold shall be supported by wire rope conforming with paragraph (a) (22) of this section, suspended from overhead supports.

(7) The free ends of the suspension wire ropes shall be equipped with proper size thimbles, secured by splicing or other equivalent means. The running ends shall be securely attached to the hoisting drum and at least four turns of

rope shall remain on the drum at all times.

(8) Guardrails not less than 2 by 4 inches or the equivalent and not less than 36 inches or more than 42 inches high, with a mid-rail, when required, of 1- by 4-inch lumber or equivalent, and toeboards, shall be installed at all open sides on all scaffolds more than 10 feet above the ground or floor. Toeboards shall be a minimum of 4 inches in height. Wire mesh shall be installed in accordance with paragraph (a)(17) of this section.

(9) When two or more scaffolds are used on a building or structure they shall not be bridged one to the other but shall be maintained at even height with platforms butting closely.

(10) Each scaffold shall be installed or relocated in accordance with designs and instructions of a registered professional engineer, and such installation or relocation shall be supervised by a competent designated person.

(i) *Single-point adjustable suspension scaffolds.*

(1) The scaffolding, including power units or manually operated winches, shall be a type tested and listed by a nationally recognized testing laboratory. Refer to §1910.399(a)(77) for definition of listed, and §1910.7 for nationally recognized testing laboratory. [1910.28(i)(1) revised by 53 FR 12121, April 12, 1988]

(2) [Revoked]

(3) All power-operated gears and brakes shall be enclosed.

(4) In addition to the normal operating brake, all-power driven units must have an emergency brake which engages automatically when the normal speed of descent is exceeded.

(5) Guards, mid-rails, and toeboards shall completely enclose the cage or basket. Guardrails shall be no less than 2 by 4 inches or the equivalent installed no less than 36 inches nor more than 42 inches above the platform. Mid-rails shall be 1 by 6 inches or the equivalent, installed equidistant between the

guardrail and the platform. Toeboards shall be a minimum of 4 inches in height.

(6) The hoisting machines, cables, and equipment shall be regularly serviced and inspected after each installation and every 30 days thereafter.

(7) The units may be combined to form a two-point suspension scaffold. Such scaffold shall comply with paragraph (g) of this section.

(8) The supporting cable shall be straight for its entire length, and the operator shall not sway the basket and fix the cable to any intermediate points to change his original path of travel.

(9) Equipment shall be maintained and used in accordance with the manufacturers' instructions.

(10) Suspension methods shall conform to applicable provisions of paragraphs (f) and (g) of this section.

(j) *Boatswain's chairs.* (1) The chair seat shall be not less than 12 by 24 inches, and of 1-inch thickness. The seat shall be reinforced on the underside to prevent the board from splitting.

(2) The two fiber rope seat slings shall be of 5/8-inch diameter, reeved through the four seat holes so as to cross each other on the underside of the seat.

(3) Seat slings shall be of at least 3/8-inch wire rope when a workman is conducting a heat producing process such as gas or arc welding.

(4) The workman shall be protected by a safety life belt attached to a lifeline. The lifeline shall be securely attached to substantial members of the structure (not scaffold), or to securely rigged lines, which will safely suspend the worker in case of a fall.

(5) The tackle shall consist of correct size ball bearing or bushed blocks and properly spliced 5/8-inch diameter first-grade manila rope.

(6) The roof irons, hooks, or the object to which the tackle is anchored shall be securely installed. Tiebacks when used shall be installed at right

angles to the face of the building and securely fastened to a chimney.

(k) *Carpenters' bracket scaffolds.*
(1) The brackets shall consist of a triangular wood frame not less than 2 by 3 inches in cross section, or of metal of equivalent strength. Each member shall be properly fitted and securely joined.

(2) Each bracket shall be attached to the structure by means of one of the following:

(i) A bolt no less than five-eighths inch in diameter which shall extend through the inside of the building wall.

(ii) A metal stud attachment device.

(iii) Welding to steel tanks.

(iv) Hooking over a well-secured and adequately strong supporting member. The brackets shall be spaced no more than 10 feet apart.

(3) No more than two persons shall occupy any given 10 feet of a bracket scaffold at any one time. Tools and materials shall not exceed 75 pounds in addition to the occupancy.

(4) The platform shall consist of not less than two 2- by 9-inch nominal size planks extending not more than 18 inches or less than 6 inches beyond each end support.

(5) Guardrails not less than 2 by 4 inches or the equivalent and not less than 36 inches or more than 42 inches high, with a mid-rail, when required, of 1- by 4-inch lumber or equivalent, and toeboards, shall be installed at all open sides on all scaffolds more than 10 feet above the ground or floor. Toeboards shall be a minimum of 4 inches in height. Wire mesh shall be installed in accordance with paragraph (a)(17) of this section.

(1) *Bricklayers' square scaffolds.*
(1) The squares shall not exceed 5 feet in width and 5 feet in height.

(2) Members shall be not less than those specified in Table D-18.

(3) The squares shall be reinforced on both sides of each corner with 1- by 6-inch gusset pieces. They shall also have braces 1 by 8 inches on both sides running from center to center of each

member, or other means to secure equivalent strength and rigidity.

(4) The squares shall be set not more than 5 feet apart for medium duty scaffolds, and not more than 8 feet apart for light duty scaffolds. Bracing 1 × 8 inches, extending from the bottom of each square to the top of the next square, shall be provided on both front and rear sides of the scaffold.

TABLE D-18 —MINIMUM DIMENSIONS FOR BRICKLAYERS' SQUARE SCAFFOLD MEMBERS

Members:	Dimensions (inches)
Bearers or horizontal members	2 by 6.
Legs	2 by 6.
Braces at corners	1 by 6.
Braces diagonally from center frame	1 by 8.

(5) Platform planks shall be at least 2- by 9-inch nominal size. The ends of the planks shall overlap the bearers of the squares and each plank shall be supported by not less than three squares.

(6) Bricklayers' square scaffolds shall not exceed three tiers in height and shall be so constructed and arranged that one square shall rest directly above the other. The upper tiers shall stand on a continuous row of planks laid across the next lower tier and be nailed down or otherwise secured to prevent displacement.

(7) Scaffolds shall be level and set upon a firm foundation.

(m) *Horse scaffolds.*
(1) Horse scaffolds shall not be constructed or arranged more than two tiers or 10 feet in height.

(2) The members of the horses shall be not less than those specified in Table D-19.

(3) Horses shall be spaced not more than 5 feet for medium duty and not more than 8 feet for light duty.

(4) When arranged in tiers, each horse shall be placed directly over the horse in the tier below.

(5) On all scaffolds arranged in tiers, the legs shall be nailed down to the planks to prevent displacement or thrust and each tier shall be substantially cross braced.

TABLE D-19—MINIMUM DIMENSIONS FOR HORSE SCAFFOLD MEMBERS

Members:	Dimensions (inches)
Horizontal members or bearers	3 by 4.
Legs...........................	$1\frac{1}{4}$ by $4\frac{1}{2}$/
Longitudinal brace between legs...........	1 by 6.
Gusset brace at top of legs....................	1 by 8.
Half diagonal braces	$1\frac{1}{4}$ by $4\frac{1}{2}$.

(6) Horses or parts which have become weak or defective shall not be used.

(7) Guardrails not less than 2 by 4 inches or the equivalent and not less than 36 inches or more than 42 inches high with a mid-rail, when required, of 1- by 4-inch lumber or equivalent and toeboards, shall be installed at all open sides on all scaffolds more than 10 feet above the ground or floor. Toeboards shall be a minimum of 4 inches in height. Wire mesh shall be installed in accordance with paragraph (a)(17) of this section.

(n) *Needle beam scaffold.* (1) Wood needle beams shall be in accordance with paragraph (a) (5) and (9) of this section, and shall be not less than 4 by 6 inches in size, with the greater dimension placed in a vertical direction. Metal beams or the equivalent conforming to paragraph (a) (4) and (8) of this section may be used.

(2) Ropes or hangers shall be provided for supports. The span between supports on the needle beam shall not exceed 10 feet for 4- by 6-inch timbers. Rope supports shall be equivalent in strength to 1-inch diameter first-grade manila rope.

(3) The ropes shall be attached to the needle beams by a scaffold hitch or a properly made eye splice. The loose end of the rope shall be tied by a bowline knot or by a round turn and one-half hitch.

(4) The platform span between the needle beams shall not exceed 8 feet when using 2-inch scaffold plank. For spans greater than 8 feet, platforms shall be designed based on design requirements for the special span. The overhang of each end of the platform planks shall be not less than 1 foot and not more than 18 inches.

(5) When one needle beam is higher than the other or when the platform is not level the platform shall be secured against slipping.

(6) All unattached tools, bolts, and nuts used on needle beam scaffolds shall be kept in suitable containers.

(7) One end of a needle beam scaffold may be supported by a permanent structural member conforming to paragraph (a) (4) and (8) of this section.

(8) Each man working on a needle beam scaffold 20 feet or more above the ground or floor and working with both hands, shall be protected by a safety life belt attached to a lifeline. The lifeline shall be securely attached to substantial members of the structure (not scaffold), or to securely rigged lines, which will safely suspend the workman in case of a fall.

(o) *Plasterers, decorators, and large area scaffolds.* (1) Plasterers', decorators' lathers', and ceiling workers' inside scaffolds shall be constructed in accordance with the general requirements set forth for independent wood pole scaffolds.

(2) Guardrails not less than 2 by 4 inches or the equivalent and not less than 36 inches or more than 42 inches high, with a mid-rail, when required, of 1- by 4-inch lumber or equivalent, and toeboards, shall be installed at all open sides on all scaffolds more than 10 feet above the ground or floor. Toeboards shall be a minimum of 4 inches in height. Wire mesh shall be installed in accordance with paragraph (a)(17) of this section.

(3) All platform planks shall be laid with the edges close together.

(4) When independent pole scaffold platforms are erected in sections, such sections shall be provided with connecting runways equipped with substantial guardrails.

(p) *Interior hung scaffolds.*

(1) [Removed]

[Sec. 1910.28(p)(1) deleted by 49 FR 5321, February 10, 1984]

(2) The suspended steel wire rope shall conform to paragraph (a)(22) of this section. Wire may be used providing the strength requirements of paragraph (a)(22) of this section are met.

(3) For hanging wood scaffolds, the following minimum nominal size material is recommended:

(i) Supporting bearers 2 by 9 inches on edge.

(ii) Planking 2 by 9 inches or 2 by 10 inches, with maximum span 7 feet for heavy duty and 10 feet for light duty or medium duty.

(4) Steel tube and coupler members may be used for hanging scaffolds with both types of scaffold designed to sustain a uniform distributed working load up to heavy duty scaffold loads with a safety factor of four.

(5) When a hanging scaffold is supported by means of wire rope, such wire rope shall be wrapped at least twice around the supporting members and twice around the bearers of the scaffold, with each end of the wire rope secured by at least three standard wire-rope clips.

(6) All overhead supporting members shall be inspected and checked for strength before the scaffold is erected.

(7) Guardrails not less than 2 by 4 inches or the equivalent and not less than 36 inches or more than 42 inches high, with a mid-rail, when required, of 1- by 4-inch lumber or equivalent, and toeboards, shall be installed at all open sides on all scaffolds more than 10 feet above the ground or floor. Toeboards shall be a minimum of 4 inches in height. Wire mesh shall be installed in accordance with paragraph (a) (17) of this section.

(q) *Ladder-jack scaffolds.* (1) All ladder-jack scaffolds shall be limited to light duty and shall not exceed a height of 20 feet above the floor or ground.

(2) All ladders used in connection with ladder-jack scaffolds shall be heavy-duty ladders and shall be designed and constructed in accordance with §1910.25 and §1910.26.

(3) The ladder jack shall be so designed and constructed that it will bear on the side rails in addition to the ladder rungs, or if bearing on rungs only the bearing area shall be at least 10 inches on each rung.

(4) Ladders used in conjunction with ladder jacks shall be so placed, fastened, held, or equipped with devices so as to prevent slipping.

(5) The wood platform planks shall be not less than 2 inches nominal in thickness. Both metal and wood platform planks shall overlap the bearing surface not less than 12 inches. The span between supports for wood shall not exceed 8 feet. Platform width shall be not less than 18 inches.

(6) Not more than two persons shall occupy any given 8 feet of any ladder-jack scaffold at any one time.

(r) *Window-jack scaffolds.* (1) Window-jack scaffolds shall be used only for the purpose of working at the window opening through which the jack is placed.

(2) Window jacks shall not be used to support planks placed between one window jack and another or for other elements of scaffolding.

(3) Window-jack scaffolds shall be provided with suitable guardrails unless safety belts with lifelines are attached and provided for the workman. Window-jack scaffolds shall be used by one man only.

(s) *Roofing brackets.* (1) Roofing brackets shall be constructed to fit the pitch of the roof.

(2) Brackets shall be secured in place by nailing in addition to the pointed metal projections. The nails

shall be driven full length into the roof. When rope supports are used, they shall consist of first-grade manila of at least three-quarter-inch diameter, or equivalent.

(3) A substantial catch platform shall be installed below the working area of roofs more than 20 feet from the ground to eaves with a slope greater than 3 inches in 12 inches without a parapet. In width the platform shall extend 2 feet beyond the projection of the eaves and shall be provided with a safety rail, mid-rail, and toeboard. This provision shall not apply where employees engaged in work upon such roofs are protected by a safety belt attached to a lifeline.

(t) *Crawling boards or chicken ladders.* (1) Crawling boards shall be not less than 10 inches wide and 1 inch thick, having cleats 1 ×1 1/2 inches. The cleats shall be equal in length to the width of the board and spaced at equal intervals not to exceed 24 inches. Nails shall be driven through and clinched on the underside. The crawling board shall extend from the ridge pole to the eaves when used in connection with roof construction, repair, or maintenance.

(2) A firmly fastened lifeline of at least three-quarter-inch rope shall be strung beside each crawling board for a handhold.

(3) Crawling boards shall be secured to the roof by means of adequate ridge hooks or equivalent effective means.

(u) *Float or ship scaffolds.* (1) Float or ship scaffolds shall support not more than three men and a few light tools, such as those needed for riveting, bolting, and welding. They shall be constructed in accordance with paragraphs (u)(2) through (6) of this section, unless substitute designs and materials provide equivalent strength, stability, and safety.

(2) The platform shall be not less than 3 feet wide and 6 feet long, made of three-quarter-inch plywood, equiva-

lent to American Plywood Association Grade B —B, Group I, Exterior.

(3) Under the platform, there shall be two supporting bearers made from 2- × 4-inch, or 1- × 10-inch rough, selected lumber, or better. They shall be free of knots or other flaws and project 6 inches beyond the platform on both sides. The ends of the platform shall extend about 6 inches beyond the outer edges of the bearers. Each bearer shall be securely fastened to the platform.

(4) An edging of wood not less than 3/4 × 1 1/2 inches, or equivalent, shall be placed around all sides of the platform to prevent tools from rolling off.

(5) Supporting ropes shall be 1-inch diameter manila rope or equivalent, free from deterioration, chemical damage, flaws, or other imperfections. Rope connections shall be such that the platform cannot shift or slip. If two ropes are used with each float, each of the two supporting ropes shall be hitched around one end of a bearer and pass under the platforms to the other end of the bearer where it is hitched again, leaving sufficient rope at each end for the supporting ties.

[Sec. 1910.29(u)(5) amended by 49 FR 5321, February 10, 1984]

(6) Each workman shall be protected by a safety lifebelt attached to a lifeline. The lifeline shall be securely attached to substantial members of the structure (not scaffold), or to securely rigged lines, which will safely suspend the workman in case of a fall.

(v) *Scope.* This section establishes safety requirements for the construction, operation, maintenance, and use of scaffolds used in the maintenance of buildings and structures.

[Section 1910.28(i)(2) revoked and Section 1910.28(v) amended at 43 FR 49726, October 24, 1978, effective November 24, 1978]

§1910.29 Manually propelled mobile ladder stands and scaffolds (towers).

(a) *General requirements—(1) Application.* This section is intended to prescribe rules and requirements for the design, construction, and use of mobile work platforms (including ladder stands but not including aerial ladders) and rolling (mobile) scaffolds (towers). This standard is promulgated to aid in providing for the safety of life, limb, and property, by establishing minimum standards for structural design requirements and for the use of mobile work platforms and towers.

(2) *Working loads.* (i) Work platforms and scaffolds shall be capable of carrying the design load under varying circumstances depending upon the conditions of use. Therefore, all parts and appurtenances necessary for their safe and efficient utilization must be integral parts of the design.

(ii) Specific design and construction requirements are not a part of this section because of the wide variety of materials and design possibilities. However, the design shall be such as to produce a mobile ladder stand or scaffold that will safely sustain the specified loads. The material selected shall be of sufficient strength to meet the test requirements and shall be protected against corrosion or deterioration.

(a) The design working load of ladder stands shall be calculated on the basis of one or more 200-pound persons together with 50 pounds of equipment each.

(b) The design load of all scaffolds shall be calculated on the basis of:

Light—Designed and constructed to carry a working load of 25 pounds per square foot.

Medium—Designed and constructed to carry a working load of 50 pounds per square foot.

Heavy—Designed and constructed to carry a working load of 75 pounds per square foot.

All ladder stands and scaffolds shall be capable of supporting at least four times the design working load.

(iii) The materials used in mobile ladder stands and scaffolds shall be of standard manufacture and conform to standard specifications of strength, dimensions, and weights, and shall be selected to safely support the design working load.

(iv) Nails, bolts, or other fasteners used in the construction of ladders, scaffolds and towers shall be of adequate size and in sufficient numbers at each connection to develop the designed strength of the unit. Nails shall be driven full length. (All nails should be immediately withdrawn from dismantled lumber.)

(v) All exposed surfaces shall be free from sharp edges, burrs or other safety hazards.

(3) *Work levels.* (i) The maximum work level height shall not exceed four (4) times the minimum or least base dimension of any mobile ladder stand or scaffold. Where the basic mobile unit does not meet this requirement, suitable out-rigger frames shall be employed to achieve this least base dimension, or provisions shall be made to guy or brace the unit against tipping.

(ii) The minimum platform width for any work level shall not be less than 20 inches for mobile scaffolds (towers). Ladder stands shall have a minimum step width of 16 inches.

(iii) The supporting structure for the work level shall be rigidly braced, using adequate cross bracing or diagonal bracing with rigid platforms at each work level.

(iv) The steps of ladder stands shall be fabricated from slip resistant treads.

(v) The work level platform of scaffolds (towers) shall be of wood, aluminum, or plywood planking, steel or expanded metal, for the full width of the scaffold, except for necessary openings. Work platforms shall be secured in place. All planking shall be 2-inch (nominal) scaffold grade minimum 1,500

f. (stress grade) construction grade lumber or equivalent.

(vi) All scaffold work levels 10 feet or higher above the ground or floor shall have a standard (4-inch nominal) toeboard.

(vii) All work levels 10 feet or higher above the ground or floor shall have a guardrail of 2- by 4-inch nominal or the equivalent installed no less than 36 inches or more than 42 inches high, with a mid-rail, when required, of 1- by 4-inch nominal lumber or equivalent.

(viii) A climbing ladder or stairway shall be provided for proper access and egress, and shall be affixed or built into the scaffold and so located that its use will not have a tendency to tip the scaffold. A landing platform shall be provided at intervals not to exceed 30 feet.

(4) *Wheels or casters.* (i) Wheels or casters shall be properly designed for strength and dimensions to support four (4) times the design working load.

(ii) All scaffold casters shall be provided with a positive wheel and/or swivel lock to prevent movement. Ladder stands shall have at least two (2) of the four (4) casters and shall be of the swivel type.

(iii) Where leveling of the elevated work platform is required, screw jacks or other suitable means for adjusting the height shall be provided in the base section of each mobile unit.

(b) *Mobile tubular welded frame scaffolds—(1) General.* Units shall be designed to comply with the requirements of paragraph (a) of this section.

(2) *Bracing.* Scaffolds shall be properly braced by cross braces and/or diagonal braces for securing vertical members together laterally. The cross braces shall be of a length that will automatically square and align vertical members so the erected scaffold is always plumb, square, and rigid.

(3) *Spacing.* Spacing of panels or frames shall be consistent with the loads imposed. The frames shall be placed one on top of the other with cou-

pling or stacking pins to provide proper vertical alignment of the legs.

(4) *Locking.* Where uplift may occur, panels shall be locked together vertically by pins or other equivalent means.

(5) *Erection.* Only the manufacturer of a scaffold or his qualified designated agent shall be permitted to erect or supervise the erection of scaffolds exceeding 50 feet in height above the base, unless such structure is approved in writing by a registered professional engineer, or erected in accordance with instructions furnished by the manufacturer.

(c) *Mobile tubular welded sectional folding scaffolds—(1) General.* Units including sectional stairway and sectional ladder scaffolds shall be designed to comply with the requirements of paragraph (a) of this section.

(2) *Stairway.* An integral stairway and work platform shall be incorporated into the structure of each sectional folding stairway scaffold.

(3) *Bracing.* An integral set of pivoting and hinged folding diagonal and horizontal braces and a detachable work platform shall be incorporated into the structure of each sectional folding ladder scaffold.

(4) *Sectional folding stairway scaffolds.* Sectional folding stairway scaffolds shall be designed as medium duty scaffolds except for high clearance. These special base sections shall be designed as light duty scaffolds. When upper sectional folding stairway scaffolds are used with a special high clearance base, the load capacity of the entire scaffold shall be reduced accordingly. The width of a sectional folding stairway scaffold shall not exceed 4 1/2 feet. The maximum length of a sectional folding stairway scaffold shall not exceed 6 feet.

(5) *Sectional folding ladder scaffolds.* Sectional folding ladder scaffolds shall be designed as light duty scaffolds including special base (open end) sections which are designed for high clear-

ance. For certain special applications the six-foot (6') folding ladder scaffolds, except for special high clearance base sections, shall be designed for use as medium duty scaffolds. The width of a sectional folding ladder scaffold shall not exceed 4 ½ feet. The maximum length of a sectional folding ladder scaffold shall not exceed 6 feet 6 inches for a six-foot (6') long unit, 8 feet 6 inches for an eight-foot (8') unit or 10 feet 6 inches for a ten-foot (10') long unit.

(6) *End frames.* The end frames of sectional ladder and stairway scaffolds shall be designed so that the horizontal bearers provide supports for multiple planking levels.

(7) *Erection.* Only the manufacturer of the scaffold or his qualified designated agent shall be permitted to erect or supervise the erection of scaffolds exceeding 50 feet in height above the base, unless such structure is approved in writing by a licensed professional engineer, or erected in accordance with instructions furnished by the manufacturer.

(d) *Mobile tube and coupler scaffolds—(1) Design.* Units shall be designed to comply with the applicable requirements of paragraph (a) of this section.

(2) *Material.* The material used for the couplers shall be of a structural type, such as a drop-forged steel, malleable iron or structural grade aluminum. The use of gray cast iron is prohibited.

(3) *Erection.* Only the manufacturer of the scaffold or his qualified designated agent shall be permitted to erect or supervise the erection of scaffolds exceeding 50 feet in height above the base, unless such structure is approved in writing by a licensed professional engineer, or erected in accordance with instructions furnished by the manufacturer.

(e) *Mobile work platforms—(1) Design.* Units shall be designed for the use intended and shall comply with the re-

quirements of paragraph (a) of this section.

(2) *Base width.* The minimum width of the base of mobile work platforms shall not be less than 20 inches.

(3) *Bracing.* Adequate rigid diagonal bracing to vertical members shall be provided.

(f) *Mobile ladder stands.*

(1) *Design.* Units shall comply with applicable requirements of paragraph (a) of this section.

(2) *Base width.* The minimum base width shall conform to paragraph (a) (3) (i) of this section. The maximum length of the base section shall be the total length of combined steps and top assembly, measured horizontally, plus five-eighths inch per step of rise.

(3) *Steps.* Steps shall be uniformly spaced, and sloped, with a rise of not less than nine (9) inches, nor more than ten (10) inches, and a depth of not less seven (7) inches. The slope of the steps section shall be a minimum of fifty-five (55) degrees and a maximum of sixty (60) degrees measured from the horizontal.

(4) *Handrails.* (i) Units having more than five (5) steps or 60 inches vertical height to the top step shall be equipped with handrails.

(ii) Handrails shall be a minimum of 29 inches high. Measurements shall be taken vertically from the center of the step.

(5) *Loading.* The load (see paragraph (a) (2) (ii) (a) of this section) shall be applied uniformly to a 3 ½ inches wide area front to back at the center of the width span with a safety factor of four (4).

§1910.30 Other working surfaces.

(a) *Dockboards (bridge plates)* (1) Portable and powered dockboards shall be strong enough to carry the load imposed on them.

(2) Portable dockboards shall be secured in position, either by being anchored or equipped with devices which will prevent their slipping.

(3) Powered dockboards shall be designed and constructed in accordance with Commercial Standard CS202-56 (1961) "Industrial Lifts and Hinged Loading Ramps published by the U.S. Department of Commerce.

(4) Handholds, or other effective means, shall be provided on portable dockboards to permit safe handling.

(5) Positive protection shall be provided to prevent railroad cars from being moved while dockboards or bridge plates are in position.

(b) *Forging machine area.* (1) Machines shall be so located as to give (i) enough clearance between machines so that the movement of one operator will not interfere with the work of another, (ii) ample room for cleaning machines and handling the work, including material and scrap. The arrangement of machines shall be such that operators will not stand in aisles.

(2) Aisles shall be provided of sufficient width to permit the free movement of employees bringing and removing material. This aisle space is to be independent of working and storage space.

[Sec. 1910.30(b)(2) amended by 49 FR 5321, February 10, 1984]

(3) Wood platforms used on the floor in front of machines shall be substantially constructed.

(c) *Veneer machinery.* (1) Sides of steam vats shall extend to a height of not less than 36 inches above the floor, working platform, or ground.

(2) Large steam vats divided into sections shall be provided with substantial walkways between sections. Each walkway shall be provided with a standard handrail on each exposed side. These handrails may be removable, if necessary.

(3) Covers shall be removed only from that portion of steaming vats on which men are working and a portable railing shall be placed at this point to protect the operators.

(4) Workmen shall not ride or step on logs in steam vats.

§**1910.31 Sources of standards**.

The standards in this Subpart D are devised from the following sources:

Standard	Source
§1910.22(a)..........	ANSI Z4.1-1968, Requirements for Sanitation in Places of Employment.
§1910.22(b) and	41 CFR 50-204.3.
§1910.22(d)	ANSI A58.1-1955, Minimum Design Loads in Building and Other Structures.
§1910.23...............	ANSI A12.1-1967, Safety Requirements for Floor and Wall Openings, Railings, and Toeboards.
§1910.24...............	ANSI A64.1-1968, Requirements for Fixed Industrial Stairs.
§1910.25...............	ANSI A14.1-1968, Safety Code for Portable Wood Ladders.
§1910.26...............	ANSI A14.2-1956, Portable Metal Ladders.
§1910.27...............	ANSI A14.3-1956, Safety Code for Fixed Ladders.
§1910.28...............	ANSI A10.8-1969, Safety Requirements for Scaffolding.
§1910.29...............	ANSI A92.1-1971, Standard for Manually Propelled Mobile Ladder Stands and Scaffolds.

Standard	Source
§1910.30(a)..........	ANSI B56.1-1969, Safety Standard for Powered Industrial Trucks.
§1910.30(b)	ANSI B24.1-1963, Safety Standard for Forging.
§1910.30(c)..........	ANSI 01.1-1954 (R-1961), Safety Code for Woodworking Machinery.

[Section 1910.31 amended at 39 FR 19468, June 3, 1974]

§1910.32 Standards organizations.

The following organizations have been referenced in this Subpart D:

American National Standards Institute, 1430 Broadway, New York, NY 10018.

Underwriters' Laboratories, Inc., 207 East Ohio Street, Chicago, IL 60611.

Factory Mutual Engineering Corp., Post Office Box 688, Norwood, MA 02062.

Appendix C

HAZARD COMMUNICATION STANDARD (PERFORMANCE STANDARD)

OSHA PERFORMANCE STANDARD (EXAMPLE)

Editor's Note: This OSHA standard, which requires employers to notify employees of the identities and hazards of chemicals with which they work, is an example of a *performance standard* that requires employers to protect workers from a particular workplace hazard, but gives the employer a measure of flexibility in meeting this requirement (for example, in developing a training program designed to meet the needs of a particular group of employees).

OCCUPATIONAL SAFETY AND HEALTH STANDARDS SUBPART Z—TOXIC AND HAZARDOUS SUBSTANCES HAZARD COMMUNICATION STANDARD

(Code of Federal Regulations, Title 29, Chapter XVII, Part 1910, Subpart Z, Section 1910.1200; Issued by 48 FR 53280, November 25, 1983; amended and corrected by 50 FR 48758, November 27, 1985; amended by 51 FR 345297, September 30, 1986; revised by 52 FR 31877, August 24, 1987)

Authority: Section 1910.1200 issued under 5 U.S.C. 553.

§1910.1200 Hazard communication.

(a) *Purpose.* (1) The purpose of this section is to ensure that the hazards of all chemicals produced or imported are evaluated, and that information concerning their hazards is transmitted to employers and employees. This transmittal of information is to be accomplished by means of comprehensive hazard communication programs, which are to include container labeling and other forms of warning, material safety data sheets and employee training.

(2) This occupational safety and health standard is intended to address comprehensively the issue of evaluating the potential hazards of chemicals, and communicating information concerning hazards and appropriate protective measures to employees, and to preempt any legal requirements of a state, or political subdivision of a state, pertaining to the subject. Evaluating the potential hazards of chemicals, and communicating information concerning hazards and appropriate protective measures to employees, may include, for example, but is not limited to, provisions for: developing and maintaining a written hazard communication program for the workplace, including lists of hazardous chemicals present; labeling of containers of chemicals in the workplace, as well as of containers of chemicals being shipped to other workplaces; preparation and distribution of material safety data sheets to employees and downstream employers; and development and implementation of employee training programs regarding hazards of chemicals and protective measures. Under section 18 of the Act, no state or political subdivision of a state may adopt or enforce, through any court or agency, any requirement relating to the issue addressed by this Federal standard, except pursuant to a Federally-approved state plan.

(b) *Scope and application.* (1) This section requires chemical manufacturers or importers to assess the hazards

216

of chemicals which they produce or import, and all employers to provide information to their employees about the hazardous chemicals to which they are exposed, by means of a hazard communication program, labels and other forms of warning, material safety, data sheets, and information and training. In addition, this section requires distributors to transmit the required information to employers.

(2) This section applies to any chemical which is known to be present in the workplace in such a manner that employees may be exposed under normal conditions of use or in a foreseeable emergency.

(3) This section applies to laboratories only as follows:

(i) Employers shall ensure that labels on incoming containers of hazardous chemicals are not removed or defaced.

(ii) Employers shall maintain any material safety data sheets that are received with incoming shipments of hazardous chemicals, and ensure that they are readily accessible to laboratory employees; and,

(iii) Employers shall ensure that laboratory employees are apprised of the hazards of the chemicals in their workplaces in accordance with paragraph (h) of this section.

(4) In work operations where employees only handle chemicals in sealed containers which are not opened under normal conditions of use (such as are found in marine cargo handling, warehousing, or retail sales), this section applies to these operations only as follows:

(i) Employers shall ensure that labels on incoming containers of hazardous chemicals are not removed or defaced;

(ii) Employers shall maintain copies of any material safety data sheets that are received with incoming shipments of the sealed containers of hazardous chemicals, shall obtain a material safety data sheet for sealed containers of hazardous chemicals received without a material safety data sheet if an em-

ployee requests the material safety data sheet, and shall ensure that the material safety data sheets are readily accessible during each work shift to employees when they are in their work area(s); and,

(iii) Employers shall ensure that employees are provided with information and training in accordance with paragraph (h) of this section (except for the location and availability of the written hazard communication program under paragraph (h)(1)(iii)), to the extent necessary to protect them in the event of a spill or leak of a hazardous chemical from a sealed container.

(5) This section does not require labeling of the following chemicals:

(i) Any pesticide as such term is defined in the Federal Insecticide, Fungicide, and Rodenticide Act (7 U.S.C. 136 et seq.), when subject to the labeling requirements of that Act and labeling regulations issued under that Act by the Environmental Protection Agency:

(ii) Any food, food additive, color additive, drug, cosmetic, or medical or veterinary device, including materials intended for use as ingredients in such products (e.g. flavors and fragrances), as such terms are defined in the Federal Food, Drug, and Cosmetic Act (21 U.S.C. 301 et seq.) and regulations issued under that Act, when they are subject to the labeling requirements under that Act by the Food and Drug Administration;

(iii) Any distilled spirits (beverage alcohols), wine, or malt beverage intended for nonindustrial use, as such terms are defined in the Federal Alcohol Administration Act (27 U.S.C. 201 et seq.) and regulations issued under that Act, when subject to the labeling requirements of that Act and labeling regulations issued under that Act by the Bureau of Alcohol Tobacco, and Firearms; and,

(iv) Any consumer product or hazardous substance as those terms are defined in the Consumer Product Safety Act (15 U.S.C. 2051 et seq.) and Fed-

217

eral Hazardous Substances Act (15 U.S.C. 1261 et seq.) respectively, when subject to a consumer product safety standard or labeling requirement of those Acts, or regulations issued under those Acts by the Consumer Product Safety Commission.

(6) This section does not apply to

(i) Any hazardous waste as such term is defined by the Solid Waste Disposal Act, as amended by the Resource Conservation and Recovery Act of 1976, as amended (42 U.S.C. 6901 et seq.), when subject to regulations issued under that Act by the Environmental Protection Agency;

(ii) Tobacco or tobacco products;

(iii) Wood or wood products;

(iv) Articles;

(v) Food, drugs, cosmetics, or alcoholic beverages in a retail establishment which are packaged for sale to consumers;

(vi) Foods, drugs, or cosmetics intended for personal consumption by employees while in the workplace;

(vii) Any consumer product or hazardous substance, as those terms are defined in the Consumer Product Safety Act (15 U.S.C. 2051 *et seq.*) and Federal Hazardous Substances Act (15 U.S.C. 1261 *et seq.*) respectively, where the employer can demonstrate it is used in the workplace in the same manner as normal consumer use, and which use results in a duration and frequency of exposure which is not greater than exposures experienced by consumers; and.

(viii) Any drug, as that term is defined in the Federal Food, Drug, and Cosmetic Act (21 U.S.C. 301 *et seq.*), when it is in solid, final form for direct administration to the patient (i.e. tablets or pills).

(c) *Definitions.*

"Article" means a manufactured item: (i)Which is formed to a specific shape or design during manufacture; (ii) which has end use function(s) dependent in whole or in part upon its shape or design during end use; and (ii)

which does not release, or otherwise result in exposure to, a hazardous chemical, under normal conditions of use.

"Assistant Secretary" means the Assistant Secretary of Labor for Occupational Safety and Health. U.S. Department of Labor, or designee.

"Chemical" means any element, chemical compound or mixture of elements and/or compounds.

"Chemical manufacturer" means an employer with a workplace where chemical(s) are produced for use or distribution.

"Chemical name" means the scientific designation of a chemical in accordance with the nomenclature system developed by the International Union of Pure and Applied Chemistry (IUPAC) or the Chemical Abstracts Service (CAS) rules of nomenclature, or a name which will clearly identify the chemical for the purpose of conducting a hazard evaluation.

"Combustible liquid" means any liquid having a flashpoint at or above 100 °F (37.8°C) but below 200°F (93.3 °C), except any mixture having components with flashpoints of 200 °F (93.3 °C), or higher, the total volume of which make up 99 percent or more of the total volume of the mixture.

"Common name" means any designation or identification such as code name, code number, trade name, brand name or generic name used to identify a chemical other than by its chemical name.

"Compressed gas" means:

(i) A gas or mixture of gases having in a container, an absolute pressure exceeding 40 psi at 70°F (21.1°C); or

(ii) a gas or mixture of gases having, in a container, an absolute pressure exceeding 104 psi at 130°F (54.4 °C) regardless of the pressure at 70°F (21.1°C); or

(iii) A liquid having a vapor pressure exceeding 40 psi at 100 °F (37.8°C) as determined by ASTM D-323–72.

"Container" means any bag, barrel, bottle, box, can, cylinder, drum, reaction vessel, storage tank, or the like that contains a hazardous chemical. For purposes of this section, pipes or piping systems, and engines, fuel tanks, or other operating systems in a vehicle are not considered to be containers.

"Designated representative" means any individual or organization to whom an employee gives written authorization to exercise such employee's rights under this section. A recognized or certified collective bargaining agent shall be treated automatically as a designated representative without regard to written employee authorization.

"Director" means the Director, National Institute for Occupational Safety and Health. U.S. Department of Health and Human Services or designee.

"Distributor" means a business, other than a chemical manufacturer or importer which supplies hazardous chemicals to other distributors or to employers.

"Employee" means a worker who may be exposed to hazardous chemicals under normal operating conditions or in foreseeable emergencies. Workers such as office workers or bank tellers who encounter hazardous chemicals only in non-routine, isolated instances are not covered.

"Employer" means a person engaged in a business where chemicals are either used, distributed, or are produced for use or distribution, including a contractor or subcontractor.

"Explosive" means a chemical that causes a sudden, almost instantaneous release of pressure, gas, and heat when subjected to sudden shock, pressure, or high temperature.

"Exposure" or "exposed" means that an employee is subjected to a hazardous chemical in the course of employment through any route of entry (inhalation, ingestion, skin contact or absorption, etc.), and includes potential (e.g. accidental or possible) exposure.

"Flammable" means a chemical that falls into one of the following categories:

(i) "Aerosol, flammable" means an aerosol that, when tested by the method described in 16 CFR 1500.45, yields a flame projection exceeding 18 inches at full value opening, or a flashback (a flame extending back to the valve) at any degree of valve opening;

(ii) "Gas, flammable" means:

(A) A gas that, at ambient temperature and pressure, forms a flammable mixture with air at a concentration of thirteen (13) percent by volume or less; or

(B) A gas that, at ambient temperature and pressure, forms a range of flammable mixtures with air wider than twelve (12) percent by volume, regardless of the lower limit;

(iii) "Liquid, flammable" means any liquid having a flashpoint below 100 °F (37.8 °C), except any mixture having components with flashpoints of 100 °F (37.8 °C) or higher, the total of which make up 99 percent or more of the total volume of the mixture;

(iv) "Solid, flammable" means a solid, other than a blasting agent or explosive as defined in §190.109(a), that is liable to cause fire through friction, absorption of moisture, spontaneous chemical change, or retained heat from manufacturing or processing, or which can be ignited readily and when ignited burns so vigorously and persistently as to create a serious hazard. A chemical shall be considered to be a flammable solid if, when tested by the method described in 16 CFR 1500.44, it ignites and burns with a self-sustained flame at a rate greater than one-tenth of an inch per second along its major axis.

"Flashpoint" means the minimum temperature at which a liquid gives off a vapor in sufficient concentration to ignite when tested as follows:

(i) Tagliabue Closed Tester (See American National Standard Method of Test for Flash Point by Tag Closed Tester, Z11.24–1979 (ASTM D 56 –79)) for liquids with a viscosity of less than 45 Saybolt University Seconds (SUS) at 100°F (37.8 °C), that do not contain suspended solids and do not have a tendency to form a surface film under test; or

(ii) Pensky-Martens Closed Tester (See American National Standard Method of Test for Flash Point by Pensky-Martens Closed Tester, Z11.7–1979 (ASTM D 93 –79)) for liquids with a viscosity equal to or greater than 45 SUS at 100 °F (37.8 °C), or that contain suspended solids, or that have a tendency to form a surface film under test; or

(iii) Setaflash Closed Tester (see American National Standard Method of Test for Flash Point by Setaflash Closed Tester (ASTMD 3278–78)).

Organic peroxides, which undergo autoaccelerating thermal decomposition, are excluded from any of the flashpoint determination methods specified above.

"Foreseeable emergency" means any potential occurrence such as, but not limited to, equipment failure, rupture of containers, or failure of control equipment which could result in an uncontrolled release of a hazardous chemical into the workplace.

"Hazardous chemical" means any chemical which is a physical hazard or a health hazard.

"Hazard warning" means any words, pictures, symbols, or combination thereof appearing on a label or other appropriate form of warning which convey the hazard(s) of the chemical(s) in the container(s).

"Health hazard" means a chemical for which there is statistically significant evidence based on at least one study conducted in accordance with established scientific principles that acute or chronic health effects may occur in exposed employees. The term "health hazard" includes chemicals which are carcinogens, toxic or highly toxic agents, reproductive toxins, irritants, corrosives, sensitizers, hepatotoxins, nephrotoxins, neurotoxins, agents which act on the hematopoietic system, and agents which damage the lungs, skin, eyes, or mucous membranes. Ap-

pendix A provides further definitions and explanations of the scope of health hazards covered by this section, and Appendix B describes the criteria to be used to determine whether or not a chemical is to be considered hazardous for purposes of this standard.

"Identity" means any chemical or common name which is indicated on the material safety data sheet (MSDS) for the chemical. The identity used shall permit cross-references to be made among the required list of hazardous chemicals, the label and the MSDS.

"Immediate use" means that the hazardous chemical will be under the control of and used only by the person who transfers it from a labeled container and only within the work shift in which it is transferred.

"Importer" means the first business with employees within the Customs Territory of the United States which receives hazardous chemicals produced in other countries for the purpose of supplying them to distributors or employers within the United States.

"Label" means any written, printed, or graphic material, displayed on or affixed to containers of hazardous chemicals.

"Material safety data sheet (MSDS)" means written or printed material concerning a hazardous chemical which is prepared in accordance with paragraph (g) of this section.

"Mixture" means any combination of two or more chemicals if the combination is not, in whole or in part, the result of a chemical reaction.

"Organic peroxide" means an organic compound that contains the bivalent-O-O-structure and which may be considered to be a structural derivative of hydrogen peroxide where one or both of the hydrogen atoms has been replaced by an organic radical.

"Oxidizer" means a chemical other than a blasting agent or explosive as defined in §1910.109(a), that initiates or promotes combustion in other materials, thereby causing fire either of itself or through the release of oxygen or other gases.

"Physical hazard" means a chemical for which there is scientifically valid evidence that it is a combustible liquid, a compressed gas, explosive, flammable, an organic peroxide, an oxidizer, pyrophoric, unstable (reactive) or water-reactive.

"Produce" means to manufacture, process, formulate, or repackage.

"Pyrophoric" means a chemical that will ignite spontaneously in air at a temperature of 130°F (54.4°C) or below.

"Responsible party" means someone who can provide additional information on the hazardous chemical and appropriate emergency procedures, if necessary.

"Specific chemical identity" means the chemical name, Chemical Abstracts Service (CAS) Registry Number, or any other information that reveals the precise chemical designation of the substance.

"Trade secret" means any confidential formula, pattern, process, device, information or compilation of information that is used in an employer's business, and that gives the employer an opportunity to obtain an advantage over competitors who do not know or use it. Appendix D sets out the criteria to be used in evaluating trade secrets.

"Unstable (reactive)" means a chemical which in the pure state, or as produced or transported, will vigorously polymerize, decompose, condense, or will become self-reactive under conditions of shocks, pressure or temperature.

"Use" means to package, handle, react, or transfer.

"Water-reactive" means a chemical that reacts with water to release a gas that is either flammable or presents a health hazard.

"Work area" means a room or defined space in a workplace where hazardous chemicals are produced or used, and where employees are present.

"Workplace" means an establishment, job site, or project, at one geographical location containing one or more work areas.

(d) *Hazard determination.*(1) Chemical manufacturers and importers shall evaluate chemicals produced in their workplaces or imported by them to determine if they are hazardous. Employers are not required to evaluate chemicals unless they choose not to rely on the evaluation performed by the chemical manufacturer or importer for the chemical to satisfy this requirement.

(2) Chemical manufacturers, importers or employers evaluating chemicals shall identify and consider the available scientific evidence concerning such hazards. For health hazards, evidence which is statistically significant and which is based on at least one positive study conducted in accordance with established scientific principles is considered to be sufficient to establish a hazardous effect if the results of the study meet the definitions of health hazards in this section. Appendix A shall be consulted for the scope of health hazards covered, and Appendix B shall be consulted for the criteria to be followed with respect to the completeness of the evaluation, and the data to be reported.

(3) The chemical manufacturer, importer or employer evaluating chemicals shall treat the following sources as establishing that the chemicals listed in them are hazardous:

(i) 29 CFR Part 1910, Subpart Z, Toxic and Hazardous Substances, Occupational Safety and Health Administration (OSHA); or

(ii) *Threshold Limit Values for Chemical Substances and Physical Agents in the Work Environment* , American Conference of Governmental Industrial Hygienists (ACGIH) (latest edition).

The chemical manufacturer, importer, or employer is still responsible for evaluating the hazards associated with the chemicals in these source lists in accordance with the requirements of this standard.

(4) Chemical manufacturers, importers and employers evaluating chemicals shall treat the following sources as establishing that a chemical is a carcinogen or potential carcinogen for hazard communication purposes:

(i) National Toxicology Program (NTP), *Annual Report on Carcinogens* (latest edition):

(ii) International Agency for Research on Cancer (IARC) *Monographs* (latest editions); or

(iii) 29 CFR Part 1910, Subpart Z, Toxic and Hazardous Substances, Occupational Safety and Health Administration.

Note.—The *Registry of Toxic Effects of Chemical Substances* published by the National Institute for Occupational Safety and Health indicates whether a chemical has been found by NTP or IARC to be a potential carcinogen.

(5) The chemical manufacturer, importer or employer shall determine the hazards of mixtures of chemicals as follows:

(i) If a mixture has been tested as a whole to determine its hazards, the results of such testing shall be used to determine whether the mixture is hazardous;

(ii) If a mixture has not been tested as a whole to determine whether the mixture is a health hazard, the mixture shall be assumed to present the same health hazards as do the components which comprise one percent (by weight or volume) or greater of the mixture, except that the mixture shall be assumed to present a carcinogenic hazard if it contains a component in concentrations of 0.1 percent or greater which is considered to be a carcinogen under paragraph (d)(4) of this section;

(iii) If a mixture has not been tested as a whole to determine whether the mixture is a physical hazard, the chemical manufacturer, importer, or employer may use whatever scientifically

valid data is available to evaluate the physical hazard potential of the mixture; and,

(iv) If the chemical manufacturer, importer, or employer has evidence to indicate that a component present in the mixture in concentrations of less than one percent (or in the case of carcinogens, less than 0.1 percent) could be released in concentrations which would exceed an established OSHA permissible exposure limit or ACGIH Threshold Limit Value, or could present a health, hazard to employees in those concentrations, the mixture shall be assumed to present the same hazard.

(6) Chemical manufacturers, importers, or employers evaluating chemicals shall describe in writing the procedures they use to determine the hazards of the chemical they evaluate. The written procedures are to be made available, upon request, to employees, their designated representatives, the Assistant Secretary and the Director. The written description may be incorporated into the written hazard communication program required under paragraph (e) of this section.

(e) *Written hazard communication program.* (1) Employers shall develop, implement, and maintain at the workplace, a written hazard communication program for their workplaces which at least describes how the criteria specified in paragraphs (f), (g), and (h) of this section for labels and other forms of warning, material safety data sheets, and employee information and training will be met, and which also includes the following:

(i) A list of the hazardous chemicals known to be present using an identity that is referenced on the appropriate material safety data sheet (the list may be compiled for the workplace as a whole or for individual work areas); and,

(ii) The methods the employer will use to inform employees of the hazards of non-routine tasks (for example, the cleaning of reactor vessels), and the hazards associated with chemicals contained in unlabeled pipes in their work areas.

(2) *Multi-employer workplaces.* Employers who produce, use, or store hazardous chemicals at a workplace in such a way that the employees of other employer(s) may be exposed (for example, employees of a construction contractor working on-site) shall additionally ensure that the hazard communication programs developed and implemented under this paragraph (e) include the following:

(i) The methods the employer will use to provide the other employer(s) with a copy of the material safety data sheet, or to make it available at a central location in the workplace, for each hazardous chemical the other employer(s) employees may be exposed to while working;

(ii) The methods the employer will use to inform the other employer(s) of any precautionary measures that need to be taken to protect employees during the workplace's normal operating conditions and in foreseeable emergencies; and,

(iii) The methods the employer will use to inform the other employer(s) of the labeling system used in the workplace.

(3) The employer may rely on an existing hazard communication program to comply with these requirements, provided that it meets the criteria established in this paragraph (e).

(4) The employer shall make the written hazard communication program available, upon request, to employees, their designated representatives, the Assistant Secretary and the Director, in accordance with the requirements of 29 CFR 1910.20(e).

(f) *Labels and other forms of warning.* (1) The chemical manufacturer, importer, or distributor shall ensure that each container of hazardous chemicals leaving the workplace is labeled, tagged or marked with the following information:

(i) Identity of the hazardous chemical(s):

(ii) Appropriate hazard warnings: and

(iii) Name and address of the chemical manufacturer, importer, or other responsible party.

(2) For solid metal (such as a steel beam or a metal casting) that is not exempted as an article due to its downstream use, the required label may be transmitted to the customer at the time of the initial shipment, and need not be included with subsequent shipments to the same employer unless the information on the label changes. The label may be transmitted with the initial shipment itself, or with the material safety data sheet that is to be provided prior to or at the time of the first shipment. This exception to requiring labels on every container of hazardous chemicals is only for the solid metal itself and does not apply to hazardous chemicals used in conjunction with, or known to be present with, the metal and to which employees handling the metal may be exposed (for example, cutting fluids or lubricants).

(3) Chemical manufacturers, importers, or distributors shall ensure that each container of hazardous chemicals leaving the workplace is labeled, tagged, or marked in accordance with this section in a manner which does not conflict with the requirements of the Hazardous Materials Transportation Act (49 U.S.C. 1801 *et seq.*) and regulations issued under that Act by the Department of Transportation.

(4) If the hazardous chemical is regulated by OSHA in a substance- specific health standard, the chemical manufacturer, importer, distributor or employer shall ensure that the labels or other forms of warning used are in accordance with the requirements of that standard.

(5) Except as provided in paragraphs (f)(6) and (f)(7) the employer shall ensure that each container of hazardous chemicals in the workplace is labeled,

tagged or marked with the following information:

(i) Identity of the hazardous chemical(s) contained therein; and

(ii) Appropriate hazard warnings.

(6) The employer may use signs, placards, process sheets, batch tickets, operating procedures, or other such written materials in lieu of affixing labels to individual stationary process containers, as long as the alternative method identifies the containers to which it is applicable and conveys the information required by paragraph (f)(5) of this section to be on a label. The written materials shall be readily accessible to the employees in their work area throughout each work shift.

(7) The employer is not required to label portable containers into which hazardous chemicals are transferred from labeled containers, and which are intended only for the immediate use of the employee who performs the transfer.

(8) The employer shall not remove or deface existing labels on incoming containers of hazardous chemicals, unless the container is immediately marked with the required information.

(9) The employer shall ensure that labels or other forms of warning are legible, in English, and prominently displayed on the container, or readily available in the work area throughout each work shift. Employers having employees who speak other languages may add the information in their language to the material presented, as long as the information is presented in English as well.

(10) The chemical manufacturer, importer, distributor or employer need not affix new labels to comply with this section if existing labels already convey the required information.

(g) *Material safety data sheets.* (1) Chemical manufacturers and importers shall obtain or develop a material safety data sheet for each hazardous chemical they produce or import. Employers shall have a material safety data sheet for each hazardous chemical which they use.

(2) Each material safety data sheet shall be in English and shall contain at least the following information:

(i) The identity used on the label, and, except as provided for in paragraph (i) of this section on trade secrets:

(A) If the hazardous chemical is a single substance, its chemical and common name(s);

(B) If the hazardous chemical is a mixture which has been tested as a whole to determine its hazards, the chemical and common name(s) of the ingredients which contribute to these known hazards, and the common name(s) of the mixture itself; or,

(C) If the hazardous chemical is a mixture which has not been tested as a whole:

(1) The chemical and common name(s) of all ingredients which have been determined to be health hazards, and which comprise 1% or greater of the composition, except that chemicals identified as carcinogens under paragraph (d)(4) of this section shall be listed if the concentrations are 0.1% or greater, and,

(2) The chemical and common name(s) of all ingredients which have been determined to be health hazards, and which comprise less than 1% (0.1% for carcinogens) of the mixture, if there is evidence that the ingredient(s) could be released from the mixture in concentrations which would exceed an established OSHA permissible exposure limit or ACGIH Threshold Limit Value, or could present a health hazard to employees; and,

(3) The chemical and common name(s) of all ingredients which have been determined to present a physical hazard when present in the mixture;

(ii) Physical and chemical characteristics of the hazardous chemical (such as vapor pressure, flash point);

(iii) The physical hazards of the hazardous chemical, including the potential for fire, explosion, and reactivity;

(iv) The health hazards of the hazardous chemical, including signs and symptoms of exposure, and any medical conditions which are generally recognized as being aggravated by exposure to the chemical;

(v) The primary route(s) of entry;

(vi) The OSHA permissible exposure limit, ACGIH Threshold Limit Value, and any other exposure limit used or recommended by the chemical manufacturer, importer, or employer preparing the material safety data sheet, where available;

(vii) Whether the hazardous chemical is listed in the National Toxicology Program (NTP) *Annual Report on Carcinogens* (latest edition) or has been found to be a potential carcinogen in the International Agency for Research on Cancer (IARC) *Monographs* (latest editions), or by OSHA;

(viii) Any generally applicable precautions for safe handling and use which are known to the chemical manufacturer, importer or employer preparing the material safety data sheet, including appropriate hygienic practices, protective measures during repair and maintenance of contaminated equipment, and procedures for cleanup of spills and leaks;

(ix) Any generally applicable control measures which are known to the chemical manufacturer, importer or employer preparing the material safety data sheet, such as appropriate engineering controls, work practices, or personal protective equipment;

(x) Emergency and first aid procedures;

(xi) The date of preparation of the material safety data sheet or the last change to it; and,

(xii) The name, address and telephone number of the chemical manufacturer, importer, employer or other responsible party preparing or distributing the material safety data sheet, who can provide additional information on the hazardous chemical and appropriate emergency procedures, if necessary.

(3) If not relevant information is found for any given category on the material safety data sheet, the chemical manufacturer, importer or employer preparing the material safety data sheet shall mark it to indicate that no applicable information was found.

(4) Where complex mixtures have similar hazards and contents (i.e. the chemical ingredients are essentially the same, but the specific composition varies from mixture to mixture), the chemical manufacturer, importer or employer may prepare one material safety data sheet to apply to all of these similar mixtures.

(5) The chemical manufacturer, importer or employer preparing the material safety data sheet shall ensure that the information recorded accurately reflects the scientific evidence used in making the hazard determination. If the chemical manufacturer, importer or employer preparing the material safety data sheet becomes newly aware of any significant information regarding the hazards of a chemical, or ways to protect against the hazards, this new information shall be added to the material safety data sheet within three months. If the chemical is not currently being produced or imported the chemical manufacturer or importer shall add the information to the material safety data sheet before the chemical is introduced into the workplace again.

(6) Chemical manufacturers or importers shall ensure that distributors and employers are provided an appropriate material safety data sheet with their initial shipment, and with the first shipment after a material safety data sheet is updated. The chemical manufacturer or importer shall either provide material safety data sheets with the shipped containers or send them to the employer prior to or at the time of the shipment. If the material safety data sheet is not provided with a shipment that has been labeled as a hazard-

ous chemical, the employer shall obtain one from the chemical manufacturer, importer, or distributor as soon as possible.

(7) Distributors shall ensure that material safety data sheets, and updated information, are provided to other distributors and employers. Retail distributors which sell hazardous chemicals to commercial customers shall provide a material safety data sheet to such employers upon request, and shall post a sign or otherwise inform them that a material safety data sheet is available. Chemical manufacturers, importers, and distributors need not provide material safety data sheets to retail distributors which have informed them that the retail distributor does not sell the product to commercial customers or open the sealed container to use it in their own workplaces.

(8) The employer shall maintain copies of the required material safety data sheets for each hazardous chemical in the workplace, and shall ensure that they are readily accessible during each work shift to employees when they are in their work area(s).

(9) Where employees must travel between workplaces during a workshift, *i.e.*, their work is carried out at more than one geographical location, the material safety data sheets may be kept at a central location at the primary workplace facility. In this situation, the employer shall ensure that employees can immediately obtain the required information in an emergency.

(10) Material safety data sheets may be kept in any form, including operating procedures, and may be designed to cover groups of hazardous chemicals in a work area where it may be more appropriate to address the hazards of a process rather than individual hazardous chemicals. However, the employer shall ensure that in all cases the required information is provided for each hazardous chemical, and is readily accessible during each work shift to em-

ployees when they are in their work area(s).

(11) Material safety data sheets shall also be made readily available, upon request, to designated representatives and to the Assistant Secretary, in accordance with the requirements of 29 CFR 1910.20 (e). The Director shall also be given access to material safety data sheets in the same manner.

(h) *Employee information and training* . Employers shall provide employees with information and training on hazardous chemicals in their work area at the time of their initial assignment, and whenever a new hazard is introduced into their work area.

(1) *Information.* Employees shall be informed of:

(i) The requirements of this section;

(ii) Any operations in their work area where hazardous chemicals are present; and,

(iii) The location and availability of the written hazard communication program, including the required list(s) of hazardous chemicals, and material safety data sheets required by this section.

(2) *Training.* Employee training shall include at least:

(i) Methods and observations that may be used to detect the presence or release of a hazardous chemical in the work area (such as monitoring conducted by the employer, continuous monitoring devices, visual appearance or odor of hazardous chemicals when being released, etc.);

(ii) The physical and health hazards of the chemicals in the work area;

(iii) The measures employees can take to protect themselves from these hazards, including specific procedures the employer has implemented to protect employees from exposure to hazardous chemicals, such as appropriate work practices, emergency procedures, and personal protective equipment to be used; and,

(iv) The details of the hazard communication program developed by the employer, including an explanation of the labeling system and the material safety data sheet, and how employees can obtain and use the appropriate hazard information.

(i) *Trade secrets.* (1) The chemical manufacturer, importer, or employer may withhold the specific chemical identity, including the chemical name and other specific identification of a hazardous chemical, from the material safety data sheet, provided that:

(i) The claim that the information withheld is a trade secret can be supported;

(ii) Information contained in the material safety data sheet concerning the properties and effects of the hazardous chemical is disclosed;

(iii) The material safety data sheet indicates that the specific chemical identity is being withheld as a trade secret; and,

(iv) The specific chemical identity is made available to health professionals, employees, and designated representatives in accordance with the applicable provisions of this paragraph.

(2) Where a treating physician or nurse determines that a medical emergency exists and the specific chemical identity of a hazardous chemical is necessary for emergency or first-aid treatment, the chemical manufacturer, importer, or employer shall immediately disclose the specific chemical identity of a trade secret chemical to that treating physician or nurse, regardless of the existence of a written statement of need of a confidentiality agreement. The chemical manufacturer, importer, or employer may require a written statement of need and confidentiality agreement, in accordance with the provisions of paragraphs (i)(3) and (4) of this section, as soon as circumstances permit.

(3) In non-emergency situations, a chemical manufacturer, importer, or employer shall, upon request, disclose a specific chemical identity, otherwise permitted to be withheld under paragraph (i)(1) of this section, to a health professional (i.e. physician, industrial hygienist, toxicologist, epidemiologist, or occupational health nurse) providing medical or other occupational health services to exposed employee(s), and to employees or designated representatives, if:

(i) The request is in writing;

(ii) The request describes with reasonable detail one or more of the following occupational health needs for the information:

(A) To assess the hazards of the chemicals to which employees will be exposed;

(B) To conduct or assess sampling of the workplace atmosphere to determine employee exposure levels;

(C) To conduct pre-assignment or periodic medical surveillance of exposed employees;

(D) To provide medical treatment to exposed employees;

(E) To select or assess appropriate personal protective equipment for exposed employees;

(F) To design or assess engineering controls or other protective measures for exposed employees; and,

(G) To conduct studies to determine the health effects of exposure.

(iii) The request explains in detail why the disclosure of the specific chemical identity is essential and that, in lieu thereof, the disclosure of the following information to the health professional, employee, or designated representative, would not satisfy the purposes described in paragraph (i)(3)(ii) of this section:

(A) The properties and effects of the chemical;

(B) Measures for controlling workers exposure to the chemical;

(C) Methods of monitoring and analyzing worker exposure to the chemical; and,

(D) Methods of diagnosing and treating harmful exposures to the chemical;

(iv) The request includes a description of the procedures to be used to maintain the confidentiality of the disclosed information; and,

(v) The health professional, and the employer or contractor of the services of the health professional (i.e. downstream employer, labor organization, or individual employee), employee, or designated representative, agree in a written confidentiality agreement that the health professional, employee, or designated representative, will not use the trade secret information for any purpose other than the health need(s) asserted and agree not to release the information under any circumstances other than to OSHA, as provided in paragraph (i)(6) of this section, except as authorized by the terms of the agreement or by the chemical manufacturer, importer, or employer.

(4) The confidentiality agreement authorized by paragraph (i)(3)(iv) of this section:

(i) May restrict the use of the information to the health purposes indicated in the written statement of need;

(ii) May provide for appropriate legal remedies in the event of a breach of the agreement, including stipulation of a reasonable pre-estimate of likely damages; and,

(iii) May not include requirements for the posting of a penalty bond.

(5) Nothing in this standard is meant to preclude the parties from pursuing non-contractual remedies to the extent permitted by law.

(6) If the health professional, employee, or designated representative receiving the trade secret information decides that there is a need to disclose it to OSHA, the chemical manufacturer, importer, or employer who provided the information shall be informed by the health professional, employee, or designated representative prior to or at the same time as, such disclosure.

(7) If the chemical manufacturer, importer, or employer denies a written request for disclosure of a specific chemical identity, the denial must:

(i) Be provided to the health professional, employee, or designated representative, within thirty days of the request;

(ii) Be in writing;

(iii) Include evidence to support the claim that the specific chemical identity is a trade secret;

(iv) State the specific reasons why the request is being denied; and,

(v) Explain in detail how alternative information may satisfy the specific medical or occupational health need without revealing the specific chemical identity.

(8) The health professional, employee, or designated representative whose request for information is denied under paragraph (i)(3) of this section may refer the request and the written denial of the request to OSHA for consideration.

(9) When a health professional, employee, or designated representative refers the denial to OSHA under paragraph (i)(8) of this section. OSHA shall consider the evidence to determine if:

(i) The chemical manufacturer, importer, or employer has supported the claim that the specific chemical identity is a trade secret;

(ii) The health professional, employee, or designated representative has supported the claim that there is a medical or occupational health need for the information; and,

(iii) The health professional, employee, or designated representative has demonstrated adequate means to protect the confidentiality.

(10) (i) If OSHA determines that the specific chemical identity requested under paragraph (i)(3) of this section is not a *bona fide* trade secret, or that it is a trade secret, but the requesting health professional, employee, or designated representative has a legitimate

medical or occupational health need for the information, has executed a written confidentiality agreement, and has shown adequate means to protect the confidentiality of the information, the chemical manufacturer, importer, or employer will be subject to citation by OSHA.

(ii) If a chemical manufacturer, importer, or employer demonstrates to OSHA that the execution of a confidentiality agreement would not provide sufficient protection against the potential harm from the unauthorized disclosure of a trade secret specific chemical identity, the Assistant Secretary may issue such orders or impose such additional limitations or conditions upon the disclosure of the requested chemical information as may be appropriate to assure that the occupational health services are provided without an undue risk of harm to the chemical manufacturer, importer, or employer.

(11) If a citation for a failure to release specific chemical identity information is contested by the chemical manufacturer, importer, or employer, the matter will be adjudicated before the Occupational Safety and Health Review Commission in accordance with the Act's enforcement scheme and the applicable Commission rules of procedure. In accordance with the Commission rules, when a chemical manufacturer, importer, or employer continues to withhold the information during the contest, the Administrative Law Judge may review the citation and supporting documentation in camera or issue appropriate orders to protect the confidentiality or such matters.

(12) Notwithstanding the existence of a trade secret claim, a chemical manufacturer, importer, or employer shall, upon request, disclose to the Assistant Secretary any information which this section requires the chemical manufacturer, importer, or employer to make available. Where there is a trade secret claim, such claim shall be made no later than at the time the information is provided to the Assistant Secretary so that suitable determinations of trade secret status can be made and the necessary protections can be implemented.

(13) Nothing in this paragraph shall be construed as requiring the disclosure under any circumstances of process or percentage of mixture information which is a trade secret.

(j) *Effective dates.* (1) Chemical manufacturers, importers, and distributors shall ensure that material safety data sheets are provided with the next shipment of hazardous chemicals to employers after September 23, 1987.

(2) Employers in the non-manufacturing sector shall be in compliance with all provisions of this section by May 23, 1988. (Note: Employers in the manufacturing sector (SIC Codes 20 through 39) are already required to be in compliance with this section.)

Appendix A to §1910.1200 Health Hazard Definitions (*Mandatory*)

[Appendix A reprinted at 52 FR 32877, August 24, 1987]

Although safety hazards related to the physical characteristics of a chemical can be objectively defined in terms of testing requirements (e.g. flammability), health hazard definitions are less precise and more subjective. Health hazards may cause measurable changes in the body —such as decreased pulmonary function. These changes are generally indicated by the occurrence of signs and symptoms in the exposed employees —such as shortness of breath, a non-measurable, subjective feeling. Employees exposed to such hazards must be apprised of both the change in body function and the signs and symptoms that may occur to signal that change.

The determination of occupational health hazards is complicated by the fact that many of the effects or signs and symptoms occur commonly in non-occupationally exposed populations, so that effects of exposure are difficult to separate from normally occurring illnesses. Occasionally, a substance causes an effect that is rarely seen in the population at large, such as angiosarcomas caused by vinyl chloride exposure, thus making it easier to ascertain that the occupational exposure was the primary causative factor. More often, however, the effects are common, such as lung cancer. The situation is further complicated by the fact that most chemicals have not been adequately tested to determine their health hazard potential, and data do not exist to substantiate these effects.

There have been many attempts to categorize effects and to define them in various ways. Generally, the terms "acute" and "chronic" are used to delineate between effects on the basis of severity or duration. "Acute" effects usually occur rapidly as a result of short-term exposures, and are of short duration. "Chronic" effects generally occur as a result of long-term exposure, and are of long duration.

The acute effects referred to most frequently are those defined by the American National Standards Institute (ANSI) standard for Precautionary Labeling of Hazardous Industrial Chemicals (Z129.1–1982) —irritation, corrosivity, sensitization and lethal dose. Although these are important health effects, they do not adequately cover the considerable range of acute effects which may occur as a result of occupational exposure, such as, for example, narcosis.

Similarly, the term chronic effect is often used to cover only carcinogenicity, teratogenicity, and mutagenicity. These effects are obviously a concern in the workplace, but again do not adequately cover the area of chronic effects, excluding for example, blood dyscrasias (such as enemia), chronic bronchitis and liver atrophy.

The goal of defining precisely in measurable terms, every possible health effect that may occur in the workplace as a result of chemical exposures cannot realistically be accomplished. This does not negate the need for employees to be informed of such effects and protected from them. Appendix B, which is also mandatory, outlines the principles and procedures of hazardous assessment.

For purposes of this section, any chemicals which meet any of the following definitions, as determined by the criteria set forth in Appendix B are health hazards:

1. *Carcinogen*: A chemical is considered to be a carcinogen if:

(a) It has been evaluated by the International Agency for Research on Cancer (IARC), and found to be a carcinogen or potential carcinogen; or

(b) It is listed as a carcinogen or potential carcinogen in the *Annual Report on Carcinogens* published by the National Toxicology Program (NTP) (latest edition); or,

(c) It is regulated by OSHA as a carcinogen.

2. *Corrosive*: A chemical that causes visible destruction of, or irreversible alterations in, living tissue by chemical action at the site of contact. For example, a chemical is considered to be corrosive if, when tested on the intact skin of albino rabbits by the method described by the U.S. Department of Transportation in Appendix A to 49 CFR Part 173, it destroys or changes irreversibly the structure of the tissue at the site of contact following an exposure period of four hours. This term shall not refer to action on inanimate surfaces.

3. *Highly toxic*: A chemical falling within any of the following categories:

(a) A chemical that has a median lethal dose (LD) *of 50 milligrams or less per kilogram of body weight when administered orally to albino rats weighing between 200 and 300 grams each.*

(b) A chemical that has a median lethal does (LD) *of 200 milligrams or less per kilogram of body weight when administered, by continuous contact for 24 hours (or less if death occurs within 24 hours) with the bare skin of albino rabbits weighing between two and three kilograms each.*

(c) A chemical that has a median lethal concentration (LC) *in air of 200 parts per million by volume or less of gas or vapor, or 2 milligrams per liter or less of mist, fume, or dust, when administered by continuous inhalation for one hour (or less if death occurs within one hour) to albino rats weighing between 200 and 300 grams each.*

4. *Irritant*: A chemical, which is not corrosive, but which causes a reversible inflammatory effect on living tissue by chemical action at the site of contact. A chemical is a skin irritant if, when tested on the intact skin of albino rabbits by the methods of 16 CFR 1500.41 for four hours exposure or by other appropriate techniques, it results in an empirical score of five or more. A chemical is an eye irritant if so determined under the procedure listed in 16 CFR 1500.42 or other appropriate techniques.

5. *Sensitizer*: A chemical that causes a substantial proportion of exposed people or animals to develop an allergic reaction in normal tissue after repeated exposure to the chemical.

6. *Toxic*. A chemical falling within any of the following categories.

(a) A chemical that has a median lethal dose (LD) *of more than 50 milligrams per kilogram but not more than 500 milligrams per kilogram of body weight when administered orally to albino rats weighing between 200 and 300 grams each.*

(b) A chemical that has a median lethal dose (LD) *of more than 200 milligrams per kilogram but not more than 1,000 milligrams per kilogram of body weight when administered by continuous contact for 24 hours (or less if death occurs within 24 hours) with the bare skin of albino rabbits weighing between two and three kilograms each.*

(c) A chemical that has a median lethal concentration (LC) *in air of more than 200 parts per million but not more than 2,000 parts per million by volume of gas or vapor, or more than 20 milligrams per liter but not more than 20 milligrams per liter of mist, fume, or dust, when administered by continuous inhalation for one hour (or less if death occurs within one hour) to albino rats weighing between 200 and 300 grams each.*

7. *Target organ effects*. The following is a target organ categorization of effects which may occur, including examples of signs and symptoms and chemicals which have been found to cause such effects. These examples are presented to illustrate the range and diversity of effects and hazards found in the workplace, and the broad scope employers must consid-

ered in this area, but are not intended to be all-inclusive.

a. Hepatotoxins: Chemicals which produce liver damage
Signs & Symptoms: jaundice; liver enlargement
Chemicals: Carbon tetrachloride nitrosamines

b. Nephrotoxins: Chemicals which produce kidney damage
Signs & Symptoms: Edema; proteinuria
Chemicals: Halogenated hydrocarbons; uranium

c. Neurotoxins; Chemicals which produce their primary toxic effects on the nervous system
Signs & Symptoms: Narcosis; behavioral changes; decrease in motor functions
Chemicals Mercury; carbon disulfide

d. Agents which act on the blood or hematopoietic system: Decrease hemoglobin function; deprive the body tissues of oxygen
Signs & Symptoms: Cyanosis; loss of consciousness
Chemicals: Carbon monoxide; cyanides

e. Agents which damage the lung: Chemicals which irritate or damage the pulmonary tissue
Signs & Symptoms: Cough; tightness in chest; shortness of breath
Chemicals; Silica; asbestos

f. Reproductive toxins: Chemicals which affect the reproductive capabilities including chromosomal damage (mutations) and effects on fetuses (teratogenesis)
Signs & Symptoms: Birth defects; sterility
Chemicals: Lead; DBCP

g. Cutaneous hazards: Chemicals which affect the dermal layer of the body
Signs & Symptoms: Defatting of the skin; rashes; irritation
Chemicals: Ketones; chlorinated compounds

h. Eye hazards: Chemicals which affect the eye or visual capacity
Signs & Symptoms: Conjunctivitis; corneal damage
Chemicals: Organic solvents; acids

Appendix B to §1910.1200, Hazard Determination (Mandatory)

[Appendix B reprinted at 52 FR 32877, August 24, 1987]

The quality of a hazard communication program is largely dependent upon the adequacy and accuracy of the hazard determination. The hazard determination requirement of this standard is performance-oriented. Chemical manufacturers, importers, and employers evaluating chemicals are not required to follow any specific methods for determining hazards, but they must be able to demonstrate that they have adequately ascertained the hazards of the chemicals produced or imported in accordance with the criteria set forth in this Appendix.

Hazard evaluation is a process which relies heavily on the professional judgment of the evaluation, particularly in the area of chronic hazards. The performance-orientation of the hazard determination does not diminish the duty of the chemical manufacturer, importer or employer to conduct a thorough evaluation, examining all relevant data and producing a scientifically defensible evaluation. For purposes of this standard, the following criteria shall be used in making hazard determinations that meet the requirements of this standard.

1. *Carcinogenicity* : As described in paragraph (d)(4) and Appendix A of this section, a determination by the National Toxicology Program, the International Agency for Research on Cancer, or OSHA that a chemical is a carcinogen or potential carcinogen will be considered conclusive evidence for purposes of this section.

2. *Human data* : Where available, epidemiological studies and case reports of adverse health effects shall be considered in the evaluation.

3. *Animal data* : Human evidence of health effects in exposed populations is generally not available for the majority of chemicals produced or used in the workplace. Therefore, the available results of toxicological testing in animal populations shall be used to predict the health effects that may be experienced by exposed workers. In particular, the definitions of certain acute hazards refer to specific animal testing results (see Appendix A).

4. *Adequacy and reporting of data.* The results of any studies which are designed and conducted according to established scientific principles, and which report statistically significant conclusions regarding the health effects of a chemical, shall be a sufficient basis for a hazard determination and reported on any material safety data sheet. The chemical manufacturer, importer, or employer may also report the results of other scientifically valid studies which tend to refute the findings of hazard.

Appendix C to §1910.1200 Information Sources (Advisory)

[Appendix C reprinted at 52 FR 32877, August 24, 1987]

The following is a list of available data sources which the chemical manufacturer importer, distributor, or employer may wish to consult to evaluate the hazards of chemicals they produce or import;

—Any information in their own company files, such as toxicity testing results or illness experience of company employees.

—Any information obtained from the supplier of the chemical, such as material safety data sheets or product safety bulletins.

—Any pertinent information obtained from the following source list (latest editions should be used):

Condensed Chemical Dictionary Van Nostrand Reinhold Co., 135 West 50th Street, New York, NY 10020.

The Merck Index: An Encyclopedia of Chemicals and Drugs
Merck and Company, Inc., 126 E. Lincoln Ave., Rahway, NJ 07065.

IARC Monographs on the Evaluation of the Carcinogenic Risk of Chemicals to Man
Geneva : World Health Organization. International Agency for Research on Cancer, 1972-Present. (Multivolume work). Summaries are available in supplement volumes, 49 Sheridan Street, Albany, NY 12210.

Industrial Hygiene and Toxicology, by F.A. Patty
John Wiley & Sons, Inc., New York, NY (Multivolume work).

Clinical Toxicology of Commercial Products Gleason, Gosselin, and Hodge

Casarett and Doull's Toxicology: The Basic Science of Poisons

Doull, Klaassen, and Amdur, Macmillan Publishing Co., Inc., New York, NY.

Industrial Toxicology, by Alice Hamilton and Harriet L. Hardy

Publishing Sciences group, Inc., Acton MA.

Toxicology of the Eye, by W. Morton Grant Charles C. Thomas, 301 –327 East Lawrence Avenue, Springfield, IL.

Recognition of Health Hazards in Industry William A. Burgess, John Wiley and Sons. 605 Third Avenue, New York, NY 10158.

Chemical Hazards of the Workplace Nick H. Proctor and James P. Hughes, J.P. Lipincott Company, 6 Winchester Terrace, New York, NY 10022.

Handbook of Chemistry and Physics Chemical Rubber Company, 18901 Cranwood Parkway, Cleveland, OH 44128.

Threshold Limit Values for Chemical Substances and Physical Agents in the Work Environment and Biological Exposure Indices with Intended Changes

American Conference of Governmental Industrial Hygienists (ACGIH). 6500 Glenway Avenue. Bldg. D-5, Cincinnati, OH 45211.

Information on the physical hazards of chemicals may be found in publications of the National Fire Protection Association, Boston, MA.

Note. —The following documents may be purchased from the Superintendent of Documents, U.S. Government Printing Office, Washington, DC 20402.

Occupational Health Guidelines NIOSH/OSHA (NIOSH Pub. No. 81–123)

NIOSH Pocket Guide to Chemical Hazards NIOSH Pocket Guide to Chemical Hazards NIOSH Pub. No. 85–114

Registry of Toxic Effects of Chemical Substances NIOSH Pub. No. 80 –102

Miscellaneous Documents published by the National Institute for Occupational Safety and Health.

Criteria documents. Special Hazard Reviews. Occupational Hazard Assessments. Current Intelligence Bulletins.

OSHA's General Industry Standards (29 CFR Part 1910)

NTP Annual Report on Carcinogens and Summary of the Annual Report on Carcinogens.

National Technical Information Service (NTIS), 5285 Port Royal Road. Springfield, VA 22161: (703) 487-4650.

BIBLIOGRAPHIC DATA BASES

Service provider	File name
Bibliographic Retrieval Services (BRS), 1200 Route 7, Latnam, NY 12110.	Biosis Previews CA Search Medlars NTIS Hazardline American Chemical Society Journal Excepta Medica IRCS Medical Science Journal Pre-Med Inti Pharmaceutical Abstracts Paper Chem
Lockheed —DIALOG Information Service, Inc. 3460 Hillview Avenue, Palo Alto. CA 94304.	Biosis Prev. Files CA Search Files CAB Abstracts Chemical Exposure Chemname Chemsis Files Chemzero Embase Files Environmental Bibliographies Enviroline Federal Research in Progress IRL Life Science Collection NTIS Occupational Safety and Health (NIOSH) Paper Chem

BIBLIOGRAPHIC DATA BASES

Service provider	File name
SDC —Orbit, SDC Information Service, 2500 Colorado Avenue, Santa Monica, CA 90406.	CAS Files Chemdex, 2,3 NTIS
National Library of Medicine, Department of Health and Human Services. Public Health Service, National Institutes of Health, Bethesda, MD 20209.	Hazardous Substances Data Bank (NSDB) Medline files Toxline Files Cancerlit RTECS Chemline
Pergamon International Information Corp., 1340 Old Chain Bridge Rd., McLean, VA 22101.	Laboratory Hazard Bulletin
Questel, Inc., 1625 Eye Street, NW., Suite 818, Washington, DC 20006.	CIS/ILO Cancemet
Chemical Information System ICI (ICIS), Bureau of National Affairs, 1133 15th Street, NW., Suite 300, Washington, DC 20005.	Structure and Nomenciature Search System (SANSS) Acute Toxicity (RTECS) Clinical Toxicology of Commercial Products Oil and Hazardous Materials Technical Assistance Data System CCRIS CESARS
Occupational Health Services, 400 Plaza Drive, Secaucus, NJ 07094.	MSDS Hazardine

Appendix D to §1910.1200 Definition of "Trade Secret" (Mandatory)

[Appendix D reprinted at 52 FR 32877, August 24, 1987]

The following is a reprint of the *Restatement of Torts* section 757, comment b (1939):

b. *Definition of trade secret.* A trade secret may consist of any formula, pattern, device or compilation of information which is used in one's business, and which gives him an opportunity to obtain an advantage over competitors who do not know or use it. It may be a formula for a chemical compound, a process of manufacturing, treating or preserving materials, a pattern for a machine or other device, or a list of customers. It differs from other secret information in a business (see §759 of the *Restatement of Torts* which is not included in this Appendix) in that it is not simply information as to single or ephemeral events in the conduct of the business, as, for example, the amount or other terms of a secret bid for a contract or the salary of certain employees, or the security investments made or contemplated, or the date fixed for the announcement of a new policy or for bringing out a new model or the like. A trade secret is a process or device for continuous use in the operations of the business. Generally it relates to the production of goods, as, for example, a machine or formula for the production of an article. It may, however, relate to the sale of goods or to other operations in the business, such as a code for determining discounts, rebates or other concessions in a price list or catalogue, or a list of specialized customers, or a method of bookkeeping or other office management.

Secrecy. The subject matter of a trade secret must be secret. Matters of public knowledge or of general knowledge in an industry cannot be appropriated by one as his secret. Matters which are completely disclosed by the goods which one markets cannot be his secret. Substantially, a trade secret is known only in the particular business in which it is used. It is not requisite that only the proprietor of the business know it. He may, without losing his protection, communicate it to employees involved in its use. He may likewise communicate it to others pledged to secrecy. Others may also know of it independently, as, for example, when they have discovered the process or formula by independent invention and are keeping it secret. Nevertheless, a substantial element of secrecy must exist, so that, except by the use of improper means, there would be difficulty in acquiring the information. An exact definition of a trade secret is not possible. Some factors to be considered in determining whether given information is one's trade secret are: (1) The extent to which the information is known outside of his business; (2) the extent to which it is known by employees and others involved in his business; (3) the extent of measures taken by him to guard the secrecy of the information; (4) the value of the information to him and his competitors; (5) the amount of effort or money expended by him in developing the information; (6) the ease or difficulty with which the information could be properly acquired or duplicated by others.

Novelty and prior art. A trade secret may be a device or process which is patentable: but it need not be that. It may be a device or process which is clearly anticipated in the prior art or one which is merely a mechanical improvement that a good mechanic can make. Novelty and invention are not requisite for a trade se-

cret as they are for patentability. These requirements are essential to patentability because a patent protects against unlicensed use of the patented device or process even by one who discovers it properly through independent research. The patent monopoly is a reward to the inventor. But such is not the case with a trade secret. Its protection is not based on a policy of rewarding or otherwise encouraging the development of secret processes or devices. The protection is merely against breach of faith and reprehensible means of learning another's secret. For this limited protection it is not appropriate to require also the kind of novelty and invention which is a requisite of patentability. The nature of the secret is, however, an important factor in determining the kind of relief that is appropriate against one who is subject to liability under the rule stated in this section. Thus, if the secret consists of a device or process which is a novel invention, one who acquires the secret wrongfully is ordinarily enjoined from further use of it and is required to account for the profits derived from his past use. If, on the other hand, the secret consists of mechanical improvements that a good mechanic can make without resort to the secret, the wrongdoer's liability may be limited to damages, and an injunction against future use of the improvements made with the aid of the secret may be inappropriate.

Appendix D
OSHA PROGRAM DIRECTIVE (EXAMPLE)

Editor's Note: This document is an example of an OSHA *program directive,* an instruction to the agency's field staff that is intended to clarify a provision in a given standard and provide guidance on citing the provision during an inspection. In this instance, the directive clarifies the meaning of a provision on fixed ladders in OSHA's standard for walking/working surfaces (see Appendix B for the text of the standard).

OSHA INSTRUCTION STD 1–1.12

June 20, 1983

Subject: Application of 29 CFR 1910.27, Fixed Ladders, to Fixed Ladders Used In Emergency Situations

A. *Purpose*. This instruction clarifies the meaning of 29 CFR 1910.27 as it applies to the protection of employees exposed to falling from fixed ladders used only as a means of escape from fire and other emergency situations.

B. *Scope*. This instruction applies OSHA-wide.

C. *Reference*. OSHA Instruction STD 1–1.3, October 30, 1978, originally dated January 18, 1977.

D. *Action*. Regional Administrators and Area Directors shall ensure that the interpretative guidelines given in this instruction are addressed when inspecting sites with fixed ladders used only during fire and other emergency situations.

E. *Federal Program Change*. This instruction describes a Federal program change which affects State programs. Each Regional Administrator shall:

1. Ensure that this change is forwarded to each State designee.

2. Explain the technical content of the change to the State designee as requested.

3. Ensure that State designees are asked to acknowledge receipt of this Federal program change in writing, within 30 days of notification, to the Regional Administrator. This acknowledgment should include a description either of the State's plan to implement the change or of the reasons why the change should not apply to that State.

4. Review policies, instructions and guidelines issued by the State to determine that this change has been communicated to State program personnel.

Routine monitoring activities (accompanied inspections and case file reviews) shall also be used to determine if this change has been implemented in actual performance.

F. *Background*. OSHA has historically established that the requirements of 29 CFR 1910.27 for cages, platforms, or similar fall prevention protection devices are not appropriate for fixed ladders on structures where the fixed ladders are used only as a means of access by fire fighters, other emergency personnel, or escape for employees in fire and other emergency situations. Sometimes these ladders are not provided with employee protection as presently required in 29 CFR 1910.27, when they are intended to be used only in an emergency. In these circumstances, it is sometimes more hazardous to install a cage, well, landing platform or ladder safety device pursuant to the standard than it is not to comply. A cage or well, etc., may interfere with fire fighting or other rescue equipment, or employee escape from fire or other emergency situations.

G. *Guidelines*. This instruction provides performance criteria for fixed ladders used only as a means of access for fire fighters and other emergency personnel, or escape for employees in fire and other emergency situations,

1. Employers must establish and implement adequate administrative controls such as barricades and signs to prevent nonemergency use of fixed ladders which are meant for fire fighter use and emergency escape only.

238

2. In the event the employer does not provide adequate administrative controls such as barricades or signs and employees use an emergency ladder for other than its intended purpose, the employer may be appropriately cited under 29 CFR 1910.27.

3. Fixed ladders not equipped with cages, landing platforms, ladder safety devices, or other forms of employee protection, in some situations may be allowed as a means of access for fire fighters and other emergency personnel, or escape for employees in fire and other emergency situations. These guidelines are provided because it may be more hazardous to comply with 29 CFR 1910.27 than not to comply.

Appendix E

U.S. Department of Labor Forms for Recording Work-Related Injuries and Illnesses

OSHA FORM 200
(LOG AND SUMMARY OF OCCUPATIONAL
INJURIES AND ILLNESSES)

OSHA FORM 101
(SUPPLEMENTARY RECORD OF INJURIES
AND ILLNESSES)

BLS FORM 200-S
(ANNUAL SURVEY)

241

INSTRUCTIONS FOR COMPLETING
THE LOG AND SUMMARY OF OCCUPATIONAL
INJURIES AND ILLNESSES

(OSHA Form No. 200)

I. Log and Summary of Occupational injuries and illnesses

Each employer who is subject to the recordkeeping requirements of the Occupational Safety and Health Act of 1970 must maintain for each establishment a log of all recordable occupational injuries and illnesses. This form (OSHA No. 200) may be used for that purpose. A substitute for the OSHA No. 200 is acceptable if it is as detailed, easily readable, and understandable as the OSHA No. 200.

Enter each recordable case on the log within six (6) workdays after learning of its occurrence. Although other records must be maintained at the establishment to which they refer, it is possible to prepare and maintain the log at another location, using data processing equipment if desired if the log is prepared elsewhere, a copy updated to within 45 calendar days must be present at all times in the establishment.

Logs must be maintained and retained for five (5) years following the end of the calendar year to which they relate. Logs must be available (normally at the establishment) for inspection and copying by representatives of the Department of Labor, or the Department of Health and Human Services, or States accorded jurisdiction under the Act. Access to the log is also provided to employees, former employees and their representatives.

II. Changes in Extent of or Outcome of injury or illness

If, during the 5-year period the log must be retained, there is a change in an extent and outcome of an injury or illness which affects entries in columns 1, 2, 6, 8, 9, or 13, the first entry should be lined out and a new entry be made. For example, if an injured employee at first required only medical treatment but later lost workdays away from work, the check in column 6 should be lined out, and checks entered in columns 2 and 3 and the number of lost workdays entered in column 4.

In another example, if an employee with an occupational illness lost workdays, returned to work, and then died of the illness, any entries in columns 9 through 12 should be lined out and the date of death entered in column 8.

The entire entry for an injury or illness should be lined out if later found to be nonrecordable. For example an injury which is later determined not to be work related, or which was initially thought to involve medical treatment but later was determined to have involved only first aid.

III. Posting Requirements

A copy of the totals and information following the fold line of the last page for the year must be posted at each establishment in the place or places where notices to employees are customarily posted. This copy

242

Published by THE BUREAU OF NATIONAL AFFAIRS, INC., Washington, D.C. 20037

must be posted no later than *February 1 and must remain in place until March 1.*
Even though there were no injuries or illnesses during the year, zeros must be entered on the totals line, and the form posted.

The person responsible for the *annual summary totals* shall certify that the totals are true and complete by signing at the bottom of the form.

IV. Instructions for Completing Log and Summary of Occupational Injuries and Illnesses

Column A- CASE OR FILE NUMBER Self-explanatory.

Column B- DATE OF INJURY OR ONSET OF ILLNESS.
For occupational injuries, enter the date of the work accident which resulted in injury. For occupational illnesses, enter the date of initial diagnosis of illness, or, if absence from work occurred before diagnosis, enter the first day of the absence attributable to the illness which was later diagnosed or recognized.

Columns C through F- Self-explanatory.

Columns 1 and 8- INJURY OR ILLNESS RELATED DEATHS.
Self-explanatory.

Columns 2 and 9- INJURIES OR ILLNESSES WITH LOST WORKDAYS.
Self-explanatory.
Any injury which involves days away from work, or days of restricted work activity, or both must be recorded since it always involves one or more of the criteria for recordability.

Columns 3 and 10- INJURIES OR ILLNESSES INVOLVING DAYS AWAY FROM WORK.
Self-explanatory.

Columns 4 and 11- LOST WORKDAYS--DAYS AWAY FROM WORK.
Enter the number of workdays (consecutive or not) on which the employee would have worked but could not because of occupational injury or illness. The number of lost workdays should not include the day of injury or onset of illness or any days on which the employee would not have worked even though able to work.
NOTE: For employees not having a regularly scheduled shift, such as certain truck drivers, construction workers. farm labor, casual labor, part-time employees, etc., it may be necessary to estimate the number of lost workdays. Estimates of lost workdays shall be based on prior work history of the employee AND days worked by employees, not ill or injured, working in the department and/or occupation of the ill or injured employee.

Columns 5 and 12- LOST WORKDAYS--DAYS OF RESTRICTED WORK ACTIVITY.
Enter the number of workdays (consecutive or not) on which because of injury or illness:

243

(1) the employee was assigned to another job on a temporary basis or

(2) the employee worked as a permanent job less than full time, or

(3) the employee worked at a permanently assigned job but could not perform all duties normally connected with it.

The number of lost workdays should not include the day of injury or onset of illness or any days on which the employee would not have worked even though able to work.

Columns 6 and 13-   INJURIES OR ILLNESSES WITHOUT LOST WORKDAYS. Self-explanatory.

Columns 7a through 7g-   TYPE OF ILLNESS. Enter a check in only one column for each illness.

TERMINATION OR PERMANENT TRANSFER-Place an asterisk to the right of the entry in columns 7a through 7g (type of illness) which represented a termination of employment or permanent transfer.

Bureau of Labor Statistics
Log and Summary of Occupational
Injuries and Illnesses

NOTE:	This form is required by Public Law 91-596 and must be kept in the establishment for 5 years. Failure to maintain and post can result in the issuance of citations and assessment of penalties. *(See posting requirements on the other side of form.)*			RECORDABLE CASES: You are required to record information about every occupational death, every nonfatal occupational illness, and those nonfatal occupational injuries which involve one or more of the following: loss of consciousness, restriction of work or motion, transfer to another job, or medical treatment (other than first aid). *(See definitions on the other side of form.)*		
Case or File Number	Date of Injury or Onset of Illness	Employee's Name	Occupation	Department		Description of Injury or Illness
Enter a nonduplicating number which will facilitate comparisons with supplementary records.	Enter Mo./day.	Enter first name or initial, middle initial, last name.	Enter regular job title, not activity employee was performing when injured or at onset of illness. In the absence of a formal title, enter a brief description of the employee's duties.	Enter department in which the employee is regularly employed or a description of normal workplace to which employee is assigned, even though temporarily working in another department at the time of injury or illness.		Enter a brief description of the injury or illness and indicate the part or parts of body affected. Typical entries for this column might be: Amputation of 1st joint right forefinger, Strain of lower back, Contact dermatitis on both hands, Electrocution—body.
(A)	(B)	(C)	(D)	(E)		(F)
						PREVIOUS PAGE TOTALS ⟶
						TOTALS (Instructions on other side of form.) ⟶

OSHA No. 200

U.S. Department of Labor

For Calendar Year 19 _____   Page ____ of ____

Company Name	Form Approved
Establishment Name	O.M.B. No. 1220-0029
Establishment Address	

Extent of and Outcome of INJURY						Type, Extent of, and Outcome of ILLNESS														
Fatalities	Nonfatal Injuries					Type of Illness								Fatalities	Nonfatal Illnesses					
Injury Related	Injuries With Lost Workdays				Injuries Without Lost Workdays	CHECK Only One Column for Each Illness *(See other side of form for terminations or permanent transfers.)*								Illness Related	Illnesses With Lost Workdays					Illnesses Without Lost Workdays
Enter DATE of death. Mo./day/yr. (1)	Enter a CHECK if injury involves days away from work, or days of restricted work activity, or both. (2)	Enter a CHECK if injury involves days away from work. (3)	Enter number of DAYS away from work. (4)	Enter number of DAYS of restricted work activity. (5)	Enter a CHECK if no entry was made in columns 1 or 2 but the injury is recordable as defined above. (6)	Occupational skin diseases or disorders (a)	Dust diseases of the lungs (b)	Respiratory conditions due to toxic agents (c)	Poisoning (systemic effects of toxic materials) (d)	Disorders due to physical agents (e)	Disorders associated with repeated trauma (f)	All other occupational illnesses (g)		Enter DATE of death. Mo./day/yr. (8)	Enter a CHECK if illness involves days away from work, or days of restricted work activity, or both. (9)	Enter a CHECK if illness involves days away from work. (10)	Enter number of DAYS away from work. (11)	Enter number of DAYS of restricted work activity. (12)		Enter a CHECK if no entry was made in columns 8 or 9. (13)
									(7)											

INJURIES   ILLNESSES

Certification of Annual Summary Totals By _____ Title _____ Date _____

OSHA No. 200   **POST ONLY THIS PORTION OF THE LAST PAGE NO LATER THAN FEBRUARY 1.**

V. Totals

Add number of entries in columns 1 and 8. Add number of checks in column 2, 3, 6, 7, 9, 10, and 13. Add number of days in columns 4, 5, 11, and 12. Yearly totals for each column (1-13) are required for posting. Running or page totals may be generated at the discretion of the employer.

If an employee's loss of workdays is continuing at the time the totals are summarized, estimate the number of future workdays the employee will lose and add that estimate to the workdays already lost and include this figure in the annual totals. No further entries are to be made with respect to such cases in the next year's log.

VI. Definitions

OCCUPATIONAL INJURY is any injury such as a cut, fracture, sprain, amputation, etc., which results from a work accident or from an exposure involving a single incident in the work environment. **NOTE:** Conditions resulting from animal bites, such as insect or snake bites or from one time exposure to chemicals, are considered to be injuries.

OCCUPATIONAL ILLNESS of an employee is any abnormal condition or disorder, other than one resulting from an occupational injury, caused by exposure to environmental factors associated with employment. It includes acute and chronic illnesses or diseases which may be caused by inhalation, absorption, ingestion, or direct contact.

The following listing gives the categories of occupational illnesses and disorders that will be utilized for the purpose of classifying recordable illnesses. For purposes of information, examples of each category are given. These are typical examples however, and are not to be considered the complete listing of the types of illnesses and disorders that are to be counted under each category.

7a. **Occupational Skin Diseases or Disorders** Examples: Contact dermatitis, eczema, or rash caused by primary irritants and sensitizers or poisonous plants, oil acne, chrome ulcers, chemical burns or inflammations. etc.

7b. **Dust Diseases of the Lungs (Pneumoconiosis)** Examples: Silicosis, abestosis and other asbestos-related diseases, coal worker's pneumoconiosis, byssinosis, siderosis, and other pneumoconioses.

7c. **Respiratory Conditions Due to Toxic Agents** Examples: Pneumonitis, pharyngitis, rhinitis or acute congestion due to chemicals, dust, gases, or fumes, farmer's lung. etc.

7d. **Poisoning (Systemic Effect of Toxic Materials)** Examples: Poisoning by lead, mercury, cadmium, arsenic, or other metals; poisoning by carbon monoxide hydrogen sulfide or other gases, poisoning by benzol, carbon tetrachloride or other organic solvents; poisoning by insecticide sprays such as parathion, lead arsenate; poisoning by other chemicals such as formaldehyde, plastics, and resins, etc.

7e. **Disorders Due to Physical Agents (Other than Toxic Materials)** Examples: Heatstroke, sunstroke, heat exhaustion, and other effects of environmental heat, freezing, frostbite, and effects of exposure to low temperatures, caisson disease; effects of ionizing radiation (isotopes. X-rays, radium); effects of nonionizing radiation (welding flash, ultraviolet rays, microwaves, sunburn), etc.

7f. **Disorders Associated With Repeated Trauma** Examples: Noise-induced hearing loss; synovitis, tenosynovitis, and bursitis, Raynaud's phenomena, and other conditions due to repeated motion, vibration, or pressure.

7g. **All Other Occupational illnesses** Examples. Anthrax, brucellosis, infectious hepatitis, malignant and benign tumors, food poisoning, histoplasmosis, coccidioidomycosis, etc.

MEDICAL TREATMENT includes treatment (other than first aid) administered by a physician or by registered professional personnel under the standing orders of a physician Medical treatment does NOT include first -aid treatment (one-time treatment and subsequent observation of minor scratches, cuts, burns, splinters, and so forth, which do not ordinarily require medical care) even though provided by a physician or registered professional personnel.

ESTABLISHMENT: A single physical location where business is conducted or where services or industrial operations are performed (for example: a factory, mill, store, hotel, restaurant, movie theater, farm, ranch, bank, sales office, warehouse, or central administrative office). Where distinctly separate activities are performed at a single physical location, such as construction activities operated from the same physical location as a lumber yard, each activity shall be treated as a separate establishment.

For firms engaged in activities which may be physically dispersed, such as agriculture: construction, transportation, communications, and electric, gas, and sanitary services, records may be maintained at a place to which employees report each day.

Records for personnel who do not primarily report or work at a single establishment, such as traveling salesmen, technicians, engineers, etc., shall be maintained at the location from which they are paid or the base from which personnel operate to carry out their activities.

WORK ENVIRONMENT is comprised of the physical location, equipment, materials processed or used, and the kinds of operations performed in the course of an employee's work, whether on or off the employer's premises.

BUREAU OF LABOR STATISTICS
SUPPLEMENTARY RECORD OF
OCCUPATIONAL INJURIES
AND ILLNESSES
FORM NO. 101

Bureau of Labor Statistics
Supplementary Record of
Occupational Injuries and Illnesses

U.S. Department of Labor

SUPPLEMENTARY RECORD OF OCCUPATIONAL INJURIES AND ILLNESSES

This form is required by Public Law 91-596 and must be kept in the establishment for 5 years.
Failure to maintain can result in the issuance of citations and assessment of penalties.

Case or File No. _____   Form Approved O M B No 1220 0029

To supplement the Log and Summary of Occupational Injuries and Illnesses (OSHA No. 200), each establishment must maintain a record of each recordable occupational injury or illness. Worker's compensation, insurance, or other reports are acceptable as records if they contain all facts listed below or are supplemented to do so. If no suitable report is made for other purposes, this form (OSHA No. 101) may be used or the necessary facts can be listed on a separate plain sheet of paper. These records must also be available in the establishment without delay and at reasonable times for examination by representatives of the Department of Labor and the Department of Health and Human Services, and States accorded jurisdiction under the Act. The records must be maintained for a period of not less than five years following the end of the calendar year to which they relate.

Such records must contain at least the following facts:

1) *About the employer*—name, mail address, and location if different from mail address.

2) *About the injured or ill employee*—name, social security number, home address, age, sex, occupation, and department.

3) *About the accident or exposure to occupational illness*—place of accident or exposure, whether it was on employer's premises, what the employee was doing when injured, and how the accident occurred

4) *About the occupational injury or illness*—description of the injury or illness, including part of body affected, and name of the object or substance which directly injured the employee, and date of injury or diagnosis of illness.

5) *Other*—name and address of physician, if hospitalized, name and address of hospital, date of report, and name and position of person preparing the report

SEE *DEFINITIONS* ON THE BACK OF OSHA FORM 200.

Employer

1 Name

2 Mail address *(No. and street, city or town, State, and zip code)*

3 Location, if different from mail address

Injured or Ill Employee

4 Name *(First, middle, and last)*   Social Security No.

5 Home address *(No. and street, city or town, State, and zip code)*

6 Age

7 Sex *(Check one)*   Male ☐   Female ☐

8 Occupation *(Enter regular job title, not the specific activity he was performing at time of injury.)*

9 Department *(Enter name of department or division in which the injured person is regularly employed, even though he may have been temporarily working in another department at the time of injury.)*

The Accident or Exposure to Occupational Illness
If accident or exposure occurred on employer's premises, give address of plant or establishment in which it occurred. Do not indicate department or division within the plant or establishment. If accident occurred outside employer's premises at an identifiable address, give that address. If it occurred on a public highway or at any other place which cannot be identified by number and street, please provide place reference locating the place of injury as accurately as possible.

10 Place of accident or exposure *(No. and street, city or town, State, and zip code)*

11 Was place of accident or exposure on employer's premises?   Yes ☐   No ☐

12 What was the employee doing when injured? *(Be specific. If he was using tools or equipment or handling material, name them and tell what he was doing with them.)*

13 How did the accident occur? *(Describe fully the events which resulted in the injury or occupational illness. Tell what happened and how it happened. Name any objects or substance involved and tell how they were involved. Give full details on all factors which led or contributed to the accident. Use separate sheet for additional space.)*

Occupational Injury or Occupational Illness

14 Describe the injury or illness in detail and indicate the part of body affected. *(E.g., amputation of right index finger at second joint; fracture of ribs; lead poisoning; dermatitis of left hand, etc.)*

15 Name the object or substance which directly injured the employee. *(For example, the machine or thing he struck against or which struck him; the vapor or poison he inhaled or swallowed; the chemical or radiation which irritated his skin; or, in cases of strains, hernias, etc., the thing he was lifting, pulling, etc.)*

16 Date of injury or initial diagnosis of occupational illness   17 Did employee die? *(Check one)*   Yes ☐   No ☐

Other

18 Name and address of physician

19 If hospitalized, name and address of hospital

Date of report   Prepared by   Official position

OSHA No. 101 (Feb. 1981)

BUREAU OF LABOR STATISTICS
OCCUPATIONAL INJURIES
AND ILLNESSES
SURVEY FORM NO. 200-S

SECTION I   ANNUAL AVERAGE EMPLOYMENT IN 1990

Enter in Section I the **average** (not the total) number of full and part time employees who worked during calendar year 1990 in the establishment(s) included in this report. If more than one establishment is included in this report, add together the annual average employment for each establishment and enter the sum. Include all classes of employees: seasonal, temporary, administrative, supervisory, clerical, professional, technical, sales, delivery, installation, construction and service personnel, as well as operators and related workers.

Annual Average employment should be computed by summing the employment from all pay periods during 1990 and then dividing that sum by the total number of such pay periods throughout the entire year. In cluding periods with no employment. For example, if you had the following monthly employment: Jan. 10, Feb. 10, Mar. 10, Apr. 5, May 5, June 5, July 5, Aug. 0, Sept. 0, Oct. 0, Nov. 5, Dec. 5, you would sum the number of employees for each monthly pay period in this case, 60) and then divide that total by 12 (the number of pay periods during the year) to derive an annual average employment of 5.

SECTION II   TOTAL HOURS WORKED IN 1990

Enter in Section II the **total** number of hours actually **worked** by all classes of employees during 1990. Be sure to include **only** time on duty. **DO NOT** include **any** non work time even though paid, such as vacations, sick leave, holidays, etc. The hours worked figure should be obtained from payroll or other time records wherever possible. If **hours worked** are not maintained separately from **hours paid**, please enter your best estimate. If actual hours worked are not available for employees paid on commission, salary by the mile, etc. hours worked may be estimated or the basis of scheduled hours or 8 hours per workweek.

For example, if a group of 10 salaried employees worked an average of 8 hours per day, 5 days a week, for 50 weeks of the report period, the total hours worked for this group would be 10 x 8 x 5 x 50 = 20,000 hours for the report period.

SECTION III   NATURE OF BUSINESS IN 1990

In order to verify the nature of business code, we must have information about the specific economic activity carried on by the establishment(s) included in your report during calendar year 1990.

Complete Parts A, B and C as indicated in Section III on the OSHA No. 200 S form. Complete Part C only if supporting services are provided to other establishments of your company. Leave Part C blank if a) supporting services are not the primary function of any establishment(s) included in this report or b) supporting services are provided but only on a **contract or fee basis** for the general public or for other business firms. **(Instructions continued on page 2)**

We estimate that it **will** take an average of 10 30 minutes to complete this form, including time for reviewing instructions, searching existing data sources, gathering and maintaining the data needed, and completing and reviewing this information. If you have any comments regarding these estimates or any other aspect of this Survey, send them to the Bureau of Labor Statistics, Division of Management Systems, (1720 0045), 441 G St. NW, Washington, DC 20212, and to the Office of Management and Budget, Paperwork Reduction Project (1220 0045). Washington, DC 20503.

INSTRUCTIONS FOR COMPLETING THE OSHA NO. 200 S FORM
1990 OCCUPATIONAL INJURIES AND ILLNESSES SURVEY
(Covering Calendar Year 1990)

Change of Ownership When there has been a change of ownership during the report period, only the records of the current owner are to be entered in the report. Explain fully under Comments, (Section VIII, and include the date of the ownership change and the time period this report covers.

Partial Year Reporting For any establishment(s) which was not in existence for the entire report year (the report should cover the portion of the period during which the establishment was in existence. Explain fully under Comments (Section VIII, including the time period this report covers.

ESTABLISHMENTS INCLUDED IN THE REPORT

This report should include only those establishments located in, or identified by, the Report Location and Identification designation which appears next to your mailing address. This designation may be a geographic area, usually a county or city, or it could be a brief description of your operation within a geographic area. If you have any questions concerning the coverage of this report, please contact the agency identified on the OSHA No. 200 S report form.

DEFINITION OF ESTABLISHMENT

An ESTABLISHMENT is defined as a single physical location where business is conducted or where services or industrial operations are performed. (For example, a factory, mill, store, hotel, restaurant, movie theatre, farm, ranch, bank, sales office, warehouse, or central administrative office.)

For firms engaged in activities such as construction, transportation, communications, or electric, gas and sanitary services, which may be physically dispersed, reports should cover the place(s) to which employees normally report each day.

Reports for personnel who do not primarily report or work at a single establishment such as traveling salesmen, technicians, engineers, etc. should cover the location from which they are paid or the base from which personnel operate to carry out their activities.

- 2 -

NOTE: If more than one establishment is included, information in Section III should reflect the combined activities of all such establishments. One code will be assigned which best indicates the nature of business of the group of establishments as a whole.

SECTION IV TESTING FOR DRUG OR ALCOHOL USE

A Check the appropriate box. Check "Yes" if your company had a formal written policy, during calendar year 1990, to test **JOB APPLICANTS and/or EMPLOYEES** for drug or alcohol use. Examples of testing policies include: "For cause", for selected jobs, random tests, as part of an annual physical, periodic tests, or testing all employees.

Drug Test A test designed to detect the presence of metabolites or drugs in urine or blood specimens.

Drugs include opioids, cocaine, cannabinoids (such as marijuana or hashish), hallucinogens, and their derivatives. Drugs for which persons have prescriptions (whether or not the prescription was legally obtained) are excluded. Please answer part B.

B Check the appropriate box. Check "Yes" only if an employee was **actually tested** for drug or alcohol use in connection with a work related injury or illness, **EVEN IF THE EMPLOYEE WAS ONE OTHER THAN THE EMPLOYEE WHO WAS INJURED OR BECAME ILL,** during calendar year 1990. Only drug or alcohol tests administered at the request of the company, whether actually administered by the company or another organization, should be considered when answering this question.

SECTION V RECORDABLE INJURIES AND ILLNESSES

Check the appropriate box. If you checked "Yes", complete Sections VI and VII on the back of the form. If you checked "No", complete only Section VII.

SECTION VI OCCUPATIONAL INJURY AND ILLNESS SUMMARY

This section can be completed easily by copying the totals from the annual summary of your 1990 OSHA No. 200 form (Log and Summary of Occupational Injuries and Illnesses). Please note that if this report covers more than one establishment, the final totals on the "Log" for each must be added and the sums entered in Section VI.

Leave Section VI blank if the employees covered in this report experienced no recordable injuries or illnesses during 1990.

If there were recordable injuries or illnesses during the year, please review your OSHA No. 200 form for each establishment to be included in this report to make sure that all entries are correct and complete before completing Section VI. Each recordable case should be included on the "Log" in only one of the six main categories of injuries or illnesses.

1 INJURY related deaths (Log column 1)
2 INJURIES with days away from work and/or restricted days (Log column 2)
3 INJURIES without lost workdays (Log column 6)
4 ILLNESS related deaths (Log column 8)
5 ILLNESSES with days away from work and/or restricted days (Log column 9)
6 ILLNESSES without lost workdays (Log column 13)

Also review each case to ensure that the appropriate entries have been made for the other columns if applicable. For example, if the case is an injury with Lost Workdays, be sure that the check for an injury involving days away from work (Log column 3) is entered if necessary. Also verify that the correct number of days away from work (Log column 4) and/or days of restricted work activity (Log column 5) are recorded. A similar review should be made for a case which is an illness with Lost Workdays (including Log columns 10, 11 and 12). Please remember that if your employees' loss of workdays is still continuing at the time the annual summary for the year is completed, you should estimate the number of future workdays they will lose and add this estimate to the actual workdays already lost. Each partial day away from work, other than the day of the occurrence of the injury or onset of illness, should be entered as one full restricted workday.

Also, for each case which is an illness, make sure that the appropriate column indicating Type of Illness (Log columns 7a-7g) is checked.

After completing your review of the individual case entries on the "Log," please make sure that the "Totals" line has been completed by summarizing Columns 1 through 13 according to the instructions on the back of the "Log" form. Then, copy these "Totals" onto Section VI of the OSHA No. 200 S form. If you entered fatalities in columns (1) and/or (8), please include in the "Comments" section a brief description of the object or event which caused each fatality.

FIRST AID

Finally, please remember that all injuries which, in your judgement, required only **First Aid Treatment**, even when administered by a doctor or nurse, should not be included in this report. First Aid Treatment is defined as one time treatment and subsequent observation of minor scratches, cuts, burns, splinters, etc., which do not ordinarily require medical care.

SECTION VII COMMENTS AND IDENTIFICATION

Please complete all parts including your area code and telephone number. Then return the OSHA No. 200 S form in the pre-addressed envelope. **KEEP** your file copy.

1990 OSHA No. 200-S

U.S. Department of Labor
Bureau of Labor Statistics for the Occupational Safety and Health Administration

Annual Occupational Injuries and Illnesses Survey Covering Calendar Year 1990

The information collected on this form will be used for statistical purposes only by the BLS, OSHA, and the cooperating State Agencies. | THIS REPORT IS MANDATORY UNDER PUBLIC LAW 91-596. FAILURE TO REPORT CAN RESULT IN THE ISSUANCE OF CITATIONS AND ASSESSMENT OF PENALTIES. | O.M.B No. 1220-0045   Approval Exp. 9/30/92

Burden Statement Located in Instructions

St.   Sch. No.   Ck.   Suf.

SIC

EDIT

Complete and return ONLY THIS FORM within 30 days

Complete this report whether or not there were recordable occupational injuries or illnesses.
PLEASE READ THE ENCLOSED INSTRUCTIONS

I. ANNUAL AVERAGE EMPLOYMENT IN 1990

Enter the average number of employees who worked during calendar year 1990 in the establishment(s) covered by this report. Include all classes of employees: full-time, part-time, seasonal, temporary, etc. See the instructions for an example of an annual average employment calculation. *(Round to the nearest whole number.)*

II. TOTAL HOURS WORKED IN 1990

Enter the total number of hours actually worked during 1990 by all employees covered by this report. DO NOT include any non-work time even though paid such as vacations, sick leave, etc. If employees worked low hours in 1990 due to layoffs, strikes, fires, etc.. explain under Comments (section VII). *(Round to the nearest whole number.)*

III. NATURE OF BUSINESS IN 1990

A. Check the box which best describes the general type of activity performed by the establishment(s) included in this report.

☐ Agriculture
☐ Forestry
☐ Fishing
☐ Mining
☐ Construction
☐ Manufacturing
☐ Transportation
☐ Communication
☐ Public Utilities
☐ Wholesale Trade
☐ Retail Trade
☐ Finance
☐ Insurance
☐ Real Estate
☐ Services
☐ Public Administration

B. Enter in order of importance the principal products, lines of trade, services or other activities. For each entry also include the approximate percent of total 1990 annual value of production, sales or receipts.

_____ %
_____ %
_____ %

C. If this report includes any establishment(s) which perform services for other units of your company, indicate the primary type of service or support provided. *(Check as many as apply.)*

1. ☐ Central administration
2. ☐ Research, development and testing
3. ☐ Storage (warehouse)
4. ☐ Other (specify)

IV. TESTING FOR DRUG OR ALCOHOL USE

A. Did the establishment(s) covered by this report have a formal **written** policy to test job applicants and/or employees for drug or alcohol use during calendar year 1990?

1. ☐ No
2. ☐ Yes

B. Were any drug or alcohol tests administered at the company's request to any employees as the result of the occurrence of a recordable work-related injury or illness during calendar year 1990?

1. ☐ No
2. ☐ Yes

V. RECORDABLE INJURIES AND ILLNESSES

Did the establishment(s) have any recordable injuries or illnesses during calendar year 1990?

1. ☐ No (Please complete section VII.)

2. ☐ Yes (Please complete sections VI and VII.)

SEE REVERSE →

RETURN REPORT TO:

U.S. Department of Labor
Bureau of Labor Statistics
OSH Survey, Mail Code 51
441 G Street, N.W.
Washington, D.C. 20212

REPORT LOCATION AND IDENTIFICATION

Complete this report for the establishment(s) covered by the description below:

Please indicate any address changes below.

OSHA No. 200-S (Revised December 1990)

VI. OCCUPATIONAL INJURY AND ILLNESS SUMMARY (Covering Calendar Year 1990)

- *Complete this section by copying totals from the annual summary of your 1990 OSHA No. 200.*
- Reminder to reverse the carbon insert before completing this side
- Leave section VI blank if there were no OSHA recordable injuries or illnesses during 1990.
- *Note: First aid for injuries even when administered by a doctor or nurse is not recordable.*

- Please check your figures to be certain that the sum of entries in columns (7a) – (7b) = (7c) + (7d) + (7e) + (7h) + (7g) = the sum of entries in columns (8) – (9) + (13)
- If you listed fatalities in columns (1) and/or (8), please give a brief description of the object or event which caused each fatality in the "Comments" section

OCCUPATIONAL INJURY CASES

INJURY RELATED FATAL-ITIES** (DEATHS)	INJURIES WITH LOST WORKDAYS				INJURIES WITHOUT LOST WORK-DAYS*
	Injury cases with days away from work and/or restricted workdays	Injury cases with days away from work	Total days away from work	Total days of restricted activity	
Number of DEATHS in col 1 of the log (OSHA No. 200)	Number of CHECKS in col 2 of the log (OSHA No. 200)	Number of CHECKS in col 3 of the log (OSHA No. 200)	Sum of the DAYS in col 4 of the log (OSHA No. 200)	Sum of the DAYS in col 5 of the log (OSHA No. 200)	Number of CHECKS in col 6 of the log (OSHA No. 200)
(1)	(2)	(3)	(4)	(5)	(6)

DEATHS

OCCUPATIONAL ILLNESS CASES

TYPE OF ILLNESS Enter the number of checks from the appropriate columns of the log (OSHA No. 200).								ILLNESS RELATED FATAL-ITIES** (DEATHS)	ILLNESSES WITH LOST WORKDAYS				ILLNESSES WITHOUT LOST WORK-DAYS*
Occupational skin diseases or disorders	Dust diseases of the lungs	Respiratory conditions due to toxic agents	Poisoning (systemic effects of toxic materials)	Disorders due to physical agents	Disorders associated with repeated trauma	All other occupational illnesses			Illness cases with days away from work and/or restricted workdays	Illness cases with days away from work	Total days away from work	Total days of restricted activity	
								Number of DEATHS in col 8 of the log (OSHA No. 200)	Number of CHECKS in col 9 of the log (OSHA No. 200)	Number of CHECKS in col 10 of the log (OSHA No. 200)	Sum of the DAYS in col 11 of the log (OSHA No. 200)	Sum of the DAYS in col 12 of the log (OSHA No. 200)	Number of CHECKS in col 13 of the log (OSHA No. 200)
(a)	(b)	(c)	(d)	(e)	(f)	(g)	(7)	(8)	(9)	(10)	(11)	(12)	(13)

DEATHS

* WITHOUT LOST WORKDAYS—CASES (WITH NO DAYS LOST) RESULTING IN EITHER: DIAGNOSIS OF OCCUPATIONAL ILLNESS, LOSS OF CONSCIOUSNESS, RESTRICTION OF WORK OR MOTION (ON THE DAY OF OCCURRENCE), TRANSFER TO ANOTHER JOB, OR MEDICAL TREATMENT BEYOND FIRST AID.

** IF YOU LISTED FATALITIES IN COLUMNS (1) AND/OR (8), PLEASE GIVE A BRIEF DESCRIPTION OF THE OBJECT OR EVENT WHICH CAUSED EACH FATALITY IN THE "COMMENTS" SECTION BELOW.

VII. REPORT PREPARED BY (Please type or print)

NAME _____

TITLE _____

SIGNATURE _____

AREA CODE _____ PHONE _____

DATE _____

COMMENTS _____

Appendix F
OSHA Inspection Procedures

Editor's Note: This appendix consists of Chapter III of the Occupational Safety and Health Administration's "Field Operations Manual," which provides guidelines to OSHA compliance officers on conducting inspections of business establishments.

FIELD OPERATIONS MANUAL
CHAPTER III — COMPLIANCE INSPECTION PROGRAMMING

(Issued by OSHA Instruction CPL 2.45B, June 15, 1989; Amended by OSHA Instruction CPL 2.45B CH–1, December 31, 1990)

A. CHSO Responsibilities.

1. The primary responsibility of the Compliance Safety and Health Officer (CSHO) is to carry out the mandate given to the Secretary of Labor, namely, "to assure so far as possible every working man and woman in the Nation safe and healthful working conditions...." To accomplish this mandate the Occupational Safety and Health Administration employs a wide variety of programs and initiatives, one of which is enforcement of standards through the conduct of effective inspections to determine whether employers are:

a. Furnishing places of employment free from recognized hazards that are causing or are likely to cause death or serious physical harm to their employees, and

b. Complying with safety and health standards and regulations promulgated under the Act.

2. The conduct of effective inspections requires identification, professional evaluation and accurate reporting of safety and health conditions and practices. Inspections may vary considerably in scope and detail, depending upon the circumstances in each case.

B. Preparation.

1. **General Planning.** It is most important that the CSHO spend an adequate amount of time preparing for an inspection.

a. CSHOs shall plan individual work schedules in advance in coordination with their supervisor reflecting the priorities in Chapter II.

b. Data available at the Area Office shall be reviewed for information relevant to the establishments scheduled for inspection. These may include inspection files, other establishment files and reference materials. When CSHOs need additional information concerning the type of industry to be inspected, the supervisor shall be consulted.

2. **Preinspection Planning.** Due to the wide variety of industries and associated hazards likely to be encountered, preinspection preparation is essential to the conduct of a quality inspection. The CSHO together with the supervisor shall carefully review:

a. All pertinent information contained in the establishment file and appropriate reference sources to become knowledgeable in the potential hazards and industrial processes that may be encountered and shall identify the personal protective equipment necessary for protection against these anticipated hazards.

b. Appropriate standards and sampling methods and, based on experience and information on file concerning the establishment, shall select the instruments and equipment that will be

256

needed for the inspection and prepare them according to the standard methods of sampling and calibration.

3. Preinspection Compulsory Process. 29 CFR 1903.4 authorizes the agency to seek a warrant in advance of an attempted inspection if circumstances are such that "preinspection process (is) desirable or necessary." The Act authorizes the agency to issue administrative subpoenas to obtain necessary evidence with no time restrictions.

a. Although agency policy is generally not to seek warrants without evidence that the employer is likely to refuse entry, the Regional Administrator may, on a case-by-case basis, authorize the Area Director to seek compulsory process in advance of an attempt to inspect or investigate whenever circumstances indicate the desirability of such warrants.

NOTE: Examples of such circumstances would be evidence of being denied entry in previous inspections, or awareness that a job will only last a short time or that job processes will be changing rapidly.

b. Administrative subpoenas may also be issued prior to any attempt to contact the employer or other person for evidence related to an OSHA inspection or investigation.

4. Inspection Materials and Equipment. The CSHO shall have all report forms and handouts available and in sufficient quantity to conduct the inspection and all assigned personal protective equipment available for use and in serviceable condition.

a. If, based on the preinspection review or upon facts discovered at the worksite, a need for unassigned personal protective equipment is identified, the supervisor shall ensure that any required equipment is provided. Prior to the inspection, the supervisor shall ensure that the CSHO has been trained in the uses and limitations of such equipment.

b. Unless an exception is authorized by the supervisor because of the nature of the worksite (e.g., a worksite where no overhead hazards, no eye hazards and/or no foot hazards are likely to be present), approved hard hats, approved safety glasses with permanently or rigidly attached side shields and approved safety shoes shall be worn by CSHOs on the walkaround phase of all inspections. This will set an example for industry and provide minimum acceptable protection for the CSHO.

c. Inspections involving the use of negative pressure respirators shall not be assigned without the CSHO's having had an adequate quantitative fit test within the last year. Since respirators with tight-fitting facepieces require the skin to be clean shaven at the points where sealing occurs, CSHOs assigned to conduct inspections which involve the use of such respirators shall not have interfering facial hair.

d. If there is a need for special or additional inspection equipment, the supervisor shall be consulted to ensure that training in the use and limitation of such equipment has been accomplished prior to the inspection. The supervisor shall ensure that a review or recheck in the use of all equipment is given to the CSHO at least once a year.

5. Expert Assistance. The Area Director shall arrange through the Regional Administrator for a specialist from within OSHA to assist in an inspection or investigation when the need for such expertise is identified. If OSHA specialists are not available, or when otherwise desirable, the Regional Administrator shall arrange for the procurement of the services of qualified consultants. For further details on the selection of experts, see Chapter VIII, D.2.

a. Expert assistance may be necessary during inspections for the implementation of engineering or administrative controls involving, but not limited to, noise, air contaminants, complicated machine guarding and construction.

b. OSHA specialists may accompany the CSHO or perform their tasks sepa-

257

rately. Outside consultants must be accompanied by a CSHO. OSHA specialists and outside consultants shall be briefed on the purpose of the inspection and personal protective equipment to be utilized.

c. All data, conclusions and recommendations from the assigned specialists shall be made part of the inspection report, including information on any resultant actions.

6. Safety and Health Rules of the Employer. 29 CFR 1903.7(c) requires that the CSHO comply with all safety and health rules and practices at the establishment and wear or use the safety clothing or protective equipment required by OSHA standards or by the employer for the protection of employees.

7. Immunization and Other Special Entrance Requirements. Many pharmaceutical firms, medical research laboratories and hospitals have areas which have special entrance requirements. These requirements may include proof of up-to-date immunization and the use of respirators, special clothing or other protective devices or equipment.

a. The CSHO will not enter any area where special entrance restrictions apply until the required precautions have been taken. It shall be ascertained prior to inspection, if possible, if an establishment has areas with immunization or other special entrance requirements. If the supervisor and CSHO cannot make a determination through consultation, the Area Director or supervisor may telephone the establishment using the following procedures. Such communication will NOT be considered advance notice. (See 29 CFR 1903.6 and C of this chapter if advance notice is to be given.)

(1) Telephone as far in advance of the proposed inspection date as possible so the employer cannot determine a time relationship between the communication and a possible future inspection.

(2) State the purpose of the inquiry and that an inspection may be scheduled in the future. DO NOT GIVE A SPECIFIC DATE.

(3) Determine the type of immunization(s) and/or special precautions required and the building or area which has restricted access.

b. If immunization is required, the supervisor shall ensure that the inspecting CSHO has the proper immunization and that any required incubation or waiting period is met prior to the inspection. Those immunizations necessary to complete inspections will be provided by the Region. (See D.8.e.(2) for procedures to follow if immunization areas are initially identified during walkaround.)

8. Personal Security Clearance. Some establishments have areas which contain material or processes which are classified by the U.S. Government in the interest of national security. Whenever an inspection is scheduled for an establishment containing classified areas, the supervisor shall assign a CSHO who has the appropriate security clearances. The Regional Administrator shall ensure that an adequate number of CSHOs with appropriate security clearances are available within the Region.

a. *Clearance Procedures.* Appropriate U.S. Department or agency security clearances, such as those required by the Department of Defense (DoD) or the Department of Energy (DoE) may be required both at civilian establishments with Government contracts requiring security areas and at Government installations that have civilian contractor operations.

(1) The Regional Administrators and Area Directors shall select the individual CSHOs who require clearance at each Regional and Area Office for Top Secret, Secret, Confidential and DoE "Q" clearances. These requirements shall be based on the number of defense contract or classified Federal Agency establishments in the area. As

an initial guideline the Regional Administrator may require one CSHO with "Top Secret" and one with a DoE "Q" clearance located at any Area Office with the need for such clearances. The Area Office may require two CSHOs with "Secret" and as many "Confidential" clearances as the Area Director may consider necessary.

(2) Area Directors and Regional Administrators shall review at least annually the security clearance needs of each Area Office. If any additional CSHO clearances are needed, the Area Director shall follow the procedures given in (3).

(3) The Area Director shall submit the names of the individuals and the type of clearance desired for each to the Director, Office of Field Programs, through the Regional Administrator.

(4) The Director, Office of Field Programs shall forward the names to the Director of Administrative Programs who shall obtain the necessary clearances and prepare a list of names of OSHA personnel cleared for access to defense plants. The list, arranged geographically, will be submitted to the DoD with copies to the appropriate Regional and Area Offices. Since the list will be sent to the 11 DoD Regional Industrial Security Ofces, a telephone verification by the plant security personnel is all that should be required upon the arrival of the CSHO.

(5) The DoE clearance list will be distributed by DoE to their field offices. Local office approval shall be obtained just before the inspections. Since these approvals are checked with the DoE Washington Office, a reasonable delay should be anticipated. However, there should be very few situations requiring access to areas under DoE security.

(6) Lists of OSHA personnel with various types of clearances shall be reviewed and updated annually. If there is any change to the list previously received under (4), a revised list shall be submitted to the Director, Office of Field Programs in accordance with the procedures in (3).

b. *Employer Resistance.* For worksites with limited areas subject to DoD security regulations, where the CSHO does not have the necessary clearance requirements, the employer shall be asked to immediately contact the cognizant DoD Regional Industrial Security Office and shall make arrangements which allow the CSHO to complete the investigation or inspection without breaching security requirements. Resistance to CSHO's with the proper clearances which can be telephonically checked shall constitute an unwarranted resistance and shall be immediately brought to the attention of the Area Director.

c. *Classified Information and Trade Secrets.* Any classified information and/or personal knowledge of such information by OSHA personnel shall be handled in accordance with the regulations of the responsible agency. The collection of such information, and the number of exposed personnel shall be limited to the minimum necessary for the conduct of such compliance activities.

C. Advance Notice of Inspections.

1. Policy. Section 17(f) of the Act and 29 CFR 1903.6 contain a general prohibition against the giving of advance notice of inspections, except as authorized by the Secretary or the Secretary's designees.

a. The Occupational Safety and Health Act regulates many conditions which are subject to speedy alteration and disguise by employers. To forestall such changes in worksite conditions, the Act, in Section 4(a), prohibits unauthorized advance notice and authorizes OSHA to enter worksites "without delay" in order to preserve the element of surprise.

b. There may be occasions when advance notice is necessary to conduct an effective investigation. These occasions are narrow exceptions to the statutory prohibition against advance notice.

c. Advance notice of inspections may be given only in the following situations:

(1) In cases of apparent imminent danger to enable the employer to correct the danger as quickly as possible;

(2) When the inspection can most effectively be conducted after regular business hours or when special preparations are necessary;

(3) To ensure the presence of employer and employee representatives or other appropriate personnel who, as determined by the Area Director, are needed to aid in the inspection; and

(4) When the Area Director determines that giving advance notice would enhance the probability of an effective and thorough inspection; e.g., in complex fatality investigations.

d. Advance notice exists whenever the Area Director sets up a specific date or time with the employer for the CSHO to begin an inspection, or to continue an inspection that was interrupted or delayed more than 5 working days as described in C.1.d.(3). It generally does not include nonspecific indications of potential future inspections.

(1) Although advance notice normally does not exist after the CSHO has arrived at the worksite, presented credentials and announced the inspection, many causes can serve to delay or interrupt the continued conduct of the inspection. For example, the employer representative on site may request a delay of entry pending the return of the president or some other higher ranking official, or sampling may have to be delayed for some reason after completion of the initial walkaround.

(a) Such delays shall be as short as possible. If an employer's (or an employee representative's) request for delay appears reasonable, the CSHO may delay or interrupt the inspection for up to an hour. The supervisor shall be contacted, if the delay lasts or is anticipated to last longer than one hour.

(b) The supervisor shall decide whether the circumstances justify a delay of more than one hour and, if so, for how long. If the delay appears reasonable, the inspection may be delayed or interrupted for the time judged necessary, but in no case for longer than 5 working days except as indicated in C.1.d.(3).

(c) In cases where screening sampling is performed and laboratory analysis of the samples is required, there shall be no more than 5 working days between receipt of screening results and the onset of full-shift sampling.

(d) The inspection shall be resumed as soon as reasonably possible. Delays or interruptions of less than 5 working days shall not require implementation of advance notice procedures.

(2) If the employer or the employee representative requests a delay which the supervisor believes is unreasonable or without sufficient justification (e.g., too long, not in good faith) or if the delay requested is for more than 5 working days except as indicated in C.1.d.(3), the CSHO shall inform the requester that agency policy does not allow for such a delay. If the employer representative continues to insist on the delay, the situation shall be treated as a refusal of entry and shall be handled in accordance with the procedures in D.1.d.(1).

(3) In unusual circumstances, the Area Director may decide that a delay of more than 5 working days is necessary; e.g., the process to be sampled may not be activated within that time or compliance personnel may not be available in the Area Office because of higher priority demands. Any situation involving a delay of more than 5 working days, whatever the justification, shall be handled as advance notice and must be approved by the Area Director. In such cases the procedures in C.2. shall be observed in addition to the following:

(a) The CSHO shall determine whether employees at the worksite are represented by a labor organization or a safety committee and, if so, who the authorized representative of employees is.

(b) The CSHO shall notify the employee representative of the delay as promptly as possible and shall keep the representative informed of future appointments or other arrangements for resuming the inspection.

(c) If more than one employer is at the worksite, authorized employee representatives of all such employers shall be notified of the delay as promptly as possible and kept informed of arrangements for resuming the inspection.

(d) The CSHO may request the employer(s) to inform the employee representatives of the delay and to notify them promptly when arrangements have been made to resume the inspection.

(e) If there is no authorized representative of employees, the procedures in C.2.h. shall be followed.

2. Procedures. In the situations described in C.1.c. and d.(3), advance notice may be given by the CSHO only after authorization by the Area Director. In cases of apparent imminent danger, however, advance notice may be given by the CSHO without such authorization if the Area Director is not immediately available. The Area Director shall be notified as soon as possible and kept apprised of all details.

a. If it is decided to provide advance notice, the CSHO shall do so by telephone or other appropriate contact. This contact normally shall be made not more than 24 hours prior to the inspection. Documentation of the conditions requiring advance notice and the procedures followed shall be included in the case file.

b. If advance notice is to be given at a construction or other multiple employer site, the CSHO shall contact the general contractor. If there are two or more general contractors, all shall be contacted. The general contractor shall be informed of the responsibility of advising all subcontractors on the site of the inspection.

c. During the telephone contact with the employer, the CSHO shall identify himself/herself, explain the purpose of the inspection, state when the inspection is expected to be conducted, ascertain the employer's normal business hours and whether special protective equipment or precautions are required. If security clearances or immunizations are necessary, the supervisor shall be notified. (See B.7. for immunization requirements and B.8. for personal security clearance.)

d. An important purpose of advance notice is to make arrangements for the presence of employer and employee representatives to aid in the conduct of an effective and thorough inspection. A responsible management official shall be requested to assist in the inspection. The CSHO shall advise the employer that Section 8(e) of the Act and 29 CFR 1903.8 require that an employee representative be given an opportunity to participate in the inspection.

e. The CSHO shall determine if employees at the establishment are represented by a labor organization(s) and if there is a safety committee with employee representatives. The CSHO shall advise the employer that, when advance notice is given, it is the employer's responsibility to notify the authorized employee representative(s) promptly of the inspection.

f. If a general contractor is contacted, it shall be pointed out that it is that contractor's responsibility to instruct each subcontractor of the obligation to notify employee representatives promptly of the inspection.

g. If the employer requests and furnishes the identity of the representative, the CSHO shall promptly inform the employee representative of the inspection and shall provide any other information necessary in accordance with 29 CFR 1903.6(b).

h. The advance notice requirement with respect to employees applies only if there is a known representative authorized by employees, such as a labor organization or a safety committee with employee representatives. If there is no authorized employee representative or if it cannot be determined with reasonable certainty who the representative is, the CSHO shall consult with a reasonable number of employees during the inspection to determine the impact or possible adverse effects of the advance notice.

D. Conduct of the Inspection.

1. Entry of the Workplace. The CSHO shall enter the establishment to be inspected with an attitude reflecting a professional, balanced, and thorough concern for safety and health.

a. *Time of Inspection.* Inspections shall be made during regular working hours of the establishment except when special circumstances indicate otherwise. The supervisor shall be contacted before entry during other than normal working hours.

b. *Severe Weather Conditions.* If severe weather conditions encountered during an inspection cause workplace activities to shut down, the inspection shall be continued at a later time as soon as weather permits.

(1) If work continues during adverse weather conditions but the CSHO decides that the weather interferes with the effectiveness of the inspection, it shall be terminated and continued when conditions improve.

(2) If work continues and the CSHO decides to continue the inspection in spite of bad weather, hazardous conditions created by the weather shall be noted since they may be the subject of later citation.

c. *Presenting Credentials.* At the beginning of the inspection the CSHO shall attempt to locate the owner, operator or agent in charge at the workplace and present credentials. On construction sites this will most often be the representative of the general contractor. In the following circumstances, the CSHO shall:

(1) When the person in charge is not present at the beginning of the inspec-

tion, identify the top management official. This person may be the foreman, leadman, gang boss or senior member of the crew.

(2) When neither the person in charge nor a management official is present, contact the employer by telephone and request the presence of the owner, operator or management official. The inspection shall not be delayed unreasonably to await the arrival of the employer representative. This delay shall not normally exceed one hour.

(3) If the person in charge at the workplace cannot be determined by (1) and (2) above, record the extent of the inquiry in the case file and proceed with the physical inspection after contacting the supervisor. If the person in charge arrives during the inspection, an abbreviated opening conference shall be held, and the person shall be informed of the status of the inspection and included in the continued walkaround.

(4) When an inspection is scheduled for a military base or other Federal facility, first contact the base commander and/or other government person in charge to inform him or her of OSHA's presence on the facility, to request permission to inspect a contractor and to invite appropriate participation.

(5) On multi-employer sites ask the superintendent, project manager or other representative of the general or prime contractor to identify the subcontractors or other contractors on the site together with the names of the individuals in charge of their operations.

(a) The CSHO shall then request that these individuals be contacted and asked to assemble in the general contractor's office or other suitable location, together with their employee representatives, if any.

(b) The inspection shall not be postponed or unreasonably delayed because of the unavailability of one or more representatives.

(c) If a Federal contracting agency representative is onsite, the general contractor shall be asked to contact the representative, advising him or her of the inspection and extending an invitation to attend the opening conference and to participate in the inspection.

d. *Refusal to Permit Inspection.* Section 8 of the Act provides that CSHOs may enter without delay and at reasonable times any establishment covered under the Act for the purpose of conducting an inspection. An employer has a right to require that the CSHO seek an inspection warrant prior to entering an establishment and may refuse entry without such a warrant.

NOTE: On a military base or other Federal government facility, the following guidelines do not apply. Instead, a representative of the controlling authority shall be informed of the contractor's refusal and asked to take appropriate action to obtain cooperation.

(1) *Refusal of Entry or Inspection.* The CSHO shall not engage in argument concerning refusal. When the employer refuses to permit entry upon being presented proper credentials or allows entry but then refuses to permit or hinders the inspection in some way, a tactful attempt shall be made to obtain as much information as possible about the establishment. (See D.1.d(5)(b) 7 for the information the CSHO shall attempt to obtain.)

(a) If the employer refuses to allow an inspection of the establishment to proceed, the CSHO shall leave the premises and immediately report the refusal to the supervisor. The Area Director shall notify the Regional Administrator.

(b) If the employer raises no objection to the inspection of portions of the workplace, the CSHO, after informing the supervisor of the partial refusal, shall normally continue the inspection, confining it to the portions concerning which the employer has raised no objections.

(c) In either case the CSHO shall advise the employer that the refusal will be reported to the supervisor and that the agency may take further action, including obtaining legal process.

(2) *Questionable Refusal.* When permission to enter or inspect is not clearly given, the CSHO shall make an effort to clarify the employer's intent.

(a) If there is doubt as to whether the employer intends to permit an inspection, the CSHO *shall not proceed* but shall contact the supervisor immediately. When the employer's intent is clarified, the CSHO shall either conduct the inspection or proceed as outlined in D.1.d.(1).

(b) When the employer hesitates or leaves for a period of time so that permission is not clearly given within one hour of initial entry, the CSHO shall contact the supervisor, who shall decide whether or not permission is being refused.

1. The CSHO may answer reasonable questions presented by the employer; e.g.; the scope of the inspection, purpose, anticipated length.

2. The CSHO shall avoid giving any impression of unyielding insistence or intimidation concerning the right to inspect.

(c) If it becomes clear that the employer is refusing permission to enter, the CSHO shall leave the establishment and contact the supervisor.

(3) *Employer Interference.* Where entry has been allowed but the employer interferes with or limits any important aspect of the inspection, the CSHO shall immediately contact the supervisor for instructions on whether or not to consider this action as a refusal. Examples of interference are refusals to permit the walkaround, the examination of records essential to the inspection, the taking of essential photographs, the inspection of a particular part of the premises, indispensable employee interviews, or the refusal to allow attachment of sampling devices.

(4) *Administrative Subpoena.* Whenever there is a reasonable need for records, documents, testimony and/or other supporting evidence nec-

essary for completing an inspection scheduled in accordance with any current and approved inspection scheduling system or an investigation of any matter properly falling within the statutory authority of the agency, the Regional Administrator may issue an administrative subpoena. (For medical records, however, see D.7.a.(4).)

(a) If a person refuses to provide requested information or evidence, the CSHO shall explain the reason for the request. If he/she continues to refuse to produce the information or evidence requested, the CSHO shall inform the person that the refusal will be reported to the supervisor and that the agency may take further legal action.

(b) If an administrative subpoena appears to be indicated, the Area Director shall prepare a subpoena for the Regional Administrator's signature. The draft subpoena, together with written supportive documentation, shall be forwarded as soon as practicable to the Regional Administrator.

(c) The Regional Administrator shall evaluate the documentation and decide whether to issue a subpoena.

(d) If the Regional Administrator, after consultation with the Regional Solicitor, believes that the subpoena should be issued, he/she shall sign it and forward the signed document to the Area Director or other local supervisor for service.

(e) The subpoena shall normally be served by personal service. In exceptional circumstances service may be by certified mail with return receipt requested.

(f) The person served may comply with the subpoena by making the information or evidence available immediately to the CSHO upon service, or by making the information or evidence available at the time and place specified in the subpoena.

(g) If the person served honors the subpoena, the inspection or other investigation shall proceed as usual.

(h) If the person served refuses to honor the subpoena, the Area Director shall proceed as usual for cases involving a refusal of entry and shall refer the matter, through the Regional Administrator, to the Regional Solicitor for appropriate action.

(5) *Obtaining Compulsory Process.* If it is determined, upon refusal of entry or upon refusal to produce required evidence, that a warrant will be sought, the Area Director shall proceed according to guidelines and procedures established in the Region for warrant applications.

(a) With the approval of the Regional Administrator and the Regional Solicitor, the Area Director may initiate the compulsory process.

(b) If the warrant is to be obtained by the Regional Solicitor, the Area Director shall transmit in writing to the Regional Solicitor, within 48 hours after the determination is made that compulsory process (warrant) is necessary, the following information:

1 Area/District Office, telephone number (FTS), and the name of supervisor involved.

2 Name of CSHO attempting inspection and inspection number, if assigned. Identify whether inspection to be conducted included safety items, health items or both.

3 Legal name of establishment and address including City, State and County. Include site location if different from mailing address.

4 Estimated number of employees at inspection site.

5 SIC Code and high hazard ranking for that specific industry within the State, as obtained from statistics provided by the National Office.

6 Summary of all facts leading to the refusal of entry or limitation of inspection, including the following:

a Date and time of entry.

b Date and time of denial.

c Stage of denial (entry, opening conference, walkaround, etc.).

7 Narrative of all actions taken by the CSHO leading up to, during and after refusal including, as a minimum, the following information:

a Full name and title of the person to whom CSHO presented credentials.

b Full name and title of person(s) who refused entry.

c Reasons stated for the denial by person(s) refusing entry.

d Response, if any, by CSHO to *c* above.

e Name and address of witnesses to denial of entry.

8 All previous inspection information, including copies of the previous citations.

9 Previous requests for warrants. Attach details, if applicable.

10 As much of the current inspection report as has been completed.

11 If a construction site involving work under contract from any agency of the Federal Government, the name of the agency, the date of the contract, and the type of work involved.

12 Other pertinent information such as description of the workplace; the work process; machinery, tools and materials used; known hazards and injuries associated with the specific manufacturing process or industry.

13 Investigative techniques which will be required during the proposed inspection; e.g., personal sampling, photographs, examination of records, access to medical records, etc.

14 The specific reasons for the selection of this establishment for the inspection including proposed scope of the inspection and the rationale:

a Imminent Danger.

• Description of alleged imminent danger situation.

• Date received and source of information.

• Original allegation and copy of typed report, including basis for reasonable expectation of death or serious physical harm and immediacy of danger.

• Whether all current imminent danger processing procedures have been strictly followed.

b Fatality/Catastrophe.

• Type of accident—fatality, catastrophe.

• Method of accident notification — telephone, news media (attach copy of report), employee representative, other.

• Number of employees involved — fatalities, injuries, number hospitalized.

c Complaint.

• Original complaint and copy of typed complaint.

• Reasonable grounds for believing that a violation that threatens physical harm or imminent danger exists, including standards that could be violated if the complaint is true and accurate.

• Whether all current complaint processing procedures have been strictly followed.

• Additional information gathered pertaining to complaint evaluation.

d Referral

• Original referral and copy of completed Referral Form, OSHA-90.

• Specific description of the hazards observed and the potential injury or illness that may result from the specific hazard.

• Specific standards that may be violated.

• Number of employees affected by the specific hazard.

• Corroborative information or other supporting material to demonstrate potential existence of a hazard and employee exposure, if known.

• Whether all current referral processing procedures have been strictly followed.

• Additional information gathered pertaining to referral evaluation.

e Programmed.

• High rate safety — general industry, maritime, construction.

• Targeted health.

• Special emphasis program — Special Programs, Local Emphasis Program, Migrant Housing Inspection, etc.

f Followup.

- Date of initial inspection.
- Details and reasons followup was to be conducted.
- Copies of previous citations on the basis of which the followup was initiated.
- Copies of settlement stipulations and final orders, if appropriate.
- Previous history of failure to correct, if any.

g Monitoring.

- Date of original inspection.
- Details and reasons monitoring inspection was to be conducted.
- Copies of previous citations on the basis of which the monitoring inspection was initiated.
- PMA request, if applicable.

(6) *Compulsory Process.* When a court order or warrant is obtained requiring an employer to allow an inspection, the CSHO is authorized to conduct the inspection in accordance with the provisions of the court order or warrant. All questions from the employer concerning reasonableness of any aspect of an inspection conducted pursuant to compulsory process shall be referred to the Area Director.

(7) *Action to be Taken Upon Receipt of Compulsory Process.* The inspection will normally begin within 24 hours of receipt of compulsory process or of the date authorized by compulsory process for the initiation of the inspection.

(a) The CSHO shall serve a copy of the compulsory process on the employer and make a separate notation as to the time, place, name and job title of the individual served.

(b) The compulsory process may have a space for a return of service entry by the CSHO in which the exact dates of the inspection made pursuant to the compulsory process are to be entered. Upon completion of the inspection, the CSHO will complete the return of service on the original compul-

sory process, sign and forward it to the supervisor for appropriate action.

(c) If physical resistance or interference by the employer is anticipated, the Area Director shall notify the Regional Administrator; and appropriate action shall be determined.

(8) *Refused Entry or Interference With a Compulsory Process.* When an apparent refusal to permit entry or inspection is encountered upon presenting the compulsory process, the CSHO shall specifically inquire whether the employer is refusing to comply with the compulsory process.

(a) If the employer refuses to comply or if consent is not clearly given (for example, the employer expresses an objection to the inspection), the CSHO shall not attempt to conduct the inspection but shall leave the premises and contact the supervisor concerning further action. The CSHO shall make notations (including all possible witnesses to the refusal or interference) and fully report all relevant facts.

(b) The Area Director shall contact both the Regional Administrator and the Regional Solicitor, either orally or in writing, as appropriate, concerning the refusal to comply or the interference.

(c) The Regional Administrator, jointly with the Regional Solicitor, shall decide what further action shall be taken.

e. *Forcible Interference with Conduct of Inspection or Other Official Duties.* It is a Federal criminal offense to kill "any officer or employee...of the Department of Labor assigned to perform investigative, inspection or law enforcement functions, while engaged in the performance of his official duties."

(1) *Agency Response.* Whenever an OSHA official or employee encounters forcible resistance, opposition, interference, etc., or is assaulted or threatened with assault while engaged in the performance of official duties, all investigative activity shall cease.

(a) The supervisor shall be advised by the most expeditious means.

(b) Upon receiving a report of such forcible interference, the Area Director or designee shall immediately notify the Regional Administrator.

(2) *Types of Interference.* Although the employer is legally entitled to refuse permission to conduct an inspection without a warrant, the Act does not permit forcible conduct against the CSHO. The following illustrates the type of forcible conduct which shall be immediately reported to the supervisor:

(a) Anyone physically holding, grabbing, pushing, shoving, or in any way limiting the official's or employee's freedom of action or choice of action. The threat of any action which limits freedom of action or choice of action is included.

(b) Anyone striking, kicking, or in any way inflicting or attempting to inflict injury, pain or shock on the official or employee. The threat of such actions is included as is oral abuse which menaces or causes concern for the official's or employee's personal safety.

(c) Anyone assaulting or threatening the official or employee with a weapon of any kind. The handling or display of weapons in a menacing manner is included.

f. *Release for Entry.* The CSHO shall not sign any form or release or agree to any waiver. This includes any employer forms concerned with trade secret information.

(1) If the employer requires that a release be signed before entering the establishment, the CSHO shall inform the employer of the Secretary's authority under Section 8(a) of the Act. If the employer still insists on the signing of a release, the CSHO shall suspend the inspection and report the matter promptly to the supervisor who shall decide if the situation is to be treated as a refusal of entry.

(2) The CSHO may sign a visitor's register, plant pass, or any other book or form used by the establishment to control the entry and movement of persons upon its premises. Such signature shall not constitute any form of a release or waiver of prosecution or liability under the Act.

(3) In case of any doubt, the CSHO shall consult with the supervisor before signing any document.

g. *Bankrupt or Out of Business.* If the establishment scheduled for inspection is found to have ceased business and there is no known successor, the CSHO shall report the facts to the supervisor. If an employer, although adjudicated bankrupt, is continuing to operate on the date of the scheduled inspection, the inspection shall proceed. An employer must comply with the Act until the day the business actually ceases to operate.

h. *Strike or Labor Dispute.* Plants or establishments may be inspected regardless of the existence of labor disputes involving work stoppages, strikes or picketing. If the CSHO identifies an unanticipated labor dispute at a proposed inspection site, the supervisor shall be consulted before any contact is made.

(1) *Programmed Inspections.* As a rule, programmed inspections will be deferred during a strike or labor dispute, either between a recognized union and the employer or between two unions competing for bargaining rights in the establishment.

(2) *Unprogrammed Inspections.* As a rule, unprogrammed inspections (complaints, fatalities, etc.) will be performed during strikes or labor disputes. However, the seriousness and reliability of any complaint shall be thoroughly investigated by the supervisor prior to scheduling an inspection to ensure as far as possible that the complaint reflects a good faith belief that a true hazard exists and is not merely an attempt to harass the employer or to gain a bargaining advantage for labor. If there is a picket line at the establishment, the CSHO shall inform the appropriate union official of the reason for the inspection prior to initiating the inspection.

i. *No Inspection.* If a scheduled inspection cannot be conducted, the CSHO shall document the reasons for not conducting the inspection, and shall include the names of persons contacted on the OSHA-1A form to be included in the case file.

2. Employee Participation. CSHOs shall determine as soon as possible after arrival whether the employees at the worksite to be inspected are represented and, if so, shall ensure that employee representatives are afforded the opportunity to participate in all phases of the workplace inspection. If an employer resists or interferes with participation by employee representatives in an inspection and this cannot be resolved by the CSHO, the employer shall be informed of the right of the employee representative to participate. Continued resistance by the employer shall be construed as a refusal to permit the inspection and the supervisor shall be contacted in accordance with D.1.d.(1).

NOTE: For the purpose of this chapter, the term "employee representative" refers to (1) a representative of the certified or recognized bargaining agent, or, if none, (2) an employee member of a safety and health committee who has been chosen by the employees (employee committee members or employees at large) as their OSHA representative, or (3) an individual employee who has been selected as the walkaround representative by the employees of the establishment.

3. Opening Conference. The CSHO shall inform the employer of the purpose of the inspection and shall obtain the employer's consent to include participation of an employee representative, as defined in D.2, when appropriate. The opening conference shall be kept as brief as possible, normally not to exceed one hour. Conditions of the worksite shall be noted upon arrival as well as any changes which may occur during the opening conference. Pursuant to 29 CFR 1903.8, the employer

and the employee representatives shall be informed of the opportunity to participate in the physical inspection of the workplace.

NOTE: An abbreviated opening conference shall be conducted whenever the CSHO believes that the circumstances at the worksite dictate that the walkaround begin as promptly as possible. In such cases the opening conference shall be limited to the bare essentials; namely, identification, purpose of the visit, and a request for employer and employee representatives. The other elements shall be fully addressed in the closing conference.

a. *Purpose of the Inspection.* The employer shall be informed as to the reason for the inspection as follows:

(1) *Imminent Danger Situations.* When responding to an alleged imminent danger situation, the CSHO is required to get to the location of the alleged hazard(s) as quickly as possible. Under these circumstances, an expedited opening conference shall be conducted by limiting activities to presenting credentials and explaining the nature, scope, and purpose of the inspection.

(a) Potential safety and health hazards that may be encountered during the inspection shall be identified and appropriate steps taken to provide for personal protection.

(b) The presence of employer and employee representatives shall be requested; however, the inspection shall not be unreasonably delayed to await their arrival.

(c) The employer shall be advised that, because of the abbreviated nature of the opening conference, there will be a more extensive discussion at the closing conference.

(d) Unreasonable delays shall be reported immediately to the supervisor.

(2) *Fatality/Catastrophe Investigations.* The employer shall be informed that an investigation will be conducted and extensive interviews with witnesses will be necessary. The purpose of an

accident investigation shall be explained, namely, to determine:

(a) The cause of the accident.

(b) Whether a violation of OSHA safety or health standards related to the accident occurred.

(c) What effect the standard violation had on the occurrence of the accident.

(d) If OSHA standards should be revised to correct the hazardous working condition that led to the accident.

(3) *Complaint Investigations.* For a complaint investigation, the CSHO shall provide a copy of the complaint(s) to the employer and the employee representatives at the beginning of the opening conference.

(4) *Referral Investigations.* During the opening conference of a referral investigation, the CSHO shall inform the employer that the investigation is a result of a referral (e.g., from another agency, from a previous OSHA inspection or in response to specific evidence of probable violations at a worksite).

(5) *Records Review.* In any inspection where a records review is to be performed to determine whether a comprehensive safety inspection of the workplace will be conducted, the CSHO either shall hold an abbreviated opening conference prior to the records inspection (safety) or shall cover the records review procedures during the regular opening conference (health). The conference shall include:

(a) Explaining the procedures for selecting an establishment and for determining whether it will be subject to a comprehensive safety inspection based on its lost workday injury case rate or on random selection or to a partial inspection based on indications of existing safety problems; and that in any case the inspection will include a review of the establishment's compliance with any applicable provisions of the Hazard Communication Standard and a brief plant tour reviewing the employer's overall safety and health management program, focusing on any high hazard areas.

(b) Providing the employer and the employee representatives, at the conclusion of this discussion, with a letter confirming these procedures and with a copy of the "Recordkeeping Requirements" booklet.

NOTE: If a comprehensive or partial safety inspection is to be conducted after the records review, a complete opening conference shall be conducted prior to the inspection.

b. *Health Inspections.* During a health inspection or, as appropriate, during a safety inspection when evaluating potential health hazards, the CSHO shall provide the employer with a copy of the letter explaining the procedures for selecting an establishment for a health inspection and shall include in the opening conference the following additional procedures:

(1) Request process flow charts and plant layouts relevant to the inspection. If the plant layout and process flow charts are not available, sketch a plant layout as necessary during the course of the initial walkaround, identifying the operations and the relative dimensions of the work area. Distribution of major process equipment, including engineering controls in use, shall also be included on the sketch.

(2) Make a brief examination of all workplace records pertinent to the inspection.

(a) If detailed review is necessary, the CSHO may wish to proceed with the initial walkaround and return later to examine the records more thoroughly.

(b) Many valuable insights can be obtained from an examination of required and other records (e.g., symptomatology which may relate to workplace exposure, frequency of injuries or illnesses, dermatitis, personal protective equipment usage, monitoring data, audiometric test results, ventilation tests, process flow charts and a list of hazardous raw, intermediate, and final product materials) to ensure a more effective inspection and such an examination shall not be omitted if it can be done.

(c) In some plants, sampling for obvious health hazards can be initiated soon after the opening conference. Details of the walkaround can be accomplished while collecting the samples.

c. *Attendance At Opening Conference.* The CSHO shall conduct a joint opening conference or separate conferences as follows:

(1) *Joint Conference.* Whenever practicable, a joint opening conference shall be held with the employer and the employee representatives (if there is an employee representative as defined as D.2. of this chapter).

(2) *Separate Conferences.* Where either party chooses not to have a joint conference, separate conferences shall be held for the employer and the employee representatives. A written summary of each conference shall be made and attached to the case file. A copy of the written summaries will be available from the Area Director upon request by the employer or the employee representative. Where it is determined that separate conferences will unacceptably delay observation or evaluation of the workplace safety or health hazards, each conference shall be brief, and if appropriate, reconvened after the inspection of the alleged hazards.

d. *Scope.* The CSHO shall outline in general terms the scope of the inspection, including private employee interviews, physical inspection of the workplace and records, possible referrals, discrimination complaints, and the closing conference(s).

e. *Handouts and Additional Items.* During the opening conference of every inspection (including records inspections), the CSHO shall provide:

(1) The employer representatives with copies of the OSHA poster and with blank OSHA-200 Forms, a copy of the standards as well as other applicable laws and regulations, and informational handouts and materials. The CSHO shall also inform the employer

representatives of procedures for obtaining additional copies of any materials of which the CSHO may not have a sufficient quantity on hand.

(2) The employee representatives with a copy of the standards, upon request, as well as other applicable laws and regulations, and informational handouts and materials. The CSHO shall also inform them that additional copies and other materials can be obtained from the local Area or District Office when the CSHO has an insufficient number on hand. The employee representatives shall be given an opportunity to read the brief introductory material before the inspection begins.

f. *Program Mix.* The CSHO shall briefly indicate that OSHA shares the employer's goal of reducing workplace injuries and illnesses, that the agency is developing a variety of different cooperative approaches which are designed to assist the employer in achieving this goal, and that a more detailed discussion will take place during the closing conference.

g. *Forms Completion.* The CSHO shall obtain available information for the OSHA-1 and other appropriate forms and complete applicable sections during the opening conference.

h. *Employees of Other Employers.* During the opening conference, the CSHO shall determine whether the employees of any other employers are working at the establishment.

(1) If there are such employees and any questions arise as to whether their employers should be included in the inspection, the CSHO shall contact the supervisor to ascertain whether additional inspections shall be conducted and what limitations there may be to such inspection activity.

(a) All high rate employers potentially present at any scheduled worksite normally shall be included within the scope of the inspection, except as indicated in (b) and (c) below. Thus, for example, all construction contractors working at a manufacturing establishment scheduled for inspection are to be included in the inspection assignment.

(b) When, however, the criteria given in Chapter IX, B.2.b(1)(d), are met a CSHO referral may be made and an inspection conducted under the guidelines outlined in Chapter IX.

(c) When a construction operation is too large to be efficiently handled during the inspection of the programmed manufacturing establishment, the operation shall be treated as a referral for inspection at a later time, in accordance with Chapter IX, B.

(2) If additional inspections are authorized, both employer and employee representatives of the other employers shall be invited to the opening conference. The inspection shall not be delayed to wait for these employer or employee representatives longer than would be reasonably necessary for either to arrive.

(3) If the site is a multi-employer site, such as construction, the CSHO shall determine during the opening conference who is responsible for providing common services available to all employees on site; e.g., sanitation, first aid, handrails, etc. It shall be pointed out to all contractors that, apart from any arrangements that may have been made, each employer remains responsible for his or her own employees.

i. *Voluntary Compliance Programs.* Employers who participate in selected voluntary compliance programs may be exempted from programmed inspections. The CSHO shall determine, in accordance with the following guidelines, whether the employer falls under such an exemption during the opening conference.

(1) *7(c)(1) and Contract Consultations.* In accordance with 29 CFR 1908.7 and Chapter IX of the Consultation Policies and Procedures Manual (CPPM), the CSHO shall ascertain at the opening conference whether an OSHA-funded consultation is in progress or whether the facility is pursuing or has received an inspection exemp-

tion through consultation under current procedures.

(a) Except as indicated in 29 CFR 1908.7(b)(2)(iv), an onsite consultation visit in progress has priority over programmed inspections.

1 For conditions covered by the employer's request for consultation, an onsite visit shall be considered in progress from the beginning of the opening conference through the end of the closing conference.

2 For conditions not covered by the employer's request, the onsite visit shall be considered in progress only while the consultant is at the place of employment.

(b) If a consultation visit is in progress, the following procedures shall be observed:

1 If the consultant is actually in the facility, the inspection shall be deferred until after the consultant's closing conference and may be carried over to the next cycle in accordance with Chapter II.

2 If the consultant has left the site but has not yet held a closing conference with the employer, the inspection shall be deferred until after the closing conference and may be carried over to the next cycle.

3 Where the period between the consultation opening conference and the closing conference exceeds 30 days, the Regional Administrator may decide that the inspection shall proceed in the interest of timely assurance of worker protection. If, after conferring with the Consultation Project Manager, the Regional Administrator determines that the consultation is being conducted properly and at a reasonable pace, the inspection normally shall be deferred until after the consultant's closing conference.

4 In all of the cases described in (a) through (c), the inspection may be carried over to the next cycle in accordance with Chapter II.

(c) If the employer is participating in the process required for exemption from inspections but has not yet received the exemption, the CSHO shall locate the "Notice of Application to Pursue an Inspection Exemption through Consultation" prominently posted. The procedures outlined in the CPPM, Chapter IX, N, shall be followed.

(d) When the employer has completed the requirements for exemption and a Certificate of Recognition has been issued by the Regional Administrator, the facility shall be removed from the Establishment Lists for a period of one year from the date of the closing conference in which the employer elected to pursue the exemption.

(e) In the event a CSHO enters a facility that is currently under an inspection exemption, the dates of the exemption on the Certificate of Recognition shall be verified and, if within the exemption period, the inspection shall be terminated (programmed) or limited (unprogrammed). The Area Director shall inform the Regional Administrator of the circumstances of the visit as soon as practicable.

(f) If the programmed inspection is scheduled for a multi-employer worksite, such as a construction site, the following guidelines apply:

1 If the general contractor has invited the consultant on site, the consultant shall be considered onsite with respect to the entire worksite.

2 If the consultant has been invited by one of the subcontractors and the scope of the consultant's visit is limited to the operations of that one subcontractor, the inspection of the entire worksite shall not be deferred; the subcontractor who has invited the consultant to visit, however, shall be excluded from the scope of the inspection.

(g) If a followup inspection (including monitoring) or an imminent danger, fatality/catastrophe, complaint or referral investigation is to be conducted, the inspection shall not be deferred; but its scope shall be limited to those areas required to complete the purpose of the investigation.

1 For imminent danger, fatality/catastrophe or formal complaint investigations the employer shall be advised that the consultant must terminate the onsite visit until the compliance inspection shall have been completed.

2 For CSHO referral or followup (including monitoring) inspections the employer shall be advised that the consultant may either continue the onsite visit in areas of the facility not covered by the investigation or terminate the consultation visit until the compliance inspection shall have been completed.

(h) When a consultant is onsite at the time of an attempted compliance inspection and the inspection is to be deferred, the establishment may be carried over to the next cycle.

(i) If an employer refuses entry at the time of a compliance inspection, the Area Director shall notify the 7(c)(1) project manager of the refusal and request that no response to a consultation request that might be received from that employer be given until OSHA decides whether to seek a warrant. The Area Director shall inform the project manager as soon as possible after the resolution of the warrant issue so that a consultation visit may be conducted if the employer should request one. The Regional Administrator may decide to allow a consultation visit to proceed in the interim if that is judged to be in the best interest of employee safety and health.

(j) The employer has no obligation to inform the CSHO of a prior consultative visit. If, however, a copy of the consultant's report is provided and the CSHO finds serious hazards during the walkaround inspection that were previously identified by the consultant, a citation shall be issued for such violations. A minimum penalty shall be proposed in such cases, however, if the employer, in good faith, is complying with the consultant's recommendations.

(2) *Voluntary Protection Programs.* The CSHO shall ascertain at the opening conference whether the workplace employer is participating in one of the currently established Voluntary Protection Programs (VPP) and has received an exemption from programmed inspections under current procedures.

(a) When the employer has completed the requirements for participation and a letter of approval has been issued by the Assistant Secretary, the facility shall be removed from the Establishment Lists for the duration of the employer's participation in the VPP.

(b) If the employer has applied for approval to participate in a VPP and has had an onsite preapproval review but has not yet received a letter of approval from the Assistant Secretary, the inspection shall be deferred until a decision on participation in the VPP has been made by the Assistant Secretary.

1 If the application is denied, an inspection shall be scheduled and conducted as usual. If the application is granted and a letter of approval is issued, the employer shall be removed from the inspection register.

2 If the onsite preapproval review has been scheduled but not yet made, the inspection shall be deferred until a final decision on the application is made. If the CSHO was not aware that an onsite review had been scheduled until arrival at the establishment, the Area Director shall be contacted for verification.

3 If the onsite preapproval review has not been scheduled, the inspection shall be conducted as usual. The Area Director shall inform the Regional Administrator of the circumstances of the visit as soon as practicable.

(c) In the event a CSHO enters a facility that has been approved for participation in a VPP and is currently under an inspection exemption, the approval letter shall be copied and the inspection terminated (programmed) or limited (unprogrammed). The employer will have received also a certificate noting the dates of approved participation and a flag proper to the particular VPP in which the workplace is participating. The Area Director shall inform the Regional Administrator of the circumstances of the visit as soon as practicable.

(d) If the programmed inspection is scheduled for a multi-employer worksite, such as a construction site, the following guidelines apply:

1 If the general contractor has applied for and has been granted approval for participation in a VPP, generally the entire worksite controlled by that general contractor will have been exempted from programmed inspections.

2 If only specific operations or portions of the workplace have been approved for participation in a VPP, the programmed inspection of the entire worksite shall not be deferred; the operations or portions of the workplace that have been approved, however, shall be excluded from the scope of the inspection.

(e) If a follow up inspection (including monitoring) or an imminent danger, fatality/catastrophe, complaint or referral investigation is to be conducted, the inspection shall not be deferred; but its scope shall be limited to those areas required to complete the purpose of the investigation.

j. *Other Opening Conference Topics.* The CSHO shall determine at the beginning of the opening conference:

(1) *Legislative Limitations.* Whether or not the employer is covered by any of the exemptions or limitations noted in the current Appropriations Act (See OSHA Instruction CPL 2.51D.) or in Chapter II.

(2) *Employer Name.* What the correct legal name of the employer is, what type of legal entity is it, and whether it is a subsidiary of any other business entity.

(3) *Coverage.* What facts show that the employer is covered under the Act; i.e., that the operations conducted at the worksite to be inspected affect interstate commerce.

(4) *Trade Secrets*. Whether the employer wishes to identify areas in the establishment which contain or might reveal trade secrets. If trade secrets are identified, the CSHO will explain that OSHA is required by law to preserve the confidentiality of all information which might reveal a trade secret in accordance with 29 CFR 1903.9. (See D.8.e.(1) for further instructions.)

(5) *Photographs*. Whether the employer has any objection to taking photographs as permitted by 29 CFR 1903.7(b). If the employer does object, the CSHO shall immediately notify the supervisor in accordance with D.1.d.(3).

(6) *Potential Hazards*. Whether there are any safety and health hazards to which the walkaround party may be exposed during the inspection. The CSHO shall ensure that all members of the inspection party are advised as to the appropriate personal protective equipment that is required based on this information.

4. Records Review. A records review for the purpose of calculating the establishment's lost workday injury (LWDI) rate shall be conducted for all inspections (safety or health), including those for which an administrative subpoena and/or warrant is being served, whether the inspection is programmed or unprogrammed. This procedure applies if the establishment is within an industry whose SIC code is on the Safety SIC List currently used for scheduling General Industry inspections or if the establishment is listed on the Low Rate Establishment List or the Nonmanufacturing Establishment List for the current fiscal year. An LWDI rate need not be calculated for an establishment if one has already been calculated during the current calendar year or if the establishment meets one of the deletion criteria for a safety inspection listed in Chapter II, E.2.b.(1)(b) *5b*.

a. *Procedures for Determining Lost Workday Injury (LWDI) Rate.* During or immediately following the opening conference, the CSHO shall request the injury and employment data described in D.4.a.(3) and (4) for use in calculating the establishment's LWDI rate. The CSHO shall advise the employer of the provisions of Section 17(g) of the Act; i.e., whoever knowingly makes any false statement, representation, or certification in any record required by the Act is subject to a fine of not more than $10,000, or by imprisonment for not more than 6 months, or both. The employer shall be given a reasonable amount of time to gather the information requested (See, however, C.l.d.(1)(a).

(1) *Reference Years*. The number of years from which injury and employment data will be used in the calculation of the LWDI rate is dependent upon the average number of employee hours worked or the average number of workers employed in the establishment during the previous 3 years.

(a) Average employee hours worked may be obtained, if available, from the employer payroll records for the years involved.

(b) Average annual employment may be determined by adding the number of workers employed in the establishment in each month included in the reference years, totaling the sum of monthly employment figures and dividing the total by the number of months involved, rounding to the nearest tenth. Count all full- and part-time workers, including seasonal, temporary, administrative, supervisory and clerical.

EXAMPLE: Monthly employment for 1980:

Jan.	0	April	30	July	0	Oct.	20
Feb.	0	May	30	Aug.	0	Nov.	20
March	20	June	0	Sept.	20	Dec.	20

Total 160

$$\frac{160 \text{ employees}}{12 \text{ months}} = 13.3 \text{ (average annual employment)}.$$

1. For establishments with an average number of employee hours worked of less than 40,000 (20 x 2,000) hours or an annual employment of 20 or fewer employees in any of the 3 preceding calendar years, use data from all 3 years.

2 For establishments with an average number of employee hours worked of 40,000 hours or more or an average annual employment of more than 20 employees in each of the 3 preceding calendar years, use data from the past 2 years.

(2) *Special Circumstances*. There may be occasions when the records required in (a) and (b) above are not available, or are only partial records. The following are examples of such circumstances and how to handle them:

(a) If injury data from any or all of the reference years are not available because the employer *was not in business* or *was not required* to keep records, the LWDI rate shall be calculated on the basis of the reference years for which data are available, with a minimum of data from 12 months. Data from the current calendar year may be used to fulfill the 12-month minimum data requirement.

(b) If the employer *was required* to maintain records in any or all of the reference years but has no records or has only partial records, LWDI rate shall not be calculated. Records from years outside of the reference years shall not be used in calculating an employer's LWDI rate. The CSHO shall advise the employer of the apparent violations of the recordkeeping requirements and proceed with the inspection.

(c) When ownership has substantially changed, records from previous owners of an establishment shall not be used in the LWDI rate calculation.

(d) If verifiable injury data is obtained, the employer shall be given the opportunity to correct or complete the OSHA-200 Form(s) whenever only minor errors are found or if no recordable injuries or illnesses occurred during the reference year(s). The LWDI rate shall be calculated from the corrected forms. Citations shall be issued for violations of the regulations.

(3) *Employment Data*. Request the number of hours worked by the employees in each of the reference years. If this information is not available, request the average annual employment. The procedure used shall be indicated in the case file.

(a) *Employee Hours*. Obtain the number of hours worked by employees in each of the reference years. Do not include any nonworking time, even though paid, such as vacations, sick leave, etc. The employer might locate such information in payroll or time records. Record the data in the narrative (OSHA-1A) section of the case file.

(b) *Average Annual Employment*. Compute the average annual employment as explained in D.4.a.(1).

(4) *Injury and Illness Records Review*. Review the OSHA-200 logs and record in the narrative section of the case file the number of LWDIs that occurred in each of the reference years. (LWDIs are defined as *injuries* involving days away from work and/or days of restricted work activity — Column 2 of the OSHA-200.) As usual, record OSHA-200 data on the OSHA-1 for the most recent full calendar year.

(a) *Illnesses*. Although cases of *illness* will not be used in calculating the LWDI rate, the CSHO conducting a safety inspection shall make note of any significant recorded illnesses and submit a health referral if appropriate. The employer and the employee representatives shall be advised of the possibility of a referral health inspection.

(b) *Verification of Records.* The CSHO shall verify the accuracy of the OSHA-200 logs by carefully checking them against workers' compensation first reports of injury or OSHA-101s and first aid records, when such first aid records are no more detailed than the type of information contained in the OSHA-101. It may also be appropriate to check OSHA-200 logs against more detailed first aid and medical records located at the establishment or at other locations.

NOTE: Access to the more detailed first aid and/or medical records may require a written medical access order or the express consent of each employee with a medical record. (See OSHA Instruction CPL 2-2.33.) Such records may be sought in cases where there is evidence of wide-spread recordkeeping violations.

1 These documents must be examined carefully to ensure that all work-related injuries and illnesses are being properly recorded on the OSHA-200.

a If time allows, all workers' compensation first reports of injury or the OSHA-101s and first aid records shall be reviewed to determine if:

• Treatment was given that could qualify as medical treatment;

• There were any lost time injuries or injuries that resulted in restricted work activities or transfer to another job;

• Any injuries resulted in loss of consciousness;

• Any illnesses were diagnosed; or

• Anything else that would indicate that a recordable injury or illness occurred.

LWDI Rate   =

Where:

LWDI's = sum of LWDI's in the reference years.

employee hours worked = sum of employee hours in the reference years.

b If all reports cannot be examined, a representative sample shall be extracted for closer review as indicated in the preceding subsection.

c If any cases noted under *a* are found, the OSHA-200 shall be checked to ensure that they have been properly recorded.

2 The company representative responsible for maintaining injury and illness records shall be interviewed to determine what the company's recording policy is. This individual shall be identified in the case file.

3 Injury and illness records shall be reviewed and verified with employee representatives or other informed employees.

4 If the verification process indicates that the OSHA-200 does not accurately reflect the lost workday injury experience at the establishment or that the employer is not properly recording injuries or illnesses, this shall be documented in the case file. Data from the log shall not be used for calculation of the LWDI rate. (See D.4.a.(2)(d) for special verification circumstances.) The CSHO shall advise the employer of the problem and proceed with the inspection.

5 If the credibility of the records has been verified, the CSHO shall proceed with the calculation of the LWDI rate.

(5) *Calculation of the LWDI Rate.* The CSHO shall calculate the LWDI rate according to the following formula:

(a) If the number of employee hours worked is available from the employer, use:

$$\frac{\text{\# LWDI's} \times 200,000}{\text{\# employee hours worked}}$$

200,000 = base for 100 full-time workers, working 40 hours per week, 50 weeks per year.

EXAMPLE: An establishment scheduled for inspection in October 1981 employed an average of 54 workers in 1980, 50 workers in 1979, and 50 workers in 1978. Therefore, injury and employment data for the 2 preceding calendar years will be used.

\# LWDI's in 1979 = 5

LWDI Rate $= \dfrac{(5 + 3) \times 200,000}{100,000 + 108,000}$

$= \dfrac{1,600,000}{208,000}$

$= 7.69$ (rounded to 7.7)

\# LWDI's in 1980 = 3

\# Employee hours worked in 1979 = 100,000

\# Employee hours worked in 1980 = 108,000

NOTE: Carry out calculations to the hundredths place and round to the tenths place. Round up for "5."

EXAMPLES: Round 6.55 to 6.6; round 4.12 to 4.1.

(b) If data on employee hours worked are not available, the following procedure is to be used to establish the number of equivalent employee hours:

1 Obtain the average number of full-time employees. (A full-time employee is one who works 40 hours per week for 50 weeks per year.)

2 Ask the employer to estimate the number of full-time equivalents corresponding to the number of part-time employees, if any.

3 Add the number of full-time equivalent employees to the average number of full-time employees.

4 Multiply the resulting sum by 2000 to obtain the approximate number of employee hours worked at the establishment.

5 Use the formula given in D.4.a.(5)(a) to calculate the employer's LWDI rate.

EXAMPLE: An employer has an average of 18 full-time employees and 7 part-time employees for the year. Five of the part-time employees work 15 hours each a week and the other two work 25 hours each a week for a total of 125 part-time hours per week. This would be equivalent to three additional full-time employees (rounding to the closest 40-hour multiple). Adding 18 and 3 gives 21 full-time equivalent employees, and, multiplying by 2000, results in approximately 42,000 employee

hours at the establishment for the year. Repeat the same procedure for each year to be considered in the LWDI rate calculation. The sum of these hours is then used as the divisor in accordance with the formula given in D.4.a.(5)(a).

b. *Interpretation of Establishment LWDI Rate.* The LWDI calculated for the establishment shall be compared to the lowest national rate for manufacturing published by BLS over the past 5 years (the BLS rate). The CSHO shall determine the scope of the inspection according to the following criteria:

(1) *LWDI Rate Below the National Rate for Manufacturing.* If the calculated LWDI rate is below the BLS rate, a comprehensive safety inspection normally shall not be conducted. (See, however, D.7.a.(2). and D.7.c.)

(a) The results of the records review, including the calculated LWDI rate, shall be given to both the employer and the employee representatives.

(b) If there is no employee representative at a worksite where a comprehensive safety inspection will not be conducted due to a low LWDI rate, the employer shall be asked to post a form letter for the employees' information for at least 3 working days.

(2) *Exception:* There may be occasions for unprogrammed inspections as well as for programmed inspections scheduled from one of the Safety SIC Lists when a comprehensive or a partial inspection may be conducted even when the establishment's LWDI rate is below the BLS rate.

(a) For establishments scheduled for inspection from the High Rate SIC List, or from the Low Rate SIC List when programmed inspections are scheduled from that list under the guidelines given in Chapter II, E.2.b.(1)(e)*4,* every tenth programmed inspection shall be a comprehensive inspection irrespective of the calculated LWDI rate for the establishment. Such inspections shall be identified as follows:

1 The inspection register shall be developed and handled in accordance with Chapter II, E.2.b.(1)(a) through (f) except that Deletion Code F shall not be applied. When the register has been set for the cycle, the listed establishments shall be numbered sequentially, beginning with "1."

2 Every tenth establishment on the register shall be identified for a comprehensive inspection.

a Additions under the procedures in Chapter II, E.2.b.(1)(f) shall not be cause to renumber the inspection register.

b If a tenth-numbered establishment cannot be inspected for some legitimate reason (i.e., a deletion code other than "F" applies to the establishment (See Chapter II, E.2.b.(1)(b) *5b*.)), it shall be deleted. There is no requirement to replace it.

3 An establishment LWDI rate shall be calculated in accordance with D.4.a.

4 Establishments with LWDI rates lower than the BLS rate shall, nevertheless, receive a comprehensive inspection.

5 CSHOs shall so inform the employer and the employee representatives and shall explain that the purpose of the program is to verify the validity of the records only inspection procedures. Any questions regarding selection or any other related issue shall be explained as well.

(b) If circumstances such as, but not limited to, those listed in (1), (2) and (3) below arise at the establishment, a partial inspection normally shall be conducted under guidelines issued by the Area Director. In general, partial inspections in response to accident reports, complaints or referrals or those made under special circumstances shall be limited to the specific areas or conditions of concern.

1 An imminent danger or a serious hazard is observed in plain view prior to or during the opening conference or in transit to an area or operation which is to be inspected.

2 During the records review it is noted that an unusual number or type of injuries has occurred in one time period, area or operation.

3 A safety complaint is filed during the opening conference by the employee representative.

NOTE: Only reports of imminent danger or formal complaints meeting all the requirements for inspection as given in Chapter IX shall be immediately investigated. Other types of complaints shall be taken by the CSHO to the Area Office for appropriate action at a later date.

(3) *LWDI Rate At or Above the BLS Rate.* A comprehensive safety inspection will be conducted.

(4) *Nonverifiable Records.* A comprehensive safety inspection will be conducted under the circumstances indicated in D.4.a.(4)(b).

(5) *Partial Injury Data.* If no injury data are available for the reference years or only partial data are available from an employer who was required to maintain records in all of the reference years, a comprehensive inspection will be conducted, subject to the instructions in D.4.a.(2) of this chapter.

NOTE: 1. A comprehensive inspection may be limited as necessary in view of resource availability and other enforcement priorities.

2. Where both safety and health programmed inspections are scheduled at the establishment, the review of injury records shall not affect the health inspection; i.e., the health inspection shall proceed as scheduled even if no

comprehensive safety inspection is to be conducted.

5. Walkaround Representatives. Those representatives designated to accompany the CSHO during the walkaround are considered walkaround representatives.

a. *Employer Representatives.* Anyone designated by the employer as a representative is acceptable. In cases of isolated or remote locations, the senior supervisor, foreman, gang boss or head technician onsite at the time of inspection is the employer representative. Subject to the guidelines given in D.6.e., every reasonable effort shall be made to afford general walkaround rights to every employer representative on a multi-employer worksite.

b. *Employee Representatives.* Subject to the guidelines in D.6.e., one or more employee representatives shall be given an opportunity to accompany the CSHO during the walkaround phase of the inspection to provide appropriate involvement of employees in the physical inspection of their own places of employment and to give them an opportunity to point out hazardous conditions. 29 CFR 1903.8(b) gives the CSHO authority to resolve disputes as to who represents the employees for walkaround purposes. The following guidelines shall be utilized for determining employee representatives:

(1) *Employees Represented by a Certified or Recognized Bargaining Agent.*

During the opening conference, the highest ranking union official or union employee representative shall designate who will participate in the walkaround.

(2) *Safety Committee.* The employee members of an established plant safety committee or the employees at large may have designated an employee representative for OSHA inspection purposes or agreed to accept as their representative the employee designated by the committee to accompany the CSHO during an OSHA inspection.

(3) *No Certified or Recognized Bargaining Agent.* Where employees are not represented by an authorized representative, where there is no established safety committee, or where employees have not chosen or agreed to an employee representative for OSHA inspection purposes whether or not there is a safety committee, the CSHO shall determine if any other employees would suitably represent the interests of employees on the walkaround.

(a) If selection of such employee representatives is impractical, the inspection shall be conducted without an accompanying employee representative; and the CSHO shall consult with a reasonable number of employees during the walkaround in accordance with the provisions of 29 CFR 1903.8 and Section 8(e) of the Act.

(b) Employees selected for interviewing shall include individuals judged knowledgeable about the area or process being inspected.

6. Special Situations.

a. *Preemption by Another Agency.* Section 4(b)(1) states that the OSH Act does not apply to working conditions over which other Federal agencies exercise statutory responsibility. The determination of preemption by another Federal agency is in many cases a highly complex matter. To preclude as much as possible any misunderstanding with other agencies and to avoid consequent adverse actions by employers (or agencies) the Area Director shall observe the following guidelines whenever a situation arises involving a possible preemption of jurisdiction question:

(1) The Area Director shall be alert to potential conicts with other agencies at all times. If a question arises, usually upon receipt of a complaint, referral, or other inquiry, the OSHA Directives System shall be consulted immediately to determine if the issue has been addressed there in a Memorandum of Understanding or other agreement with the agency involved.

(2) If not, the Area Director shall consult with the Regional Administra-

tor who shall provide clarification of the issue after consulting with the Regional Solicitor, if appropriate, or with the other Federal agency's local or Regional Office.

NOTE: Routine contact with other Federal agencies at the local and regional levels is highly desirable where Section 4(b)(1) issues may arise. Regional Administrators and Area Directors shall maintain active liaison with their counterparts in other agencies to ensure full cooperation in the event a situation requires clarification.

(3) If the Regional Office is unable to clarify the issue, it shall be referred to the Director, Office of Field Programs.

(4) At times an inspection may have already begun when the Section 4(b)(1) question arises. In such cases the CSHO shall interrupt the inspection and contact the supervisor for guidance.

(5) If, following an inspection, there remains any doubt as to OSHA coverage, the proposed citation and penalty shall be cleared with the Regional Solicitor, through the Regional Administrator, and, if necessary, the Director of Compliance Programs, prior to issuance.

(6) If it is determined that OSHA does not have jurisdiction, the case shall be referred to the appropriate agency if there is reason to believe that violations may exist.

b. *Labor Relations Disputes.* The CSHO shall not become involved in labor relations disputes either between a recognized union and the employer or between two or more unions competing for bargaining rights. However, if there is a recognized union, the highest ranking official available will designate the authorized walkaround representative even though another union may be seeking recognition.

c. *Expired Collective Bargaining Agreement.* When a union contract has expired, the CSHO shall assume that the incumbent union remains as the bargaining agent unless that union is decertified, officially replaced, or has abandoned bargaining agent status.

d. *Employee Representatives Not Employees of the Employer.* Walkaround representatives authorized by employees will usually be employees of the employer. If, however, a nonemployee (union official, industrial hygienist, safety engineer, or other experienced safety or health person) is designated by the employees as their representative to accompany the CSHO during the inspection, such a person normally shall be accorded walkaround rights consistent with 29 CFR 1903.8(c). Questionable circumstances, including delays of more than one hour, shall be referred to the supervisor. A non-employee representative shall be cautioned by the CSHO not to discuss matters pertaining to operations of the employer during the inspection.

e. *More Than One Representative.* At establishments where more than one employer is present or in situations where groups of employees have different representatives, it is acceptable to have a different employer/employee representative for different phases of the inspection. More than one employer and/or employee representative may accompany the CSHO throughout or during any phase of an inspection if the CSHO determines that such additional representatives will aid and not interfere with the inspection (29 CFR 1903.8(a)).

(1) Whenever appropriate to avoid a large group, the CSHO shall encourage multiple employers to agree upon and choose a limited number of representatives for walkaround accompaniment purposes. If necessary, during the inspection, employer representatives not on the walkaround shall be contacted to participate in particular phases of the inspection.

(2) As an alternative, the CSHO shall divide a multi-employer inspection into separate phases; e.g., excava-

tion, steel erection, mechanical, electrical, etc., and encourage different employer representatives to participate in different phases, as appropriate.

(3) The same principles shall govern the selection of employee representatives when several are involved.

f. *Disruptive Conduct.* The CSHO may deny the right of accompaniment to any person whose conduct interferes with a full and orderly inspection (29 CFR 1903.8(d)). If disruption or interference occurs, the CSHO shall use professional judgment as to whether to suspend the walkaround or take other action. The supervisor shall be consulted if the walkaround is suspended. The employee representative shall be advised that during the inspection matters unrelated to the inspection shall not be discussed with employees.

g. *Trade Secrets.* The CSHO shall ascertain from the employer if the employee representative is authorized to enter any trade secret area(s). If not, the CSHO shall consult with a reasonable number of employees who work in the area (29 CFR 1903.9(d)).

h. *Classified Areas.* In areas containing information classified by an agency of the U.S. Government in the interest of national security, only persons authorized to have access to such information may accompany a CSHO (29 CFR 1903.8(d)). The CSHO must also have the proper security clearances to enter these areas.

i. *Apparent Violations Observed Prior to the Walkaround.* When an apparent violation is observed by the CSHO prior to the walkaround, it shall be noted. All such apparent violations shall be rechecked during the walkaround and cited if appropriate. When possible, serious violations shall be rechecked and documented immediately at the commencement of the walkaround.

j. *Use of Tape Recorders.* The use of tape recorders during the required conferences may inhibit the free exchange of information, and care shall be exercised in their use. Tape recorders may be used by the CSHO only after authorization by the supervisor.

(1) The use of tape recorders may be authorized whenever circumstances justify it, such as where there is conflicting evidence indicating that the preservation of statements is advisable or where securing signed statements from affected employees will delay the expeditious completion of the investigation.

(2) The tape recorder shall not be used in locations where it may be hazardous.

(3) If the employer, employer representative, affected employees, or any other witnesses object to recording their statements during any part of the investigation, the inspection shall be continued without the tape recorder.

7. Inspection of Records and Posting. Every inspection of an employer required to keep injury and illness records, including followup inspections, shall include an examination and verification of such records. Examination of other records and of the posting requirements shall be performed as appropriate in accordance with current procedures.

NOTE: For unprogrammed inspections (including followup inspections) at an establishment where a records review has already been performed during the current calendar year, the CSHO need only review the illness and injury records since the last inspection. The OSHA-200 data need not be entered on the OSHA-1 unless:

1. The OSHA-200 data was not available at the time of the last inspection but has now become available; or

2. The calendar year has changed since the last inspection and new OSHA-200 data is available.

a. *Records.* The CSHO shall comply with the records review procedures that follow for all inspections, programmed or unprogrammed, of employers required to keep the records in question. Findings shall be documented in the case file.

(1) *Injury and Illness Records.* Irrespective of the establishment's LWDI rate, all injury and illness records required by 29 CFR 1904 (if not already reviewed during the records review) shall be examined. Medical and first aid records may also be reviewed under a written medical access order as described in D.4.a(4)(b)*1*.

NOTE: The CSHO shall *not* request access to the Bureau of Labor Statistics survey questionnaire (OSHA-200S) or even ask if the employer has participated in the survey program.

(2) *Hazard Communication.* For all safety and health inspections, regardless of the LWDI rate, the CSHO shall determine if the employer is covered by the hazard communication standard. If so, the CSHO shall ensure that the applicable requirements of 29 CFR 1910.1200 have been met and that the program is effective. (See OSHA Instruction CPL 2-2.38B.) This shall be done even if the establishment LWDI rate is below the BLS average. Citations for violations of the standard shall be issued in accordance with the provisions of Chapter II, B.5.c. To ensure that the employer has an effective hazard communication program, the following shall be performed:

(a) The CSHO shall confirm his/her analysis regarding recordkeeping and training by conducting employee interviews and documenting their responses in the case file.

(b) The CSHO shall conduct a brief tour of the facility to confirm compliance with the following elements of the hazard communication standard:

1 The existence of a written hazard communication program.

2 The required list of hazardous chemicals.

3 The existence of and reliance upon hazard determination procedures.

4 The existence and availability of material safety data sheets in the work area.

5 Inplant and shipped container labeling programs.

6 The effectiveness of required training.

(3) *Access to Employee Exposure and Medical Records.* During all health inspections and safety inspections when designated by the supervisor, whatever the LWDI rate, the CSHO shall determine if applicable exposure and medical records are being maintained in accordance with the medical surveillance recordkeeping requirements of applicable standards or of 29 CFR 1910.20. CSHO access to the employee medical records is authorized under 29 CFR 1913.10(b)(4) for the limited purpose of verifying employer compliance with those requirements. Review of the content of such medical records may require a written access order or express employee consent. (See OSHA Instructions CPL 2-2.32 and CPL 2-2.33.)

(4) *Other Records.* Any other records which fall within the scope of the inspection and which are related directly to the purpose of the inspection (29 CFR 1903.3(a)) shall be examined. These may include, but are not limited to:

(a) Required certification records properly completed and any available equipment inspection and maintenance records;

(b) Medical surveillance or monitoring records, employee exposure records and other medical records not falling under D.7.a.(3).

NOTE: Whenever circumstances indicate or whenever assigned by their supervisors, adequately cross-trained CSHOs conducting a safety inspection shall also conduct a survey of records required by various health standards to be maintained by the employer. These required records may be evaluated by the CSHO at the site or may be copied for examination by the health staff.

(c) Safety committee minutes; checklists; records of inspections conducted by plant safety and health committees, insurance companies, or consultants; if voluntarily supplied by the employer.

(d) Variance documentation.

b. *Posting.* The CSHO shall determine if posting requirements are met in accordance with 29 CFR 1903 and 29 CFR 1904. These include, but are not limited to:

(1) OSHA poster informing employees of their rights and obligations under the Act.

(2) Log and Summary of Occupational Injuries and Illnesses during the month of February.

(3) Current citations, if any.

(4) Petitions for Modifications of Abatement Date (PMAs).

c. *Additional Information to Supplement Records Review.* It is OSHA policy that all safety and health inspections, including "records only" inspections, include an entry into and survey of the workplace. The information gathered during this survey will supplement the records review and serve to confirm or revise the determination as to whether the inspection's scope should be expanded.

(1) Accordingly, for all safety and health inspections, regardless of the LWDI rate, the CSHO shall review the employer's overall safety and health management program and specific programs such as those related to personal protective equipment and respiratory protection to evaluate their effectiveness and identify deficiencies.

(2) This review shall include a brief survey of the workplace, focusing on any high hazard areas. This survey will normally be conducted in conjunction with the tour of the facility to assess hazard communication compliance described at A.7.a.(2)(b).

(3) The inspection shall be expanded to either a partial or a comprehensive inspection, following consultation with the Area Director, based on the following factors:

(a) Lack of a comprehensive safety and health management program. (See D.8.a.(2) and Chapter III Appendix, "Narrative," B.18.)

(b) Significant deficiencies in specific programs such as respiratory protection programs, hazard communication, wire rope inspection for cranes, and fire protection programs.

(c) Serious violations of safety and health standards uncovered during the plant tour.

(d) Concentrations of injuries or illnesses in specific areas of the plant.

(e) Significant past history of serious safety and health violations at the plant.

(4) If it is determined to expand the inspection to either a partial or comprehensive inspection, the employer shall be immediately so notified.

(5) Observed violations shall be documented and cited appropriately. The scope of the inspection as recorded on the OSHA-1 shall be "records only" UNLESS citations are issued for violations of standards OTHER THAN 29 CFR 1904 or 29 CFR 1910.1200.

8. Walkaround Inspection. The main purpose of the walkaround is to identify potential safety and/or health hazards in the workplace. The CSHO shall conduct the inspection in such a manner as to eliminate unnecessary personal exposure to hazards and to minimize unavoidable personal exposure to the extent possible.

a. *General Procedures.* It is essential during the walkaround portion of every inspection for the CSHO to:

(1) Become familiar with plant processes, collect information on hazards, observe employees' activities and interview them as appropriate.

(a) For health inspections, a preliminary tour of the establishment normally shall be accomplished before any decision to conduct an in-depth industrial hygiene investigation.

(b) Such a preliminary walkaround shall survey existing engineering controls and collect screening samples, when appropriate, to determine the need for full-scale sampling.

1 If screening reveals potentially high exposure levels, a comprehensive health inspection shall be conducted.

2 If screening samples must be sent to the laboratory for analysis, the employer shall be so informed.

a If the laboratory results show that potentially high employee exposure levels exist, full-scale sampling of the potentially hazardous areas will be conducted.

b If the results are negative, the file will be closed.

(2) Evaluate the employer's safety and health program (whether written or not) as follows:

(a) By ascertaining the degree to which the employer is aware of potential hazards present in the workplace and the methods in use to control them;

1 What plans and schedules does the employer have to institute, upgrade and maintain engineering and administrative controls?

2 What is the employer's work practices program?

(b) By determining employee knowledge of any hazards which exist in the establishment; the extent to which the employer's program covers the precautions to be taken by employees actually or potentially exposed to plant hazards; emergency procedures and inspection schedules for emergency personal protective equipment; the program for the selection, use and maintenance of routine personal protective equipment; and the overall quality and extent of the educational and training program and the degree of employee participation in it.

1 Compliance with the training requirements of any applicable safety and/or health standard shall be determined.

2 The following specific elements of the establishment safety and health program shall be evaluated in the detail appropriate to the circumstances of the inspection:

a Comprehensiveness. Evaluate the degree to which the employer's safety and health program addresses the full range of hazards normally encountered in the employer's operations. This is an overall evaluation and shall take into account the evaluations of the remaining categories. Indicate whether the program is written.

b Communication. Evaluate the employees' awareness of and access to the safety and health program, taking into account the principal means by which the program is communicated to them (e.g., oral instructions, booklets, memorandums, posters, etc.). Consider whether safety meetings are held by the employer, their frequency and the persons conducting them (e.g., crew foremen, intermediate level supervisors, safety director, etc.). The effectiveness of these means shall be considered in the evaluation.

c Enforcement. Evaluate the degree to which safety and health rules are actually enforced, taking into account the principal methods used (e.g., warnings, written reprimands, disciplinary action, discharge, etc.) and the effectiveness of these methods. Determine whether there is a staff (or one specific person) with assigned safety or health responsibilities and consider the effectiveness of the staff's performance.

d Safety/Health Training Program. Evaluate separately any safety and health training programs the employer has. Factors to be considered include the need for special training in view of the hazards likely to be encountered or of specific requirements for such training and the need for ongoing or periodic training or retraining of employees.

e Investigations. Evaluate the employer's efforts to make accident/injury/illness investigations and indicate whether adequate corrective and preventive actions are taken as a result.

(3) Record all facts pertinent to an apparent violation on the appropriate compliance worksheets. Apparent violations shall be brought to the attention of employer and employee representatives at the time they are documented.

(a) All notes, observations, analyses, and other information shall be either recorded on the worksheet or attached to it.

1 Because this documentation is required for each instance of an alleged violation, the CSHO shall normally use one worksheet to describe each instance as it is noted.

2 If identical violations of the same standard or of several related standards are noted in one general location in the establishment and if the documentation is essentially the same, all of those violations may be treated as a single instance description and only one worksheet need be completed for that instance.

3 Photographs, sketches, and descriptions that are attached to the worksheet are part of the inspection record and shall be noted on the form. The original field notes, as a basic documentation of the violation, shall be attached to the worksheet and retained in the case file.

(b) The CSHO shall provide as much detailed information as practical to establish the specific characteristics of each violation as follows:

1 Describe the observed hazardous conditions or practices (i.e., the facts which constitute a hazardous condition, operation or practice and the essential facts as to how and/or why a standard is allegedly violated). SpecifWW]cally identify the hazards to which employees have been or could be exposed. Describe the type of accident which the violated standard was designed to prevent in this situation, or note the name and exposure level of any contaminant or harmful physical agent to which employees are, have been or could be exposed. If more than one type of accident or exposure could reasonably be predicted to occur, describe the one which would result in the most serious injury or illness. For the type of accident described, include:

a All factors about the violative condition which could significantly affect the nature and severity of the resulting injuries (e.g., "fall of 20 feet onto pro-

truding rebar"; "fall into water-filled excavation").

b Other factors which could affect the probability that an injury would occur, such as:

● Proximity of the workers to the point of danger of the operation.

● Stress producing characteristics of the operation (e.g., speed, heat, repetitiveness, noise, position of employee).

c For contaminants and physical agents, any additional facts which clarify the nature of employee exposure.

d The identification of the equipment and process which pose the hazards; i.e., serial numbers, equipment types, trade names, manufacturers, etc. Include a sketch when appropriate.

e The specific location of the violation; e.g.:

● Building No. 3, second floor, column no. 6.

● Machine Shop, N.E. corner, Department 12.

● Foundry, N.W. corner, shakeout area.

f State the nature of the more serious types of injury or illness which it is reasonably predictable could result from the accident or health exposure.

● Thus, the entry for the "fall from 20 feet onto protruding rebar" might read "death from multiple injuries." For exposure to asbestos, the entry might read, "asbestosis, cancer and death."

● Broad categories of injuries and health effects (such as "electric shock," "burns," or "lacerations") shall be qualified to indicate whether the injuries or health effects are major or minor.

● In identifying the illnesses which a standard regulating exposure to an air contaminant or harmful physical agent is designed to prevent in a particular worksite, it may be necessary to consider not only the level of exposure but also the frequency and duration of exposure to the contaminant or agent.

g Evaluate the probability of an injury and explain the selection of probability and severity factors.

h Any specific measurements taken during the inspection (e.g., "20 ft. distance from top of scaffold platform to ground level"; "employee standing 2 ft. from unguarded floor edge"; "employee seated 2 ft. from source of metal fumes") which will further document the nature of the hazardous conditions and operations.

● Describe how measurements were taken during the inspection.

● Identify the measuring techniques and equipment used and those who were present; i.e., employee or employer representative who observed the measurements being taken.

● Include calibration dates and description of calibration procedures used, if appropriate.

i Exposure facts so as to present a picture of employee exposure to the hazard for each particular occupation, including:

● The occupation and the employer of the exposed employees if the employer is different from the one on the corresponding OSHA-1.

● The number of exposed employees in that occupation.

● The length of time that the alleged violation has existed.

● The duration and frequency that the employees are exposed (e.g., 2hrs./wk).

● The name, address (with zip code) and telephone number of at least one exposed employee in each occupation. If necessary, signed and dated witness statements shall be obtained and attached to the worksheet.

EXAMPLE: A radial arm saw has been on a construction site for 3 months and has never been guarded during that time. All of the employer's 14 carpenters on the job use the saw. One of the carpenters in John Doe. Total use of the saw on a daily basis is approximately 4 hours.

j Any facts which establish that the employer knew of the hazardous condition or could have known of that condition with the exercise of reasonable diligence. Enter any facts which show that:

● The employer actually knew of the hazardous condition which constitutes the violation. In this regard, a supervisor represents the employer and supervisory knowledge amounts to employer knowledge.

● The employer could have known of the hazardous condition if all reasonable steps had been taken to identify hazards to which employees may have been exposed. As a general rule, the CSHO can presume that the employer could have discovered the condition through the exercise of reasonable diligence.

NOTE: If the CSHO has reason to believe that the violation may be a willful violation, facts shall be included to show that the employer knew that the condition existed and, in addition, knew that, by law, he had to do something to abate the hazard (e.g., the employer was previously cited for the same condition; a CSHO had already told the employer about the requirement; knowledge of the requirement was brought to the employer's attention by an employee safety committee, etc.). Also include facts showing that, even if he was not consciously violating the Act, the employer was aware that the violative condition existed and made no reasonable effort to eliminate it.

k Any pertinent employer or employee remarks made during the walkaround and/or the closing conference, especially comments directly related to the instance described.

● Include employer comments which may be characterized as admissions of the specific violations described.

● Include any other facts which may assist in evaluating the situation or in reconstructing the total picture in preparation for testimony in possible legal actions.

● Include any additional comments (by the CSHO), particularly any explanation of abatement of dates when necessary (e.g., when longer than 5 days for a serious violation or when an abatement period exceeding 30 days is recommended for an item).

2 If employee exposure (either to safety or health hazards) is not observed, state facts on which the determination is made that an employee has been or could be exposed. In appropriate cases, state what the employer could have or should have done to be in compliance. When violations are grouped, described the reasons for grouping. If a specific type of hazard exposure is caused by the combination of violations, describe it in sufficient detail.

3 If the cited employer neither created nor controlled the violative condition, state the name and relationship of the responsible party; e.g., prime contractor, electrical subcontractor, building owner or equipment lessor. Describe any steps taken by the cited employer to have the condition corrected.

b. *Health Inspections.* There are special documentation requirements for health inspections. (See Appendix, Narrative, OSHA - 1A Form, Industrial Hygiene Inspection Outline.) During such inspections, the CSHO shall:

(1) Record all relevant information concerning potential exposure to chemical substances or physical hazards such as symptomatology, duration and frequency of the hazard, pertinent employee comments, sources of potential health hazards, locations of employees pertinent to the inspection, types of engineering controls, use of personal protective devices including respirators, ear and eye protection, clothing etc.; and collect Material Safety Data Sheets where available and appropriate.

(2) Observe employee activities throughout the establishment, concentrating particularly on potentially hazardous areas, and

(a) Estimate numbers of employees at each operation to be evaluated, indicating whether they are engaged in stationary or transient activities.

(b) Interview employees.

(c) Record the duration and frequency of cyclic work processes, describing potential exposures during each phase of the cycle.

(3) Request and evaluate information on the following aspects of the employer's occupational safety and health program (Findings shall be discussed in detail at the closing conference.):

(a) *Monitoring.* The employer's program for monitoring safety and health hazards in the establishment should include a program for self-inspection. The CSHO shall discuss the employer's maintenance schedules and inspection records. Additional information shall be obtained concerning such employer activities as sampling and calibration procedures, ventilation measurements, preventive maintenance programs for engineering controls, laboratory services, use of industrial hygienists and accredited laboratories. Compliance with the monitoring requirement of any applicable standard shall be determined.

(b) *Medical.* The CSHO shall determine whether the employer provides the employees with preplacement and periodic medical examinations. The medical examination protocol shall be requested to determine the extent of the medical examinations and, if applicable, compliance with the medical surveillance requirements of any applicable standard.

(c) *Recordkeeping.* The CSHO shall determine the extent of the employer's recordkeeping program. This is not to be limited to OSHA-required records, but shall be extended to information pertinent to the inspection such as:

1 If records pertaining to employee exposure and medical records are being preserved in accordance with 29 CFR 1910.20, and

2 Where a specific standard has provisions for employee access to the records, whether the results of environmental measurements and medical examinations are accessible to the affected employees.

(d) *Compliance.* The employer's compliance program may include engineering, work practice and administrative controls and the use of personal protective equipment. The CSHO shall identify as follows:

1 Engineering Controls. Pertinent engineering controls consist of substitution, isolation, ventilation and equipment modification.

2 Work Practice and Administrative Controls. These control techniques include personal hygiene, housekeeping practices and rotation of employees.

a There should be a program of employee training and education to utilize work practice controls effectively. Where pertinent, the CSHO shall obtain a detailed description of such controls.

b The CSHO shall evaluate the overall effect of such practices and programs, considering the employees' knowledge of their exposures.

c Rotation of employees as an administrative control requires employer knowledge of the extent and duration of exposure.

3 Personal Protective Equipment. An effective personal protective equipment program should exist in the plant. A detailed evaluation of the program shall be made to determine compliance with the specific standards which require the use of protective equipment (e.g., 29 CFR 1910.95, 1910.132, 1910.134).

(e) *Regulated Areas.* The CSHO shall investigate compliance with the requirements for regulated areas as specified by certain standards.

1 Regulated areas must be clearly identified and known to all appropriate employees.

2 The regulated area designations must be maintained according to the prescribed criteria of the applicable standard.

(f) *Emergency Procedures.* The CSHO shall evaluate the employer's emergency program.

1 When standards provide that specific emergency procedures be developed where certain hazardous substances are handled, the evaluation shall determine if:

a Potential emergency conditions are included in the written plan.

b Emergency conditions have been explained to employees.

c There is a training scheme for the protection of affected employees including use and maintenance of personal protective equipment.

2 Where hazardous substances are handled for which there are no standards requiring emergency procedures, the CSHO shall, nevertheless, determine if such procedures have been established. (See OSHA Instruction CPL 2-2.45.)

(4) *Collecting Samples.* The CSHO shall determine as soon as possible after the start of the inspection whether sampling is required by utilizing the information collected during the walkaround and from the preinspection review.

(a) If sampling is necessary, a sampling strategy shall be developed by considering potential chemical and physical hazards, number of samples to be taken, and the operations and locations to be sampled.

1 There shall be no undue delay between development of the sampling strategy and the actual sampling or between receipt of the results of spot or screen sampling and full-shift sampling, when the results indicate its necessity. (See C.1.d.)

2 If a delay of more than 5 working days is unavoidable, the reasons for the delay shall be included in the case file. Such situations shall be handled in accordance with C.1.d.(3).

(b) When work schedules other than the usual 8-hour day are encountered;

e.g., 4 10-hour days per week, the following procedures shall be used when the standard itself does not cover such exposures:

1 Sampling for 8-hour exposure levels shall be performed as usual; separate sampling shall be conducted to determine any additional exposure beyond the 8 hours.

2 The results from the 8-hour sampling shall be compared to the Permissible Exposure Level (PEL) to determine whether or not an overexposure exists.

3 If it appears that the 8-hour exposure limits do not provide adequate protection from health hazards when longer workday schedules are used, the Area Director shall contact the Regional Administrator for additional instructions on further sampling that may be indicated as well as for guidance on evaluation of sampling data.

4 The Regional Administrator, in such cases, shall contact the Director of Technical Support through the Director, Office of Field Programs for assistance in determining appropriate sampling procedures and in evaluating the resulting data.

(c) If either the employer or the employee representative requests sampling results, summaries of the results shall be provided to the requesting representative as soon as practicable after consultation with the supervisor.

c. *Taking Photographs.* Photographs shall be taken whenever the CSHO judges there is a need. Developed photographs shall be properly labeled and placed in the case file.

NOTE: The CSHO shall ensure that using flash or spark-producing equipment will not be hazardous and that employees are not unexpectedly startled by the use of flash equipment.

d. *Employee Interviews.* A free and open exchange of information between the CSHO and employees is essential to an effective inspection. Interviews provide an opportunity for employees to point out hazardous conditions and, in general, to provide assistance as to what violations of the Act may exist and what abatement action should be taken.

(1) *Purpose.* Section 8(a)(2) of the Act authorizes the CSHO to question any employee privately during regular working hours in the course of an OSHA inspection. The purpose of such interviews is to obtain whatever information the CSHO deems necessary or useful in carrying out the inspection effectively. Such interviews, however, shall be conducted within reasonable limits and in a reasonable manner and shall be kept as brief as possible. Individual interviews are authorized even when there is an employee representative.

(2) *Employee Right of Complaint.* Even when employees are represented on the walkaround, the CSHO may consult with any employee who desires to discuss a possible violation. Upon receipt of such information, the CSHO shall investigate the alleged violation, where possible, and record the findings.

(a) 29 CFR 1903.10 affords any employee an opportunity to bring any condition believed to violate a standard or Section 5(a)(1) of the Act to the attention of the CSHO during an inspection.

(b) In certain instances, the employer and/or the employee walkaround representative may not be able to provide all the necessary information regarding an accident or possible violation. The CSHO shall consult with employees while conducting the walkaround inspection and shall arrange for interviews, where these are considered useful, with employees who may have knowledge of pertinent facts.

(3) *Time and Location.* Interviews normally will be conducted during the walkaround; however, they may be conducted at any time during an inspection.

(a) *Workplace.* If requested by the employee and considered useful by the CSHO, additional consultation shall be scheduled at a mutually convenient time. In retail or service establishments or in continuous production operations (e.g., assembly line), interviews shall be scheduled to afford minimum interference with the employee's duties and the employer's business operations.

(b) *Other Than Workplace.* Interviews may be held at the employee's home, the OSHA Area Office, or at any other suitable place in the community where privacy can be maintained.

(4) *Privacy.* At the time of the interview employees shall be asked if they desire the interview to be in private. Whenever an employee expresses a preference that an interview be held in private, the CSHO shall make a reasonable effort to honor that request. Even in the absence of such a request, every reasonable effort shall be made to conduct interviews with employees in private.

NOTE: "In private" refers to the exclusion of the employer representative, not the employee representative unless the employee expresses a desire to be interviewed out of hearing of both the employer and the employee representatives.

(5) *Interview Statements.* Interview statements shall be obtained whenever the CSHO determines that such statements would be useful in documenting adequately an apparent violation.

(a) Interviews shall normally be written, and the employee shall be encouraged to sign and date the statement. The CSHO shall assure the employee that the statement will be held confidential to the extent allowed by law. Following are some examples of situations where the CSHO shall normally obtain written statements:

1 When there is an actual or potential controversy between the employer and employee as to a material fact concerning a violation.

2 When there is a conflict or difference among employee statements as to the facts.

3 When there is a potential willful or repeated violation.

4 In accident investigations, when attempting to determine if apparent vio-

lation(s) existed at the time of the accident.

(b) Interview statements shall normally be written in the first person and in the language of the employee. The wording of the statement shall be understandable to the employee and reflect only what has been brought out in the interview.

1 Any changes or corrections shall be initialed by the employee; otherwise, the statement shall not be changed, added to or altered in any way.

2 The statements shall end with wording such as: "I have read the above, and it is true to the best of my knowledge." The employee shall sign and date the statement and the CSHO shall then sign it as a witness.

3 If the employee refuses to sign the statement, the CSHO shall note such refusal on the statement. The statement shall, nevertheless, be read to the employee and an attempt made to obtain agreement. A note that this was done shall be entered into the case file.

(c) If the employee interview has been recorded, the conversation shall be transcribed; the transcription shall meet the requirements of D.8.d.(5)(a) and (b).

e. *Special Circumstances.*

(1) *Trade Secrets.* Trade secrets are matters that are not of public or general knowledge. A trade secret is any confidential formula, pattern, process, equipment, list, blueprint, device or compilation of information used in the employer's business which gives an advantage over competitors who do not know or use it.

(a) *Policy.* It is essential to the effective enforcement of the Act that the CSHO and all OSHA personnel preserve the confidentiality of all information and investigations which might reveal a trade secret.

(b) *Restrictions and Controls.* When the employer identifies an operation or condition as a trade secret, it shall be treated as such. Information obtained in such areas, including all negatives, photographs and OSHA documentation forms shall be labeled:

"ADMINISTRATIVELY CONTROLLED INFORMATION" "RESTRICTED TRADE INFORMATION"

1 Under Section 15 of the Act, all information reported to or obtained by a CSHO in connection with any inspection or other activity which contains or which might reveal a trade secret shall be kept confidential. Such information shall not be disclosed except to other OSHA officials concerned with the enforcement of the Act or, when relevant, in any proceeding under the Act.

2 Title 18 of the United States Code, Section 1905, provides criminal penalties for Federal employees who disclose such information. These penalties include fines of up to $1,000 or imprisonment of up to one year, or both, and removal from office or employment.

3 Trade secret materials shall not be labeled as "Top Secret," "Secret," or "Confidential," nor shall these security classification designations be used in conjunction with other words unless the trade secrets are also classified by an agency of the U.S. Government in the interest of national security.

(c) *Photographs.* If the employer objects to the taking of photographs because trade secrets would or may be disclosed, the CSHO should advise the employer of the protection against such disclosure afforded by Section 15 of the Act and 29 CFR 1903.9. If the employer still objects, the CSHO shall contact the supervisor.

(2) *Areas Requiring Immunization.* If, during an inspection, a nonimmunized CSHO encounters an area requiring immunization, the CSHO shall not enter that area but shall note a description of the area, immunization required, employees exposed, location and other pertinent information in the case file.

(a) *Nonimmunized CSHO.* The CSHO shall consult with the supervisor about scheduling a properly immunized CSHO for an immediate or later inspection, as applicable. The CSHO shall then complete the inspection of all other areas of the establishment.

(b) *Nonimmunized Walkaround Representative.* If, during an inspection, a properly immunized CSHO finds that walkaround representatives of employers and employees are not properly immunized and, therefore, not authorized in the area, a reasonable number of employees and the supervisor of that area shall be consulted concerning workplace health and safety. (See B.7. for additional information.)

(3) *Violations of Other Laws.* If a CSHO observes apparent violations of laws enforced by other government agencies, such cases shall be referred to the appropriate agency.

9. Closing Conference. At the conclusion of an inspection, the CSHO shall conduct a closing conference with the employer and the employee representatives. (On multi-employer worksites, the CSHO shall decide whether separate closing conferences will be held with each employer representative.) A joint closing conference shall be held with the employer and the employee representatives whenever practicable. Where either party wishes to have a separate conference or where it is not practical to hold a joint closing conference, separate closing conferences shall be held. A written summary of each conference shall be included in the case file. A copy of the written summaries will be available from the Area Director upon request by the employer or the employee representatives.

a. *General.* The CSHO shall describe the apparent violations found during the inspection and indicate the applicable sections of the standards which may have been violated. Copies of the standards shall be given to both the employer and the employee representatives (if not already given during the opening conference). During the closing conference, both the employer and the employee representatives shall be advised of their rights to participate in any subsequent conferences, meetings or discussions.

(1) Since the CSHO may not have sample results prior to the first closing conference, a second closing conference shall be held by telephone or in person to inform the employer and the employee representatives whether the establishment is in compliance.

(a) If the results indicate noncompliance, apparent violations, correction procedures, and interim methods of control shall be discussed.

(b) Even if the employer is in compliance, sample results which equal or exceed 50 percent of the permissible exposure limit and any recommendations of the CSHO on good safety and health practices shall be discussed with the employer and the employee representatives.

(2) When closing conferences are delayed pending receipt of sampling data or for any other reason, the employee representative shall be afforded an opportunity to participate in such delayed conferences.

(3) The strengths and weaknesses of the employer's occupational safety and health program shall be discussed at the closing conference.

(4) During the discussion of apparent violations the CSHO shall note any comments on the OSHA-1B and obtain input for establishing correction dates.

(5) The CSHO shall advise the employee representatives that:

(a) Under 29 CFR 2200.20 of the Occupational Safety and Health Review Commission regulations, if the employer contests, the employees have a right to elect "party status" before the Review Commission.

(b) They must be notified by the employer if a notice of contest is filed.

(c) They have 11(c) rights. (See D.9.b.(12).)

(d) They have a right to contest the abatement date. (See D.9.b.(4)(a)2.) Such contest must be in writing and must be filed within 15 working days after receipt of the citation.

b. *Specific.* During the closing conference the CSHO shall give the employer the publication, "Employer Rights and Responsibilities Following an OSHA Inspection," which explains the responsibilities and courses of action available to the employer if a citation is received. The CSHO shall then briefly discuss the information in the booklet and answer any questions. All matters discussed during the closing conference shall be documented in the case file, including a note describing printed materials distributed.

(1) *Citation Issued.* If citations are issued, the original shall be sent to the employer representative at the establishment. In the case of a nonfixed worksite, the original normally shall be sent to the worksite and a copy sent to the employer's headquarters. If it is clear that the employer representative at the worksite does not receive mail deliveries or will not be at the site at the time of delivery, the circumstances shall be documented in the case file; and the original shall be sent to the location designated as most appropriate by the employer representative at the site. In addition, copies shall be sent to any other employer representatives as requested by the attending employer representative.

NOTE: The original citation shall be sent by certified mail, return receipt requested.

(a) The "Employer Rights and Responsibilities" publication (OSHA-3000) shall also be provided with each copy of the citation, and the employer shall be urged to read both the citation and the publication carefully. If the employer has any questions regarding a citation, the employer may contact the OSHA Area Director at the address on the citation.

(b) Letters informing the employer of the right to an informal conference and of the requirement that any Notice of Intent to Contest must be in writing shall be sent with each copy of the citation.

(c) Notification of assessment of interest, additional charges for nonpayment and administrative costs shall be included with each copy of the citation whenever there is an associated proposed penalty.

(d) If the employer is a contractor on a military base or other government facility, copies of the citation shall be sent to the base commander or other government officer in charge.

(2) *Citation Posting.* The citation or a copy of it must be posted at or near the place where each violation occurred to inform the employees of hazards to which they may be exposed. If, because of the nature of the employer's operation, it is not practical to post the citation at or near the place where each violation occurred, the citation must be posted in a prominent place where it will be readily observed by all affected employees. The citation must remain posted for 3 working days or until the violation is corrected, whichever is longer.

(a) If the citation is amended as a result of an informal conference or other procedure, a copy of the amended citation must be posted along with a copy of the original citation.

(b) Even if contested, a copy of the citation still must be posted.

(c) If there is an authorized employee representative at the establishment, copies of the original citation and any subsequent citation amendments shall be sent to that representative as soon as possible after receipt of these documents by the employer. The appropriate informal conference letter shall be sent with each copy of the citation.

(3) *Complying with Citation and Notification of Penalty.* If the employer does not contest the citation and the penalty and it becomes a final order, then:

(a) The cited conditions must be abated by the dates set in the citation, and

(b) The penalty must be paid if one was proposed.

(4) *Contesting Citation and Notification of Penalty.* The CSHO shall advise the employer that the citation, the penalty and/or the abatement date may be contested if, in good faith, the employer does NOT agree to the citation, penalty or abatement date.

(a) *Notice of Contest.* The CSHO shall tell the employer that, in order to contest, the Area Director must be notified in writing within 15 working days after receipt of the citation and notification of penalty (Working days are Monday through Friday, excluding Federal holidays.) It shall be emphasized that a notice of intent to contest given orally will not satisfy this requirement to give written notification.

NOTE: The written notification must be postmarked no later than the 15th working day after receipt of the citation.

1 Employer Contest. This written notification, called a Notice of Intent to Contest, must clearly state what is being contested — which item of the citation, the penalty, the correction date, or any combination. The CSHO shall ask the employer to read the pamphlet accompanying the citation for additional details.

a If the employer wishes only a later abatement date and there is a valid reason, the Area Director should be contacted. The Area Director may issue an amended citation changing an abatement date prior to the expiration of the 15-working-day period without the employer's filing a contest.

b If the employer contests only the penalty or only some of the citation items, all uncontested items must still be abated by the dates indicated on the citation and the corresponding penalties paid within 15 days of notification.

2 Employee Contest. The CSHO shall indicate that the Act provides that employees or their authorized representative(s) have the right to contest in writing any or all of the abatement dates set for a violation if they believe the date(s) to be unreasonable.

NOTE: The definition of employees' authorized representative is found on Page III-20.

(b) *Contest Process.* The CSHO shall explain that, when the Notice of Intent to Contest is properly filed, the Area Director is required to forward the case to an independent agency, the Occupational Safety and Health Review Commission (the Review Commission) at which time the case is officially in litigation.

1 Upon receipt of the Notice of Intent to Contest, the Review Commission will assign the case to an administrative law judge, who will schedule a hearing in a public place close to the workplace.

2 The Review Commission will inform the employer of the procedural requirements which must be observed throughout the proceedings.

3 The administrative law judge may uphold, modify or eliminate any item of the citation or the penalty which the employer has challenged.

(5) *Informal Conference.* The CSHO shall advise those attending the closing conference:

(a) That a request for an informal conference with the OSHA Area Director is strongly encouraged. The informal conference provides an opportunity to:

1 Resolve disputed citations and penalties without the necessity of recourse to the contest litigation process which can be time-consuming and expensive;

2 Obtain a more complete understanding of the specifWW]c safety or health standards which apply;

3 Discuss ways to correct the apparent violations;

4 Discuss questions concerning proposed penalties;

5 Discuss problems with proposed abatement dates;

6 Discuss problems concerning employee safety and health practices;

7 Learn more of other OSHA program projects and services available;

8 Obtain answers to other questions.

(b) That, if a citation is issued, an informal conference or the request for one does not extend the 15-working day period in which the employer or the employee representative may contest.

(c) That an oral statement of disagreement with or intent to contest a citation, penalty or abatement date during an informal conference will not take the place of the required written notice of intent to contest.

(d) That the employer representative(s) have the right to participate in any informal conference or negotiations between the Regional Administrator or Area Director and the employees.

(e) That the employee representative(s) have the right to participate in any informal conferences or negotiations between the Regional Administrator or Area Director and the employer in accordance with the guidelines given in G. of this Chapter.

(6) *Penalties.* The CSHO shall explain that penalties must be paid within 15 working days after the employer receives the citation and notification of penalty. If, however, the employer contests the citation and/or the penalty in good faith, the penalties need not be paid for those items contested until a final decision is made.

(7) *Abatement Action.* The CSHO shall explain the following:

(a) For violations the employer does not contest, the employer is expected to notify the Area Director promptly by letter that the cited conditions have been corrected by the abatement date set in the citation. Failure to do so may trigger a followup inspection. The notification must explain the specific action taken with regard to each violation and the approximate date the corrective action was completed. (See E.4. and Chapter II, E.1.b.(2).)

(b) When the citation permits an extended time for abatement, the employer must ensure that employees are adequately protected during this time. For example, the citation may require the immediate use of personal protective equipment by employees while engineering controls are being installed. The employer may be requested to send periodic progress reports on actions to correct these violations.

(8) *Petition for Modification of Abatement Date.* The CSHO shall advise the employer that abatement dates are established on the basis of the information available at the time the citations are issued. When uncontrollable events or other circumstances prevent the employer from meeting an abatement date and the 15-working-day contest period has expired, a petition may be submitted in writing for modifications of the abatement date. Further information on petitions for modifications of abatement dates is included in the pamphlet accompanying any citation that is received. Details may be obtained from the Area Director.

(9) *Followup Inspection.* The CSHO shall explain that:

(a) If the employer receives a citation, a followup inspection may be conducted to verify that the employer has:

1 Posted the citation as required.

2 Corrected the violations as required in the citation.

3 Adequately protected the employees during multistep or lengthy abatement periods.

4 Taken appropriate administrative or engineering abatement steps in a timely manner.

(b) The employer also has a continuing responsibility to comply with the Act. Any new violations discovered during a followup inspection will be cited.

(10) *Failure to Abate.* The CSHO shall explain that to achieve abatement by the date set forth in the citation, it is important that corrective efforts be promptly initiated. The employer shall be reminded that, under the Act, additional penalties of up to $1,000 per day per violation may be proposed if the employer is found during a followup inspection to have failed to abate by the time required on the OSHA-2 any violations which have not been contested.

(11) *False Information.* The CSHO shall explain that, if the employer knowingly provides false information relating to efforts to correct cited conditions or in records required to be maintained or in any other matter related to the Act, criminal penalties are specified in the Act.

(12) *Employee Discrimination.* The CSHO shall emphasize that the Act prohibits employers from discharging or discriminating in any way against an employee who has exercised any right under the Act, including the right to make safety or health complaints or to request an OSHA inspection. Complaints from employees who believe they have been discriminated against will be evaluated by OSHA. If the investigation discloses a probable violation of employee rights, OSHA may initiate legal action on behalf of employees whose rights have been violated.

(13) *Variance.* The CSHO shall explain that the Act permits, and the agency encourages, the employer to apply to OSHA for a temporary variance from a newly promulgated standard if the employer is unable to comply by the effective date because of the unavailability of materials, equipment, or technical personnel. The employer also is encouraged to apply for a permanent variance from a standard if the employer believes that the facilities or methods of operation at the establishments under consideration are at least as safe and healthful as would be ensured by the OSHA standard. All variance applications must be submitted in writing and must include all applicable items specified in 29 CFR 1905. More complete information on variances may be obtained from the Area Director.

(14) *SBA Loans.* If asked by the employer, the CSHO shall explain that SBA does not currently provide either direct or guaranteed loans for OSHA compliance.

(15) *De Minimis Violations.* The CSHO shall discuss all conditions noted during the walkaround considered to be de minimis, indicating that such conditions are subject to review by the Area Director in the same manner as apparent violations but, if finally classified as de minimis, will not be included on the citation. In addition, the CSHO shall explain to the employer and employee representatives that a condition is considered to be de minimis when it has direct or immediate relationship to employee safety and health or when it is apparent that the employer is complying with the clear intent of the standard but deviates in a minor, technical or trivial way. Employer comments shall be noted on the OSHA-1B. (See Chapter IV, B.6.)

(16) *Referral Inspection.* When applicable, the CSHO shall explain that apparent serious violations which have been observed during the inspection, but which are not within the scope of the CSHO's expertise, will be subject to referral to the supervisor and, as a result, additional inspections may be scheduled at a later date.

(17) *Consultative Services.* The CSHO shall explain thoroughly the consultative services available to the employer, including confidentiality provisions, safety and health program assistance, training and education service and the inspection exemption program. Onsite consultation may be sought concerning any and all citation items that have become final orders as well as items not involving citations. Such consultation may be of help when specialized or extensive abatement measures appear to be required.

(18) *Other Agency Services and Programs.* The CSHO shall briefly explain the various other services and programs currently in effect in the agency and shall provide copies of program descriptions to any interested employer. Examples are the following:

(a) *Voluntary Protection Programs.* These programs are designed for those employers want to cooperate with the agency to demonstrate the importance of functioning internal safety and health systems for the prevention of injuries and illnesses. OSHA encourages program participants to set realistic goals for the elimination or reduction of workplace hazards and for improved safety and health planning and programming. In all of the programs that have been developed thus far, as in all agency initiatives, OSHA insists that participation in any of these programs shall not in any way diminish existing employer or employee rights and responsibilities under the Act. The three currently existing programs are:

1 The STAR Program,

2 The MERIT program, and

3 The DEMONSTRATION program.

(b) *Employer Abatement Assistance.* The employer shall be made aware in greater detail of OSHA's commitment to aid as much as practicable in the process of correcting workplace hazards. Any questions regarding abatement can be discussed with the employer during the closing conference with more complete information provided as necessary as soon as possible after the completion of the inspection. (See F. for more details)

(c) *Training and Education Programs.* The CSHO shall inform the employer of any OSHA-funded training and education programs that are available, including those from the OSHA Training Institute and those from "New Directions" grantees.

E. Abatement.

1. Period. The abatement period shall be the shortest interval within which the employer can *reasonably* be expected to correct the violation. An abatement date shall be set forth in the citation as a specific date, not a number of days. When the abatement period is very short (i.e., 5 working days or less) and it is uncertain when the employer will receive the citation, the abatement date shall be set so as to allow for a mail delay and the agreed-upon abatement time. When abatement is witnessed by the CSHO during the inspection, the abatement period shall be "Immediately upon receipt" of the citation.

2. Reasonable Abatement Date. The establishment of an abatement date requires the exercise of maximum professional judgment on the part of the CSHO.

a. The exercise of this judgment shall be based on data found during the inspection and/or whatever subsequent information gathering is deemed necessary. In all cases, the employer shall be asked for any available information relative to the time required to accomplish abatement and/or any factors unique to the employer's operation which may have an effect on the time needed for abatement.

b. All pertinent factors shall be considered in determining what is a reasonable period. The following considerations may be useful in arriving at a decision.

(1) The gravity of the alleged violation.

(2) The availability of needed equipment, material, and/or personnel.

(3) The time required for delivery, installation, modification or construction.

(4) Training of personnel.

3. Abatement Periods Exceeding 30 Calendar Days. Abatement periods exceeding 30 calendar days should not normally be necessary, particularly for safety violations. Situations may arise, however, especially for health violations, where extensive structural changes are necessary or where new equipment or parts cannot be delivered within 30 calendar days. When an initial abatement date is granted that is in excess of 30 calendar days, the reason shall be documented in the case file. Initial abatement dates in excess of one year from the citation issuance date may not be granted by the Area Direc-

tor without prior approval of the Regional Administrator.

4. Verification of Abatement. The Area Director is responsible for determining if abatement has been accomplished. When abatement is not accomplished at the time of the inspection or the employer does not notify the Area Director by letter of the abatement, verification shall be determined by telephone, documentation shall be included in the case file as to the specific corrective action taken for each violation cited. (See D.9.b.(7)(a) and Chapter II, E.1.b.(2).)

5. Effect of Contest Upon Abatement Period. In situations where an employer contests either (1) the period set for abatement or (2) the citation itself, the abatement period generally shall be considered not to have begun until there has been an affirmation of the citation and abatement period. In accordance with the Act, the abatement period begins when a final order of the Review Commission is issued, and this abatement period is not tolled while an appeal is ongoing unless the employer has been granted a stay by the court. In situations where there is an employee contest of the abatement date, the abatement requirements of the citation remain unchanged.

a. Where the Review Commission or a court alters the abatement period, the abatement period as altered shall be the applicable abatement period.

b. Where an employer has contested only the amount of the proposed penalty, the abatement period continues to run unaffected by the contest.

c. Where the employer does not contest, he must abide by the date set forth in the citation even if such date is within the 15-day notice of contest period. Therefore, when the abatement period designated in the citation is 15 days or less and a notice of contest has not been filed, a followup inspection of the worksite may be conducted for purposes of determining whether abatement has been achieved within the time period set forth in the citation. A failure to abate citation may be issued on the basis of the CSHO's findings.

d. Where the employer has filed a notice of contest to the initial citation within the proper contest period, the abatement period does not begin to run until the entry of a final Review Commission order. Under these circumstances, any followup inspection within the contest period shall be discontinued and a failure to abate citation shall not be issued.

NOTE: There is one exception to the above rule. If an early abatement date has been designated in the initial citation and it is the opinion of the CSHO and/or the Area Director that a situation classified as imminent danger is presented by the cited condition, appropriate imminent danger proceedings may be initiated notwithstanding the filing of a notice of contest by the employer.

6. Feasible Administrative, Work Practice and Engineering Controls in Health Inspections. Where applicable (generally, during health inspections), the CSHO shall discuss control methology with the employer during the closing conference.

a. *Engineering Controls.* Engineering controls consist of substitution, isolation, ventilation and equipment modification.

(1) Substitution may involve process change, equipment replacement or material substitution.

(2) Isolation results in the reduction of the hazard by providing a barrier around the material, equipment, process or employee. This barrier may consist of a physical separation or isolation by distance.

(3) Ventilation controls are more fully discussed in the OSHA Technical Manual, OSHA Instruction CPL 2-2.20B.

(4) Equipment modification will result in increased performance or change in character, such as the application of sound absorbent material.

b. *Administrative Controls.* Any procedure which significantly limits daily exposure by control or manipulation of the work schedule or manner in which work is performed is considered a means of administrative control. The use of personal protective equipment is *not* considered a means of administrative control.

c. *Work Practice Controls.* Work practice controls are a type of administrative controls by which the employer modifies the manner in which the employee performs assigned work. Such modification may result in a reduction of exposure through such methods as changing work habits, improving sanitation and hygiene practices, or making other changes in the way the employee performs the job.

d. *Feasibility.* Abatement measures required to correct a citation item are feasible when they can be accomplished by the employer. The CSHO, following current directions and guidelines, shall inform the employer, where appropriate, that a determination will be made as to whether engineering or administrative controls are feasible.

(1) *Types of Feasibility.* In general there are two types of feasibility determinations that OSHA must make with regard to potential abatement methods. Each will be discussed separately.

(2) *Technical Feasibility.* Technical feasibility is the existence of technical know-how as to materials and methods available or adaptable to specific circumstances which can be applied to cited violations with a reasonable possibility that employee exposure to occupational hazards will be reduced.

(a) Sources which can provide information useful in making this determination are the following:

1 Similar situations observed elsewhere where adequate engineering controls do, in fact, reduce employee exposure.

2 Written source materials or conference presentations that indicate that equipment and designs are available to reduce employee exposure in similar situations.

3 Studies by a qualified consulting firm, professional engineer, industrial hygienist, or insurance carrier that show engineering controls are technically feasible.

4 Studies and materials collected and prepared by the Directorate of Compliance Programs, the Directorate of Technical Support and/or the Assistant Regional Administrator for Technical Support.

5 Equipment catalogs and suppliers that indicate engineering controls are technically feasible and are available.

6 Information provided by other government agencies when their regulations apply to the operations involved and which may affect or limit the design or type of controls that may be used for abatement.

(b) OSHA's experience indicates that feasible engineering or administrative controls exist for most hazardous exposures.

(c) The Regional Administrator is responsible for making determinations that engineering or administrative controls are not feasible.

(3) *Economic Feasibility.* Economic feasibility means that the employer is financially able to undertake the measures necessary to abate the citations received. The CSHO shall inform the employer that, although the cost of corrective measures to be taken will generally not be considered as a factor in the issuance of a citation, it will be considered during an informal conference or during settlement negotiations.

(a) If the cost of implementing effective engineering, administrative, or work practice controls or some combination of such controls, would seriously jeopardize the employer's financial condition so as to result in the probable shut down of the establishment or a substantial part of it, an extended abatement date shall be set when postponement of the capital expenditures would have a beneficial effect on the financial performance of the employer.

(b) If the employer raises the issue that the company has other establishments or other locations within the same establishment with equipment or processes which, although not cited as a result of the present inspection, nevertheless would require the same abatement measures as those under citation, the economic feasibility determination shall not be limited to the cited items alone. In such cases, although the employer will be required to abate the cited items within the time allowed for abatement, the opportunity to include both the cited and the additional items in a long-range abatement plan shall be offered.

(c) When additional time cannot be expected to solve the employer's financial infeasibility problem, the Area Director shall refer the problem to the Regional Administrator who shall consult with the Director, Office of Field Programs. (See E.8.c.)

e. *Reducing Employee Exposure.* Whenever feasible engineering, administrative or work practice controls can be instituted even though they are not sufficient to reduce exposure to or below the permissible exposure limit (PEL), nonetheless, they shall be required in conjunction with personal protective equipment to reduce exposure to the lowest practical level.

7. Long-term Abatement Date for Implementation of Feasible Engineering Controls. In situations where it is difficult to set a specific abatement date when the citation is originally issued; e.g., because of extensive redesign requirements consequent upon the employer's decision to implement feasible engineering controls and uncertainty as to when the job can be finished. The CSHO shall discuss the problem with the employer at the closing conference and, in appropriate cases, shall encourage the employer to seek a future informal conference with the Area Director when further information is available.

a. *Final Abatement Date.* The CSHO and the Area Director shall make their best judgment as to a reasonable abatement date. A specific date for final abatement shall, in all cases, be included in the citation. The employer shall not be permitted to propose an abatement plan setting his own abatement dates. If necessary, an appropriate petition may be submitted later by the employer to the Area Director to modify the abatement date.

b. *Employer Abatement Plan.* The employer is required to submit an abatement plan outlining the anticipated long-term abatement procedures.

(1) Such a plan may be submitted for consideration by the Area Director before setting the citation abatement date.

(a) In that case, the citation may be delayed for a brief period with a notation explaining the delay placed in the case file.

(b) If it appears that the citation might be delayed beyond 6 months from the date of alleged violation, the citation shall be issued prior to full consideration of the plan; but the employer shall be given the opportunity to provide as much input as practicable in the setting of the abatement period.

(2) Whether or not plan is submitted before issuing a citation, an abatement plan shall be provided for in the citation in addition to a final abatement date.

(3) When the plan is submitted, if the engineering or administrative corrections proposed by the employer appear to be all that are feasible based on the current technology, this fact may be stipulated and agreed to between OSHA and the employer.

(a) Such an agreement shall permit assurances in advance to the employer that the establishment will be in compliance where the provisions of the plan are fully implemented.

(b) It shall be made clear in the agreement that the employer is not relieved from instituting further engineering (or administrative) controls as they become technically feasible, if it is likely that such further controls will

lower employee exposure when exposure without personal protective equipment (PPE) remains over the PEL.

(c) In all situations where an agreement is proposed, the advice of the Regional Solicitor shall be sought on the legal implications.

(d) If an agreement is acceptable, the Regional Solicitor shall be requested to assist in drafting the agreement. Agreements having interregional implications shall be cleared with the Director, Office of Field Programs.

8. Multistep Abatement. Citations with multistep abatement periods normally will be issued only in those situations in which ultimate abatement will require the implementation of feasible engineering controls, as distinguished from feasible administrative controls or the use of PPE. Multistep abatements shall be based on the conditions cited and related feasibility considerations.

a. *General.* A step-by-step program for abatement provides a tool for the CSHO to monitor abatement progress after a citation has been issued, for the employer to make abatement decisions and to set up schedules efficiently, and for the employees to understand the changes being made to the working environment.

(1) Although abatement of an air contaminant citation normally requires the implementation of feasible engineering and/or administrative controls, abatement may be accomplished in rare cases through the use of PPE, even when engineering or administrative controls are feasible. (See E.8.c.(3).)

(2) In such cases the Regional Administrator shall contact the Directorate of Compliance Programs through the Office of Field Programs prior to approving final abatement through the use of PPE.

b. *Interim and Long-range Abatement.* When the cited employer is found to have no effective personal protection program, in addition to long-term abatement through the use of feasible administrative or engineering controls, proper abatement will include a short-term requirement that appropriate PPE be provided.

(1) The Area Director, in issuing the citation, shall set a short-range abatement date for prompt temporary protection to employees pending formulation and implementation of long-range feasible engineering and/or administrative controls. Short-range administrative controls and PPE shall be specified in the citation as the interim protection. (See Chapter V, B.2.b.(7).)

(2) If it has been determined that the employer will use engineering controls to achieve abatement, a specific date shall be set by which the employer can reasonably be expected to implement engineering controls, including enough time for the development of engineering plans and designs for such controls, as well as necessary construction or installation time.

c. *Considerations.* In providing for multistep abatement the following factors shall be taken into consideration:

(1) In general, engineering controls afford the best protection to employees, and the employer shall be required to utilize such controls in all instances to the extent feasible. The noise standards and 29 CFR 1910.1000 require the use of either engineering or administrative controls if any such controls are feasible. Engineering and work practice controls are to be used in preference to respirators and other personal protective equipment. In certain circumstances, administrative controls can be successful in controlling employee exposure to contaminants; e.g., maintenance operations involving toxic substances can sometimes be performed at night in the absence of the usual production staff.

NOTE: Employee rotation is an administrative control that OSHA prohibits as a method of complying with the permissible exposure limits of carcinogens.

(2) Economic feasibility is a major issue to be considered when imposing such controls. Requirements that would threaten the economic viability of an entire industry cannot be considered economically feasible under the OSH Act.

(3) OSHA may decide not to require engineering controls for abatement but to allow the use of PPE to abate the violation, at least until such time as engineering controls become a less significant burden for the company when the following conditions are met:

(a) If significant reconstruction of a single establishment involving a capital expenditure which would seriously jeopardize the financial condition of the company is the only method whereby the employer could achieve effective engineering controls;

(b) If there are no feasible administrative or work practice controls; and

(c) If adequate personal protective equipment or devices are available.

(4) Proper evaluation of the economic feasibility of engineering or administrative controls does not require the Area Director to understand all available economic information before deciding that the issue of potential economic infeasibility is involved. It is sufficient that the employer produce evidence of economic hardship adequate to convince the Area Director that abatement by such controls would involve considerable financial difficulty.

(5) Whenever an employer complains that an unbearable economic burden would result from implementation of engineering or administrative controls, the Area Director shall request evidence from the employer.

(a) Such evidence shall address the reasonableness of the estimated costs of engineering or administrative controls, including installation, maintenance, and lost productivity, whenever applicable, as well as the progress of the employer compared to that of the industry in installing such controls.

(b) The relative costs of engineering or administrative controls versus PPE may also be provided. Such comparisons shall take replacement costs into account.

(6) The Area Director shall discuss the problem with the Regional Administrator, whenever appropriate. The Regional Administrator shall determine whether engineering controls are economically infeasible. In cases with potential national implications, the decision (together with supporting evidence) shall be brought to the attention of the Director of Compliance Programs through the Director of Field Programs.

(7) In those limited situations where there are no feasible engineering or administrative controls, full abatement can be allowed by PPE.

9. Petitions for Modification of Abatement Date (PMA). 29 CFR 1903.14a governs the disposition of PMAs. If the employer requests additional abatement time after the 15-working-day contest period has passed, the following procedures for PMAs are to be observed:

a. *Filing Date.* A PMA must be filed in writing with the Area Director who issued the citation no later than the close of the next working day following the date on which abatement was originally required.

(1) If a PMA is submitted orally, the employer shall be informed that OSHA cannot accept an oral PMA and that a written petition must be mailed by the end of the next working day after the abatement date. If there is not sufficient time to file a written petition, the employer shall be informed on the requirement of E.9.a.(2).

(2) A late petition may be accepted only if accompanied by the employer's statement of exceptional circumstances explaining the delay.

b. *When a PMA is Anticipated.* Whenever a citation for engineering controls or other violation which the Area Director believes can reasonably be expected to give rise to a future PMA, the following procedures shall apply:

(1) A followup date 45 days prior to the final abatement date shall be entered into the information retrieval system used by the Area Office. When that followup date arrives, the file shall be pulled and reviewed by the supervisor and the CSHO involved.

(2) After review the Area Director shall contact the employer to determine abatement progress. Information on the status of abatement shall be obtained and documented in the case file. The potential need for additional time shall be discussed with the employer. If the employer indicates that more time will be necessary to complete correction of the citations, this need shall be documented; and the procedures for seeking a PMA shall be explained.

c. *Requirements for a PMA.* If a letter is received from an employer requesting a modification of an abatement date, the Area Director shall ensure that all of the following five requirements listed in 29 CFR 1903.14a are set forth in sufficient detail in the employer's petition:

(1) All steps taken by the employer and the dates of such action in an effort to achieve compliance during the prescribed abatement period.

(2) The specific additional abatement time estimated to achieve compliance.

(3) The reasons such additional time is necessary, including the unavailability of professional or technical personnel or of materials and equipment, or because necessary construction or alteration of facilities cannot be completed by the original abatement date.

(4) Interim steps being taken to safeguard the employees against the cited hazard during the abatement period.

(5) Written certification, including a copy of the posted and served petition and the date upon which such posting and service was made, that a copy of the petition addressing, as appropriate, each of the requirements set forth in (1) through (4) of this subsection:

(a) Has been posted in a conspicuous place near the location where the violation occurred or where all affected employees will have notice thereof. The petition shall remain posted for 10 working days.

(b) Has been served on the authorized representative of affected employees where affected employees are represented by an authorized representative.

d. *Failure to Meet All Requirements.* If the employer's letter does not meet *all* the requirements of E.9.c., a letter spelling out these requirements and identifying the missing elements shall be sent to the employer within 10 working days, specifying a reasonable amount of time for the employer to return the completed PMA.

(1) If no response is received or if the information returned is still insufficient, a second attempt (by telephone or in writing) shall be made. The employer shall be informed of the consequences of a failure to respond adequately; namely, that the PMA will not be granted and the employer may, consequently, be found in failure to abate.

(2) If the employer responds satisfactorily by telephone and the Area Director determines that the requirements for the PMA have been met, appropriate documentation shall be placed in the case file.

e. *Abatement Efforts.* The Area Director shall take the steps necessary to ensure that the employer is making a good faith attempt to bring about abatement as expeditiously as possible.

(1) Where engineering controls have been cited or required for abatement, a monitoring inspection shall be scheduled to evaluate the employer's abatement efforts. Failure to conduct a monitoring inspection shall be fully explained in the case file.

(2) Where no engineering controls have been cited but more time is needed for other reasons not requiring assistance from OSHA, such as delays in receiving equipment, a monitoring visit need not normally be scheduled.

(3) Monitoring inspections shall be scheduled as soon as possible after the initial contact with the employer (See E.9.b.(2).) and shall not be delayed until actual receipt of the PMA.

(4) The CSHO shall decide during the monitoring inspection whether sampling is necessary and, if so, to what extent; i.e., spot sampling, short-term sampling, or full-shift sampling.

(5) The CSHO shall include pertinent findings in the narrative along with recommendations for action. To reach a valid conclusion when recommending action, it is important to have all the relevant factors available in an organized manner. The following factors shall be considered:

(a) Progress reports or other indications of the employer's good faith, demonstrating effective use of technical expertise and/or management skills, accuracy of information reported by the employer, and timeliness of progress reports.

(b) The employer's assessment of the hazards by means of surveys performed by in-house personnel, consultants and/or the employer's insurance agency.

(c) Other documentation collected by area office personnel, including verification of progress reports, success and/or failure of abatement efforts, and assessment of current exposure levels of employees.

(d) Employer and employee interviews.

(e) Specific reasons for requesting additional time including specific plans for controlling exposure and specifWW]c calendar dates.

(f) Personal protective equipment.

(g) Medical Programs.

(h) Emergency action plans.

NOTE: Not all these factors will be pertinent in every PMA review. Neither are all the factors listed which must be considered in every case.

f. *Delayed Decisions.* Although OSHA policy is to handle PMAs as expeditiously as possible, there are cases where the Area Director's decision on the PMA is delayed because of deficiencies in the PMA itself, a decision to conduct a monitoring inspection and/or the need for Regional Office or National Office involvement. Requests for additional time (e.g, 45 days) for the Area Director to formulate a position shall be sent to the Review Commission through the Regional Solicitor. A letter conveying this request shall be sent at the same time to the employer and the employee representatives.

g. *Area Office Position on the PMA.* After 15 working days following certification of the PMA posting, the Area Director shall determine the Area Office position, agreeing with or objecting to the request. This shall be done within 10 working days following the 15 days (if additional time has not been requested from the Review Commission). The following action shall be taken:

(1) If the PMA requests an abatement date which is one year or less from the issuance date of the citation, the Area Director has the authority to approve or object to the petition.

(2) Any PMA requesting an abatement date which is more than one year from the issuance date of the citation requires the approval of the Regional Administrator as well as the Area Director.

(3) If the PMA is approved, the Area Director shall notify the employer and the employee representatives by letter.

(4) If, after a second contact with the employer, the information required under E.9.c. continues to be substantially insufficient, the Area Director shall contact the Regional Administrator who, after consultation with the Regional Solicitor, shall object to the PMA. The relevant documentation shall be filed with the Review Commission in accordance with 29 CFR 1903.14a(d).

(5) If supporting evidence justifies it (e.g., employer has taken no meaningful abatement action at all or has otherwise exhibited bad faith), the Area Director or the Regional Administrator, as appropriate and after consultation

with the Regional Solicitor, shall object to the PMA. In such a case, all relevant documentation shall be sent to the Review Commission in accordance with 29 CFR 1903.14a(d). Both the employer and the employee representatives shall be notified of this action by letter, with return receipt requested.

(a) The letters of notification of the objection shall be mailed on the same date that the agency objection to the PMA is sent to the Review Commission.

(b) When appropriate, after consultation with the Regional Solicitor, a failure to abate notification may be issued in conjunction with the objection to the PMA.

NOTE: If no objection is filed within the time frame in E.9.g, the PMA is automatically granted even if not explicitly approved.

h. *Employee Objections.* Affected employees or their representatives may file an objection in writing to an employer's PMA with the Area Director within 10 working days of the date of posting of the PMA by the employer or its service upon an authorized employee representative.

(1) Failure to file such a written objection within the 10-working-day period constitutes a waiver of any further right to object to the PMA.

(2) If an employee or an employee representative objects to the extension of the abatement date, all relevant documentation shall be sent to the Review Commission.

(a) Confirmation of this action shall be mailed (return receipt requested) to the objecting party as soon as it is accomplished.

(b) Notification of the employee objection shall be mailed (return receipt requested) to the employer on the same day that the case file is forwarded to the Commission.

F. Employer Abatement Assistance.

1. Policy. CSHOs shall offer appropriate abatement assistance during the walkaround as to how workplace hazards might be eliminated. The information shall provide guidance to the employer in developing acceptable abatement methods or in seeking appropriate professional assistance.

2. Type of Assistance. The type of abatement assistance provided will depend on the needs of the employer and the complexity of the hazard. Where standards specify abatement methods, such as guarding of belts and pulleys, the CSHO shall, at a minimum, ensure that the employer is aware of the specifications. For more complex problems, the CSHO shall offer general information on types of controls or procedures commonly used to abate the hazard. Alternative methods shall be provided whenever possible. (See E.6 for more specific requirements on health inspections).

3. Disclaimers. The employer shall be informed that:

a. The employer is not limited to the abatement methods suggested by OSHA;

b. The methods explained are general and may not be effective in all cases; and

c. The employer is responsible for selecting and carrying out an effective abatement method.

4. Procedures. Information provided by OSHA to assist the employer in identifying possible methods of abatement for alleged violations shall be provided to the employer as it becomes available or necessary. The issuance of citations shall not be delayed.

a. *Assistance Provided During An Inspection.* CSHOs shall utilize their knowledge and professional experience in providing the employer with abatement assistance during the inspection.

(1) Before leaving an inspection site and, preferably, during the walkaround when an apparent violation is noted, CSHOs shall determine whether the employer wishes to discuss possible means of abating apparent violations. The discussion may continue at the closing conference.

(2) CSHOs shall briefly document abatement information provided to the employer or the employer's negative response to the offer of assistance on the appropriate OSHA-1B Form.

b. *Assistance Provided After An Inspection.* If a CSHO cannot provided assistance during an inspection or if the employer has abatement questions after the inspection, the Area Director shall ensure that additional information, if available, is obtained and provided as soon as possible to the employer. Any communications with the employer shall be documented in the case file.

5. Services Available to Employers. Employers requesting abatement assistance shall be informed that OSHA is willing to work with them even after citations have been issued. In addition, the employer shall be made aware of the availability, free of charge, of State onsite consultation services funded by OSHA.

G. Informal Conferences.

1. General. Pursuant to 29 CFR 1903.19, the employer, any affected employee or the employee representative may request an informal conference.

NOTE: An informal conference may not be scheduled after receipt of a written Notice of Intent to Contest without prior approval of the Regional Solicitor. If the intent to contest is not clear, the Area Director shall contact the employer for clarification.

2. Procedures. Whenever an informal conference is requested by the employer, an affected employee or the employee representative, both parties shall be afforded the opportunity to participate fully. If the requesting party objects to the attendance of the other party, separate informal conferences shall be held. During the conduct of a joint informal conference, separate or private discussions shall be permitted if either party so requests.

a. *Notification of Participants.* After an informal conference has been scheduled, the Area Director shall notify the affected parties of the date, time and place, by telephone and, if considered useful, in writing.

(1) The employer shall be requested to complete and post the form found at the end of the informal conference letter until after the informal conference has been held.

(2) Documentation of the Area Director's actions notifying the parties of the informal conference shall be placed in the case file.

b. *Telephone Conferences.* The agency believes that better settlements can be arrived at by means of personal conferences between the Area Director and the employer; consequently, informal conferences shall normally not be held by telephone.

(1) When circumstances exist (e.g., the employer or the employee representatives would be required to travel long distances, there is insufficient time remaining for travel or only the penalty amount is likely to be at issue) which the Area Director believes will justify a telephone conference, such circumstances shall be documented in the case file.

(2) If a telephone conference is held all of the procedures regarding notification of affected parties, participation of OSHA officials, conduct of the conference, documentation of discussions, and decision-making, outlined in G.2.a, c, d, and e, shall be followed as far as practicable.

(3) The reasons justifying any departures from those procedures shall be explained in the case file.

c. *Participation by OSHA Officials.* The inspecting CSHOs and their supervisors shall be notified of an upcoming informal conference and, if practicable, given the opportunity to participate in the informal conference (unless, in the case of the CSHO, the Area Director anticipates that only a penalty adjustment will result). They shall be advised of any changes made by the Area Di-

rector in the event that they were unable to participate.

(1) In order to ensure that discussions of any possible settlement or modifications to the citation(s) and/or penalty may be completely and accurately recalled, at least one other OSHA employee (in addition to the Area Director) shall be present at the informal conference. This employee may be the CSHO, supervisor, a clerical staff member, or other assigned person.

(2) The Area Director shall ensure that notes are made indicating the basis for any decisions taken at or as a result of the informal conference. It is appropriate to tape record the informal conference and to use the tape recording in lieu of written notes, but the tape recording is not a substitute for the second OSHA conference participant.

d. *Conduct of the Informal Conference.* The Area Director shall conduct the informal conference in accordance with the following guidelines:

(1) *Opening Remarks.* The opening remarks shall include discussions of the following:

(a) Purpose of the informal conference.

(b) Rights of participants.

(c) Contest rights and time restraints.

(d) Limitations, if any.

(e) Settlement of cases.

(f) Other relevant information.

(2) *Conference.* The conference shall include discussion of any relevant matters including citations, safety and health programs, conduct of the inspection, means of correction, and penalties, in accordance with the following:

(a) All parties shall be encouraged to participate fully so their views can be properly considered.

(b) Positions on all issues discussed shall be fully considered before making a determination regarding possible settlement of the case in accordance with current OSHA procedures.

(c) OSHA representatives shall make every effort to assist both the employer and the affected employees and/or their representatives to improve safety and health in the workplace.

(3) *Closing.* At the conclusion of the discussion the main issues and potential courses of action shall be summarized. A written summary of the informal conference shall be provided to all participants as soon as practicable following its conclusion. A copy of the summary, together with any other relevant notes or tapes of the discussion made by the Area Director, shall be placed in the case file.

e. *Decisions.* At the termination of the informal conference, the Area Director shall make a decision as to what action is appropriate in the light of facts brought up during the conference.

(1) When preparing to make a decision to settle a case, the Area Director shall make a reasonable effort to obtain the views of the employee representative, if there is one and if he/she was not in attendance at the conference. (There is no need to contact the employee representative if only a penalty adjustment is involved.)

(2) Changes to citations, penalties or abatement dates normally shall be made by means of an informal settlement agreement in accordance with current OSHA procedures; the reasons for such changes shall be documented in the case file.

(3) Employers shall be informed that they are required by 29 CFR 1903.19 to post copies of all amendments to the citation resulting from informal conferences. Employee representatives must also be provided with copies of such documents. This regulation covers amended citations, citation withdrawals and settlement agreements.

(4) Affected parties shall be notified of the results and/or decisions of the informal conference in accordance with current OSHA procedures.

(5) The CSHOs who conducted the inspection and their supervisors shall be informed of the results and/or decisions of informal settlement agreements and/or amended citations.

(6) For more detail on settlement agreements, see Chapter V, H.

f. *Failure to Abate.* If the informal conference involves an alleged failure to abate, the Area Director may set a new abatement date in the informal settlement agreement, documenting for the case file the time that has passed since the original citation, the steps that the employer has taken to inform the exposed employees of their risk and to protect them from the hazard, and the measures that will have to be taken to correct the condition.

(1) Once a new abatement date has been set, a modification of abatement date following current IMIS procedures shall be entered into the data system.

(2) A letter shall be sent to the employer reminding him/her in the strongest possible terms that abatement is legally required if no written notice of contest is submitted within the contest period for the Notification of Failure to Abate Alleged Violation.

(3) The employer shall also be reminded that if there is any problem in meeting the new abatement date after it becomes a final order, a written PMA *must* be filed with the Area Director in accordance with E.9.a.

H. Followup Inspections.

1. Inspection Procedures. The primary purpose of a followup inspection is to determine if the previously cited violations have been corrected. There shall be no additional inspection activity unless, in the judgment of the CSHO, there have been significant changes in the workplace which warrant further inspection activity. In such a case, the supervisor shall be consulted.

2. Failure to Abate. A failure to abate exists when the employer has not corrected a violation for which a citation has been issued or has not complied with interim measures involved in a multistep abatement within the time given.

a. *Initial Followup.* The initial followup is the first followup inspection after issuance of the citation.

(1) If a violation is found not to have been abated, the CSHO shall inform the employer that the employer is subject to a Notification of Failure to Abate Alleged Violation and proposed additional daily penalties while such failure or violation continues.

(2) Failure to comply with enforceable interim abatement dates involving multistep abatement shall be subject to a Notification of Failure to Abate Alleged Violation.

(3) Where the employer has implemented some controls, but other technology was available which would have brought the levels of airborne concentrations or noise to within the regulatory requirements, a Notification of Failure to Abate Alleged Violation normally shall be issued. If the employer has exhibited good faith, a late PMA for extenuating circumstances may be considered in accordance with E.9.a.(2).

(4) Where an apparent failure to abate by means of engineering controls is found to be due to technical infeasibility, no failure to abate notice shall be issued; however, if proper administrative controls, work practices or personal protective equipment are not utilized, a Notification of Failure to Abate Alleged Violation shall be issued.

(5) There may be times during the initial followup when, because of an employer's flagrant disregard of a citation or an item on a citation, or other factors, it will be apparent that additional administrative enforcement actions will be futile. In such cases, action shall be initiated under Section 11(b) of the Act in the U.S. Court of Appeals. The Area Director shall notify the Regional Administrator, in writing, of all the particular circumstances of the case for referral to the Regional Solicitor.

b. *Second Followup.* Any subsequent followup after the initial followup dealing with the same violations is a second followup.

(1) After the Notification of Failure to Abate Alleged Violation has been issued, the Area Director shall allow a reasonable time for abatement of the violation before conducting a second followup. If the employer contests the proposed additional daily penalties, a followup inspection shall still be scheduled to ensure correction of the original violation.

(2) If a second followup inspection reveals the employer still has not corrected the original violations, a second Notification of Failure to Abate Alleged Violation with additional daily penalties shall be issued if the Area Director after consultation with the Regional Administrator and Regional Solicitor, believes it to be appropriate. If a Notification of Failure to Abate Alleged Violation and additional daily penalties are not to be proposed, the Area Director shall immediately contact the Regional Administrator, in writing, detailing the circumstances so the matter can be referred to the Regional Solicitor for action, as appropriate, in the U.S. Court of Appeals in accordance with Section 11(b) of the Act.

3. Reports. The applicable identification and description sections of the OSHA-1B/1B-IH Form shall be used for documenting correction of willful, repeated and serious violations and failure to correct items during followup inspections. If violation items were appropriately grouped in the OSHA-1B/1B-IH in the original case file, they may be grouped on the followup OSHA-1B; if not, individual OSHA-1B/1B-IH Forms shall be used for each item. The correction of other-than-serious violations may be documented in the narrative portion of the case file.

a. *Proper Documentation.* The correction circumstances observed by the CSHO shall be specifically described in the OSHA-1B/1B-IH, including any applicable dimensions, materials, specifications, personal protective equipment, engineering controls, measurements or readings, or other conditions. Brief terms such as "corrected" or "in compliance" will not be accepted as proper documentation for violations having been corrected. When appropriate this written description shall be supplemented by a photograph to illustrate correction circumstances. Only the item description and identification blocks need be completed on the followup OSHA 1B/1B-IH with an occasional inclusion of an applicable employer statement concerning correction under the employer knowledge section, if appropriate.

b. *Sampling.* The CSHO conducting a followup inspection to determine compliance with violations of air contaminants and noise standards shall decide whether sampling is necessary, and if so, what kind; i.e., spot sampling, short-term sampling or full-shift sampling. If there is reasonable probability of an issuance of a Notification of Failure to Abate Alleged Violation, full-shift sampling is required.

c. *Narrative.* The CSHO shall include in the narrative the findings pursuant to the inspection, along with recommendations for action. In order to reach a valid conclusion when recommending action, it is important to have all the pertinent factors available in an organized manner.

d. *Failure To Abate.* In the event that any item has not been abated, complete documentation shall be included on an OSHA-1B.

4. Followup Files. The followup inspection reports shall be included with the original (parent) case file.

I. Conduct of Monitoring Inspection (PMAs and Long-Term Abatement).

1. General. An inspection shall be classified as a monitoring inspection when a safety/health inspection is conducted for one or more of the following purposes:

a. To determine the progress an employer is making toward final correction.

b. To ensure that the target dates of a multistep abatement plan are being met.

c. To ensure that an employer's petition for the modification of abatement dates is made in true and good faith and that the employer has attempted to implement necessary controls as expeditiously as possible.

d. To ensure that the employees are being properly protected until final controls are implemented.

e. To ensure that the terms of a permanent variance are being carried out.

f. To provide abatement assistance for items under citation.

2. Procedures. Monitoring inspections shall be conducted in the same manner as followup inspections as described in H.

APPENDIX

NARRATIVE, OSHA-1A, FORM.

A. General. The OSHA-1A form shall be used to record information relative to organized employee groups, authorized representatives of employees, management officials contacted, management representatives accompanying CSHOs on the walkaround inspection and other persons contacted during the course of an inspection.

1. The OSHA-1A Form shall also be used to record other pertinent data about the inspection whenever indicated by Chapter III or by the professional judgment of the CSHO or the supervisor.

2. All data recorded on the OSHA-1A Form shall be as complete and accurate as circumstances require.

B. Comments. If additional space is needed to complete any item, use the space in item 20, Additional Comments, on the back of the form. When using the back, always precede the entry with the appropriate data item number which is being continued.

ITEM		INFORMATION NEEDED
1.	Establishment Name.	Enter the establishment name from the Inspection Report, OSHA-1 Form.
2.	Inspection Number.	Enter the inspection number from the OSHA-1.
3.	Type of Legal Entity.	Indicate whether the employer is a corporation, partnership, sole proprietorship, etc. (Do not use the word, "owner.") If the employer named is a subsidiary of another firm, indicate that.
4.	Type of Business or Plant.	Give the employer's principal business at the workplace being inspected. For example, the employer's business may be the manufacture of automobiles and trucks, but the workplace being inspected may be the wheel manufacturing plant. In such a situation "wheel manufacturing" is the correct entry for this item.
5.	Additional Citation Mailing Addresses.	Record any additional destinations for copies of the Citation requested by the employer representative. Include in these spaces only addresses not listed on the OSHA-1.
6.	Names and Addresses of all Organized Employee Groups.	List the organizational names, addresses and telephone numbers of all authorized employee groups. In the case of a union, enter the local number. If there are no employee group representatives, enter "none." In the column marked "CM," check the "Y" block if a copy of the Citation is to be mailed to the employee group named. The Citation will be mailed to the representative belonging to that group named in item 7 unless otherwise indicated.

ITEM	**INFORMATION NEEDED**

7. Authorized Representatives of Employees.

Show individual names and addresses of authorized representatives of employees, their telephone numbers, organizations and titles. In the column marked "WA," check the "Y" block by each representative's name if that person participates in the walkaround. If an authorized representative takes part in only a portion of the walkaround, check the "Y" box and indicate in which portions of the walkaround that individual participates (e.g., "electrical shop, warehouse") or the percentage of time during which the individual takes part in the walkaround (e.g., "60%").

If there is no organized group to represent employees but affected employees have, nevertheless, designated a person to represent them for the purpose of OSHA inspections, show that person's name and complete the other requested information.

8. Employer Representatives Contacted.

List the names, titles and functions of all employer representatives contacted. Under "Function," enter one or more of the indicated codes to describe the type of activity engaged in by the contacted official.

In the "WA" column, check "Y" alongside of each official's name if the official takes any part in the walkaround.

9. Other Persons Contacted.

If, during the inspection, other persons are interviewed for any reason, give their names and the other information requested on the form.

10. Coverage Information.

Provide substantiation of OSHA coverage of the establishment to be inspected in detail sufficient to the case. Information provided shall be specific; e.g., do not say simply "trades with out-of-State firms." The State of incorporation and the address of the home office may be sufficient to establish an operation affecting interstate commerce. Such substantation of coverage need only be done for the initial inspection of an establishment.

312   *Primer on Occupational Safety and Health*

ITEM   **INFORMATION NEEDED**

The following are examples of statements which serve the purpose of providing coverage information:

a. "This establishment daily ships goods that it manufactures to ABC Corp., Detroit, Michigan, and weekly receive goods from XYZ Suppliers, Inc., Linden, New Jersey."

b. "This establishment performs contract work or supplies parts for firms which are engaged in the production of goods for interstate commerce; e.g., company supplies plastic junction boxes to General Electric for national distribution."

c. "This firm currently has worksites located in Savannah, Georgia, Columbia, South Carolina, and Washington, D.C. The firm purchases reinforcing steel made by HBZ Co., Jacksonville, Florida."

11. Date & Time of Entry.

Enter the date and time of day marking the initial arrival at the establishment.

12. Date & Time Walkaround Began.

Enter the date and time of day that the walkaround inspection began.

13. Date & Time Closing Conference Began.

Enter under (1) the date and time of the beginning of the onsite closing conference held at the termination of the walkaround. Enter under (2) the date and time of the final closing conference held either onsite or by phone.

14. Date & Time of Exit.

Enter the date and time of day of departure from the establishment.

15. Followup Inspection Recommended.

Check "Yes" or "No" to indicate whether a followup inspection appears necessary according to the guidelines given in Chapters II and III. Briefly state the reason for the recommendation. If "yes," also indicate the items which require a followup. The reason for recommending a followup must be placed on the OSHA-1B relating to that item.

ITEM	INFORMATION NEEDED

16. CSHO Signature and Date.

Upon completion of the OSHA-1A Form, sign and date it. If more than one OSHA-1A Form is completed, sign each one of them.

17. Accompanied By.

If a third party (not an employee) participates in the inspection (e.g., a CSHO trainee, OSHA National or Regional Office representative, an outside consultant, a Local or National Union representative), enter that party's name and affiliation.

18. Evaluation of Safety and Health Program.

Circle the appropriate evaluation code (0 = nonexistent; 1 = Inadequate; 2 = Average; 3 = Above Average; Y = Yes; N = No). Mark "NA" for all items not applicable to the establishment. Explain code selections in item 20 whenever a more detailed explanation is necessary.

Careful completion of this item will be particularly important where the CSHO believes or is told that employee failure to follow established safety and health policies and procedures led to the observed violations of the Act. When rating the effectiveness of the employer's program, select an evaluation code on the basis of how a safety or health professional would classify it in light of the program characteristics, not on the basis of comparison with the programs of other similar employers. The instructions relating to each program element are as follows:

a. *Comprehensiveness.* Evaluate the degree to which the employer's safety and health program addresses the full range of hazards normally encountered in the employer's operations. This category shall reflect the overall evaluation of the employer's safety and health program. It shall take into account, therefore, the evaluations given to the following categories. Indicate whether the program is written.

ITEM	INFORMATION NEEDED

b. *Communication.* Evaluate the employees' awareness of and access to the safety and health program, taking into account the principal means by which the program is communicated to them (e.g. oral instructions, booklets, memorandums, posters, etc.) and their effectiveness.

c. *Enforcement.* Evaluate the degree to which safety and health rules are actually enforced, considering the principal methods used (e.g., verbal warnings, written reprimands, disciplinary action, discharge, etc.) and their effectiveness.

d. *Safety/Health Training Program.* Evaluate separately any safety and health training programs the employer has. Factors to be considered include the need for special training in view of the hazards likely to be encountered or of specific requirements for such training and the need for ongoing or periodic training or retraining of employees.

e. *Investigations.* Evaluate the employer's efforts to make accident/injury/illness investigations and indicate whether adequate preventive actions are taken as a result.

f. *Records.* Circle the form-type which indicates the records maintained and retained by the employer. If "Supplementary Health" is circled, specify the forms maintained.

g. *Notice to Employees.* Indicate whether the notice to employees (poster) is posted.

h. *Add'l Comments.* Add any pertinent comments related to the employer's safety and health program that will help in the overall evaluation of the program.

ITEM	INFORMATION NEEDED
19. Closing Conference Checklist.	Indicate if no violations were found and if all of the items listed were discussed or performed during the closing conference. If not, indicate in item 20 why an omitted item was not applicable or why a complete discussion of an item was not necessary.

Subitem 3 shall be checked when all relevant subjects in the "Employer Rights and Responsibilities" booklet were discussed, including employee rights. Subitem 6 includes a discussion of all services available through the Full Service Area Office or through other voluntary compliance programs offered by the Agency.

Indicate in subitem 8 whether a closing conference was held with employee representatives and whether it was held jointly or separately from that of the employer. |
| 20. Additional Comments. | Include in this section any supportive information from the opening or closing conference substantiating the employer's general attitude, any general admission of violations and any agreement about abatement dates. Note any unusual circumstances encountered during any phase of the inspection. Indicate the scope of the inspection and the reasons justifying it. If advance notice was given, explain why, to whom and the date such notice was given. Use this space for any of the other items on the Form which require additional comment. In general, place in this space any relevant comments related to the inspection or called for by other guidelines in the FOM. |

INDUSTRIAL HYGIENE INSPECTION OUTLINE

This Inspection Outline is to be used during all health inspections as a guide for the collection of information that is required according to the FOM but which is not recorded on other forms included in the case file.

The outline is intended as a guide for completion of the case file. Current information which is included and readily accessible elsewhere in the case file or in other case files need not be rewritten although a reference will usually be appropriate. All currently accurate information that will be necessary or useful for the review process shall be included; the outline is not intended merely to generate additional paperwork. A narrative covering the items described below shall be entered under item 20, Additional Comments, for all health inspections. Additional blank pages can be used if necessary.

A. Nature and Scope of the Inspection.

1. Reason for inspection if not fully indicated on the OSHA-1;

2. Background information including everything of current concern to the present inspection; e.g., open citations, variances, etc.;

3. Information concerning the scope of the inspection; and, if a complete health inspection is not to be conducted, a brief explanation of the reasons why not.

B. Opening Conference. Any unusual circumstances encountered; e.g. advance notice (including to whom given, date and employee or employee representative notied), presentation of credentials (if other than highest ranking employer representative), selection of management and employee representation for walkaround, extent of the initial walkaround, etc.

C. Workplace Observations.

1. Operations observed during the initial walkaround including:

a. Significant process information including information on all potentially hazardous operations observed, including both chemicals used (with their approximate volumes, when significant) and physical agents encountered which may (potentially) affect employee health;

b. Location of potentially exposed employees with an indication as to whether or not sampling is to be conducted and, if not, why not;

c. Proposed action and/or conclusions relating to potential hazards and complaint or referral items (e.g., citations will be issued, sampling will be conducted or is not necessary, a safety referral will be made, no additional ac-

tion, etc.) together with supporting reasons.

2. Plant layout including a sketch made during the initial walkaround if the establishment does not have a layout chart or the equivalent available; the sketch shall include, as a minimum, building numbers or names, pertinent operation (process) areas with type of operation or process (including flow chart) indicated, distribution of major process equipment, including any engineering or administrative controls (when pertinent) and relative dimensions of the work area.

D. Occupational Health Program. An adequate description of the employer's health program shall be included in each case file. Supporting notes shall include CSHO observations of program enforcement as well as relevant comments made by management or employees regarding safeguards, precautions, protective equipment, routine procedures used for protection in plant processes, training efforts, experience of employee illness or symptoms, etc. Specific comments shall be made on each of the following program elements, as appropriate:

1. Monitoring program (who, how, analysis, schedules and results);

2. Medical program (frequency, protocols and records);

3. Education and training programs (extent, emergency procedures);

4. Recordkeeping program (types, duration and accessibility to employees);

5. Compliance program (hazard control);

a. Engineering/administrative controls;

b. PPE program;

c. Regulated area procedures;

d. Emergency procedures;

e. Written compliance plan;

6. Personal hygiene facilities and practices;

7. Labeling and posting policy and procedures.

E. Closing Conference(s) including any pertinent details, such as whether a joint conference was held with employer and employee representatives as well as comments regarding explanations given (and to whom) on available inspection results, discussions of general control guidelines and recommendations made (with date), and other general comments, including comments on good faith and cooperation. Notes regarding additional closing conferences shall also be included here.

U.S. Department of Labor
Occupational Safety and Health Administration

Inspection Number

Reporting ID

NOTICE

of

Alleged Imminent Danger (to Employer(s) and Employees)

An inspection has been conducted of a place of employment in which employees of employer(s) are working, located at _____

and described as follows _____

On the basis of this inspection, it is alleged that an imminent danger to employees exists in that A DANGER EXISTS WHICH COULD REASONABLY BE EXPECTED TO CAUSE DEATH OR SERIOUS PHYSICAL HARM IMMEDIATELY or before the imminence of such danger can be eliminated through the enforcement procedures otherwise provided by the Occupational Safety and Health Act of 1970 (29 U.S.C. 651 et seq.), hereinafter referred to as the Act.

In accordance with the provisions of Section 13(c) of the Act, the employer(s) and all employees affected by these conditions constituting an alleged imminent danger are being informed of the possible danger by the posting of this Notice of Alleged Imminent Danger near the condition(s) described below. The employer(s) and

all affected employees are likewise being informed that it will be recommended to the Secretary of Labor that he seek the judicial relief provided by the Act.

The Act provides that the United States District Court is empowered upon petition of the Secretary of Labor, to order the employer(s) to take such action as is necessary to avoid, correct, or remove this alleged imminent danger, including, where necessary, the removal of employees from the dangerous area.

This notice does not constitute a Citation of alleged violations or Notification of Proposed Penalty. Appropriate Citations or a Notification of Proposed Penalty will be issued to the employer(s).

Description of Alleged Imminent Danger

This Notice of Alleged Imminent Danger must remain posted until removed by a representative of the Occupational Safety and Health Administration.

Signed and dated at _____

this _____ day of _____ . 19 ____

Compliance Safety and Health Officer
Occupational Safety and Health Administration
U.S. Department of Labor

Previous Edition Obsolete

Form OSHA 8
Rev (4-84)

Narrative

U.S. Department of Labor
Occupational Safety and Health Administration

1. Establishment Name

2. Inspection Number

3. Type of Legal Entity

4. Type of Business or Plant

5. Additional Citation Mailing Addresses

(1) Name

Attn:

Street Address

City _____ State _____ Zip _____

(2) Name

Attn:

Street Address

City _____ State _____ Zip _____

6. Names and Addresses of All Organized Employee Groups:	C M	7. Authorized Representatives of Employees:		W A
Name	□ Y	Name	Tele. No.	□ Y
Local No.	Tele. No.	Organization	Title	
Address		Home Address		
	Zip Code		Zip Code	
Name	□ Y	Name	Tele. No.	□ Y
Local No.	Tele. No.	Organization	Title	
Address		Home Address		
	Zip Code		Zip Code	

8. Employer Represent- I – Credentials Presented C – Closing Conf.
atives Contacted: O – Opening Conf. M – Other Mgmt. Official

Name	Title	Function	W A	9. Other Persons Contacted:
			□ Y	Name, Occupation & Affiliation
			□ Y	Home Address Tele. No.
			□ Y	Zip Code
			□ Y	Name, Occupation & Affiliation
10. Coverage Information				Home Address Tele. No.
				Zip Code

11. Date & Time of Entry	12. Date & Time Walkaround Began	13. Date & Time Closing Conference Began (1) (2)	14. Date & Time of Exit

15. Follow-up Inspection Recommended:
Yes □ No □ Reason

16. CSHO Signature & Date	17. Accompanied by

Previous Editions Obsolete

OSHA-1A (10-84)

NOTICE OF ALLEGED IMMINENT DANGER, OSHA-8 FORM.

A. General. Before a CSHO issues a Notice of Alleged Imminent Danger, OSHA-8 Form, the Area Director shall be informed of all circumstances regarding the imminent danger situation and shall give approval in accordance with the procedures in Chapter VII, C.4.

1. This form is the means by which the CSHO officially informs the employers and the affected employees that an imminent danger exists.

a. The form shall be signed by the CSHO and posted at or near the area in which the exposed employees are working.

b. The file copy of the OSHA-8 Form will be attached to the OSHA-1 Form and kept in the case file.

2. The CSHO shall personally post the OSHA-8 Form at or near the area in which the exposed employees are working. If the employer refuses to allow the CSHO to post the notice, then the CSHO shall immediately contact the Area Director for instructions.

B. Instructions. When authorized by the Area Director to post the OSHA-8 Form, the CSHO shall first complete the form in accordance with the instructions which follow.

1. The area or regional stamp shall have been already imprinted on the form in the lower left-hand corner prior to issuance to the CSHO.

2. The official name and address of the establishment being inspected shall be typed or clearly handwritten in the upper left-hand corner of the form. The inspection number and reporting ID of the employer most directly affected by the OSHA-8 posting shall be entered into the blocks at the upper right-hand corner.

3. On the line provided at the top of the form show the address and the name or designation of the workplace or portion of the workplace inspected.

4. The hazards to which employees are exposed shall be described briefly under the "Description of Alleged Imminent Danger" heading of the form. This shall be done in nontechnical language so that all employees who may be exposed can understand the danger.

5. The lines provided for signing and dating the form shall include the location where the OSHA-8 Form was posted and the time and date of posting. The CSHO shall sign where indicated.

6. Only one OSHA-8 Form shall be posted at or near each imminent danger area in which the exposed employees are working. In cases where there are more than one employer, a file copy of the form shall be attached to each employer's OSHA-1 Form as part of the case file.

7. If, during an inspection, more than one Notice of Alleged Imminent Danger, OSHA-8 Form, are issued to the employer, number the notices consecutively in the upper right-hand corner and show the number of pages. This will necessitate writing in the word "Number" and after that the number of the notices. For example, three OSHA-8 Forms are issued during one inspection. The forms would then show: "Number 1, page 1 of 3; Number 2, page 2 of 3; and Number 3, page 3 of 3."

PHOTO MOUNTING WORK-SHEET, OSHA-89 FORM.

A. General. This form shall be used by the CSHO to mount photographs taken during an inspection.

B. Instructions. On the left side of each form there is space for two photographs to be mounted; in the right column of each form, the required information related to each photograph shall be supplied as follows:

Inspection Number. Enter the inspection number from the OSHA-1 Form in the upper right-hand corner.

ITEM	INFORMATION NEEDED
1. Photo ID Number.	Enter the appropriate roll and frame number (roll/frame) of the photo as recorded in Item 21 on the related OSHA-1B Form.
2. Date/Time.	Enter the date and time that the photo was taken.
3. Citation Number.	From the OSHA-1B Form, enter the number of the citation in which the employer was cited for the violation depicted in the photograph. If no specific violation is pictured, enter N/A.
4. Item Number.	From the OSHA-1B Form, enter the item number of the violation depicted in the photograph.
5. Instance No.	From the OSHA-1B Form, enter the instance of the violation depicted in the photograph.
6. Location: Photo and Photographer).	Describe (or diagram) the position of the photographer in relation to the hazard depicted and locate the hazard in the worksite. Identify the photographer by name, if other than the primary CSHO assigned to the inspection.
7. Description.	Describe in appropriate detail the violation depicted, and the environment of the worker; identify employees photographed (unless already identified on the related OSHA-1B) and any other relevant factors. If, during the analysis of the photo, the CSHO discovers violations not noted during the inspection, these shall be noted; and the employer informed of the problem so that it may be corrected. This shall be done even though that violation is not included in any citation issued for that inspection.

ITEM	INFORMATION NEEDED
8. CONFIDENTAL MATERIALS.	Mark "X" in the block provided if a trade secret could be revealed by the photograph. This is necessary for disclosure determinations and must be supported on the related worksheet, OSHA-1B Form. Future printing of this Form will difWW]erentiate "Trade Secret" from security classified materials.

Photo Mounting Worksheet   **U.S. Department of Labor**
Occupational Safety and Health Administration

Inspection Number

| 1. Photo ID Number | 2. Date/Time | |
| 3. Citation Number | 4. Item Number | 5. Instance No |

6. Location (Photo and Photographer)

7. Description

8. ☐ Confidential Materials   Cont

| 1. Photo ID Number | 2. Date/Time | |
| 3. Citation Number | 4. Item Number | 5. Instance No |

6. Location (Photo and Photographer)

7. Description

8. ☐ Confidential Materials   Cont

OSAA Form 89 — Contd.

Continued

NOTE TAKING SHEET, OSHA-94 FORM.

A. General. This Note Taking Sheet is designed as a continuation of item 20 of the OSHA-1A, Additional Comments. The front of the form is lined and the back is imprinted with a grid, which may be used for graphs, drawings, sketches and the like.

B. Instructions. Whenever additional space is needed beyond that provided by the OSHA-1A, the CSHO shall use the OSHA-94 Form. The form shall be completed in accordance with the directions which follow.

1. *Company.* The name of the employer shall be entered in the first block at the top of the form. This name shall correspond with the name recorded in item 8 of the OSHA-1.

2. *Inspection Location.* The site address shall be entered in this block, corresponding with the address given an item 10 of the OSHA-1.

3. *Inspection Number.* The inspection number from the OSHA-1 shall be entered in this block.

4. *Pagination.* If, during an inspection, more than one Note Taking Sheet, OSHA-94 Form, is used, number the notices consecutively in the upper right-hand corner and show the number of pages. This will necessitate writing in the number of the pages. For example, three OSHA-94 Forms are used during one inspection. The forms would then show: "Page 1 of 3; Page 2 of 3; and Page 3 of 3."

| Note Taking Sheet (| | U.S. Department f Labor
Occupational Saf Health Administration | ◆ |
| Company | Inspection Location | | Inspection Number |

OSHA 94 Form — Contd.

INSPECTION CASE FILE ACTIVITY DIARY
(Suggested Format)

A. General. The Inspection Case File Activity Diary is designed to provide a ready record and summary of all actions relating to a case.

1. As directed in Chapter I, C.3.1., it shall include a chronological record of significant actions taken affecting the case, beginning with the opening conference and ending with the closing of the case when all outstanding penalties have been paid and abatement requirements have been met.

2. Maintenance of the diary is the responsibility of the Area Director and Supervisor. All significant contacts with the employer and other persons or entities involved in the case shall be noted.

3. The format shown here is a model for a form to be proposed at later date; pending the adoption of an official form, the actual diary shall be reproduced by the Area Office. The diary may be modified to meet local needs, but it must include at least the information specified in the model.

B. Instructions. The Inspection Case File Activity Diary shall be displayed prominently in the case file for audit purposes, and shall contain at least the types of information specified below at B.1.-7. If using the model form, complete it in accordance with the instructions that follow.

1. *Company.* The name of the employer shall be entered in the first block at the top of the form. This name shall correspond with the name recorded in item 8 of the OSHA-1.

2. *Inspection Location.* The site address shall be entered in this block, corresponding with the address given in item 10 of the OSHA-1.

3. *Inspection Number.* The inspection number from the OSHA-1 shall be entered in this block.

4. *Date.* Enter the date of each significant action being recorded.

5. *Action.* Briefly describe the action taken.

6. *Initials.* Enter the initials of the person recording the action.

7. *Pagination.* The Inspection Case File Activity Diary may comprise as many pages as needed. If more than one sheet is used, number the pages consecutively in the upper right-hand corner and show the number of pages.

U.S. Department of Labor
Occupational Safety and Health Administration

INSPECTION CASE FILE ACTIVITY DIARY

Pg. ___ of ___

Company:	Inspection Location:	Inspection Number:	
DATE:	ACTION:		INITIALS

SUGGESTED FORMAT

Appendix G

OSHA/EPA Memorandum of Understanding

OSHA MEMORANDUM OF UNDERSTANDING (EXAMPLE)

Editor's Note: This document is an example of an OSHA *memorandum of understanding*, in which OSHA and another federal agency clarify their respective areas of responsibility and outline how they plan to coordinate enforcement activities under their respective statutes. This memorandum represents an agreement between OSHA and the Environmental Protection Agency.

MEMORANDUM OF UNDERSTANDING BETWEEN THE OCCUPATIONAL SAFETY AND HEALTH ADMINISTRATION AND THE ENVIRONMENTAL PROTECTION AGENCY ON MINIMIZING WORKPLACE AND ENVIRONMENTAL HAZARDS
(November 23, 1990)

I. Purpose

The purpose of this interagency Memorandum of Understanding (MOU) is to establish and improve the working relationship between the Office of Enforcement of the Environmental Protection Agency (EPA) and the Occupational Safety and Health Administration (OSHA) of the Department of Labor. The goals of the agencies are to improve the combined efforts of the agencies to achieve protection of workers, the public, and the environment at facilities subject to EPA and OSHA jurisdiction; to delineate the general areas of responsibility of each agency; to provide guidelines for coordination of interface activities between the two agencies with the overall goal of identifying and minimizing environmental or workplace hazards.

This MOU establishes a process and framework for notification, consultation and coordination between EPA and OSHA to aid both agencies in identifying environmental and workplace health and safety problems and to more effectively implement enforcement of our national workplace and environmental statutes.

This MOU is intended to improve the information exchange relating to job-site safety and health, protection of the public health and environment thereby reducing the potential for workplace related injury, death, and environmental contamination. This MOU implements OSHA's authority under the Occupational Safety and Health Act of 1970 (OSH Act) and EPA's general and statute-specific authorities to enter into agreements with other federal agencies to further the legislative objectives of Congress and the President.

II. Background & Responsibilities

EPA and OSHA have the statutory responsibility to ensure the safety and health of the public and America's workforce through the timely and effective implementation of a number of federal laws and implementing regulations. In some areas, the responsibilities of the agencies are separate and distinct. In others, they are complementary. EPA and OSHA wish to work together to maximize the efforts of both agencies to ensure the efficient and effective protection of workers, the public, and the environment.

A. *EPA Responsibilities*

EPA responsibilities include the protection of public health and the environment by assuring compliance with federal environmental statutes and regulations. Agency functions are performed through standards setting and rulemaking; technical reviews; audits and studies; conduct of public hearings; issuance of permits and licenses; compliance inspections; investigations and

Published by THE BUREAU OF NATIONAL AFFAIRS, INC., Washington, D.C. 20037

enforcement; and evaluation of operating experience and research.

B. *OSHA Responsibilities*

OSHA is responsible for enforcing the OSH Act, 29 U.S.C. 651 *et. seq.* The goal of the OSH Act is to assure so far as possible every working man and woman in the nation safe and healthful working conditions. To achieve that purpose, the Act provides broad authority for a variety of activities and programs designed to reduce the number of occupational safety and health hazards at places of employment. Among these is the authority to promulgate mandatory safety and health standards for private sector workplaces, and to conduct inspections of such workplaces to determine compliance with the Act and with OSHA standards. When violations are found, OSHA is authorized to issue citations to employers, propose penalties, and require abatement of hazards. In cases involving imminent dangers, OSHA is authorized to seek injunctive relief in U.S. District Court. In states which have elected to administer State occupational safety and health programs, or "State plans," the Act requires OSHA to conduct a continuing evaluation of State operations and, in certain circumstances, to provide a program of concurrent federal OSHA enforcement.

C. *Applicable Statutes*

Under the OSH Act, 29 U.S.C. 651, every employer has a general duty, under section 5(a)(1), to furnish employment and a place of employment which is free from recognized hazards that are causing, or likely to cause, serious physical harm. Every employer is also required, under section 5(a)(2), to comply with occupational safety and health standards promulgated by OSHA. In addition, employers must comply with regulations prescribed by OSHA under section 8 of the Act, which pertains to the conduct of workplace inspections among other things, and must furnish such records and other information as may be requested under section 24 of the Act.

Principal EPA laws include but are not limited to:

The Asbestos Hazard Emergency Response Act;

15 U.S.C. 2641; governing the removal of asbestos.

The Clean Air Act;

42 U.S.C. Sections 7401 to 7642; governing the release of air pollutants.

The Clean Water Act;

33 U.S.C. 1251 to 1387; governing the pre-treatment and release of pollutants to water.

The Comprehensive Environmental Response, Compensation and Liability Act;

42 U.S.C. Sections 9601 to 9675; governing the release of hazardous substances and the abatement of toxic and hazardous waste sites.

The Emergency Planning & Community-Right-To-know Act;

42 U.S.C. Sections 11001 to 11050; governing the storage, use and disposal of toxic and hazardous chemicals, including the reporting of accidental releases.

The Resource Conservation and Recovery Act;

42 U.S.C. Sections 6901 to 6992k; governing the storage and disposal of hazardous wastes.

The Safe Drinking Water Act;

42 U.S.C. Sections 300f to 300j-26; governing the treatment and distribution of potable water.

The Federal Insecticide, Fungicide & Rodenticide Act;

7 U.S.C. Sections 136 to 136y; governing the manufacture and use of toxic and hazardous chemicals used for pest control.

The Toxic Substances Control Act;

15 U.S.C. Sections 2601 to 2671; governing the manufacture, use, distribution in commerce and disposal of commercial chemicals.

The Underground Injection Control Act; governing the disposal of toxic and hazardous waste products.

The Organotin Paint Act; governing the use and disposal of marine paints having toxic constituents.

III. General Operating Procedures For Interagency Activity

In recognition of the agencies' statutory authorities and responsibilities enumerated above, the following procedures will be followed:

A. *Coordination*

1. There will be the fullest possible cooperation and coordination between EPA and OSHA, at all organizational levels, in developing and carrying out training, data and information exchange, technical and professional assistance, referrals of alleged violations, and related matters concerning compliance and law enforcement activity to ensure that health and well-being of the Nation's workforce, the general public, and the environment.

2. By January 1, 1991, and by the beginning of each succeeding fiscal year, EPA and OSHA will develop an annual workplan to identify and define the priorities to be addressed during the year. This workplan will include an identification of specific types of facilities to be jointly addressed during the year.

3. EPA and OSHA will exchange names and phone numbers of appropriate agency headquarters, regional and field personnel, including personnel in OSHA area offices, and in state program offices. All information will be kept up to date by both agencies. Each EPA and OSHA Regional Office will designate a point of contact for carrying out interface activities. Each agency agrees to prepare and distribute to all field personnel a suitable directive outlining a policy concerning the effective implementation of this MOU, and to identify appropriate points of contact. In order to aid in the enforcement and issue-referral process, the agencies will update this information as the need arises and will ensure that managers and field personnel are provided with a copy of this MOU and the relevant directive.

4. Resolution of interagency policy issues concerning this MOU and specific areas of implementation will be coordinated between EPS'a Office of Enforcement and OSHA's Directorate of Policy. Resolution of issues concerning inspection and enforcement activity involving both EPA and OSHA jurisdiction also will be coordinated by EPA's Office of Enforcement and OSHA's Directorate of Policy.

B. *Inspections*

1. EPA and OSHA may conduct joint inspections as necessary to carry out the legislative purposes of the respective statutory authorities. Such inspections may be in accordance with an annual workplan which is developed by the two agencies and identifies areas for joint initiatives. Such inspections may also be scheduled on an *ad hoc* basis such as in investigations following accidents or fatalities or injuries to workers resulting from reported activities or situations subject to either EPA OR OSHA jurisdiction.

2. EPA and OSHA inspectors, in the course of conducting separate inspections, may discover situations involving potential violations of the other agency's laws or regulations. In those instances, referrals to the appropriate office will be undertaken as described below.

C. *Referrals*

1. For law enforcement purposes, OSHA and EPA shall develop a regular system to track and manage referrals of potential violations, allegations of violations, or situations requiring inspection, evaluation or followup by either Agency, as appropriate.

2. Although EPA does not conduct inspections for occupational safety, in the course of an EPA inspection, EPA personnel may identify safety concerns within the area of OSHA responsibility or may receive complaints about the safety or health of employees related to their working conditions. In such instances, EPA will bring the matter to the attention of OSHA designated con-

tacts in the Regional Office. EPA inspectors are not to perform the role of OSHA inspectors; however, they will refer worker health and safety issues to OSHA pursuant to the procedures set forth in this MOU and implementing agency directives. In the case of worker complaints, EPA will disclose the name of individuals to OSHA but will not further disclose the name and the identity of the employee. When such instances occur within OSHA State-plan States' jurisdiction, the OSHA Regional Ofce will refer the matter to the State for appropriate action.

3. OSHA will inform the EPA Regional Administrator or appropriate EPA office of matters which appear to be subject to EPA jurisdiction when these come to their attention during Federal or State safety and health inspections or through worker complaints. Although not exhaustive, the following are examples of matters that would be reported to the EPA:

a. Worker allegations of significant adverse reactions to a chemical or chemical substance which poses a potential hazard to public health or the environment.

b. Accidental, unpermitted, or deliberate releases of chemicals or chemical substances beyond the workplace.

c. Unsafe handling, storage, or use practices involving chemicals, chemical substances, or waste materials in apparent violation of EPA-administered laws.

d. Other readily detectible potential violations of EPA-administered laws, such as by-passing treatment systems.

e. Asbestos dispersal or contamination affecting the public or the environment.

4. EPA shall respond to referrals from OSHA, and OSHA shall respond to referrals from EPA, concerning potential violations of the other agency's requirements, when appropriate, by conducting investigations in a timely manner. Referrals shall be evaluated and appropriate action will be taken.

5. OSHA will work to facilitate referrals of potential violations of EPA regulations to EPA and will encourage the relevant State agencies in those States which operate their own occupational safety and health programs (under a plan approved by OSHA under Section 18 of the OSH Act) also to make such referrals. EPA will work to facilitate referrals to OSHA or OSHA State-plan States of potential violations of occupational health and safety standards or regulations discovered by federal or state environmental inspection activities.

6. EPA and OSHA will conduct periodic meetings, as necessary, to report on the progress of actions taken on the other agency's referrals and to evaluate the effectiveness of the referral system and operating procedures. Both agencies agree to establish a system to monitor the progress of actions taken on referrals.

7. OSHA will encourage State-plan States to respond to referrals from EPA and State agencies concerning potential violations of the States' occupational safety and health standards or regulations by conducting investigations in a timely manner. OSHA will further encourage State-plan States to participate in all training and information-sharing activities established under this MOU.

D. *Data Exchange*

EPA and OSHA agree to exchange information relating to complaints, inspections of investigations, violations discovered, imposition of civil monetary penalties, or other legal actions taken to enforce pertinent laws and regulations, and all other information necessary to ensure effective and coordinated law enforcement. This MOU contemplates data exchange through both hard copy and computer data bases, in accordance with procedures to be established in a separate agreement.

E. *Training*

EPA and OSHA will cooperate in developing and conducting periodic training programs for each other's personnel in the respective laws, regulations, and compliance requirements of each agency, as appropriate, to ensure that valid referrals are made when potential violations are found and to support joint enforcement and inspection initiatives. This MOU contemplates exchanges of appropriate training materials and information and development of specialized training activities in accordance with procedures to be established in a separate agreement.

IV. Period of Agreement

This MOU shall continue in effect unless modified in writing by mutual consent of both parties or terminated by either party upon 30 days advance written notice to the other.

This MOU does not preclude either Agency from entering into separate agreements setting forth procedures for other special programs which can be addressed more efficiently and expeditiously by special agreement.

V. Implementation

Nothing in this Agreement is intended to diminish or otherwise affect the authority of either agency to implement its respective statutory function. This Agreement is effective upon signature by both parties.

U.S. Department of Labor
Occupational Safety & Health Administration
Gerard F. Scannell
Assistant Secretary
Elizabeth Dole
Secretary of Labor
NOV. 23 1990
Dated
U.S. EPA
Office of Enforcement
James M. Strock
Assistant Administrator
William K. Reilly,
Administrator
NOV. 23 1990
Dated

Appendix H

U.S. Department of Labor Area Offices for the Occupational Safety and Health Administration

U.S. DEPARTMENT OF LABOR REGIONAL OFFICES FOR THE OCCUPATIONAL SAFETY AND HEALTH ADMINISTRATION

REGION I (CT,* MA, ME, NH, RI, VT*)
133 Portland Street
1st Floor
Boston, MA 02114
Telephone: (617) 565-7164

REGION II (NJ, NY,* PR,* VI*)
201 Varick Street, Room 670
New York, NY 10014
Telephone: (212) 337-2378

REGION III (DC, DE, MD,* PA, VA,* WV)
Gateway Bldg., Suite 2100
3535 Market Street
Philadelphia, PA 19104
Telephone: (215) 596-1201

REGION IV (AL, FL, GA, KY,* MS, NC,* SC,* TN*)
1375 Peachtree Street, N.E.
Suite 587
Atlanta, GA 30367
Telephone: (404) 347-3573

REGION V (IL, IN,* MI,* MN,* OH, WI)
230 South Dearborn Street
Room 3244
Chicago, IL 60604
Telephone: (312) 353-2220

REGION VI (AR, LA, NM,* OK, TX)
525 Griffin Street, Room 602
Dallas, TX 75202
Telephone: (214) 767-4731

REGION VII (IA,* KS, MO, NE)
911 Walnut Street, Room 406
Kansas City, MO 64106
Telephone: (816) 426-5861

REGION VIII (CO, MT, ND, SD, UT,* WY*)
Federal Bldg., Room 1576
1961 Stout Street
Denver, CO 80294
Telephone: (303) 844-3061

REGION IX (AMERICAN SAMOA, AZ,* CA,* GUAM, HI,* NV,* TRUST TERRITORIES OF THE PACIFIC)
71 Stevenson Street, 4th Floor
San Francisco, CA 94105
Telephone: (415) 744-6670

REGION X (AK,* ID, OR,* WA*)
1111 Third Avenue, Suite 715
Seattle, WA 98101-3212
Telephone: (206) 442-5930

U.S. DEPARTMENT OF LABOR AREA OFFICES FOR THE OCCUPATIONAL SAFETY AND HEALTH ADMINISTRATION

ALABAMA

Birmingham, AL 35216
2047 Canyon Road–Todd Mall
Telephone: (205) 731-1534

Mobile, AL 36693
3737 Government Blvd.
Suite 100
Telephone: (205) 690-2131

ALASKA

Anchorage, AK 99513-7571
Federal Bldg., USCH Room 211
222 West 7th Ave., #29
Telephone: (907) 271-5152

ARIZONA

Phoenix, AZ 85016
3221 North 16th St.–Suite 100
Telephone: (602) 640-2007

ARKANSAS

Little Rock, AR 72201
Savers Bldg.—Suite 828
320 West Capitol Avenue
Telephone: (501) 324-6291

CALIFORNIA

San Francisco, CA 94105
71 Stevenson St.
Suite 415
Telephone: (415) 744-7120

COLORADO

Denver, CO 80204
1244 Speer Blvd.
Colonnade Center, Suite 360
Telephone: (303) 844-5285

CONNECTICUT

Hartford, CT 06103
Federal Office Building
450 Main Street—Rm. 508
Telephone: (203) 240-3152

FLORIDA

Fort Lauderdale, FL 33324
Jacaranda Executive Court
8040 Peters Rd., Bldg. H-100
Telephone: (305) 424-0242

Jacksonville, FL 32216
3100 University Blvd., South
Telephone: (904) 791-2895

Tampa, FL 33602
700 Twiggs Street—Rm. 624
Telephone: (813) 228-2821

GEORGIA

Savannah, GA 31401
1600 Drayton Street
Telephone: (912) 944-4393

Tucker, GA 30084
Bldg. 7, Suite 110
La Vista Perimeter Office Park
Telephone: (404) 493-6644

HAWAII
Honolulu, HI 96850
300 Ala Moana Blvd., Suite
  5122
Telephone: (808) 541-2685

IDAHO
Boise, ID 83702
3050 N. Lake Harbor Lane
Suite 134
Telephone: (208) 334-1867

ILLINOIS
Calument City, IL 60409
1600 167th St.,—Suite 12
Telephone: (708) 891-3800

Des Plaines, IL 60018
2360 E. Devon Avenue
Suite 1010
Telephone: (708) 803-4800

North Aurora, IL 60542
344 Smoke Tree Business Park
Telephone: (708) 896-8700

Peoria, IL 61614-1223
2001 West Willow Knolls Rd.
Suite 101
Telephone: (309) 671-7033

INDIANA
Indianapolis, IN 46204
46 East Ohio Street—
  Rm. 423
Telephone: (317) 331-7290

IOWA
Des Moines, IA 50309
210 Walnut Street—Rm. 815
Telephone: (515) 284-4794

KANSAS
Wichita, KS 67202
216 N. Waco—Suite B
Telephone: (316) 269-6644

KENTUCKY
Frankfort, KY 40601
John C. Watts Fed. Bldg.—
  Rm. 108
330 W. Broadway
Telephone: (502) 227-7024

LOUISIANA
Baton Rouge, LA 70806
2156 Wooddale Blvd.
Hoover Annex—Suite 200
Telephone: (504) 389-0474

MAINE
Augusta, ME 04330
U.S. Federal Bldg.
40 Western Ave.—Rm. 121
Telephone: (207) 622-8417

MARYLAND
Baltimore, MD 21201
Federal Bldg.—Rm. 1110
Charles Center, 31 Hopkins
  Plaza
Telephone: (301) 962-2840

MASSACHUSETTS
Springfield, MA 01103-1493
1145 Main Street—Rm. 108
Telephone: (413) 785-0123

Braintree, MA 02184
639 Granite Street
4th Floor
Telephone: (617) 565-6924

Methuen, MA 01844
Valley Office Park
13 Branch Street
Telephone: (617) 565-8110

MICHIGAN
Lansing, MI 48917
801 South Waverly Rd.
Suite 306
Telephone: (517) 377-1892

MINNESOTA
Minneapolis, MN 55401
110 South 4th Street—Rm. 425
Telephone: (612) 348-1994

MISSISSIPPI
Jackson, MS 39269
Federal Bldg.—Suite 1445
100 West Capitol Street
Telephone: (601) 965-4606

MISSOURI
Kansas City, MO 64106
911 Walnut St.—Rm. 2202
Telephone: (816) 426-2756

St. Louis, MO 63120
4300 Goodfellow Blvd.—Bldg. 1
Telephone: (314) 263-2749

MONTANA
Billings, MT 59101
19 N. 25th Street
Telephone: (406) 657-6649

NEBRASKA
Omaha, NE 68106
Overland-Wolf Bldg.—Rm. 100
6910 Pacific Street
Telephone: (402) 221-3182

NEVADA
Carson City, NV 98701
1413 N. Carson Blvd., 1st Floor
Telephone: (702) 885-6963

NEW HAMPSHIRE
Concord, NH 03301
279 Pleasant Street
Suite 201
Telephone: (603) 225-1629

NEW JERSEY
Avenel, NJ 07001
Plaza 35—Suite 205
1030 Saint Georges Ave.
Telephone: (201) 750-3270

Hasbrouck Heights, NJ 07604
Teterboro Airport
Professional Bldg., 2nd Floor
500 Route 17 South
Telephone: (201) 288-1700

Marlton, NJ 08053
Marlton Executive Park
701 Route 73 South, Bldg. 2
Suite 120
Telephone: (609) 757-5181

Parsippany, NJ 07054
299 Cherry Hill Road
Telephone: (201) 263-1003

NEW MEXICO
Albuquerque, NM 87102
320 Central Ave., S.W.
Suite 5613
Telephone: (505) 776-3411

NEW YORK
Albany, NY 12207
Leo W. O'Brien Federal Bldg.
Clinton Ave. & N. Pearl St.
Rm. 132
Telephone: (518) 472-6085

Bowmansville, NY 14026
5360 Genesee Street
Telephone: (716) 684-3891

Bayside, NY 11361
42–40 Bell Blvd. 5th Floor
Telephone: (718) 279-9060

New York, NY 10007
90 Church Street—Rm. 1407
Telephone: (212) 264-9840

Syracuse, NY 13260
100 S. Clinton Street—Rm. 1267
Telephone: (315) 423-5188

Terrytown, NY 10591
660 White Plains Road
4th Floor
Telephone: (914) 683-9530

Westbury, NY 11590
990 Westbury Rd.
Telephone: (516) 334-3344

NORTH CAROLINA
Raleigh, NC 27601
Century Station—Rm. 104
300 Fayetteville Street Mall
Telephone: (919) 856-4770

NORTH DAKOTA
Bismarck, ND 58501
Federal Bldg.—Rm. 348
P.O. Box 2439
Telephone: (701) 250-4521

OHIO
Cincinnati, OH 45246
36 Triangle Park Drive
Telephone: (513) 841-4132

Cleveland, OH 44199
Federal Office Bldg.—Rm. 899
1240 East Ninth Street
Telephone: (216) 522-3818

Columbus, OH 43215
Federal Office Bldg.—Rm. 620
200 N. High Street
Telephone: (614) 469-5582

Toledo, OH 43604
Federal Office Bldg.—Rm. 734
234 North Summit Street
Telephone: (419) 259-7542

OKLAHOMA
Oklahoma City, OK 73102
420 West Main Place—Suite 725
Telephone: (405) 231-5351

OREGON
Portland, OR 97204
1220 S.W. Third Ave.—Rm. 640
Telephone: (503) 326-2251

PENNSYLVANIA
Allentown, PA 18102
850 N. 5th Street
Telephone: (215) 776-0592

Erie, PA 16506
Suite B-12
3939 West Ridge Road
Telephone: (814) 453-4351

Harrisburg, PA 17109
Progress Plaza
49 N. Progress Street
Telephone: (717) 782-3902

Philadelphia, PA 19106
U.S. Custom House—Rm. 242
Second and Chestnut Street
Telephone: (215) 597-4955

Pittsburgh, PA 15222
Federal Bldg.—Room 1428
1000 Liberty Ave.
Telephone: (412) 644-2903

Wilkes-Barre, PA 18701
Penn Place—Rm. 2005
20 North Pennsylvania Ave.
Telephone: (717) 826-6538

PUERTO RICO
Hato Rey, PR 00918
U.S. Courthouse & FOB
Carlos Chardon St.—Room 559
Telephone: (809) 766-5457

RHODE ISLAND
Providence, RI 02903
380 Westminster Mall
Room 243
Telephone: (401) 528-4669

SOUTH CAROLINA
Columbia, SC 29201
1835 Assembly Street
Rm. 1468
Telephone: (803) 765-5904

TENNESSEE
Nashville, TN 37215
2002 Richard Jones Rd.
Suite C-205
Telephone: (615) 736-5313

TEXAS
Austin, TX 78701
611 East 6th Street—Rm. 303
Telephone: (512) 482-5783

Corpus Christi, TX 78401
Government Plaza—Rm. 300
400 Mann Street
Telephone: (512) 888-3257

Dallas, TX 75228
8344 East R.L. Thornton
  Freeway
Suite 420
Telephone: (214) 320-2400

Fort Worth, TX 76180-7604
North Star 2 Bldg.
Suite 430
8713 Airport Freeway
Telephone: (817) 885-7025

Houston, TX 77004
2320 La Branch Street—
  Rm. 1103
Telephone: (713) 750-1727

Lubbock, TX 79401
Federal Bldg.—Rm. 421
1205 Texas Avenue
Telephone: (806) 743-7681

UTAH
Salt Lake City, UT 84165-0200
1781 South 300 West
Telephone: (801) 524-5080

VIRGINIA
Norfolk, VA 23510
FOB, Rm. 835
200 Granby Mall
Mail Drawer 486
Telephone: (804) 441-3820

WASHINGTON
Bellevue, WA 98004
121 107th Ave., N.E.
Telephone: (206) 553-7520

WEST VIRGINIA
Charleston, WV 25301
550 Eagan Street—Rm. 206
Telephone: (304) 347-5937

WISCONSIN
Appleton, WI 54915
2618 North Ballard Road
Telephone: (414) 734-4521

Madison, WI 53713
2934 Fish Hatchery Rd.
Suite 225
Telephone: (608) 264-5388

Milwaukee, WI 53203
Suite 1180
310 West Wisconsin Ave.
Telephone: (414) 297-3315

U.S. DEPARTMENT OF LABOR DISTRICT OFFICES FOR THE OCCUPATIONAL SAFETY AND HEALTH ADMINISTRATION

REGION III
Washington, D.C. 20002
Suite 440
820 First St., N.E.
Telephone: (202) 523-1452

Wilmington, DE 19801
U.S. Dept. of Labor—OSHA
1 Rodney Square—Suite 403
920 King Street
Telephone: (302) 573-6115

REGION V
Belleville, IL 62220
218A West Main Street
Telephone: (618) 277-5300

Eau Claire, WI 54701
500 Barstow Street
Room B-9
Telephone: (715) 832-9019

REGION VII
Mission, KS
5799 Broadmoor
Suite 338
Telephone: (913) 236-2681

REGION IX
Sacramento, CA 95815
105 El Camino Blvd., 1st Floor
Telephone: (916) 978-5641

San Diego, CA 92123
5675 Ruffin Road, Suite 330
Telephone: (619) 569-9071

*These states and territories operate their own OSHA-approved job safety and health programs (Connecticut and New York plans cover public employees only). States with approved programs must have a standard that is identical to, or at least as effective, as the Federal standard.

GLOSSARY

Abatement   The action of correcting a safety or health violation cited by OSHA in an inspection. (*See also* Abatement Date.)

Abatement Date   A deadline set by OSHA on a citation, by which an employer must correct a cited violation.

Action Level   A specific concentration of a hazardous substance at which employers are required by OSHA to begin protective steps for exposed workers, including regular monitoring to measure ongoing exposure, and use of engineering controls and personal protective equipment to reduce exposure.

ANPRM   (Advance Notice of Proposed Rulemaking) A notice by OSHA in the *Federal Register* in which the agency announces that it is considering a new standard on a specific workplace hazard and asks for comments on whether a standard is indeed needed, and if so, what provisions it should include. (*See also* NPRM.)

CASPA   (Complaint about State Plan Administration) A formal complaint to OSHA alleging problems or shortcomings in the administration of a state occupational safety and health program.

Certification   An official acknowledgement by OSHA that a state has taken steps to put into place all the elements needed to assume responsibility for setting and enforcing its own workplace safety and health regulations under a state plan agreement. (*See also* State Plan.)

Closing Conference   A meeting between OSHA inspectors and management representatives after an OSHA inspection, at which the inspector discusses any violations found in the inspection and any penalties for those violations. (*See also* Opening Conference.)

Criteria Document   A NIOSH report (submitted to OSHA as a recommendation for a new standard) that provides detailed information on a particular type of workplace hazard and recommends measures needed to protect workers from that hazard.

CSHO   A compliance safety and health officer, or OSHA inspector.

Current Intelligence Bulletin   A NIOSH report that summarizes current information on a particular type of workplace hazard.

Developmental Period   A phase in the approval process for a state plan in which the state is allowed to begin its own health and safety enforcement, under the eye of OSHA and usually concurrently with OSHA enforcement, while taking steps to meet all the goals set forth in the plan. (*See also* State Plan.)

FACOSH   (Federal Advisory Council on Occupational Safety and Health) An organization of management and employee representatives from federal agencies that advises OSHA on policy issues pertaining to health and safety in federal workplaces.

FMSHRC   (Federal Mine Safety and Health Review Commission) An independent, quasi-judicial panel that adjudicates employer challenges to MSHA citations.

Generic Standard   An OSHA standard that regulates a variety of workplace hazards, instead of a specific hazard (for example, a standard that sets exposure limits for several chemicals, rather than limits for one particular chemical).

Hazard Communication   A federal standard that requires employers to inform employees about the presence and effects of hazardous materials in their workplaces. (*See also* Right-to-Know.)

HHE   (Health Hazard Evaluation) An investigation by the National Institute for Occupational Safety and Health of an occupational health problem at a work site, performed at the request of an employee or employee representative.

Horizontal Standard   An OSHA standard that can pertain to several different types of industries.

MSHA   (Mine Safety and Health Administration) The agency in the U.S. Department of Labor that has responsibility for setting and enforcing safety and health standards for the mining industry under the Federal Mine Safety and Health Amendments Act of 1977.

NACOSH   (National Advisory Committee on Occupational Safety and Health) A 12-member organization of employer and employee representatives and health and safety professionals, which advises OSHA on policy issues.

NIOSH   (National Institute for Occupational Safety and Health) An agency in the U.S. Department of Health and Human Services that has the lead federal role under the Occupational Safety and Health Act for performing and supporting workplace health and safety research.

Notice of Contest   A notice in which the employer expresses its intention to challenge a citation by OSHA alleging that the employer has violated an agency standard.

NPRM (Notice of Proposed Rulemaking) A notice by OSHA in the *Federal Register* in which the agency proposes a new standard and requests public comment on it. (*See also* ANPRM.)

Opening Conference A meeting between OSHA inspectors and management representatives before an OSHA inspection, in which the inspectors discuss the reasons for the inspection and employer and employee rights in the process. (*See also* Closing Conference.)

OSHA (Occupational Safety and Health Administration) The agency in the U.S. Department of Labor responsible for enforcing the Occupational Safety and Health Act of 1970. (The acronym sometimes also is used to refer to the Act.)

OSHA 101 A government form, required by OSHA, that contains detailed information on individual work-related injury or illness cases.

OSHA 200 A government form, required by OSHA, on which an employer records work-related injuries and illnesses among its employees every year; also called the employer's log of injuries and illnesses.

OSHRC (Occupational Safety and Health Review Commission) An independent, quasi-judicial federal panel that adjudicates employer challenges to OSHA citations.

PEL (Permissible Exposure Limit) An OSHA limit for worker exposure to a harmful substance or physical agent, deemed by the agency to be the highest level at which an employee may be exposed without harmful effects.

Performance Standard A standard that sets general requirements for protecting employees from a workplace hazard, allowing employers to choose their own means for complying with the regulation.

Programmed Inspections Workplace inspections scheduled by OSHA based on a system for randomly selecting a certain number of sites for inspection every year.

Regional Administrators The directors of the ten OSHA regional offices across the United States.

Right-to-Act The concept that workers should have the legal right to refuse—without fear of being fired or otherwise reprimanded—to perform a task they believe would expose them to serious injury.

Right-to-Know Employees' rights under state regulations to be informed about the presence and effects of hazardous materials in their workplaces. (*See also* Hazard Communication.)

Settlement An agreement in which an employer and OSHA resolve a challenge by the employer to an OSHA citation without pursuing their dispute through adjudication; generally under such agreements, the employer (usually with the stipulation that its action does not constitute an acknowledgment that a violation occurred) agrees to correct the conditions cited by OSHA in return for the agency reducing the severity of the citation and the amount of the penalty.

Specification Standard   A standard that sets detailed requirements for protecting employees from a workplace hazard.

State Plan   An agreement with OSHA under which a state assumes responsibility for setting and enforcing its own occupational safety and health regulations.

TLVs   (Threshold Limit Values) Guidelines by the American Conference of Governmental Industrial Hygienists, which represent airborne concentrations of substances and representative conditions under which employees, generally, may be repeatedly exposed without suffering adverse health effects. TLVs formed the basis for some 400 air contaminant exposure limits issued by OSHA in 1971 and revised in 1989.

Variance   An OSHA order that allows a company—either temporarily or permanently—to use means other than those required under an OSHA standard to protect its employees from a hazard, as long as those methods are at least as effective as those required by OSHA.

Vertical Standard   An OSHA standard pertaining to a specific industry, such as construction or maritime trades.

VPP   (Voluntary Protection Program) An agreement with OSHA in which a company voluntarily pledges to develop a comprehensive safety and health program for an individual work site, in return for which the agency exempts the site from scheduled inspections.

BIBLIOGRAPHY

Ashford, Nicholas. *Crisis in the Workplace. Occupational Disease and Injury: A Report to the Ford Foundation*. Cambridge, MA: MIT Press, 1976.

Berman, Daniel M. *Death on the Job: Occupational Health and Safety Struggles in the United States*. New York: Monthly Review Press, 1978.

Bokat, Stephen A., and Horace A. Thompson III, eds. *Occupational Safety and Health Law*. Washington, D.C.: The Bureau of National Affairs, Inc., 1988.

Brodeur, Paul. *Expendable Americans*. New York: Viking Press, 1974.

Bureau of National Affairs, Inc., *The Job Safety and Health Act of 1970*. Washington, D.C.: The Bureau of National Affairs, Inc., 1971.

Changing Technologies in the Workplace. Berkeley, CA: California Policy Seminar, University of California, 1990.

Collins, Jeremiah A., and Robert C. Gombar. *Occupational Safety and Health Law, 1987–88 Supplement*. Washington, D.C.: The Bureau of National Affairs, Inc., 1989.

Hamilton, Alice. *Exploring the Dangerous Trades*. Boston: Little-Brown, 1943; Boston: Northeastern University Press, 1985.

Landrigan, Philip J., and Irving J. Selikoff, eds. *Occupational Health in the 1990s: Developing a Platform for Disease Prevention*. New York: New York Academy of Sciences, 1989. (Annals of the New York Academy of Sciences, Volume 572.)

Lofgren, Don J. *Dangerous Premises: An Insider's View of OSHA Enforcement*. Ithaca, NY: ILR Press; School of Industrial and Labor Relations, Cornell University, 1989.

McCaffrey, David P. *OSHA and the Politics of Health Regulation*, New York: Plenum Press, 1982.

Mendeloff, John. *Regulating Safety: An Economic and Political Analysis of Occupational Safety and Health Policy.* Cambridge, MA: MIT Press, 1979.

Mintz, Benjamin W. *OSHA: History, Law, and Policy.* Washington, D.C.: The Bureau of National Affairs, Inc., 1984.

Nelkin, Dorothy, and Michael S. Brown. *Workers at Risk: Voices from the Workplace.* Chicago: University of Chicago Press, 1984.

Noble, Charles. *Liberalism at Work: The Rise and Fall of OSHA.* Philadelphia: Temple University Press, 1986.

Northrup, Herbert R., Richard L. Rowan, and Charles R. Perry. *The Impact of OSHA.* Philadelphia: The University of Pennsylvania, 1978. (Wharton School, Industrial Research Unit, Labor Relations and Public Policy Series, No. 17.)

Occupational Safety and Health: Seven Critical Issues for the 1990s. Washington, D.C.: The Bureau of National Affairs, Inc., 1989.

Smith, Robert Stewart. *The Occupational Safety and Health Act, Its Goals and Its Achievements.* Washington, D.C.: American Enterprise Institute for Public Policy Research, 1976.

"Symposium—Workplace Safety for the 1990s," *Northern Kentucky Law Review* 17, No. 1 (Fall, 1989).

TABLE OF CASES

INDEX

355

State prosecution authority
99
State standards 95–96
Steiger, William 4
Strike with pay 77
Sullivan, Lenore 2
Superfund Amendments and
Reauthorization Act
(SARA) 9, 125–26
Surface Transportation Act of
1982 84–85

T

Temporary variance order
23–24
Threshold limits values 17
Toxic substance 6, 11, 12, 13,
16
clean-up 35
exposure records 33–34
medical records 34–35
NIOSH list 113
Trade secrets 41–43
Transportation, Department
of 132, 133

U

Union Carbide Corporation
65
Unions *See* Labor unions
United Mine Workers of
America 122
Unprogrammed inspections
50–51
Unreasonable search and
seizure 54

V

Vertical standards 13, 14, 15
Vessel inspection 134
Violations
categories 62–63
criminal 63, 73
de minimus 62–63
failure to abate 64
inspection 59
multiple 63
other-than-serious 63, 64
repeat 63
serious 63, 64
willful 63, 64, 65, 73
Voluntary protection
programs (VPP) 53

W

Walkaround 58
Walking-working surfaces 12,
Appendix B
Walsh-Healey Act of 1936 2,
17
Williams, Harrison 3
Written access order 39–41

Y

Yarborough, Ralph 3